WARRIOR,
KING,
SERVANT,
SAVIOR

Warrior, King, Servant, Savior

*Messianism in the Hebrew Bible
and Early Jewish Texts*

Torleif Elgvin

WILLIAM B. EERDMANS PUBLISHING COMPANY
GRAND RAPIDS, MICHIGAN

Wm. B. Eerdmans Publishing Co.
4035 Park East Court SE, Grand Rapids, Michigan 49546
www.eerdmans.com

© 2022 Torleif Elgvin
All rights reserved
Published 2022
Printed in the United States of America

Book design by Leah Luyk

28 27 26 25 24 23 22   1 2 3 4 5 6 7

ISBN 978-0-8028-7818-2

Library of Congress Cataloging-in-Publication Data

A catalog record for this book is available from the Library of Congress.

The publication of this book has received support from NLA University College.

Contents

Contents

Preface

In this book I trace the development of royal and Davidic ideology in biblical texts from the tenth to the first century BCE and the development of a multi-faceted messianism from the time of the exile onward. In the Bible, messianism and eschatology are interrelated. Thus, my presentation of messianism will be set within the wider hope for the future and the eschaton throughout biblical history. The structure of the book is primarily chronological—but at times overruled by thematic considerations.

Messianism in the Hebrew Bible should not be read independently from texts and developments during the second and first centuries. The transmission and procession of biblical texts were dynamic, and the borders of the Ketuvim were fluid until well after the turn of the era. Scholars of the Hebrew Bible need to interact with the pluriform evidence of biblical scrolls from Qumran and the wider Jewish tradition of the Second Temple period. Consequently, in chapters 5–7 I do not discern between biblical and non-biblical texts.

I include a final chapter on Jewish messianism in the first millennium after the turn of the era to show how textual lines from biblical and early Jewish texts continue in Jewish tradition. Apart from pointing to some intertextual links, the book does not thematize messianism in the New Testament—a subject well covered in the literature.

Biblical history can be read as history of religion or revelation history. The same goes for the unfolding of Israel's messianic hope in this book. I read the Hebrew Bible from the perspective of revelation history, as it was perceived and received by the scribes and editors of the Bible in Second Temple times. For some of us, tracing lines of developments in biblical history may mean trying to see the footsteps of the God of Israel in his interaction with his people through history—available to us in texts formatted through the minds and transmitted through the pens of scribes, prophets, Levites, and others—writers who convey their interpretation of the nation's encounter with God. As Durham (1987, xi) says about his traversal of the book of Exodus, to me this traversal of royal, messianic, and eschatological texts "is a trip across holy ground." However, readers who prefer to read this book within the paradigm of history of religion or secular history will have no difficulty in doing so.

To a large extent I use literary criticism combined with historical information and archaeological insights to unfold the editorial growth of biblical texts. Identification of stages in the literary growth of a text can reveal changing theological perspectives throughout the editorial processes. It is my hope that readers who identify with a Jewish or Christian faith tradition will not get lost in details of literary criticism but will enjoy seeing how various Israelite scribes through changing historical circumstances gave their specific colors to the pluriform messianic hopes that radiate from the biblical writings.

When it comes to the understanding of prophecy, a theological approach can diverge radically from a secular one. Can a prophet reveal secrets of the human heart or events of the future? Are oracles updated after certain events to fit historical reality? In my perspective, both are possible. The Bible includes *vaticinium ex eventu* texts, where history is camouflaged as foreseen in prophecy, such as Dan 11. In other cases, a prophetic oracle could be updated after certain events of history had occurred. However, if one encounters the biblical text from a theological or history-of-revelation perspective, one should not exclude that a prophet may be able to foresee events in the future—which seems to be a presupposition in much modern secularly influenced scholarship. For Thomas Aquinas, a prophet (in biblical times or in the church) can predict future events or reveal divine insight about the present (*Summa Theologica*, Part II-II question 172; *De Veritate*, question 12.3). He connects a prophetic gift with a spiritual sensitivity, a special elevation of the mind. The Holy Spirit moves the mind and thought of the prophet so that he understands, speaks, and acts accordingly.

Sweeney (1996, 22) notes that a prophetic oracle is "based on a revelatory experience or vision; it is analytical in character, and it is spoken in response to a particular situation in human events." Thus, prophetic oracles should be interpreted in light of their sociopolitical context in history. The meaning of an oracle should make sense for the prophet and, in most cases, also for his listeners or close to contemporary readers.

To come as close as possible to the sociopolitical context in which the texts developed, this book is in active dialogue with archaeological research relevant for understanding the history of Israel and Judah. I am indebted to

Mordechai Aviam, Andrea Berlin, Tali Erickson-Gini, Omer Sergi, Dvir Raviv, Itzhaq Shai, Samuel R. Wolff, and Boaz Zissu for information and feedback on the archaeological evidence. Discussions with Omer Sergi taught me a lot, and Omer generously shared a large number of publications (by himself and others) with me.

This book was finished during the Covid-19 pandemic, when library services were hampered. Therefore, there are relevant scholarly contributions to which I likely should have referred, which I was not able to check.

Biblical translations regularly follow or adapt the NRSV. I also use the 1985 NJPS *Tanakh* and often provide my own translation. For the Septuagint I mainly follow the *New English Translation of the Septuagint* (NETS). For translation of the apocrypha I also consult the Jerusalem Bible.

I tried to make the main text not too heavy a read. Particulars in the scholarly discussion are often relegated to the footnotes and in some cases to excursuses.

I would like to express my gratitude to Anders Jørgen Bjørndalen, Hartmut Gese, and Moshe Weinfeld, teachers who set a lasting mark in my study of the Hebrew Bible, and to my teachers in the field of the Dead Sea Scrolls, David Flusser, Geza Vermes, and Emanuel Tov. Thanks are due to Lida Panov, Samuel R. Wolff, and William Schniedewind, who gave me access to prepublication copies of articles; to Michael Langlois for feedback on linguistic and paleographical issues; to David M. Carr, who carefully read through and commented on chapters 1–5; to Tammy and Reuven Soffer for making the maps; and not least to my copyeditor, David Aiken, and the patient and diligent Eerdmans staff for copyediting and preparing the book for publication.

Figures

Abbreviations

DJD	Discoveries in the Judaean Desert (a series of text editions of Dead Sea Scrolls published by Clarendon Press)
DtrH	Deuteronomistic History
G	Septuagint (e.g., GIsa 7:14 means Isa 7:14 in its Greek form)
M	Masoretic Text (e.g., MJer 30:21 means Jer 30:21 in its Masoretic Hebrew form)
NETS	New English Translation of the Septuagint
NJPS	*Tanakh: The Holy Scriptures: The New JPS Translation according to the Traditional Hebrew Text*. Philadelphia: Jewish Publication Society, 1985.
NRSV	New Revised Standard Version

Notes for the Reader

- Documentation of secondary sources uses the author-date method. The sources, with full bibliographic info, are listed at the back of the book.
- Bible verses are cited using numbers in the Hebrew Bible; when the numbers differ, the English Bible number is listed in square brackets following the Hebrew Bible number; for example, Isa 9:5 [9:6]; Hos 2:1–3 [1:10–2:1].
- It is usually clear from the context which era a date is from, so BCE and CE are appended only when necessary.
- Abbreviations of Dead Sea Scrolls are cited according to *The SBL Handbook of Style*, 2nd ed. (Atlanta: SBL Press, 2014).
- Names (both personal and geographical) appearing in the Bible are spelled according to the NRSV. Nonbiblical names follow standard Israeli spelling.
- In various situations, ≈ means similar, = means equal/identical, ≠ means different from, || means parallel text.

Son of David

Before the 1990s, some scholars doubted the existence of David and Solomon as historical figures. This changed with the 1993 discovery of the Tel Dan inscription and André Lemaire's 1994 reading *bêtdāwīd* on the Mesha Stela (see below). Today few would deny that the "house of David," the royal Judahite dynasty, was indeed founded by David. For good reasons, however, biblical scholars and archaeologists have doubted the historical accuracy of the biblical stories of David and Solomon, stories that received their literary form at a later stage.

As of today, no scholarly consensus has been reached on statehood in tenth-century Israel and Judah. From archaeology, one can clearly identify ninth-century markers of statehood in Israel to the north and Judah to the south. Adding to this, during the last few years a growing number of archaeologists have pointed to such markers also in tenth-century Judah.

Was There a Judahite or United Kingdom in the Tenth Century?

Was there a "united kingdom" under David and Solomon—a kingdom that encompassed the Israel tribes to the north and Judah to the south? Or is this concept an idealized construction invented by later scribes connected to the royal Judahite echelon? On this, scholars disagree.

Davidic and messianic texts in the Bible point to David and Solomon as their foundation. The contents and profile of the son of David texts remain, even if the nature and extent of the Davidic and Solomonic state remain in the dark. But can elements of this theology be traced back to these two kings as historical figures or to their being in close memory? Can we find markers of statehood in Judea to the south or the central highlands to the north? Further, can a historical kernel in the David traditions be acknowledged? Can we identify Israelite settlements in Judah and Benjamin in this early period? Subsequent to a discussion of these issues, a short survey of the continued history of the kingdom of Judah provides the background for the ideological development of the David and son of David traditions.

Early Archaeological Markers

Khirbet Qeiyafa

Since 2007 archaeologists have unearthed the fortified village of Khirbet Qeiyafa in the Elah Valley, 32 km southwest of Jerusalem. This stronghold marked the border of some kind of early Israelite state, facing the large Philistine city of Gath. According to the excavator Yosef Garfinkel, C^{14} analysis indicates that the site was built slightly before 1000 and destroyed around 980–970.

Cultural markers point to Judahite inhabitants, not to the northern tribal entity of the highlands.[1] The town was organized within a massive circular casemate wall with a width of 4 m (a casemate wall is a double wall divided into room sections, often with houses attached to the wall on the inside). Agricultural products were stored in pottery jars, with marks on their handles typical of Judahite administration and tax collection (Garfinkel and Mumcuoglu 2016, 10–28; Garfinkel 2017, 2020). Including a governor residence or palace and large storehouses, Qeiyafa must have been planned and built by a joint Judahite body, some kind of a state. The risky location, ca. 9 km from hostile Gath, would only be chosen by a territorial entity for strategic reasons.

Qeiyafa may be the strongest indication of the beginnings of a Judahite state—in the late eleventh or early tenth century. David is the obvious candidate for heading such a state: "In the summer of 2013, a central palace structure dated to the time of King David was discovered at Khirbet Qeiyafa. The structure stands in a prominent location at the top of the site, its area is about a thousand square meters, and the thickness of its walls shows that it stood several stories high. . . . If an outlying city on the western edge of the

---

1. In contrast, Finkelstein and Fantalkin connect Qeiyafa with the Saulide entity in Benjamin and the northern highlands. They date the destruction to the mid-tenth century, possibly caused by Shishak (Finkelstein and Fantalkin 2012; Fantalkin and Finkelstein 2017). C^{14}-dating suggests a date of destruction around 956–942 (2017, 53–60).

Kingdom of Judah contained such a structure, it is all the more likely that the kingdom's capital, Jerusalem, contained no less impressive structures" (Garfinkel and Mumcuoglu 2016, 99).

At Qeiyafa, the archaeologists unearthed three aniconic cult rooms. The first contained two standing stones, a basalt altar, a limestone basin, and a libation vessel. In the third were found two artifacts characterized by Garfinkel as temple models, one in stone and another in pottery. Each artifact may be understood as a miniature temple entrance, located within a frame with three recesses. Garfinkel compares these recessed frames with ancient entrances to temples and tombs as well as details in the description of Solomon's Temple in 1 Kgs 7:4–5 (Garfinkel and Mumcuoglu 2016, 28–60, 80–84, 99): "The Khirbet Qeiyafa stone model . . . shows that the biblical text, 'And there were three rows of *sequfim*, facing each other three times' should be understood as an elaborate entranceway decorated with triple recessed frames, in the typical style of entranceways in the ancient Near East" (Garfinkel and Mumcuoglu 2016, 82). For Garfinkel, these architectural parallels suggest that the biblical tradition of a tenth-century temple in Jerusalem indeed reflects historical memory.

Qeiyafa must have been a thorn in the eye of Philistine Gath, the largest city around. The Philistines did not tolerate its existence for long. After its downfall, the Judahites built Beth-shemesh 10 km northeast from Gath (Bunimovitz and Lederman 2017, 30–34) and, slightly later, Tel Burna to its south (Shai 2017).

Two fragmentary inscriptions were found in Qeiyafa; the larger contained five lines. Another tenth-century inscription was unearthed in Beth-shemesh, and one in Jerusalem—all written in early alphabetic script, the immediate ancestor of the Old Hebrew script. Bureaucratic or literary Biblical Hebrew is still not there, but not far away.

Jerusalem

What about Jerusalem, which according to biblical texts became David's capital? In the City of David, boulders from a monumental tenth-century building have been unearthed immediately west of the "stepped-stone-structure" that slopes down toward the Kedron Valley. The stepped-stone-structure was constructed in a continuous process during the late eleventh and early tenth centuries.[2] According to Mazar (2010, 34–46), the combination of

---

2. Sergi 2017, 2–5. "The Stepped Stone Structure and the Large Stone Structure to

the stepped-stone-structure and the monumental building was either the fortress of Zion that David captured (2 Sam 5:7) or David's palace. For other scholars, the monumental building may be dated to any time during the tenth century and could be either Davidic or Solomonic. At least by the time of Solomon, tenth-century Jerusalem was a town with a monumental citadel.[3] Pottery from Iron Age IIA shows that the town soon expanded to the Ophel ridge north of the City of David, with the establishment of a large administrative quarter.[4]

To the north of Jerusalem, numerous new rural settlements were founded in the Benjamin plain in the eleventh century, and most of the older sites were still settled. For Sergi (2017, 4–8; 2020, 63), the stepped structure and the citadel constituted a power symbol of the Jerusalem king vis-à-vis these settlements, settlements that likely had to provide manpower to build this structure. The citadel demonstrated the existence of the newly born Jerusalem kingdom, soon to be known as the "house of David."

In the second half of the tenth century, many Benjaminite sites to the north were abandoned, while Mizpah experienced growth and stood out as the main site of the northern Benjamin plain. This process shows northern Benjamin as a border region between two emerging kingdoms: Judah to the south and Ephraim/Israel to the north. The settlements of southern Benjamin were clearly allied with Jerusalem (Sergi 2017, 8–12).

---

its west were part of a single monumental archaeological complex that was constructed either toward the end of Iron Age I (eleventh to early 10th cent. B.C.E.) or during the Early Iron Age IIA (main part of 10th cent. B.C.E.)" (Mazar 2020, 139–46 at 146). "The magnitude and uniqueness of the combined 'Stepped Structure' and the 'Large Stone Structure' are unparalleled anywhere in the Levant between the 12th and the 9th centuries BCE" (Mazar 2010, 45).

3. "The archaeological evidence shows that Jerusalem was the main political center in the region during the 10th century B.C.E. . . . Much of this monumental architecture, at least the imposing structures in the City of David, was already standing by the 10th cent. B.C.E. and set Jerusalem apart from other urban centers of the southern Levant at that time" (Mazar 2020, 149). For Sergi (2020, 63), the stepped structure demonstrates that a centralized political rule was established in Jerusalem around 1100, an entity that dominated the Benjamin region to the north.

4. "Since this pottery is not yet fully published, a more precise date within Iron Age IIA (10th–9th cent. B.C.E.) cannot yet be established"; "The 'Ophel' administrative quarter (was) including a gate complex protected by the monumental Warren Tower, a fortification wall to its east, storage rooms and several significant buildings north of this wall" (Mazar 2020, 147, 149).

Other Sites

According to 2 Chr 11:5–10, Solomon's son Rehoboam fortified fifteen towns in Judea and Benjamin, Lachish being one of them. A fortified city wall was recently unearthed in Lachish, demonstrating that Lachish indeed was fortified for the first time in the late tenth century (Garfinkel 2020; Mazar 2020, 148). Tenth-century Israelite settlements have further been identified at Arad, Beer-sheba, Gezer,[5] Tel Harasim,[6] and Tel Zayit (Tappy 2017, 164–70). Then there are settlements going through a transition from Canaanite to Judahite (Gezer, Beth-shemesh, Tel 'Eton, Tel Beit-mirsim, Tel Halif), and some Judean settlements that were established in either the late tenth or early ninth century (e.g., Tel Burna).[7] Whether the tenth-century settlement at Mozah, 6 km west of Jerusalem, was established by Judeans so far remains an open question (Kisilevitz and Lipschits 2020; see p. 44).

5. Ortiz and Wolff 2017, 78–100; Mazar 2020, 148. According to Samuel R. Wolff (personal communication), Canaanite Gezer (Iron I) was destroyed and then rebuilt in Iron IIA (tenth century) as a well-fortified Israelite city with monumental buildings. A late tenth-century destruction of this stratum (8) was likely caused by the Shishak campaign. The city was more modestly rebuilt in the ninth century and subsequently destroyed by Hazael. The domestic units of stratum 7 are not built as the Israelite four-room house and may continue local Canaanite household tradition (Ortiz and Wolff 2017, 90–95, 100). The city destroyed by Tiglath-pileser in 734 (stratum 6) belonged to the Northern Kingdom and evinces intensive trade contacts with Phoenicia. Fifty *lamelek* stamp handles from stratum 5 demonstrate that Gezer was incorporated in the Judahite state under Ahaz or Hezekiah. Koch (2017, 195–96) provides this archaeological timetable: Iron I (1100–1000), Early Iron IIA (1000–900), Late Iron IIA (900–800), Iron IIB (800–587).

6. Tel Harasim was excavated from 1990 to 2000. An unfortified Israelite settlement was established at the end of the tenth century not far from Philistine Timna. It was fortified by the mid-ninth century and destroyed by the end of the same century (by Philistines or Hazael?) (Givon 2008).

7. For a survey, see Koch 2017, 195–96. According to Faust and Katz (2015, 91–92), the early triangle of Tel 'Eton, Tel Beit-mirsim, and Tel Halif demonstrates close interaction and a clear Canaanite identity. Subsequently, a transition into the Judahite kingdom is evident, as in the case of Beth-shemesh: "The inhabitants (of Tel 'Eton) slowly changed their identity and gradually assimilated and became Judeans" (Faust and Katz 2015, 95). The Judahite phase of Tel 'Eton most likely goes back to the tenth century, and the settlement would soon be fortified. For Tel Burna, see Shai 2017. In a personal communication he adds: the fortifications were constructed in the ninth century, but waiting for C[14] data, the question about how much earlier the site was occupied still remains open. Faust (2013, 209–10) attributes the growth of settlements in the Shephelah in Iron Age I to the developing Judean or united kingdom. Koch (2017, 191–92) disagrees, arguing that the archaeological evidence is too sparse for such an overall theory.

The excavators of En Hazeva, biblical Tamar in the Negev, have identified a small Judean fortification tower from the tenth century, built over by a small fortress in the ninth or eighth century, which again was covered up by a larger fortress in the seventh century.[8]

Summing up, archaeological evidence from Jerusalem, Qeiyafa, and sites such as Beth-shemesh, Lachish, Gezer, Tel Zayit, Arad, Beer-sheba, Tel ʿEton, and Tamar shows the existence of a small Judean state throughout the tenth century (cf. Faust 2014, 11–34); the same is evinced by settlement patterns of the eleventh/tenth centuries around Jerusalem.

This survey of early Judahite settlements in the south doesn't imply that all these settlers had an ethnic or tribal identity as belonging to "Judah." In the eleventh and tenth centuries, the connotations of "Judah" might refer more to a region than to a clan-based tribal entity (cf. Lipschits 2020, 168). Judeans did not come from nowhere—there is some cultural continuity from Canaanite society to the early proto-Israelite villages many archaeologists identify in the highlands. Both in the north and the south, Canaanite towns and settlements could slowly acquire an Israelite identity—indeed, Ezekiel reminds his people that "your origin and your birth were in the land of the Canaanites" (16:3). At the same time, ceramic types from this period can be identified as Israelite, different from Philistine and Canaanite.

At the coast and in the lower Shephelah, there were Philistine cities and towns with a distinct identity.[9] However, it remains an open question

---

8. The tenth-century tower gave way for the ninth- or eighth-century fortress (50 m × 50 m), which again was covered up when the next fortress (100 m × 100 m) was built around the late seventh century. Based on pottery and comparative structures, Tali Erickson-Gini identifies the tenth-century fortification as Israelite. Excavations in 2005–8 and 2013–20 revealed a previously unknown eleventh-century settlement of industrial character. Copper from Faynan was cast here, and local-type vessels contained copper slag. This early settlement may have been Edomite (as Faynan), but Erickson-Gini hesitates to conclude about the identity of these settlers—the site revealed a number of items that suggest links to Arabia. Further, the latest vessel in this earliest stratum was of a Judean type (all personal communication from Tali Erickson-Gini, excavator 2013–20).

9. Coming from the west, and mainly from the Aegeans, the Philistines established themselves in the Levant in the early twelfth century. Pottery, cultic practices, and architecture evince a distinctive culture of their own. In the subsequent centuries, social, economic, and political changes stimulated a process of acculturation, leading to increased cultural similarity between the Philistines and their neighbors. Despite this trend, the Philistines did not lose their cultural core or assimilate into Canaanite or Israelite society, retaining a distinct cultural and political identity throughout the Iron Age (Stone 1995; cf. Koch 2020).

whether settlements further inland regarded themselves as "Canaanite," "Judean," or "allied with Ekron or Gath" during the eleventh and tenth centuries. Philistine pottery has been found at non-Philistine settlements in the Shephelah—trade and communication were crossing cultural borders. Settlements in the Shephelah may have been oscillating between Jerusalem and Philistia, where, in the tenth century, Gath replaced Ekron as the major Philistine center.[10] With the development of the Judahite state throughout the ninth century, the connotations of "Judah" would soon signal ethnic identity, as evinced in the tribal blessings in Gen 49.

The development of Israelite polities in the tenth century can be compared with their neighbors to the east, where there are indications of emerging statehood in the eleventh/tenth centuries. The excavation of the copper mines at Faynan in the Arava Valley shows traces of an Edomite kingdom in the late eleventh and tenth centuries (cf. Gen 36:31: "the kings who reigned in Edom before any Israelite king reigned" [my translation]). At Khirbet en-Nahas, an early tenth-century monumental fortress measuring 70 m × 70 m has been unearthed, suggesting an organized political entity behind it. There was organized copper mining here from ca. 1300, run by the Edomite tribes themselves after the pullout of the Egyptian overlords around 1140, with development into large-scale industrial production in the tenth/ninth century (Levy, Najjar, and Ben-Yosef 2014a, 93–130, 231; Ben-Yosef et al. 2019).[11] The copper installations at Timna, 105 km further south, used the same mining technology and belonged to the same political entity (Ben Yosef et al. 2012, 2019; Levy 2020). With Edomite tribes uniting into a regional polity, a similar effort among Israelite tribes would make sense.

10. Sergi and de Hulster (2016, 7–10) argue that tenth- to eighth-century Geshurite settlements north and east of the Sea of Galilee could shift their loyalty between Damascus and Samaria dependent on the relative strength of these two kingdoms. The identity and political loyalty of the inhabitants of the Shephelah could have been similarly flexible.

11. "The technology in Timna and Faynan, evident as early as the eleventh century BCE . . . suggests that an overarching political body existed in the region already at this time. Further centralization of this political body is evident in changes observed toward 1000 BCE" (Ben-Yosef et al. 2019). "During the tenth century BCE . . . local complex societies (kingdom/small state) were present in the southern Levant at this time" (Levy, Najjar, and Ben-Yosef 2014a, 232). Mazar (2016, 101–3) points to a possible trade link with the city of Rehov (south of the Lake of Galilee). This thriving Canaanite (and later Israelite) city produced yearly ca. 400 kg of honey and 60 kg of beeswax. Beeswax was a necessary ingredient in the casting of copper.

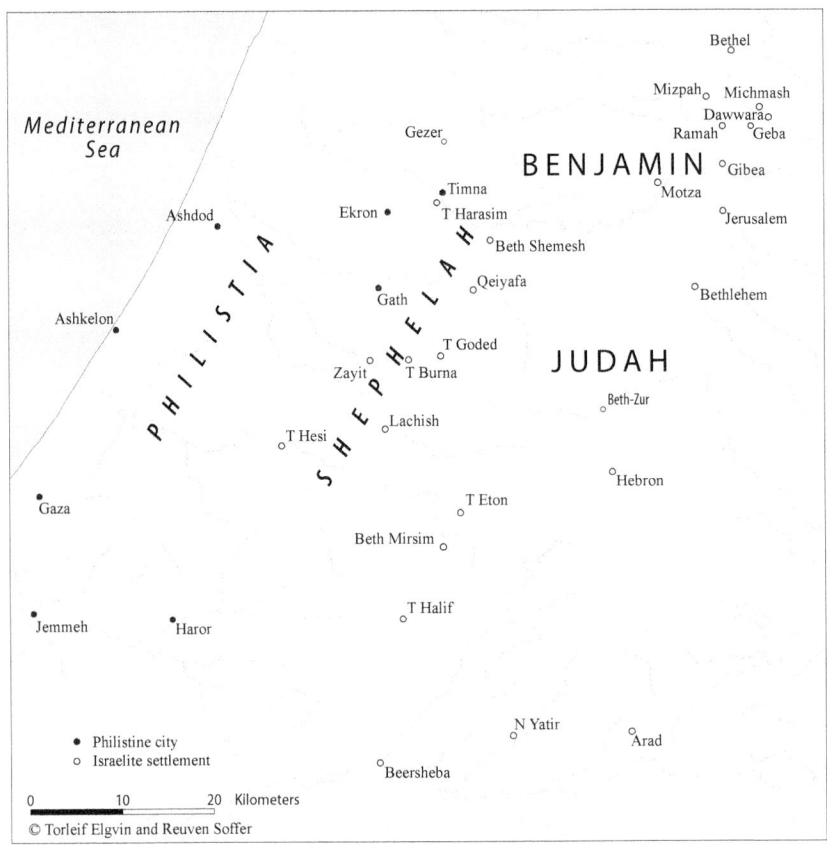

Figure 1. Philistine cities and southern Israelite settlements in the tenth and early ninth centuries.

Khirbet ed-Dawwara—a fortlike settlement established in the eleventh century and abandoned in the late tenth century.

Beth-zur—the 1957 excavations found a prosperous settlement in the twelfth/eleventh centuries and a substantial decline toward the end of the tenth century (Sellers 1958). Fortifications from Rehoboam's time were not identified (cf. 2 Chr 11:7). A renewed growth in the ninth century could likely be explained by the developing Judahite kingdom.

Tel Burna—an existing Judean settlement fortified in the ninth century.

Tel 'Eton, Tel Beth Mirsim, Tel Halif—Canaanite settlements that became Judahite around the late tenth century.

Tamar—a small tenth-century Judahite fort at Tamar (located outside the map, 27 km southwest of the Dead Sea; cf. fig. 2 on p. 63).

Gath, Gezer, Tel Zayit, Tel Harasim—destroyed in the late ninth century, likely by Hazael of Damascus (2 Kgs 12:18 [12:17]).

Texts and Inscriptions in the Geopolitical Landscape of the Tenth and Ninth Centuries

The two main components of the David traditions in the historical books are the Saul-David narratives ("David's rise to power") and the Succession Narrative (2 Sam 9–20; 1 Kgs 1–2). Some scholars argue that features of the milieu described in the Saul-David narratives best fit the historical patterns of the tenth/early ninth centuries (Na'aman 1996; Blum 2010, 64–73; Sergi 2020, 74–75).[12]

First, literary features suggest a historical core in the narratives. Blum (2010, 68–70) asks, With the Solomon dynasty in power, why would scribes so thoroughly describe David's nasty behavior vis-à-vis Uriah in the affair with Bathsheba (2 Sam 11–12)? The legendary founder of the dynasty would be remembered for adultery, betrayal, and murder. Blum concludes that essential features of the narrative plot and of the overall tendency fit either the tenth century or the beginning of the ninth.[13]

Second, archaeologists point to settlement patterns. Sergi (2017, 4–8; 2020, 63) argues that the stories of David's rise to power align with settlement patterns in the Benjamin and Jerusalem regions in the late eleventh/early tenth centuries: the growing number of settlements in the Benjamin plain appears as hinterland for the rapidly growing Jerusalem, with monumental buildings that reflect the capital's power.[14]

---

12. "The stories in 1 Sam 16–2 Sam 5, like those in 1 Sam 9–14, are, therefore, consistent with the social and political reality in south Canaan during the tenth through ninth centuries BCE" (Sergi 2020, 74).

13. "Why does the image of the dynastic founder David remain oscillating between disaster-bearing weakness and admirable piety and human greatness? . . . The author of our narrative felt a *need* to present the main actors as he did. . . . The basic reason for such a need must be that there was some knowledge or memory in the world of the addressees, too virulent and too politically dangerous to be ignored by silence. . . . The very core of such knowledge: the king's marriage with the wife of a fallen officer and the birth of his future successor by that woman. This could give rise *inter alia* to questions regarding Solomon's legitimacy. Is it by chance that David's malicious deeds in 2 Samuel 11 actually ensure Solomon's royal descent?" (Blum 2010, 69–70).

14. "These traditions concur well with the archaeological picture portrayed above, according to which the Iron IIA saw the growth of Jerusalem as the main political center among the rather isolated cluster of rural settlements between Jerusalem and Bethel . . . as these traditions are well embedded in the political and social realia of southern Canaan in the early Iron Age, they preserve, at least in their essence (but not in their details!) an authentic memory regarding the formation of Judah" (Sergi 2020, 82–83).

Third, the geopolitical tensions between the settlement hub around Jerusalem and that of Gibeon/Gibeah is brought to bear. For Oswald (2020), the Saul-David narrative has a probable origin in a tenth-century rivalry between a Benjamin polity in Gibeon/Gibeah and a Judean polity centered in Jerusalem. The first is in the texts connected with the house of Saul, the second with David. David's power base was the highlands south of the territory of Ephraim, from the Benjamin plateau to Bethlehem, while that of Saul was from Gibeah (in the Benjamin plateau) and to the north.

Sergi (2020, 66–73) notes that the geographical scope of the early Saul tradition is the Benjamin region and the southern Ephraim hills, with one excursion to Gilead, while the heartland of the later kingdom of Israel is absent—which would be strange if the stories were given literary form by Samaria scribes. This geographical scenario confirms Saul's Benjaminite background and suggests the viewpoint of Jerusalem scribes well versed in Benjaminite history, as southern Benjamin early on had been allied with Jerusalem.[15] The scene of David's rise to power and his service in Saul's court is the same southern region.[16] Historically, "Saul and David tried to establish their hegemony over the same group of people: the Israelites residing in the Jerusalem-Benjamin highlands" (Sergi 2020, 81).

Fourth, relations to two neighboring polities point to the tenth and ninth centuries. The Philistine city of Gath has a prominent role in the stories of David, both in the Saul-David narratives and the Succession Narrative (Halpern 2001, 69; Finkelstein and Silberman 2006a, 38–39; Blum 2010, 64–73). Gath was the larger of the Philistine coastal cities until it was destroyed by Hazael of Damascus in the late ninth century—suggesting that the roots of the Succession Narrative should be sought in the tenth or ninth century and that the literary formation hardly can be later than ca. 800.

---

15. Sergi (2020, 66–69) finds a historical core in early Saul tradition (1 Sam 9:1–10:16; 11:1–15; 13:1–14:52; 31:1–13). The present form of the Saul narrative reflects a pro-Davidic and Jerusalemite perspective and was formed in a scribal school in Jerusalem not later than the early eighth century. "The early traditions about Saul and David preserve the memory of a struggle for power in the early monarchic period: the rise of dynastic monarchy in Jerusalem was the result of a struggle between two Israelite ruling families engaged in an attempt to establish their political hegemony over their own Israelite kinsmen settled in the regions north and south of Jerusalem" (Sergi 2020, 83).

16. "A similar portrayal of Israel as a kinship group residing in the region of Jerusalem and Benjamin also characterizes the stories about David's rise and especially the stories about David's service in Saul's court (1 Sam 18–19, see also 2 Sam 5:1–2)" (Sergi 2020, 80).

In the north, the early polity of Geshur was located around the northern end of the Sea of Galilee. Joshua 13:13 states: "The Israelites did not drive out the Geshurites or the Maacathites; but Geshur and Maacath live within Israel to this day."[17] The later capital of Geshur, et-Tell (often problematically identified with Bethsaida; cf. Notley and Aviam 2020), was founded in the eleventh century and destroyed in the 920s either by Pharaoh Shishak or by the Arameans (Arav 2020). Other centers of this Geshurite entity were Kinrot, Tel Hadar, and En Gev, sites where settlement came to an end around the mid-tenth century before they flourished anew from the late ninth century (cf. Sergi and Kleinman 2018). In the early period, Kinrot was the strongest urban center, while eighth-century et-Tell was a large and well-fortified city.[18]

One of David's wives was Maacah, daughter of King Talmai of Geshur. She gave birth to Absalom, who later found refuge in Geshur (2 Sam 3:3; 13:37–38). A memory of such a marriage for David primarily makes sense in the tenth century and can hardly be ascribed to a late fabrication of a Davidic foundation story for the kingdom of Judah. Thus, the presence of Absalom

17. Maacath/Abel-beth-maacah, north in the Hula Valley, is close to today's border between Israel and Lebanon (cf. 2 Sam 10:6; 20:15; 1 Kgs 15:20; 2 Kgs 15:29). Abel-beth-maacah was incorporated in the Northern Kingdom under the Jehu dynasty by Joash or Jeroboam II (Panitz-Cohen and Mullins 2016, 165).

18. Based on the last seasons at et-Tell, excavation leader Rami Arav (2020) maintains that stratum VI shows a substantial city in the eleventh/tenth century, coming to an end in the 920s. Sergi and Kleiman (2018) identify an early sociopolitical entity around the Sea of Galilee that came to an end by the mid-tenth century, with centers in Tel Hadar, En Gev, et-Tell, and Kinrot (with the latter as political center). With the limited evidence available to them from et-Tell stratum VI (eleventh/tenth century), they date the *state* of Geshur, with et-Tell as capital, to the next period with substantial settlement of these four sites, that of the late ninth and early eighth century, a state subordinate to the kingdom of Aram, ruled by Hazael of Damascus. This would mean that elements of the David stories reflect political realities of that time (for Sergi and Kleiman, the David-Maacah story would reflect the early eighth century). Eighth-century et-Tell, founded by the Arameans (possibly by Hazael), was a strong city encompassing the largest city gate excavated in the Levant—possibly the city gate pictured in Tiglath-pileser's relief from Nineveh, now in the British Museum (Arav 2020). Sergi and de Hulster (2016, 7–10) see the region north and east of the Sea of Galilee as a settlement hub where local rulers shifted loyalty between Damascus and Samaria, dependent on the relative strength of these two kingdoms. Under Hazael, the Geshurites were allied with Aram, while the Jehu dynasty dominated the region in the eighth century. Culturally and socially, the inhabitants remained closer to the Arameans—a sanctuary for the moon god has been unearthed in eighth-century et-Tell. All these sites were devastated in Tiglath-pileser's 733 campaign.

and Maacah in the David narrative is a strong indication of a historical core in the David narratives.

Fifth, the role of Benjaminites in the power struggle between the house of Saul and the house of David is instructive. Blum (2010, 64–73) argues that texts describing Benjaminites in active opposition to David (2 Sam 16:5–13; 19:16–24 [19:15–23]; 20:1–2; 1 Kgs 2:46) give meaning only in the second half of the tenth century and testify to some kind of a united kingdom under David and Solomon.[19] Verses 1–2 of 2 Sam 20 demonstrate Benjamin's strong voice among the Israel tribes, with the Benjaminite Sheba initiating a revolt against David. Later, Benjamin would follow Jeroboam and the Israel tribes in their break with the son of Solomon (1 Kgs 11:31–32; 12:16–17).

Sixth, the texts evince both tensions and bridge-building efforts between Judah in the south and the tribal-based union of the Israel tribes to the north. There is a historical memory in the sources that David was made "king over Israel" (2 Sam 5:1–3, 17), not "king over Judah"—an editorial addition notes that the Hebron-based David was king over Judah for seven and a half years (2:11). A tribal alliance based in the central highlands, moving away from the house of Saul, came to Hebron and made a temporary covenant with David to be their king. "The accumulated stories of David in the books of Samuel define him above all by his rule over Israel . . . these memories inhere in material that knows David only as king of Israel" (Fleming 2012, 98).

Then, what is the background of David, early known as leader of a band of outcasts? Sergi (2020, 81) notes that David is identified as an Israelite (1 Sam 18:18; 27:12; 2 Sam 5:1) belonging to the Ephrathite clan of Bethlehem (1 Sam 17:12),[20] which means that his Bethlehem clan belonged to one of the Israel tribes: "Nowhere in the stories of his rise to kingship is David identified as a Judahite." If the Israel tribes recognized that one of their own had seized power in Judah and conquered the Jebusite stronghold Jerusalem, a decision to make him king of Israel would be easy to understand.[21] Later, when

---

19. "Apart from the time of David and Solomon itself, I see one period in which such a memory-based, anti-Davidic atmosphere in Benjamin could have fatal consequences for the Davidic dynasty: that is the first four or five decades after Solomon, when we see an enduring struggle between the two kingdoms for the territory of Benjamin" (Blum 2010, 65–67 at 67).

20. The same term, *'eprātî* (not "Ephraimite" as translations often render it), is used about Jeroboam I (1 Kgs 11:26 according to all textual witnesses). 1 Kgs 11:28 connects Jeroboam with the house of Joseph.

21. Oswald (2020, 95) disagrees: in the Saul-David narratives, the house of Benjamin with the Saulides stands against the house of Judah that follows David (1 Sam 22:7; 2 Sam

the state of ninth-century Judah was ruled by the house of David, David's clan became identified as part of the tribe of Judah, as evinced by the tribal blessing in Gen 49:8–12 and Mic 5:1 [5:2].

Israel's covenant with David was not dynastic; the house of David or his descendants are not mentioned. Two generations later, Rehoboam needed to negotiate with "all Israel" to be acclaimed as their king but failed (1 Kgs 12:1–24). David's attempt to merge the north with the south proved too fragile in the long run. The socioeconomic contrast between the larger and wealthier population of the central hill country and the poor and under-populated south, which even claimed dynastic leadership, may have played a role.[22]

When were these narratives crystallized in oral form, and when and where did they receive their literary form? For Sergi, the stories were written down by Jerusalem scribes of the established Judean kingdom in the late ninth century: "The stories about the rise of David in 1 Sam 16–2 Sam 5 . . . should be read for what they are: a story about the rise of Israelite monarchy. . . . These traditions are a literary product of an intellectual elite that should be dated to the period after the formation of the territorial kingdom centered on Jerusalem (second half of the ninth century BCE)" (Sergi 2020, 82).

For Oswald, the core narrative was crystallized in oral form at a time when Benjamin was allied with Jerusalem, before the rise of the Omrides who would dominate the Benjamin region. Preserving memories from the tenth century, the oral narrative found its shape in the early ninth century. At that time (around 900) southern Benjamin had become subject to the Judean kingdom, when King Asa of Judah "built Geba of Benjamin and Miz-pah" (1 Kgs 15:22; cf. Jer 41:9). From this time onward, the narrative was

---

2:10; 20:1). Here I part with Sergi: in their power struggle against Benjamin, the Judahites could easily have accepted as their leader a strong outsider who had built his power base in their territory.

22. "In the 10th century, the sedentary population of the Judean Hills was only ca. 3 percent of the total population of the country, as compared to ca. 10 percent in the 8th century B.C.E. and ca. 20 percent in the 7th century B.C.E. David's power (and Solomon's after him) did not stem, therefore, from a solid sedentary population, but from the special composition of the population of Judah (which still had, at that time, a strong non-sedentary element), and from the personality of the monarch. The demographic dispersal of the 10th century may also explain one of the reasons for the division of the United Monarchy—the much larger and wealthier population of the northern part of the central hill country arose against the dynasty of the poor and underpopulated south" (Finkelstein 1993, 63). For Finkelstein's later views of the united monarchy, see p. 61 n. 6.

an essential part of the dynastic self-conception of Judah. With the fall of Samaria in 722 and Benjamin again being attached to Judah, the narrative would gain importance: it would underline the primacy of the Judean kingdom and its dynasty, so that the Benjaminites should submit to Jerusalem and accept the house of David as their legitimate rulers. Thus, for Oswald (2020), the narrative found its literary form around 720, when there definitely was an advanced literate milieu in Jerusalem.[23]

While differing in many details, these scholars identify historical roots of the Saul-David stories and the Succession Narrative in the tenth century. There is no agreement on the time of literary formation, but this is not essential for my analysis of the developing royal ideology in Jerusalem. Schniedewind's identification of early archival documents from Solomon's time (see p. 22) evinces the presence of scribal resources in Jerusalem around the mid-tenth century. Similarly, an early core in 2 Sam 7 and a possible dating of some royal psalms to the late tenth or early ninth century could point to early literary formation of the David narratives. The expansion of Jerusalem with new administrative quarters around the early ninth century would point in the same direction.

Neighboring nations would soon designate the new Judean state as the "house of David." The mention of "house of David" and references to Israel in the Moabite Mesha Stela (ca. 840) and Tel Dan Inscription[24] of the Aramean

---

23. Finkelstein (2013, 155–56) would concur: early oral versions of the history of David's rise and the Succession History were written down in the late eighth century. In contrast, Van Seters (1983, 277–91) and Sweeney (2001, 93–107) ascribe the Succession Narrative to Deuteronomistic editors in the seventh century.

24. The authenticity of the Tel Dan inscription should not be taken for granted. It could be another example of a forged artifact "planted" into an excavation. The inscription gives the impression that the Dan region belonged to the house of Israel before it was retaken by the Aramean King Hazael around 840, as 1 Kgs 12:29 may suggest. However, Hazor—the Omrides' northern border fortress—was located 27 km to the south, and archaeological analysis suggests that Dan was included in the Northern Kingdom only by Jeroboam II in the early eighth century. It was Hazael who built the large city of stratum III. The earlier site was modest and populated by an indigenous group; Phoenician and Aramean influences and the presence of a non-Israelite cult can be recognized (Arie 2008; Thareani 2016, 2019). The three pieces of the stela were not found during regular stratigraphic excavations. Pieces 1 and 2B were identified not when their asserted strata were cleared out but rather a year later (respectively in 1993 and 1994), while piece 2A was identified in debris removed in a wheelbarrow (G. Cook, undated; Biran 1994a, 5; 1994b, 22; Biran and Naveh 1995, 2; Shanks 1999, 89). Further, the inscription came to light just in time to enter the debate about King David as a historical figure.

King Hazael (ca. 835) hardly make sense without David being the first king of the Judean dynasty. "House of David" was the common denomination for the Judean state and its dynasty (1 Kgs 12:16; Isa 7:2).

> I am Mesha, son of Chemosh, king of Moab, from Dibon. . . . Omri was king of *Israel* and oppressed Moab during many days, and Chemosh was angry with his aggressions. His son succeeded him, and he also said, "I will oppress Moab." In my days he said, "Let us go, and I will see my desire upon him and his house," and Israel said, "I shall destroy it forever." Now Omri took the land of Madeba and occupied it in his day and in the days of his son, forty years. And Chemosh had mercy on it in my time. . . . And the *men of Gad* dwelled in the country of Ataroth from ancient times,[25] and the king of Israel fortified Ataroth for himself. I assaulted the city, captured it and killed all the warriors. Chemosh and Moab came in possession of the city.[26] I carried away from there the fire hearth of its beloved and hauled it before Chemosh in Qariyot. . . . And Chemosh said to me, "Go take Nebo from *Israel*!" And I went in the night and fought against it from the break of day till noon and took it, and I killed seven thousand men. I did not kill the women and maidens, for I devoted them to Ashtar-Chemosh. I took from it the vessels of Yhwh and offered them before Chemosh. And the *king of Israel* fortified Jahaz and occupied it when he made war against me. Chemosh drove him out before me, and I took from Moab two hundred men in all and placed them in Jahaz, and took it to annex it to Dibon. . . . As for Horonaim, the *house of David* dwelt there, on the ancient descent.[27] And Chemosh said to me, "Go down, make war against Horonaim, and take it!" And I assaulted it and took it, for Chemosh restored it in my days. (Mesha Stela)

> And the *king of I[s]rael* previously entered my father's land, [and] Hadad made me king. . . . [I killed Jeho]ram son [of Ahab,] *king of Israel*, and [I] killed [Ahaz]iahu son of [Jehoram, *kin]g of the house of David*, and I set

---

25. Here, the "men of Gad" are indigenous residents of the Madaba plain, a region now brought under Moabite rule, while biblical texts consider Gad an Israelite tribe. Borders and ethnic identity may be fluid in this early period. "This tribe might still have been independent between Israel and nascent Moab" (Blum 2020, 217).

26. Translation of lines 23–29 based on Blum 2020, 212–13.

27. Lemaire (1994) suggests the reading *bêtdāwīd* ("house of David") in line 31 of the Mesha Stela, a reading accepted by a majority of the scholars and now confirmed by multispectral imaging of the stele and early squeezes of it; see Langlois 2019a.

[their towns into ruins and turned] their land into [desolation.] (Tel Dan inscription, lines 3–4, 7–10)

David may emerge from the shadows of history as dominating a small territory between Mizpah and Hebron with an extension to the Shephelah (cf. Qeiyafa) and, by covenant with the highland tribes to the north, elected as their king.

The Israel Tribes of the North

The Israel that enters into covenant with David, the military commander of the south—whence do they come? What are the historical roots of the tribal entity of the central highlands that appears under the name "Israel"? In the late tenth or early ninth century these tribes appear in history as the core and power base of the Northern Kingdom (see chap. 2).

The Merenptah Stela from 1207 evinces a tribal entity, not identified with any city-state in Canaan, with the name Israel. For Egypt, this Israel was an opponent worth celebrating in victory.

The continued history of this tribal Israel is not at all clear. The Israelites are commonly connected with two hundred small highland villages appearing in the twelfth, eleventh, and tenth centuries (Faust 2014, 65–109, 227–34; Gadot 2019). These villages appear after the collapse of the earlier city-states around the beginning of the twelfth century, with the 1177 attack by the Sea Peoples and a prolonged period of drought as main causes for the sociopolitical changes in the Levant (Cline 2020). The city plan with houses constructed in a circle around an open space, resembling a nomadic camp, betrays links to a nomadic prehistory. In pottery design, archaeologists identify both new traits and features common with earlier Canaanite culture in the region. In the subsequent centuries, potters continued to develop these designs throughout the history of the Northern and Southern Kingdoms. The architecture of the "four-room house" appears as another cultural marker from these villages that remained in Israel and Judah until 722 and 587.

In Judg 4–5 (the battle and Song of Deborah and Barak), the tribes emerge more clearly. The poetic units of Judg 5 carry traits of archaic Biblical Hebrew, which suggests that they preserve true memories from the early eleventh century (Hendel and Joosten 2018, 101–4).

The earlier battle account in Judg 5:12–22 does not mention Israel but names the tribes involved, "the people of Yhwh" (5:13): Ephraim, Benjamin,

Machir, Zebulun, Issachar, Reuben, Gilead, Dan, Asher, and Naphtali. This ten-tribe list bears archaic features with its inclusion of Machir and Gilead— in later lists reduced to clans within Manasseh and replaced with the tribes Manasseh and Gad. Judah, Simeon, and Levi are not mentioned.

The poem betrays weaknesses in a tribal union that was expected to appear as a unified community and as the one people of Yhwh. Only six tribes respond to the call to battle; four choose to stay home. The tribes staying home are geographically distant: Reuben and Gilead are across the Jordan herding their flocks, while Dan and Asher, located at the seacoast, are busy with ships and trade. "Far from a political-cultic unity, Israel is a diffuse network of autonomous tribes who may or may not join together for common interests against a common enemy" (Hendel and Joosten 2018, 104).

In the introductory hymn in Judg 5:2–11, we find phrases such as "Yhwh, he from Sinai," "Yhwh, the god of Israel," "a mother in Israel," "rulers of Israel," "the rural folks in Israel." The sociocultural context appears as rural and oral: "By the watering places they recount the righteous deeds of Yhwh, the righteous deeds of his rural folks in Israel." The full composite text of the Song of Deborah intends to fashion a common identity of this early Israel (Hendel and Joosten 2018, 104).

Monroe and Fleming (2019, 19) identify an early "Little Israel" concentrated in the highlands between Jerusalem and the Jezreel Valley, an entity that in the tenth century appears in the accounts of the kingdoms of Saul and David, the geography of which was tied to the central highlands. This "Little Israel" developed into a "Greater Israel" in the early ninth-century kingdom of the house of Omri.

In the early sources, Benjamin is one of the Israel tribes. After the emergence of the two kingdoms, the plain of Benjamin was contested border territory. The settlements of southern Benjamin became allied with Jerusalem as it rose to power around 1100 (Sergi 2017, 8–12). But from the late tenth century, Benjamin sided with the Israel tribes of the north, even though the tribe was wooed by the Jerusalem rulers. For a short period in the early ninth century, Judah ruled the southern Benjamin region (1 Kgs 15:17–22).

The House of Saul

With extensive Saul traditions present in the Deuteronomistic History (hereafter DtrH), there must be a historical kernel behind the traditions of his kingdom, centered in the southern highlands. Israel appears as a tribal or clan union that chooses the Benjaminite Saul as its king (1 Sam 8–10). Terms such as "Israel," "the land of Israel," "territory of Israel," "all Israel," and "children of Israel" are integral to the Saul narratives: "Two episodes in . . . the old Saul northern royal tradition—the rescue of Jabesh and battle of Michmash—refer to a group of people or an entity named Israel" (Finkelstein 2019, 12; 1 Sam 11:7–8, 13; 13:4–6, 13, 19).[28]

Saul rose to power as military leader and liberator (11:15; 14:47). In sociological terms, he appears more as a leader of a tribal confederation than head of a bourgeoning state.[29] In the texts there is no trace of a capital, a central bureaucracy, or a professional army. The house of Saul appears in the texts with a claim for royal leadership over a tribal union, and "chiefdom" would be a fitting designation for this rule.

Saul appears as the elected head of kinship groups denoting themselves as *Israel*. But did he really rule "all Israel," the tribes that inhabited the highlands between Bethel and the Jezreel Valley? His home turf remained Benjaminite territory; he ruled from Gibeah, northwest of Jerusalem, which had grown in power after the downfall of Shechem in the late eleventh century. For Sergi, the early Saul tradition does not see him ruling the region of Shechem and Samaria, the later heartland of the Omride kingdom. It rather "tells how Saul came to rule his Israelite kinsmen residing in the Benjamin plateau" (Sergi 2020, 78).

According to 2 Sam 2:8–9, the house of Saul ruled a larger territory: Saul's son Ishbaal[30] ruled "toward Gilead, toward the Ashurites, and toward Jezreel; over Ephraim, over Benjamin, (that means), over all Israel" (my translation). Gilead (east of the Jordan), the Jezreel Valley, and the Ashurites (= Geshur or those of Asher?) represent the directions in which his rule extended (Monroe and Fleming 2019, 22).[31] Finkelstein (2020, 46–47) asserts that Saul ruled the highlands up to the Jezreel Valley. His will to dominate also the north is indicated by his death in the battle of the Gilboa hills and

---

28. "The name *Israel* is mentioned fourteen times in 1 Sam 13–14 (the stories about Saul's wars with the Philistines). In most of these cases the term clearly refers to a group of people; that is, in 1 Sam 13–14 it is a designation for a kinship group and not for a territorial polity. The text identifies the Israelites as a composite of clan/tribal society settled in the Benjamin plateau and in the southern Ephraim hill country" (Sergi 2020, 78).

29. One may compare the copper industry at Faynan in the Arava Valley, probably organized by a tribal confederation from the Egyptian pullout in 1140 until the development of a proto-kingdom in the late eleventh century (Ben-Yosef et al. 2019; Levy 2020).

30. G renders his name as *Eisbaal*; M changes *baʿal* to *bōšet* ("shame").

31. The meaning and location of "the Ashurites" are not clear. Latin and Syriac give more meaning, reading Geshur.

the campaign to Jabesh-Gilead with initial mustering of the forces at Bezek east of the Jordan.

Elements in the David narratives confirm that the house of Saul was a dynasty with a claim on kingship in Israel. For the biblical editors, the Saulides had been replaced as legitimate rulers of Israel by the house of David. They made it clear that the line of Saul faded out of history, explicitly noting that Saul's daughter Michal bore no children (2 Sam 6:23). According to 21:1–14, David allowed the Gibeonites to kill seven descendants of Saul, while 2 Sam 4 reports the death of Saul's son Ishbaal, who had ruled for two years after the death of Saul—killed without David's initiative.

Texts from Genesis and the Prophets

David had a power base in Judah to the south and, by covenant, was elected by the northern tribes as "king of Israel." Do other early texts identify memories of a union between the Israelite tribes and Judah to the south?

The Jacob and Joseph narratives in Genesis may bear on this question. These sagas of the Northern Kingdom envisage an Israel comprising both north and south, with Joseph in the first place. Judah is part of the all-Israel tribal system, and it is noteworthy that Benjamin is associated with Joseph, the ancestor of the northern tribes Ephraim and Manasseh—as Benjamin was connected to Judah both in the early tenth century and the post-722 period. These texts preserve the memory of an early union that included the central northern tribes as well as Judah (Weingart 2019, 29).

The same twelve tribes are listed in Jacob's tribal blessings in Gen 49. According to 49:10–12, both the present and future rulers stem from Judah—which will be set above the other tribes and the neighboring nations. The blessings preserve tradition of the Israel tribes from the time of the Northern Kingdom, while the royal blessing on Judah likely was elaborated by Jerusalemite scribes after 722. Still, Judah appears in the fourth place of the tribes, suggesting that Judah could have been more briefly described in the earlier version or that Judah had a firm place as number four in a tribal list.

Three eighth-century prophets preserve memories of an early connection between Judah and Israel. The Jerusalemite Isaiah remembers the days when "Ephraim turned away from Judah" (7:17 NJPS) and talks about "both houses of Israel" (8:14), thus echoing "a claim that the house of David never gave up its heritage as onetime rulers of Israel" (Fleming 2012, 48–49).

The northern prophet Hosea envisages a restoration when Israel and Judah will come together under a common leader (2:2 [1:11])—probably preserving a memory of an earlier union. Hosea remembers a time when Ephraim and Judah were laboring together (Laato 2016, 510–13):

> Ephraim was a trained heifer that loved threshing,
> I placed a yoke upon her sleek neck.
> Ephraim will go first,
> and Judah will plow,
> Jacob shall do the harrowing! (Hos 10:11, my translation)

Both Amos and the book named after him reflect a concept of two sister-nations under Yhwh. Amos came from Tekoa in the south and carried out his prophetic ministry in Bethel of the north. His book opens with Yhwh roaring as a lion from Zion/Jerusalem—the lion was a symbol of the divine in the ancient Near East—with a message of judgment on Israel (2:6–16). In the mouth of Amos the southerner, Yhwh of Zion addresses the northern nation as "my people Israel" (8:2) and proclaims that "the end has come upon my people Israel." And in the exilic additions to the book, 9:11–12 and 9:13–15 (see pp. 112–14), the reestablishment of the fallen booth of David (9:11–12) is connected to the restoration of "my people Israel."

Traditions of David as "king of Israel"; a memory of a union between the two houses of Israel in Isaiah, Hosea, and (probably) Amos; and tribal traditions reflected in Genesis—all point to an early communion between the northern and southern entities, likely connected to David in the early tenth century.[32]

David, Solomon, and the Davidic Kingdom

With David secured as a historical figure, ruling a temporary union between northern tribes and Judah in the south, one may surmise that his successor indeed was Solomon, although no extrabiblical references to Solomon have been identified.

---

32. Sergi (2017, 8–12) might formulate it differently: early on, Jerusalem/Judah was allied only with Benjamin and the southern Ephraim highlands. Subsequently, "Israel and Judah developed separately, side by side, throughout the 10th to the 9th century BCE" (Sergi 2020, 65).

How large was the state of David and Solomon? David's rule may have extended from Qeiyafa and Hebron in the south and—through his alliance with the Israel tribes—likely included the central highlands south of the Jezreel Valley. These regions would subsequently have been the power base for Solomon's kingdom.

The choice of Jerusalem, a place that belonged neither to Judah nor to Benjamin, as capital was strategically ingenious—none of the tribes could claim the capital as their own. Traditions from the northern tribes would in time find their home in Jerusalem.

The ark of the covenant was a symbol of God's presence for the northern tribes—located in Shiloh until the Philistine wars in the early eleventh century. According to 1 Sam 6–7, the Judahites of Beth-shemesh were not comfortable hosting the "ark of Yhwh" and asked the Benjaminites of Kiriath-jearim to take responsibility for it (cf. Josh 18:28). In Kiriath-jearim, the ark had come back to the tribes of Israel. David's later transfer of the ark to Zion is a powerful symbol of the union he tried to establish between Judah and "all Israel." His decision to house the ark in a tabernacle, a nonpermanent structure that could be moved around, demonstrates that the time was not ripe for building a central temple (2 Sam 6:17; 7:2).

Biblical reports that David ruled Edom or Moab hardly reflect historical reality (2 Sam 8:14 ∥ 1 Chr 18:13; 1 Chr 18:2 ≈ 2 Sam 8:2–3). These verses may preserve a memory of the rule of the northern Omrides in the ninth century or reflect the reality of Hasmonean times.

David is portrayed as a king with his own elite force of mercenaries (2 Sam 8:18; 15:18; 20:7, 23), with a core stemming from David's gang of outcasts in his early years. The lists of David's officials in 2 Sam 8:16–18 and 20:23–26 appear as early archival texts. Together, these factors point to the early history of a kingdom in the making.[33]

The book of 1 Kings preserves archival lists and documents reflecting political structures with bureaucracy and regional officers and tax collectors,

33. In their analysis of sociopolitical structures in Edom, Levy, Najjar, and Ben-Yosef (2014a, 289) distinguish between chiefdom, kingdom, and state. A kingdom is a politically organized community or major territorial unit ruled by a king (in Semitic tradition, *melek* ["king"] was the common term for a leader of a territorial entity) and with political organization involving the jurisdiction over a region. Kingdoms can also connote a palace, government, military, monumental construction, and social stratification, but the extent of political hegemony and size is left vague. State or empire denotes a social organization of exceptional size and complexity. In tenth-century Edom, they identify a complex society (kingdom/small state) (Levy, Najjar, and Ben-Yosef 2014a, 3, 232; 2014b, 985, 992).

which give meaning only in the time of Solomon (4:2–19). The king used resources gathered through taxes and by levying corvée on the northern tribes to build persistent state structures (Blum 2010, 73).

Schniedewind notes archaic features in the list of twelve administrative districts (4:7–19): the list is organized around early clan-based tribal structures and ignores the (probably later) twelve-tribe division (six of the twelve tribes are listed, seven if one counts Gilead; cf. Judg 5:17; see pp. 16–17).[34] This list indicates that Solomon also ruled the northern tribes. Schniedewind (1999, 24) concludes that the classic characteristics of an early state emerged only in the Solomonic period.

He further argues that early Israelite scribal curricula were influenced by cuneiform traditions that were in active use both in Mesopotamia and Egypt (Schniedewind 2019; cf. Blum 2010, 71–72). In the late Bronze Age, Akkadian language and cuneiform script were the media for international communication. This system fell out of use in the Iron Age and was replaced with early attempts of developing specific scripts for the local languages (Gzella 2015, 20–22; Sergi and de Hulster 2016, 3–4). The earliest documents written by court scribes in Jerusalem may have been written in cuneiform script, before they turned to Old Hebrew.

The descriptions in DtrH of the extension of the state under David and Solomon should be interpreted as "preached, ideal history." At the same time, these narratives may reflect that scribes in the smaller seventh-century kingdom of Judah preserved a memory of a larger, united territorial entity under these two kings. Memories of the extension of the large ninth-century Omride state, brought to the south by northern scribes after 722, also set their stamp on the narratives.

The developing polities of Judah, Israel, and Edom caused Pharaoh Shishak to campaign in Canaan and Transjordan, either in the time of Solomon (1 Kgs 9:16) or more probably that of his son Rehoboam (14:25–27; Finkelstein 2002; Krause 2020, 119–26). If the campaign coincided with Rehoboam's reign, the invasion may be dated to around 925.[35] According to

---

34. Schniedewind 2022 identifies copies of archival documents from the tenth century from David's and Solomon's time: 2 Sam 8:16–18; 20:23–26; 1 Kgs 4:2–6, 7–19; 7:41–46 (list of temple items and metal casting in the Jordan Valley); 9:15–19 (Solomon's building projects). In 1 Kgs 14:25–27 he identifies an archive text from Rehoboam's reign. The tribal names recurring in 4:7–19 are Ephraim, (Ramoth-)gilead, Napthali, Asher, Issachar, Benjamin, and Judah.

35. Shishak's rule is traditionally dated to 945–924. Biblical texts (some based on archival sources) clearly connect Shishak with Rehoboam and Jeroboam (1 Kgs 11:40). A

Shishak's Karnak record, the campaign primarily focused on the territory of Israel, including Benjamin, while Jerusalem was subject only to tribute (cf. 14:26). Krause (2020, 127) suggests that Shishak's campaign opened the way for Rehoboam to gain supremacy over the Benjamin region and push the border against Israel northward.

For Weingart, the core of the Jeroboam/Rehoboam narrative (1 Kgs 11:26–40; 12:1–20) is pre-Deuteronomistic: one can note a positive view of Jeroboam and the establishment of the Northern Kingdom alongside a critical perspective on Solomon and Rehoboam. Davidic rule over more than one tribe is rejected. Thus, the Jeroboam/Rehoboam narrative has origins in the north before 722. At the same time, one can observe echoes of the narratives of David's rise to the throne that show knowledge of the Saul-David stories (Weingart 2020). Referring to Becker (2000, 216), who reads 1 Kgs 12 as a justification of the God-willed existence of two states, Weingart rhetorically asks: "If the coexistence of two separate states was a matter that needed explanation, does this not require at least the concept of a unified state in the background?" (2020, 150).

Subsequent to the (ascribed) time of Solomon, in the late tenth and early ninth centuries there was a continued power struggle between Judah in the south and Israel in the north, with Benjamin as contested border region (Sergi 2017, 15; Krause 2020, 126–27). Finding momentum when King Baasha of Israel and Ben-hadad of Damascus fought over the dominion of the northern Jordan Valley around 900, King Asa of Judah gained territory to the north, and "built Geba of Benjamin and Mizpah" (1 Kgs 15:17–22).

Throughout the ninth century, Jerusalem continued to grow and remained "the most developed urban center in the region, with well-built fortifications and structures" (Lipschits 2020, 167–68).[36] The kingdom expanded too. For geopolitical reasons, the region between Mizpah and Jerusalem had in earlier centuries been separated from the southern highlands around Hebron. This would now change. The Davidic dynasty united these two south-

---

scarab bearing the name Sheshonq was found in 2006 at a stronghold 5 km from the Edomite copper production site Khirbet en-Nahas. During his campaign, Shishak took control of the copper production at Timna and en-Nahas (Levy, Najjar, and Ben-Yosef 2014b, 748–49, 983–93).

36. See Uziel and Gadot 2017. Sergi (2020, 65) notes: "Throughout the Iron IIA the power and strength of Jerusalem grew steadily, reflecting the accumulation of economic and consequently also political wealth in the hands of its ruling dynasty: the house of David."

ern regions of the hill country and took the name Judah from its southern parts. From there the kingdom expanded into the Shephelah and the lowlands (Lipschits 2020, 168–71): "The integration of the southern territory into the kingdom of Jerusalem, the establishment of the kingdom of Judah, and the later integration of the lowland into that kingdom, probably in the second half of the ninth century, were the most important achievements of the Davidic kings" (Lipschits 2020, 168–69). From the late tenth century and until the Syro-Ephraimite war in 734–732, the house of Israel was the larger and more powerful of the sister nations. Throughout its history, Israel held the territory from the north all the way to Bethel and Jericho. Judah remained the smaller brother.

In the mid-eighth century Uzziah bolstered Judah's dominion in the south. From his time, a number of fortresses guarding the eastern and southern borders have been identified. Then, the fall of Samaria led to a large influx of northerners to Jerusalem and central Judea. Hezekiah used the momentum to campaign to the north to secure the Benjamin hills for the Judean kingdom (cf. Hos 5:8–11) but was likely not able to establish a permanent foothold there. However, Gezer, earlier belonging to Israel, was incorporated in the Judean state under Ahaz or Hezekiah (see p. 5 n. 5). Hezekiah's expansion toward Philistia (2 Kgs 18:7–8) was halted by Sennacherib's 701 campaign. And by 732 and 715, Israel and Philistia were divided into Assyrian provinces (see figure 4, p. 63).

Sennacherib left the Shephelah devastated—likely one of the factors that led to the demographic growth in central Judea. In the late eighth and especially the seventh centuries, archaeologists identify a substantial development of the district around Jerusalem, with a growth of towns, villages, hamlets, and agricultural installations (Lipschits 2020, 169).

Only with the demise of the Assyrian Empire in the 630s and 620s was Josiah able to secure the territory up to the Bethel-Jericho line for Judah. Thus, the territory of greater Benjamin was for the first time fully included in Judah. And with the Assyrian withdrawal, Josiah could again establish Judean presence in the Shephelah (Lipschits 2020, 173–77).

This kingdom of Judah, changing through the centuries, is the scene of the development, editing, and reediting of hymns and oracles related to the present or future son of David. With an eye to the sociopolitical realities in the Levant, there seems to be a large gap between political reality and a royal theology that would easily be deemed fully utopian.

Figure 2. The Northern Kingdom and Judea in the mid-ninth century BCE.

Tirzah—a strong urban center from around 900; destroyed around 850 and remained in ruins.

Shechem—destroyed in the early tenth century and only sparsely settled during the tenth and ninth centuries.

Kedesh and Abel-beth-maacah—included in the Northern Kingdom only around 800, under the Jehu dynasty.

Gath—the largest Philistine city, destroyed by Hazael in the late ninth century.

Ancient Near Eastern Tradition on the Divinely Installed King

Royal traditions connected to the house of David are indebted to Mesopotamian and Egyptian traditions. The links between these traditions demonstrate early scribal interaction between Israelite scribes in Jerusalem and their counterparts in the east and west.

Mesopotamian Texts

Among relevant Mesopotamian texts we find oracular texts from nineteenth-century Eshnunna, eighteenth-century Mari, and Assyrian texts from the late second millennium. (In the texts quoted here, particularly relevant terms are italicized.) In an Eshnunna oracle from the nineteenth century, the goddess Kititum speaks to her king Ibalpiel:

> Because you always have my name in your mouth, I will continually open the secrets of the gods for you. At the advice of the gods and by the decree of Anu, *the country is given you* to rule. . . . You will ransom the riches of the upper and lower country. Your wealth shall not diminish . . . I, Kititum, have established a protective spirit for you, and *will strengthen the foundations of your throne. May your ear hear my voice*! (Laato 1998, 41)

Among eighteenth-century texts from Mari, a city-state on the Euphrates, there are texts with oracles delivered by cult prophets. In one, the god Adad speaks emphatically to King Zimri-Lim, vassal king under Yarim-Lim, father of Hammurabi: Adad has fostered Zimri-Lim, restored him to his father's throne, and promises him a continued dynasty if the king obeys the will of his god and provides Adad with a sanctuary. Adad has given the king a throne and a palace and requires the king to provide him with an inheritance, a permanent temple. As in tenth-century Jerusalem, there is a movement from the earlier nomadic tent shrine to the monarchic model with a royal temple (Malamat 1980):

> Am I not Adad, Lord of Halab, who has raised you . . . and made you regain the throne of your father's house? . . . This is what I demanded from you: when a wronged man or woman cries out to you, stand and let his case be judged! What I have communicated to you, you will do! *You will heed my word and [I will give you] the land* from the ri[sing of the sun to its setting]. (Text B [Malamat 1980])

Am I not [Ad]ad, Lord of Kallassu, who *reared him between my loins*[37] and restored him to the throne of his father's house? After I restored him to the throne of his father's house, *I have given him a residence*. Since I restored him to the throne of his father's house, I will *ask him to provide an inheritance for me*. Should he not provide it, am I not master of throne, territory and city? What I have given, I can take away. *If he satisfies my desire and heeds my word, I shall give him throne upon throne*, house upon house, territory upon territory, city upon city. And I shall give him the land from the rising of the sun to its setting. . . .

Now, the diviner of Adad—the Lord of Kallassu—is guarding the *tent-shrine* of Alahtum,[38] which shall be the lot of his inheritance. (Text A [Malamat 1980])

There is a long time between nineteenth-century Eshnunna, eighteenth-century Mari, and tenth-century Jerusalem. But the close parallels between this Mari oracle and Judean royal tradition suggest that similar traditions on king, god, and sanctuary were common in Mesopotamian city-states throughout the second millennium and subsequently filtered through to Judean scribes.

Assyrian building inscriptions from the late second millennium promise an eternal dynasty to the king who is both ruler and priest:

You (the gods) granted him [Tiglath-pileser I] leadership, supremacy and valour, you pronounced *forever his destiny of dominion* as powerful as his *priestly progeny for service* in Ehursagkurkurra. (Laato 1998, 38–40 at 39)

Tiglath-pileser I (1114–1076) prays for earthly blessings, for victory over his enemies, and that his dynasty forever should stand as ruling priests for the gods of Asshur:

Because I made plans without easing . . . may the gods Anu and Adad faithfully have mercy on me . . . may they heed my fervent petitions, *grant abundant rain and rich years* during my reign . . . may they *subdue under*

---

37. "Reared him between my loins" (lit., "between my testicles")—cf. Yhwh conceiving and giving birth to the king in Ps 2 and Ps 110. Adad may here be depicted in the form of a bull—in the iconography, Adad is sometimes shown standing upon the back of a bull or personified as a bull.

38. Cf. "the Levites encamping around the tabernacle" in the wilderness (Num 1:53, my translation).

*me all enemy lands, rebellious mountain regions and rulers who are hostile
to me.* May they pronounce *a blessing of favor over me and my priestly
progeny.* May they *firmly place my priesthood in the presence of the god*
Asshur and their great divinity *forever* like a mountain. (Laato 1998, 40)

Dedicating a temple to Asshur, Shalmaneser I (1274–1245) prayed that
the god who has received his temple from the royal builder will provide for
him an everlasting dynasty:

When Asshur, the lord, enters the temple and joyfully takes his place
on high, may he see the brilliant work of the temple and rejoice. May he
receive my prayers and hear my supplications. May he *for eternity* decree with his mighty voice *abundance* during my reign and a destiny of
well-being for my vice-regency and the *vice-regency of my progeny.* (Laato
1998, 39)

Egyptian Texts

In Egypt, we encounter a father-son relation between god and the king. The
title "son of [the solar god] Re" is attested as early as the third millennium.
Four texts from the mid-second millennium describe divine conception of
the new king.

A condensed presentation of this myth is found in "Myth of the Procreation and Birth of the King" (fifteenth century). In this text, Amon,
king of the gods, decides to procreate a new king over the entire world.
Disguised as the queen's husband, he enters her bed and conceives the
coming crown prince. His odor (a euphemism for his semen) impregnates the queen's limbs. Subsequently, Amon commands the god Khnum
to create the child in Amon's likeness, and the pregnancy is proclaimed
to the queen. After the birth of the prince, Amon addresses the child
and acknowledges his fatherhood. In the pictorial circle of carved reliefs,
Amon is portrayed embracing the newborn child that is sitting on his lap
(Granerød 2010a, 325–26).[39]

In the coronation accounts of Hatshepshut (1507–1458) and Amenhotep
III (1386–1349), Amon takes the form of the king and has intercourse with
the queen, filling her with "his dew." In the coronation account of Horem-

---

39. For a Mesopotamian parallel, cf. "I reared him between my loins" in the Mari text.

heb (around 1315), the coming pharaoh has divine qualities even as a child. In these three cases, the succession to the throne was contested, which may explain the promotion and preservation of these coronation stories (Roberts 1997, 126–29)—cf. 2 Sam 7 and Ps 2 as possible apologetic texts for Solomon and his house as legitimate heirs of David. Although the new king is described as conceived by the god, these are coronation texts for the acclaimed king, not texts rejoicing over the birth of a crown prince or promotion texts for one throne pretender among others (see pp. 81–85 on Isa 9:5–6 [9:6–7]).

During the coronation, royal symbols and a "divinely written decree" were given to the new pharaoh. In the decree, Amon addresses the king and proclaims: "*You are my son, today I have begotten you.*" Subsequently Amon addresses the divine council and introduces his royal son to them, and the gods acclaim that a divine son is born—an acclamation that may enlighten the understanding of "a son is born to us" (Isa 9:5 [9:6]).

The close echoes[40] of these Egyptian concepts in Ps 2 and Ps 110 demonstrate that the Egyptian myth of divine procreation was still promoted around the tenth century and directly influenced Judean coronation liturgies. It is often argued that the Egyptian king physically was regarded as "the son of Re/Amon" walking on earth. Conceived by his god, the king was the physical offspring of the deity and carried divine nature. In contrast, biblical literature would (in polemic reception) not attribute divine nature to the king and rather understand the God-king relation in adoption categories (e.g., von Rad 1947; Alt 1950).

Roberts (1997, 116–17, 126–29) tends to disagree: the stories about divine conception of the king were also then understood for what they are—mythological stories with a symbolic message. The Egyptians regarded pharaoh's *office* as divine but did not ascribe divine nature to the king. Any individual king was a transitory figure, while kingship was eternal. Thus, the difference between Egyptian and Judean royal ideology is not necessarily so great.

How were early Israelite scribes reasoning when they imported and adapted traditions on foreign kings and their pagan gods from a polytheistic setting into a Yahwistic framework, either within a monotheistic or

---

40. For stylistic reasons I regularly use the term "echo" in a general way, without referring to literary theorists' discerning between "quotation," "allusion" (a consciously created marker of an earlier text in a later one), and "echo" (evoking an earlier text without intending to enrich one's own thereby).

monolatric theological model?[41] From a systematic-theological viewpoint, one could argue that God or earthly scribes used the natural revelation—structures in the created world—as means for the special revelation to God's people. With the institution of kingship in place, scribes would naturally draw analogies with ideologies of neighboring kingdoms and their dynasties' legitimation of power. With reflected monotheistic voices such as Amos, Deuteronomy, and Deutero-Isaiah, epithets and characteristics of other gods would be adopted and transferred to Yhwh, perceived as Lord of heaven and earth.

The Son of David as Yhwh's Viceroy

The central texts in the development of the son of David theology in the Judean kingdom have probable roots back to David and Solomon. I tend to date the source of 2 Sam 7 to the tenth century; the core of Pss 2, 110, and 21 to the late tenth or ninth century; and Ps 72 to the late eighth or seventh century.[42]

Two texts—2 Sam 7 and Ps 2—are the foundational texts for royal Judean theology and the election of the Davidic line. Parallels in Egyptian tradition suggest a dating of the core of these texts to the early kingdom, between the tenth and (at the latest) the early seventh centuries.

The Succession Narrative (2 Sam 9–20; 1 Kgs 1–2) fits tenth-century reality in Judah and cannot be later than the early ninth century. What about 2 Sam 7? In my view, the main elements in the Nathan promise could well go back to the time of David and preserve memory of an early prophetic oracle, the earliest building stone of the son of David tradition.

---

41. Some biblical scholars, who postulate an evolutionary development in Israelite faith from early monolatry or some kind of polytheism (some find reminiscences of a consort for Yhwh in texts and inscriptions) to the reflected monotheism of Deuteronomy and Deutero-Isaiah, hardly recognize the frequent belief in a "high god" or an original creator god among archaic tribes, recognized by scholars of religion.

42. "In sum, there is good reason to believe that all or part of Psalms 2, 21, 45, 72, 89, and 110 preserve royal traditions from Judah and Israel's earliest monarchal past. . . . [T]he bulk of these texts correlate with features of pre-Israelite royal ideology and have good claim to be among Judah's earliest written literature, a literature written to envision and script the social transition toward the monarchy in general and from one monarch to another in particular" (Carr 2011, 394–95).

Alternatively, the father-son and adoption terminology could have been developed by scribes of the Solomonic echelon as an apology for Solomon as David's legitimate successor or belong to the early post-Solomon period. In the latter case, 2 Sam 7 would be a foundational text for the claim of Solomon and the Solomonic line to the Jerusalem throne.[43]

For modern eyes and for historians of religion, 2 Sam 7 can be viewed as a sociopolitical apology for the claim by the line of Solomon to be legitimate rulers in Judea, arguing against opponents that this dynasty is elected by God, perhaps also trying to woo the neighboring tribe of Benjamin.

In a theological perspective, which perceives the development of biblical tradition as God-given revelation through the unfolding events of earthly history, one could ask: Could Yhwh, who elected Israel and Judah, intervene in human history and put his stamp on the family in power with promises of divine presence? It remains a paradox that the house of David remained in power for more than four hundred years in the tiny and politically weak state of Judah, while new dynasties regularly took over the throne of the Northern Kingdom. And as we know, the Davidic promises set a lasting stamp on messianic traditions in Judaism and Christianity.

2 Samuel 7: An Eternal House for David, a House for Yhwh?

The text of 2 Sam 7:5–16 has undergone editing, which makes it difficult precisely to reconstruct the earlier source. In 7:16, the M text may represent a clarification vis-à-vis the Greek, while the opposite could be the case in 7:11.[44] Here are the main differences between these two recensions (my translations):

43. Schniedewind (1999, 28) notes that Nathan's oracle serves three overt purposes: (1) it legitimizes David over Saul, (2) it justifies the monarchy as a divine institution, (3) it legitimizes the dynasty of David and Solomon.

44. Since Samuel R. Driver's 1890 commentary, the Greek text of Samuel has generally been considered superior to M. The David-Goliath narrative in 1 Sam 16:14–18:30 may be considered an exception. Here G[B] is substantially shorter than M, and I follow those scholars who consider the G *Vorlage* as a later, harmonizing recension (see pp. 174–75).

M	G
[5]Go and tell my servant David: Thus says Yhwh: *Are you really the one* to build me a house to dwell in?	[5]Go and tell my servant David: Thus says the Lord: You shall not build me a house for me to dwell in,
[6]I have not dwelled in a house since the day I brought up the children of Israel from Egypt to this day, but I have been moving around in a tent and a tabernacle.	
[7]Wherever I have moved around among all the children of Israel, did I ever speak to any leader in Israel, whom I commanded to shepherd my people Israel, saying, "Why have you not built me a house of cedar?"	
[8]. . . Thus says Yhwh of hosts: I took you *from the pasture, from following* the sheep, to be leader of my people Israel,	[8]. . . I took you from the sheepfold to be leader of my people Israel,
[9]and I have been with you wherever you went and cut off all your enemies from before you and made you renowned like the great ones of the earth.	
[10]And I will appoint a place for my people Israel and will plant them, so that they may live in their own place, and be disturbed no more; and evildoers shall afflict them no more, as formerly,	
[11]from the time I appointed judges over my people Israel; and I will give you rest from all your enemies. Now Yhwh declares to you that *Yhwh will make you a house.*	[11]. . . the Lord proclaims to you that you will build him a house.

M	G
¹²When your days are fulfilled and you lie down with your ancestors, I will raise up your offspring after you, who shall come forth from your body, and I will establish his kingdom,	
¹³/he shall build a house for my name/ and I will establish the throne of *his kingdom* forever.	¹³. . . and I will establish his throne forever.
¹⁴I will be a father to him, and he shall be a son to me. When he commits iniquity, I will punish him with a rod such as mortals use, with blows inflicted by men.	
¹⁵But my steadfast love will not depart from him, *as I took it from Saul,* whom I put away from before you.	¹⁵But I will not take my mercy from him, as I took it from those whom I removed from [walking] before me.
¹⁶*Your house and your kingdom* shall be made sure forever before me; your throne shall be established forever.	¹⁶And his house and his kingdom shall be made sure forever before me, and his throne shall be restored forever.

The chapter displays two separate but interrelated oracles: 7:5–7, which rejects David's offer to build a house for Yhwh, and 7:8–16, where Yhwh promises David to build him a house. The second oracle cannot be properly understood without the first and should be read as a contrasting sequel to the former, on the background of the storyline in 7:1–3, where David expresses his intention to build a permanent sanctuary for Yhwh.

Bayīt ("house") is a keyword recurring throughout the chapter: the king's luxurious house in 7:1–2 (in contrast to the tent of Yhwh), the negation of a house for Yhwh in 7:5–7, Yhwh making a permanent house for David in 7:11, "your [David's]house and your kingdom" in 7:16—with "house" in 7:11 and 7:16 designating a Davidic dynasty.

"He [your son] shall build a house for my name" in 7:13a appears as a later addition that moves the divine command to build the sanctuary back to the foundation oracle for the Solomonic dynasty. The same goes for 7:11b in G, which likely changed "Yhwh declares to you that *Yhwh* will make *you* a house" (M) to "the Lord proclaims to you that *you* will build *him* a house"—that is, through his son, David will indirectly be a temple builder. Here the Greek or its *Vorlage* clarifies an ambiguous statement—since the M text of 7:11c could be read "for he will build a house for you, O Yhwh."

"His house and his kingdom" in the G text of 7:16 refers to the house of Solomon and could fit a tenth-century strife about Solomon as David's legitimate successor, while M's "your house and your kingdom" may represent a clarification: the text should refer to the house of David, the designation of the lasting dynasty.

In 7:6–11, the terms "my people Israel," "the children of Israel," or cognates appear seven times. This is noteworthy since the oracle became a foundational text for the kingdom of Judah. The text probably preserves the memory of David being elected "king of Israel" and again points to a tenth-century background for the oracle.

Second Sam 7:13b may be a later explication, declaring that the sins of Solomon's later years would not nullify the divine promise. A similar statement appears in 1 Kgs 11:11–13: because of Solomon's sins, Yhwh will tear the kingdom away from the house of David, but only when his son will be in charge. However, Yhwh will leave him one tribe and a smaller kingdom, "for the sake of my servant David and for the sake of Jerusalem, which I have chosen." In the time of later kings with their shortcomings, the oracle would still uphold the lasting character of the Davidic dynasty.[45]

There are thematic parallels with the royal Mesopotamian texts quoted above: "I will strengthen the foundations of your throne" (Eshnunna); "I have given him a residence," "I will ask him to provide an inheritance for me," "I shall give him throne upon throne" (Mari); "you pronounced forever his destiny of dominion," "may they firmly place my priesthood in the presence of the god Asshur and their great divinity forever," "subdue under me all enemy lands, rebellious mountain regions and rulers who are hostile to me" (Assyria). In Mari, the god restored the king to his father's

---

45. This will be different in the postexilic David-and-Zion Ps 132:11–14, which looks back on the breakdown of state and kingship (see pp. 165–67): Yhwh's oath and covenant with David will secure the dynasty's lasting character only "if your sons keep my covenant and my decrees." In contrast, Yhwh's election of Zion as his eternal resting place will never be nullified.

throne—according to Nathan's words David was taken from the sheepfold to be leader of Yhwh's people. The Mesopotamian texts promise the king a lasting dynasty in the presence of the gods, as does the Nathan oracle.

"I will be a father to him, and he shall be a son to me" is an ancient formula of adoption or sonship.[46] The oracle proclaims that the coming king will be declared a son of Yhwh. In this text, we do not encounter mythological language about conception by divine semen or any heavenly intervention in his mother's womb.

Schniedewind (1999, 30) notes that Isaiah takes for granted the promise to David (7:1–17; 9:1–6 [9:2–7]). Thus, the text must be earlier than the eighth century. How much earlier?

> The sociopolitical context of the emerging monarchy is a compelling sociopolitical context for the Promise to David.
>
> So central is the rewriting of this promise within and outside DtrH that it is difficult to place its origin later than the Davidic and Solomonic period. Indeed, the promise itself points to the United Monarchy, which lasted less than a century.
>
> The ambivalence about building the temple in 1 Sam 7:5–7 . . . is tied precisely to the pastoral and nomadic origins of the Israelites in vv. 6–11. There seems to be little point in locating such an ambivalence in a much later period . . . when the Jerusalem temple was a long established *fait accompli*. (Schniedewind 1999, 30, 34, 47)

I concur with Schniedewind: whenever its precise time of origin, the original Nathan oracle functioned as tenth-century apologetic for Solomon as David's legitimate successor and for Jerusalem's claim to sovereignty over the whole nation (Schniedewind 1999, 47).

What is 2 Sam 7 saying about building a permanent temple? The primary focus is the divine election of the Davidic dynasty. The role of the temple in the oracle is more ambiguous. Apart from "you will build him a house" (G7:11) and 7:13a, there is no other mention of building a temple for Yhwh—

---

46. On (declaration of) adoption in Mesopotamia and Judah as possible background for 2 Sam 7:14 and Ps 2:7, see Roberts 1997, 115–26; Tigay 1971; Paul 1979–80. In Mesopotamian literature there is ample evidence for declarations of dissolution of adoption ties, such as "you are not my father" and "you are not my son." In biblical legal corpora, however, there is no mention of adoption. "The very institution of adoption was rare—if at all existent—in Israel" (Tigay 1971, 300–301). Thus, a Judean court scribe would not easily find a local model for the adoption metaphor.

in 7:5–7, Yhwh is comfortable dwelling in a tent. And 7:13a interrupts the logical flow and can be isolated as an exegetical addition by a Deuteronomistic hand (Schniedewind 1999, 35–36).[47]

The seventh chapter of 2 Sam reflects the transition from a pastoral and seminomadic culture to an agrarian and sedentary lifestyle. David is transformed from shepherd to prince, a collection of tribes is now "my people Israel" (Schniedewind 1999, 38–39). Until the transfer of the ark to Zion, the ark of God and the divine presence was also nomadic. God was "moving about in a tent and a tabernacle" (7:6).

Schniedewind suggests that the fresh tribal union was not keen to establish one central sanctuary: "The diverse clans and tribes of Palestine needed a common political ideology to knit their new union together, apparently, they did not need a common religious focal point at this time" (1999, 18). In 2 Sam 7, "the vision of a Davidic monarchy had to be stated unequivocally, the status of the royal Jerusalem temple was allowed to remain ambiguous" (1999, 39).

The earlier version of the two oracles clearly did not contain any passage about building a temple. Both 2 Sam 7:13a and the G version of 7:11b reflect editing in hindsight: the temple has been there for a long time, so its divine legitimation should be expressed in this foundational oracle. The synthesis of royal ideology and Zion theology of Ps 2 and Ps 110 is still not there—which in itself is an indication of the early date of the Nathan oracle.

Building a central temple would seal the claim of the king and capital of sovereignty over the tribes spread around in the land—which could explain the hesitance toward building a temple in 2 Sam 7, again a feature pointing to the antiquity of the oracle. "While foreshadowing the eventual construction of a royal temple in Jerusalem, it also acknowledges the multiplicity of sacred sites characteristic of pastoral nomads" (Schniedewind 1999, 49–50 at 50).

47. Only here does Schniedewind find a Deuteronomic hand, which demonstrates the early date of the oracle. 2 Sam 7:10 ("I will appoint *a place* for my people Israel and will plant them") uses the term *māqōm* of the land, a term that in Deuteronomic usage consistently points to the place of the temple (Deut 12:5; Schniedewind 1999, 36–37). Thus, most of the oracle is clearly pre-Deuteronomistic. However, 2 Sam 7:13a reflects the Deuteronomic concept of (only) Yhwh's *name* dwelling in the temple. The Greek suggests a *Vorlage* where "for my name" was added in the editorial process: *hûʿ yibneh lî bayît—lišəmî* ("he will build me a house—for my name").

Psalm 2: Coronation in Zion—Conceived and Begotten by Yhwh

The parallels with 2 Sam 7 indicate that Ps 2 is an early coronation psalm, preserving essential elements of the Jerusalem enthronement liturgy (for the following, cf. Hossfeld and Zenger 1993, 49–54; Roberts 1997; Granerød 2010a). Different from 2 Sam 7, kingship is here essentially connected with Zion and the temple, and the language is more mythological and closer to Egyptian concepts. The central verses run as follows:

> [1]Why do nations assemble,
> and peoples plot vain things?
> [2]The kings of the land set themselves,
> the rulers take counsel together
> against Yhwh and his anointed.
> [3]"Let us burst their bonds asunder,
> and cast their ropes from us." . . .
> [5]He will speak to them in his wrath. . . .
> [6] "I have conceived[48] my king on Zion, my holy mountain."
> [7]"I will tell of the decree of Yhwh:
> He said to me, 'You are my son, today I have begotten you.
> [8]Ask me, and I will make the nations your heritage
> and the far corners of the land your possession.'[49]
> [9]You shall break them with a rod of iron,
> and dash them in pieces like a potter's vessel." (Ps 2:1–3, 5–9,
>   my translation)

Building on earlier scholars, Spieckermann argues that the royal ideology of Ps 2 and Ps 72 is indebted to Egyptian tradition and should be dated to the early centuries of the Judean kingdom. Following and partly transforming Egyptian concepts, the Judean king comes in the closest conceivable relationship with the divine Father. Yhwh is bearing, "giving birth," to the suc-

48. The verb *nāsak* means pouring out a liquid; here it is a metaphor for the male semen; cf. the use of *yālad* ("begetting") in the subsequent verse (Granerød 2010a, 326–34). Such a terminology represents a clear allusion to the Egyptian myth. Most translations follow G: "I was installed king."

49. One can translate either "to the ends/far corners of the land" or "to the ends of the earth." In the early centuries of the Judean kingdom, one would, with the regions around in view, probably read the former. In contrast, a postexilic messianic rereading would go for the latter.

cessor to the throne in the act of enthronement. The "today" of 2:7–9 points to divine adoption on the coronation day, not to a bodily divine-human conception. Thus, the metaphor of conception and birth is used without suggesting deification of the king when the psalm proclaims royal participation in divine power. In Ps 2, we encounter Yahwist theologians who adopted the Egyptian father-son relationship, moved it out of the divine sphere, and reclaimed it for the relation between Yhwh and the Judean king (Feldmeier and Spieckermann 2011, 55–57). Similarly, Craig notes (2004, 67) that the words "I have begotten you" implies a new birth of a divine nature without making the king divine in any sense. As argued above, the "divinization" of pharaoh in Egyptian thinking is likely exaggerated. And it may be too shallow to understand 2:7 in adoption categories (see the critique in Roberts 1997, 116–28).

The "decree of Yhwh" that declares divine sonship (2:7–9) should be understood in light of Egyptian customs: during the coronation, the crown and a "divinely written decree" were given to the new pharaoh, outlining the five royal names and declaring the king as the deity's son (von Rad 1947; Roberts 1997). The statements "I have conceived my king on Zion, my holy mountain" and "you are my son, today I have begotten you" are close recasts of the Egyptian coronation ritual. Amon's words to Horemheb "you are my son, the heir who came forth from my flesh" are closely paralleled in the psalm.

The expression "Zion, my holy mountain" points to the temple as location of the coronation. In the ancient Near East, the sanctuary was often conceived as the mountain of God. In Ugarit, the dwelling of El is the mountain of the north (≈ Ps 48:3 [48:2]). The Bible points to Zion as the mountain of Yhwh, source of life and abundance (cf. Pss 46:5 [46:4]; 48:2–3 [48:1–2]).

In contrast to 2 Sam 7, there is in Ps 2 an intimate connection between Yhwh's adopting or begetting the new king and the temple as the place of divine presence, which suggests that some time has passed since the Nathan oracle. Royal ideology and Zion theology are intertwined. The temple and its importance are well established.

When was the psalm written? While earlier scholars tended to date it to the time of David or Solomon, recent scholars are more uncertain about its time of composition. Not only does the conscious adaptation and transformation of Egyptian royal ideology suggest that some time has passed since the Nathan oracle, but the expressed Zion theology demonstrates that the temple is a well-established institution. Psalm 2 reflects active interaction with Egyptian royal ideology by the scribes of the fresh Judean bureaucracy.

Characterizing Zion as God's holy mountain—as in Ugarit—demonstrates an active dialogue with ancient Near Eastern temple concepts. The development and integration of a Zion/temple theology with royal ideology that comes to the forefront in Ps 2 would necessarily need some time. But similar to 2 Sam 7, Ps 2 could also be understood as a defense for Solomon and Rehoboam as the rightful heirs to the Davidic throne, which might suggest a late tenth-century date.

Schniedewind (1999, 69) argues that Ps 2 is pre-Deuteronomistic and suggests Hezekiah's time as an option. Nations assembling against the king on Zion (2:1–3) would indeed be a well-known theme in the aftermath of the Syro-Ephraimite war in 734–732 (the war that led to the Assyrian invasion of Damascus, Israel, and Transjordan). However, the psalm is in dialogue with Egyptian, not Assyrian, royal ideology. While influence of Egyptian imagery still could be felt in eighth-century Judah (Keel and Uehlinger 1998, 177–281, 350–54), such a profile makes a time of composition before the rise of Assyria in the mid-eighth century more probable.

The form *yəlidtîkā* ("I have begotten you") belongs to Classical Biblical Hebrew of First Temple times. Only in Classical Biblical Hebrew can the *qal* of *yālad* ("to give birth") be used also with a male subject. Later one would consistently use the *hiphil* for the male who "begets/causes to bear" and the *qal* for the mother who "bears" (Hendel and Joosten 2018, 19). A dating of this psalm to the postexilic period remains problematic.[50]

In the framework of the coronation liturgy, the king proclaims Yhwh's promise to him (2:7–9): "today" he has been born anew and made son of the divine. He has been given rule in the land and dominion over the nations around. "Breaking the nations with a rod of iron and dashing them in pieces like a potter's vessel" are themes from Egyptian and Mesopotamian royal

50. In 1993, Zenger understood Ps 2 (with 2:1–9 as original core) as a postexilic psalm influenced by Egyptian and Hellenistic royal ideology and Neo-Assyrian royal propaganda: the psalm was written around 300 as an introduction to the messianic psalter (Pss 2–89). Through these words the small Judean community proclaimed its vision of hope: the Davidic covenant is still valid, and Yhwh will uphold his promise to extend his kingdom through his king from Mount Zion. The authors of the psalm drew inspiration from 2 Sam 7 and Pss 18, 20, 21, 45 (Hossfeld and Zenger 1993, 50–51). Against such a late dating, Spieckermann argues that in postexilic times the father/son metaphor does not refer to the king but rather to Yhwh's relationship to righteous Israelites (Feldmeier and Spieckermann 2011, 55–65). In 2008, however, Zenger dated Ps 2 and the earliest form of Ps 110 to preexilic times (Hossfeld and Zenger 2008, 204–5). For Carr (2011, 387–88), 2:6–9 is an early stratum that reflects Egyptian tradition, while other parts of the psalm may be relatively late.

ideology: scarabs and temple reliefs portray the king beating his enemies to the ground, and shattering pottery is a common Egyptian symbol for defeating enemies.

Psalm 2:1–3 brings into the scene powers of chaos in the form of rebellious kings and nations. This theme is probably taken over from Egyptian coronation rituals, where the call of pharaoh was to restore order and harmony in the land. Psalm 2 may be one of the earliest texts about the nations threatening Zion, a motif recurring in 46:7 [46:6]; 76:4–7 [76:3–6]; Isa 17:12–14; 30:28–33. Against the nations, Yhwh speaks a word of power that breaks their might, here "I have conceived my king on Zion, my holy mountain"—Yhwh's victorious voice recurs in other texts (Pss 46:11 [46:10]; 76:13 [76:12]; Isa 17:13; 30:30).

According to Ps 2, the earthly Davidic king is adopted or conceived into sonship and appointed deputy of the heavenly Yhwh, the true ruler of the land. Yhwh will make the Jerusalem king rule the lands around and the surrounding nations to submit to Yhwh's elected king. In contrast to the Egyptian rule that the nation should obey pharaoh, the son of Amon-Re, the king of Zion instructs kings and rulers to serve and submit to Yhwh (2:11–12).

In Hellenistic times, Ps 2 was placed as a "messianic preamble" to an early collection of psalms, 3–72 or 3–89 (see p. 177). At this stage the scene is not the Judean king ruling the land and the nations around but a future messianic king receiving global rule from Yhwh, the lord of all nations.[51] This hope of a future king would be proclaimed at a time Judea was a small and powerless temple province, helpless booty in the fight between mighty empires.

Can we trace other early foundational texts for the temple? In his discussion of the posthistory of 2 Sam 7, Schniedewind (1999, 40–46) identifies three tenth-century liturgies or liturgical fragments that refer to the election of David and the temple: 1 Kgs 8:12–13; Ps 89:4–19 [89:3–18]; and Ps 132. The Zion-centered theology of Ps 132 should more likely be dated to the postexilic period, while there may be some early royal material in the exilic Ps 89 (see pp. 108, 165–67). But 1 Kgs 8:12–13 could possibly be an ancient text connected to the Jerusalem temple:

---

51. Zenger suggests that 2:10–12 was added when, first, Ps 1 and thereafter Ps 2 were placed as a preamble to Pss 3–89. The instruction to serve and obey Yhwh should be read in harmony with the Torah-centered Ps 1: when the nations come to Zion and submit to the Torah they will get through the eschatological judgment (cf. Isa 2:2–4; 60:10–14; Zech 14:16–19; Hossfeld and Zenger 1993, 50, 54).

> Then Solomon said:
> "Yhwh has said that he would dwell in thick darkness.
> I have built you an exalted house,
> a place for you to dwell in forever." (NRSV adapted)

The canonical version of Solomon's Temple dedication prayer in 1 Kgs 8 reveals three stages with different theological emphases, with 8:12–13 as the earliest. First Kgs 8:14–21 gives expression to the Deuteronomic idea of Yhwh's name dwelling in the temple; 8:22–61 first repeats the promise to David (8:24–26) and continues expressing that Yhwh dwells in the heavens and from his lofty abode can focus his eyes on the house where his name dwells (8:26–30).

In the earliest prayer, 8:12–13, it is God himself that dwells in the temple. "Dwelling" in an earthly abode echoes 2 Sam 7:5–6, which confirms that God can dwell in an earthly abode such as a tent or tabernacle. Here we encounter a pre-Deuteronomistic prayer that should be dated somewhere between the tenth and the eighth centuries. Weinfeld (1972, 35) characterizes these two verses as an "ancient song . . . apparently recited by Solomon during the temple inauguration ceremonies," and Schniedewind (1999, 43–44) concurs that this prayer may well date to the Solomonic period.

Psalm 110: Enthroned with Yhwh

Zenger rightly regards Ps 110:1–3, 5–7 as a preexilic royal psalm. Psalm 110:4 breaks the logical sequence between 110:1–3 and 110:5–7 and should be categorized as a postexilic interpretative addition (for the following, cf. Hossfeld and Zenger 2011, 140–56). Psalm 110:3 has been a scholarly headache. The text of M is knotty and reflects scribal tampering with an earlier recension. It runs as follows (my translation):

> Your people willingly on the day of your power in majestic
>   holiness.
> From the womb, from the dawn, to you—dew, your young age.

Stretching the Hebrew text, translations commonly go for something like

> Your people come willingly in majestic holiness
> on the day of your power.

> From the womb, from the dawn,
> yours was the dew of youth.

Taking the Greek and Syriac versions into account, an earlier Hebrew form may be reconstructed. With some slight modifications, the consonantal text can be read:

> There was dignity with you on the day of your birth.
> On holy mountains, from the womb of the morning star,
> like dew I have begotten you.[52]

Leaving 110:4 aside as a postexilic interpretative addition, the original psalm would run:

> About David, a psalm.
> A word of Yhwh to my lord,
> "Sit at my right hand
> while I make your enemies your footstool."
> ²Yhwh stretches out from Zion your mighty scepter:
> "Rule in the midst of your foes!
> ³There was dignity with you on the day of your birth.
> On holy mountains, from the womb of the morning star,
> like dew I have begotten you."
> ⁵Yhwh is at your right hand,
> he will shatter kings on the day of his wrath.
> ⁶He will execute judgment among the nations,
> heaping up corpses,
> he will shatter heads over the wide earth.

52. Cf. Hossfeld and Zenger 2011, 142–43, 149. In contrast to M's *yaldutêkā* ("your young age"), G, Syriac, and some Hebrew manuscripts read *yəlidtîkā* ("I have begotten you")—with a male subject this usage is characteristic of early Biblical Hebrew and supports an early dating of the psalm. One can further read *hîlêkā* ("your birth") for *ḥêlêkā* ("your forces"). *Bəhadrê-qōdeš* ("in majestic holiness/in the glory of the holy sanctuary") may be a scribal change from *bəharərê-qōdeš* ("on holy mountains"); cf. "Zion, my holy mountain" in 2:6 (graphically, *resh* and *dalet* may appear almost identical). For the enigmatic *ləkā ṭal* one may read *qəṭal* ("like dew"). Peshitta reads: "With you is glory on the day of force. In holy splendor, from the womb I bore you, child, from the beginning" (my translation); and G: "With you is rule on the day of your power among the splendors of the holy ones. From the womb, before the Morning-star, I brought you forth" (NETS).

⁷He will drink from the stream on his way.
Therefore, he holds his head high.

The earlier form of 110:3 refers back to 2:6–7: in the coronation, Yhwh conceives and begets the new king. The words "like dew I have begotten you" echo royal Egyptian mythology where Amon impregnates the queen with "his dew." Zenger proposes that the superscription *ləd̄āwīd* could be translated "about David/the Davidic king" and reflect the hope for a future powerful Davidic king during the time of the Judahite kingdom. This king has an intimate relation to Yhwh, who from heaven will bring the neighboring peoples into subjugation. Among the editorially connected David psalms 108–10, the motif of victory over enemies appears in 108:8–14 [108:7–13].

According to 110:1–3, Yhwh appoints the king as his coregent, sitting on the throne above, to the right of the heavenly ruler. This image is closely related to Egyptian models and is more easily dated to preexilic times. In Egypt, pharaoh is frequently pictured sitting or standing alongside a main god. The scepter is the symbol of royal power, given by Yhwh to his king. While in Ps 2 the king is portrayed as Yhwh's deputy, a kind of viceroy on earth, here the king appears enthroned with God in the heavenly realms, ruling together with Yhwh.

Making defeated enemies a footstool of the victorious king sitting at his throne is a well-known image in the ancient Near East: in Ps 18:39 [18:38] the enemies fell under David's feet, and in Josh 10:24 Joshua's commanders put their feet on the necks of the defeated kings. The term "footstool" can be connected with the divine throne (e.g., Ps 99:5), so the drama of 110:1–2 goes on in the heavenly realms.

In 110:5–7, Yhwh appears as the heavenly warrior who gives victory to his earthly king, similar to 2:8–9. In Ps 2, the king is the acting warrior, while Yhwh himself takes on this role in Ps 110. Psalm 110:7 either refers to the earthly victorious king or more likely elaborates the anthropomorphic description of Yhwh as fighter in 110:5–6.

The terms "holy mountains" and "from Zion" point to the temple as place of the coronation and, due to the divine presence, as source for the king's continued reign. The Zion theology of Ps 2 and Ps 110 can be compared with the idea of the Priestly source that the divine glory/presence of Yhwh is dwelling in the temple and contrasts the Deuteronomic concept of (only) Yhwh's *name* dwelling there. The temple is the place where Yhwh is "enthroned over the cherubs" (Ps 99:1; cf. Exod 25:20–22; Ps 22:4 [22:3]; Isa 6:1–3).

From around 900 there was a sanctuary in Mozah (6 km west of ancient Jerusalem) and for a great part of the eighth century in Arad. The Arad temple was likely discontinued with Hezekiah's reform (Herzog 2010, 169–97),[53] while the Mozah sanctuary remained in use until the Babylonian conquest. Kisilevitz and Lipschits (2020; cf. Kisilevitz 2015) suggest that the large Mozah temple (19 m × 13 m) was built by a strong local group. At least by the late eighth century, the site and the temple would be part of the economic and administrative system of Judah and officially sanctioned.[54] Situated in a fertile spot in the Sorek Valley, Mozah was an agricultural and administrative center supplying foodstuff to Jerusalem.

These temples are not mentioned in the biblical text, while they apparently were sponsored by the state, probably together with other local sanctuaries. The royal or Zion psalms do not care at all about these other Yahwist shrines.

With time, when the Sinai tradition on the "mountain of Yhwh" of the northern tribes became integrated into Judean theology, one would read "Zion, my holy mountain" in a continuum with the idea of Yhwh's presence at Sinai: the divine presence in the Zion temple would recall Yhwh's presence at Sinai—Yhwh's glory descended first at Sinai and subsequently over the tabernacle and the temple (Exod 24:16; 34:5; Num 9:15–23; 1 Kgs 8:10–11; Ps 50:1–6). In Exodus, the encounter with the divine—heaven touching earth—realized at Mount Sinai, has a living continuation in the divine presence in the tabernacle (Durham 1987, 354–55). And again, the tabernacle—at home in Zion since David's time—foreshadows the Jerusalem temple.

An echo of Ps 110 appears in the plea for the Judean king that was added to Ps 80 in the late seventh century: "Let your hand be upon the man at your right hand, the son of humankind you made strong for yourself!" (80:18 [80:17], my translation; see p. 73). And two David psalms proclaim that the king is upheld by Yhwh's right hand (18:36 [18:35]; 20:7 [20:6]).

---

53. At Tel Beer-sheba, remnants of a horned altar made of hewn stones were found in secondary use in a stratum from the eighth century. Herzog (2010, 176–78) suggests that Beer-sheba had a sanctuary similar to that in Arad and that both were abolished before Sennacherib's 701 campaign, likely connected with Hezekiah's reform.

54. Tel Motza has been identified with biblical Mozah—according to Josh 18:26 a town in Benjaminite territory. A number of silos shows the site's importance as an agricultural center. An earlier cultic structure was identified under the temple that was constructed ca. 900. The ground plan of the temple is typical for the ancient Levant: a temple courtyard with an open-air altar of unhewn stones, from which an entrance leads into a long hall with an elevated podium to the west (here without any separation wall between the holy place and the holy of holies).

A rereading and extension of the psalm is evident around the third century. With the addition of v. 4, the psalm describes a future messiah with a priestly job description:[55]

> Yhwh has sworn and will not change his mind,
> "You are a priest forever according to the order of Melchizedek."
> (NRSV adapted)

The firm oath of Yhwh to keep the Davidic dynasty makes more sense after the collapse of the Judean kingdom, when this promise of Yhwh would have been questioned. This confirmation of the divine oath appears as a response to 89:20–52 [89:19–51] that questions the lasting validity of the divine promise, referred to as an oath in 89:36–38 [89:35–37]. The same term appears in 132:11, in another psalm that responds to Ps 89.

In 110:4, a priestly role is ascribed to the future messianic ruler. A possible source for this idea appears in Ezekiel's blueprint for restoration, which includes a ruler with priestly functions—but without a Davidic pedigree (Ezek 45:7–8; 46:1–18; see p. 123). The third-century M version of Jer 30:18–22 elaborates this theme in a particular way, reinterpreting a Davidic messiah in the earlier G-related recension as a priestly messianic ruler (see pp. 111–12, 150–52).

By proclaiming that his priestly ministry follows the order of Melchizedek, the central figure of the psalm is rooted in the prehistory of Jerusalem, where Abraham encountered Melchizedek, king and priest in Salem (Gen 14:17–24). Thus, the promise of the messianic king is rooted not only in the promise to David but in the patriarchal age and connected to Melchizedek, conceived as "founding father" for kingship and priesthood in Jerusalem.

By the third century, the high priest was both religious and civil leader of the Judeans, and a priestly messianism had gained more importance. This may be a factor behind this attribution of priestly features to a psalm on the Davidic messiah. Some scholars suggest that Ps 110:4 was phrased as legitimation for the Hasmonean rulers who combined the offices of ruler/king and high priest. More likely, the Hasmonean Simon used this existing (full) psalm as legitimation for taking full authority in Judea in 142 (see p. 219).

The idea of a viceroy enthroned with Yhwh and given power and authority on earth will recur in Dan 7 and a messianic text from Qumran, 4Q521

---

55. Carr (2011, 388–89) identifies much ancient material in the psalm, with 110:4 legitimating the early Judean king as high priest: "Psalm 110 is one of the better candidates for containing remnants of Judah's most ancient monarchal traditions" (2011, 389).

(see pp. 200–202). A particular rereading of this psalm with its war image is evident in the second century, when vv. 1–4 were read as an address by God to Melchizedek—the semidivine commander of God's heavenly army, who in the end time will defeat the powers of evil and redeem the elect people of God (see p. 253).

An alternative view of the relation between the Melchizedek texts, Ps 110 and Gen 14:18–20, is advocated by Granerød. He dates all of Ps 110 to the time of the Judean kingdom and reads *malkî-ṣedeq* not as a personal name but rather as "my king is righteousness/loyalty" and translates: "You are a priest forever. For my sake my king is loyal." As David and Solomon at times performed in the cult, such a reading would make sense in First Temple times.

In postexilic times, however, the word *'adonî* ("my lord") in 110:1 was identified with Abraham. Since the central figure of the psalm is involved in warfare, the psalm was connected with the warlike Abraham in Gen 14:1–17 (at a time when 14:18–20 was not written). When *malkî-ṣedeq* then was read as the personal name Melchizedek, biblical editors felt the need to fill out the Abraham story of Gen 14 with verses that explained the role of Melchizedek vis-à-vis Abraham. Genesis 14:18–20 should therefore be considered a late midrashic addition to the biblical text, instigated by postexilic scribes' reading of Ps 110 (Granerød 2010b).[56]

At a certain stage, 110:3 was seen as too mythological and rewritten into the enigmatic and less provocative form of M:

> Your people (come) willingly in majestic holiness
> on the day of your power.
> From the womb, from the dawn, yours (was) the dew of youth.[57]

The focus is changed from the mythological description of the king's divinely given "birth" to the people of the king coming forward on the day of mustering or battle. The king's youthful power is a promise of victory and abundance. Hossfeld and Zenger suggest the same third-century

---

56. Granerød's monograph is based on a 2008 PhD thesis from Oslo, defended the same year that Zenger's German commentary on Ps 110 was published. Thus, neither of these two scholars could consult the work of the other.

57. Reading *'ammakā* ("your people") instead of *'imkā* ("with you") and likely connecting *bəhadrê-qōdeš* to the first part of the verse, not the second. *Yaldutêkā*, although spelled as a plural (keeping the consonants from *yəlidtîkā*), means "your young age," not "your young ones."

scribal circle behind the censoring of v. 3 and the addition of v. 4 (Hossfeld and Zenger 2011, 146–47). However, the rewriting of v. 3 instead reflects "censoring" in Hasmonean times, when the psalm was used as legitimation for the combined priestly and princely office of the ruler. The proto-M version of v. 3 does not fit a third-century context—it makes more sense in the time of the warring Hasmoneans Simon (142–135) and John Hyrcanus (135–105).[58]

From these psalms and other biblical texts one can deduct the main elements and liturgical themes in the investiture of a new king: anointing (2 Sam 2:4; 5:3; 1 Kgs 1:39), adoption or fathering by Yhwh (Ps 2:7), name giving (an Egyptian custom; cf. Isa 9:5 [9:6]), recitation of the divine decree (Ps 2:7), the king's proclamation (2:7–9), being appointed to Yhwh's right hand (110:1), handing over crown regalia (21:4 [21:3]; 110:2), and being enclothed with royal garments (21:6 [21:5]; Hossfeld and Zenger 2005, 204–5).

Psalm 21: Crowning and Adorning the King

Psalm 21:2–14 [21:1–13] contains ancient material. In the process of transmission, divine promises to the king on victory over his enemies were rephrased and focused directly on the Lord (my translation):

> [2]In your strength the king rejoices, Yhwh,
> how greatly he exults in your help!
> [3]You have given him his heart's desire,
> and have not withheld the request of his lips.
> [4]For you set him before you, bestowing rich blessings,
> you set a crown of fine gold on his head.
> [5]He asked you for life; you gave it to him—
> length of days forever and ever.
> [6]His glory is great through your help,
> splendor and majesty you bestow on him.

---

58. G shows that the earlier reading was affirmed in Alexandria in the early first century BCE, and the Syriac shows that the same was the case in Edessa in the late second century CE. Psalm 110 is not represented among the forty-two psalm scrolls from the Judean Desert. The large amount of variation among the *Hexapla* texts of this verse suggests a fluid Hebrew tradition up to the second century CE.

⁷You bestow on him blessings forever,
in your presence you make him rejoice.
⁸For the king trusts in Yhwh,
through the steadfast love of the Most High he shall not be
moved.
⁹Your hand will find out all your enemies,
your right hand will find out those who hate you.
¹⁰You will make them like a fiery furnace when you appear.
Yhwh will swallow them up in his wrath, fire will consume them.
¹¹You will destroy their offspring from the earth,
their children from among humankind.
¹²If they plan evil against you,
if they devise mischief, they will not succeed.
¹³For you will put them to flight,
you will aim at their faces with your bows.
¹⁴Be exalted, Yhwh, in your strength!
We will sing and praise your power.

Scholars point out parallels to this psalm in texts from Egypt, the El-Amarna correspondence, Akkadian texts, and Ugaritic texts: the king is given his heart's desire, including a long life (21:3, 5 [21:2, 4]); God crowns him with gold and bestows him with splendor and majesty—alluding to being adorned with royal garments of glory (21:4, 6 [21:3, 5]); he is brought into God's presence (21:4, 7 [21:3, 6]). Here God is painted in the role of the great emperor who personally crowns and adorns his viceroy; such a description in anthropomorphic terms is more likely in the early period. Thus, the bulk of the psalm echoes royal ideology and installation liturgies in the ancient Near East.⁵⁹

In 21:9–13 [21:8–12] Yhwh is fighting his enemies and putting them to flight. These verses have likely transformed into hymnic praise of an earlier divine promise to the king that he will prevail over his foes, as in 2:8–9 (Hossfeld and Zenger 1993, 140; Carr 2011, 389–90). With this transformation, 21:14 [21:13] would be a natural closure.

59. "The psalm echoes elements of ancient royal ideology seen in various contexts, from the hymn of Thutmoses IV to requests for long life at Ugarit and more recent northwest Semitic royal inscriptions. These echoes, along with parallels to major elements of other potential early royal psalms, make Psalm 21 another probable source of Judah's most ancient royal traditions" (Carr 2011, 390).

Psalm 72: Implementing Yhwh's Righteousness in the Land

Psalm 72 is a mixture of Egyptian and Neo-Assyrian royal motifs that suggest the late eighth or seventh century as time of composition. After Tiglath-pileser III's campaigns in the Levant in 734–732, the kingdom of Judah had to navigate in the shadow of the Assyrian superpower (2 Kgs 16:7–18). In its polemical reception of Assyrian themes, the psalm draws up a Yahwistic alternative to Assyrian ideology, similar to Deuteronomy's adaptation and transformation of Assyrian vassal treaties and concepts of covenant (for the following, cf. Hossfeld and Zenger 2005, 201–20).

I follow Zenger's separation of a seventh-century royal psalm in Ps 72:1–7, 12–14, 16–17a. He ascribes the additive redaction of the psalm to fourth-century editors that combined earlier psalm scrolls into the messianic psalter of Pss 2–89 (Hossfeld and Zenger 2005, 207–8).[60]

The doxology of 72:18–19 is not an integral part of the psalm, but rather a conclusion to the collection of Pss 42–72. The final colophon in 72:20, "end of the prayers of David, son of Jesse (Isai)" (my translation), is likely a second-century marker of the end of the first scroll of a long Davidic psalter—to include the full Psalter into one scroll would be materially difficult (Willgren 2016, 196–201, 237–41, 379).

The superscript "for/about Solomon" was added in a late redaction. Seen together with the concluding colophon "end of the prayers of David, son of Jesse," it could suggest that the psalm in the second century was read as a prayer by David for his son—the Greek translation (early first century) reads *eis salōmōn* ("for Solomon"; Hossfeld and Zenger 2005, 211, 219). The seventh-century royal psalm might have run like this:

> About Solomon.
> [1]O God, endow the king with your judgments,
> he who is a king's son with your loyal justness,
> [2]that he may judge your people with righteousness,
> your lowly ones with justice.
> [3]Let the mountains produce well-being for the people,

60. In contrast, Carr finds preexilic royal motifs all through the psalm: "Psalm 72 seems to be part of a broader stream of Egyptian, Mesopotamian, and other royal traditions that focus on the king as the bringer of justice and fertility. These ancient nonbiblical royal traditions likewise feature grandiose claims of dominion, tribute, and fame, integral elements of the psalm (e.g., Ps 72:8–11)" (2011, 393–94).

the hills, the reward of justice.
⁴Let him champion the lowly among the people,
deliver the needy folk and crush the oppressor.
⁵May his days be long as the sun shines,⁶¹
while the moon lasts, generations on end.
⁶He shall be like rain falling on a mown field,
a downpour of rain in the land.
⁷Righteousness shall flourish in his time,⁶²
peace and welfare abound till the moon is no more. . . .
¹²For he saves the needy who cry out,
the lowly who have no helper.
¹³He cares about the poor and needy,
he brings the needy deliverance.
¹⁴He redeems them from oppression and violence,
the shedding of their blood touches his heart.
¹⁶May there be abundant grain in the land, to the tops of the
    mountains,
the crops thrive like the forest of Lebanon,
and men sprout up in towns like the grass of the field.
¹⁷ᵃMay his name endure forever
and get offspring as long as the sun lasts.

In contrast to Ps 2 and Ps 110, Zion is not an explicit theme in Ps 72. However, the paradisiac conditions in the land described in 72:3, 6, 16 could suggest a link to the temple, as images of paradise and temple converge in ancient Near Eastern and Israelite tradition.

Different from the psalms discussed above, the early version of Ps 72 is a prayer for the king. Liturgical elements that could point to a coronation ceremony cannot be identified, but such a prayer could easily have been recited during the investiture of a new king. If the psalm indeed was recited at this specific occasion, its use should not be restricted to such a ceremony.

The dialogue with Assyrian tradition is transparent but not provocative in form. As earthly representative of the sun god Shamash, the Assyrian king

61. Reading with G ("he will endure") *wəyaʾărîk* ("he [i.e., his days] will be long") for M *yîrāʾûkā* ("they will fear you"). In most scribal hands, *waw* and *yod* are penned in an almost identical fashion: G reads the word opening with *waw* and *yod*, while M reads two *yods*.

62. One can read either *yiprāḥ ṣadîq* ("the righteous shall flourish") with M or *yiprāḥ ṣedeq* ("righteousness shall flourish") with G, Syriac, and some Hebrew manuscripts.

shall implement the divinely given order on earth, rule with righteousness, and inaugurate a time of harmony, fruitfulness, and well-being. He opposes the powers of chaos and fights nations that disturb the harmony of the Assyrian Empire. The kingdom was instituted during the act of creation:

> Ea spoke to Belet-ili: "Belet-ili, lady of the great gods, you created common man. Now make the king, the ruling man! Surround his whole figure with good, make his features harmonious, make his body lovely!" Then Belet-ili made the king, the ruling man. The gods gave the king the fighting spirit. Anu gave him his crown, Enlil his throne, Nergal his weapons, Ninurta his terrifying radiance, Belet-ili his beauty. (adapted from Hossfeld and Zenger 2005, 212)

According to the creation myth Enuma Elish, "the king shall do on earth what Marduk did in the heavens." The gods endow the king with scepter and ring, signs of his dignity, and with divinely given power. The prologue to the Law of Hammurabi (ca. 1810–1750) prescribes that the king shall implement justice, protect the poor, destroy the wicked, and care for the well-being of the nation. The rightly consecrated king will be a source for paradisiac fertility; he will rise up as the sun god to enlighten the land (Hossfeld and Zenger 2005, 212). As in Egypt, the king is the normative lawgiver.

In polemic reception with the ideology of the superpower, in Ps 72 the Davidic king is the divinely ordained mediator, first of righteousness in rule and judgment and second of harmony and fruitfulness in nature—the second would follow from the first. In contrast to other royal psalms and their ancient Near Eastern models, there is no warlike imagery in Ps 72 (Carr 2011, 394).

In 72:5, sun and moon are elements of creation, as is the rain watering the fields in the subsequent verse—a hidden polemic against the Assyrian Shamash as well as the moon god, worshiped in the Levant. In Assyria, Shamash was the source and guarantee for righteousness and justice—a role taken over by Yhwh (72:1).

In Ps 72 as in other texts, a Yahwistic transformation of oriental royal ideology is transparent: Yhwh, not the king, is the normative lawgiver. The word *mišpāṭîm* ("judgments") in 72:1a is the term for legal prescriptions in the Covenant Code and Deuteronomic Law, and the verse qualifies Yhwh as originator of law and legal prescriptions for his people. The king will execute *Yhwh's* righteousness (*ṣədāqâ*; 72:1b), not his own. The king shall judge *Yhwh's* people rightly and plead the cause of *Yhwh's* lowly ones (72:2;

the verb *dîn* has connotations of judgment, rule, and pleading the cause of another). *Ṣedeq* and *mišpāṭ*, righteousness and justice (72:2), are a common pair that signals Yhwh's justice and ethical norms that should be implemented in the land.

Psalm 72:2–4 and 72:12–14 bring the king's responsibility for the poor and downtrodden into focus. With a late eighth- or seventh-century dating, Isaiah's pleading for the lowly ones and harsh oracles against the elite's oppression of the poor provide a sociocultural background for the admonition expressed in these verses (Isa 5:7, 8, 23; 10:1–4). While the Assyrian king fights the powers of chaos in his wars against other nations, Yhwh's consecrated king shall eliminate the oppressors in the land.

Psalm 72:5–7 unfolds the consequences when the king implements Yhwh's righteousness and justice in his nation—the harmony of creation will spread in the land. Psalm 72:5 combines a "long live the king" prayer with a lasting horizon: "As long as the sun shines, while the moon lasts, generations on end"—bringing the continued dynasty into focus. Psalm 72:7 parallels the terms *ṣedeq* ("righteousness") and *šālôm*, which has connotations of peace, well-being, and wholeness. According to 72:7, *šālôm* shall abound—and *šālôm* is connected with the righteous king to be born in Isa 9:5 [9:6] and (the likely exilic) Mic 5:4 [5:5].

Psalm 72:12–14 repeats the king's duty to protect and care for the poor, which will again lead to blessing in the land, rich crops, and folks thriving in the cities (72:16).

Psalm 72:8–11 displays features that separate these verses as a literary addition. Psalm 72:12–14 flows more easily as a continuation of 72:1–7 than of 72:8–11. The theme of the king and his people—essential in 72:1–7, 12–17a—is not present in 72:8–11. The same goes for the king as protector of the poor and the fruitfulness of the land. In the earlier core, the king is the mediator of blessings, the movement is outward—from the king. In 72:8–11, however, there is a movement inward—from the nations toward the king. The main theme in these verses is the universal dimension of the kingdom and the nations submitting to the king, absent in the earlier core. Thematically, 72:15 and 72:17b are congenial with this second literary stratum (Hossfeld and Zenger 2005, 209):

> [8]Let him rule from sea to sea,
> from the Great River to the ends of the earth.
> [9]Let desert dwellers kneel before him,
> and his enemies lick the dust.

> [10]Let kings of Tarshish and the islands pay tribute,
> kings of Sheba and Seba offer gifts.
> [11]Let all kings fall down before him,
> and all nations serve him. . . .
> [15]So let him live, and receive gold of Sheba,
> let prayers for him be said always,
> blessings on him invoked at all times. . . .
> [17b]Let men invoke his blessedness upon themselves,
> let all nations pronounce him blessed.

These verses reflect a developed, postexilic messianism that draws on other biblical promises, such as Isa 2:2–4; 49:23; 60:1–22; 66:18–21; Mic 7:14–17. In Ps 72:8, the king's dominion stretches from the Great River Euphrates to the ends of the earth, that is, to the ends of the known, civilized world. Tarshish signals the western end in maritime perspective, Sheba and Seba (in southern Arabia) the far ends of the Orient. "From the Great River to the ends of the earth" takes up the promise of Gen 15:18 to Abraham, that God would give to his seed all the land from the Brook of Egypt (Wadi El Arish) to the Great River. The blessing formula of Ps 72:17b will, again, take up the Abraham blessing of Gen 12:2–3. Thus, in the time of the messianic king, the promises to Israel's forefather will be realized.

This late part of the psalm may be compared with postexilic reading of Ps 2 and Ps 110. In my reading of Ps 2 as a tenth/ninth-century royal psalm, the conspiring nations are the peoples around Judea, and the king is promised these nations as heritage and the far corners of the land as possession. In postexilic times, "the kings of the land" (2:2) would be read as "the kings of the earth," and *'apsê-'āreṣ* ("the far corners of the land"; 2:8) as "the ends of the earth," leading to the promise "I will make the nations your heritage and the ends of the earth your possession."

Psalm 2:8–9 describes a conquering Davidic king, and 110:5–6 a warlike Yhwh conducting the battle for his earthly king, as does the edited version of Ps 21. In contrast, in the postexilic section of Ps 72, the Davidic messiah is portrayed as a peaceful emperor who receives the homage of kings and nations—an image recurring in Zech 9:9–10—with one of these two texts alluding to the other.

The canonical versions of Ps 110 and Ps 72 evince how royal Judean ideology in postexilic times—in the tiny and powerless temple province of Yehud—was transformed into a futuristic messianism with utopic traits. In Ps 110, the inclusion of 110:4 adds a priestly dimension to the king's job description. In Ps 72, the inclusion of 72:8–11, 15, 17b makes the king a universal ruler before whom all nations pay homage, in the image of emperors such as the Persian king or Alexander the Great. The Targum would later make this messianic reading explicit, rendering the opening prayer "O God, endow the king messiah with your judgments," and regard the name of the messiah as preexistent: "his name existed before the sun and will be remembered forever" (72:17).

When discussing the postexilic growth of these two psalms, the terms *intertextuality, hypertextuality,* and *transtextuality* are pertinent.

Genette's wider concept *transtextuality* is fruitful, with subcategories *intertextuality* (the actual presence of one text in another, such as quotation), *metatextuality* (commentary), *hypertextuality* (one text [the *hypertext*] is integrally based on and transforms another text [the *hypotext*], such as allusion), *architextuality* (a text's relation to other texts through participation in shared genres, types, and modes) (Genette 1997, 1–10; Rosenberg 2016, 16–19).

As for hypertextuality, the subcategories *continuation* (completing an unfinished hypotext)[63] and *sequel* (offering new episodes following a complete hypotext) are particularly relevant for the rereading of earlier texts in the Hebrew Bible. *Transformation* occurs when plot, characters, and motifs in a narrative are transferred to a new textual context.

The postexilic additions to Ps 110 and Ps 72 evince intervention by scribal editors who saw the form of the psalm transmitted to them as an unfinished hypotext that required a continuation that would complete the text and update it according to messianic ideas of their time.

---

63. Rabbinic midrash can often be classified as a continuation that completes what is supposed to be lacking in the biblical source.

Royal Ideology
in the Northern Kingdom

After the fall of the Northern Kingdom, royal traditions from the Northern Kingdom ("the house of Israel" and its tribes) filtered into Judea and were transformed by Judean scribes to conform more with Jerusalem tradition. Texts with origins in the north set their trace in Judean royal tradition both before and after the fall of Jerusalem in 587.

Northern Scribes Fleeing to the South

Archaeological evidence indicates that Jerusalem grew substantially during the late eighth century, accompanied by a large increase in the population of central Judea. Based on the settled area of the city and the number of identified settlements around, it is estimated that the population of Jerusalem grew from around 10,000 to 40,000 and that of central Judea from 100,000 to 200,000.[1] Broshi (1974), Schniedewind (1999, 51; 2003), and Finkelstein (2008; 2015) argue for a sudden, massive growth of the city due to an influx of refugees from the destroyed Northern Kingdom after the Assyrian campaigns in 734–732 and 725–722. Slightly in contrast, Na'aman (2007, 2014) argues for a slow, natural growth of the city throughout the second half of the eighth century—while agreeing that groups of refugees from the north flowed into Judah.

Schniedewind (1999, 52) adds that the influx of disposed Judeans after Sennacherib's 701 campaign should also be taken into account. A devastation of the Shephelah was followed by a substantial growth in small rural settlements around Jerusalem.

---

1. Archaeologists can identify decline or growth in population, but precise calculation of population density in ancient sites remains difficult.

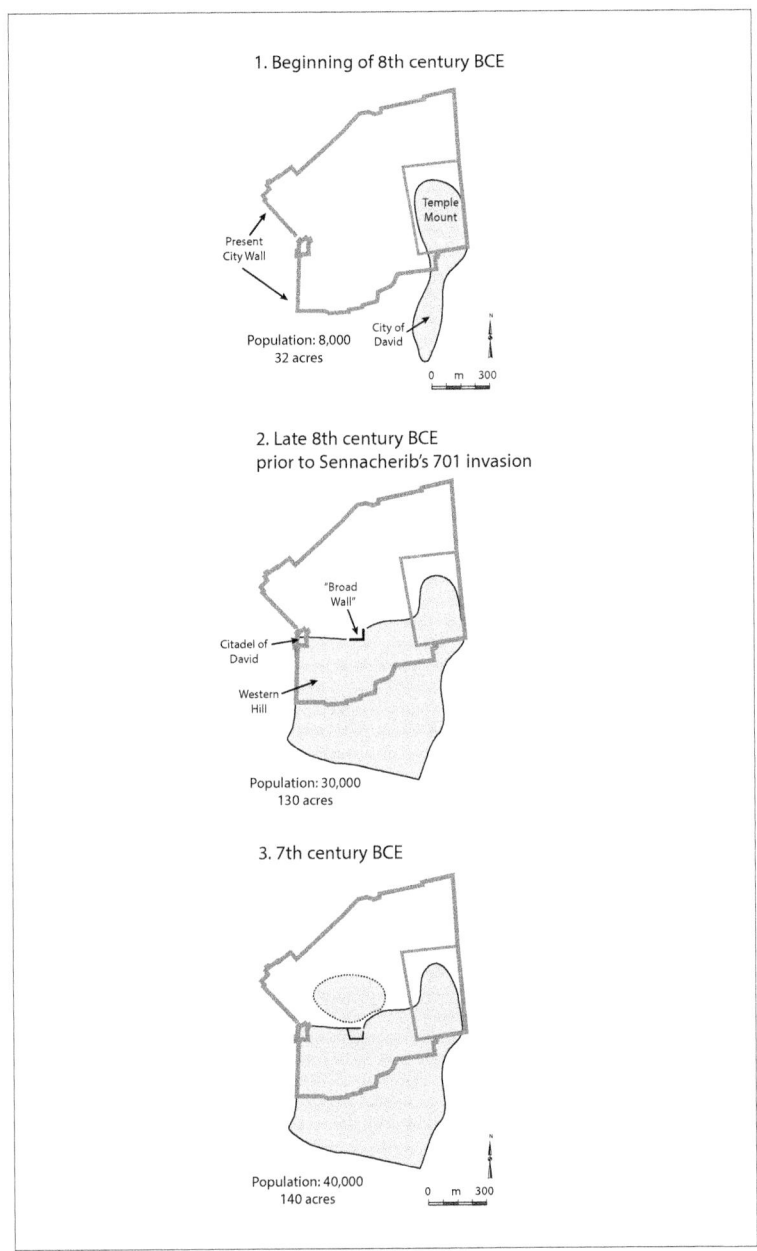

1. Beginning of 8th century BCE

Present
City Wall

Temple
Mount

City of
David

Population: 8,000
32 acres

0   m   300

2. Late 8th century BCE
prior to Sennacherib's 701 invasion

"Broad
Wall"

Citadel of
David

Western
Hill

Population: 30,000
130 acres

3. 7th century BCE

Population: 40,000
140 acres

0   m   300

Figure 3. The growth of Jerusalem during the eighth century BCE.

Hezekiah's cult reform (2 Kgs 18:1–5) would concentrate economic, political, and cultic power in Jerusalem. Specifically, the centralization also aimed at assembling the northern tribes around Jerusalem's royal house (Finkelstein and Silberman 2006b; Herzog 2010, 196–97). The king made efforts to integrate the northerners into Judean society. He named his son Manasseh, the name of one of the leading tribes of the north. His grandson Amon married into a family from Jotbah in Galilee (2 Kgs 21:19).

Presence of northerners in the upper echelon of Judahite society can be noted in the biblical text, with Shebna as one example (Isa 22:15; 37:2) (Schniedewind 2004, 69; Rendsburg and Schniedewind 2010). Mendel-Geberovich, Chalaf, and Uziel (2020, 170–75) suggest that a skillfully engraved bulla recently unearthed in the City of David, reading "For Ahiav son of Menaham," belonged to an elite scribe of northern origin since it carries the names of two northern kings, Ahab and Menahem.

From his viewpoint in the Shephelah, the prophet Micah castigates the role of northern leaders in Jerusalem (Schniedewind 1999, 53):

> Hear this, you rulers of the house of Jacob
> and chiefs of the house of Israel,
> who abhor justice and pervert all equity,
> who build Zion with blood and Jerusalem with wrong!
> (Mic 3:9–10)

The Bible includes large textual traditions with origins in the Northern Kingdom from the ninth and eighth centuries (Carr 2011, 472–83; Fleming 2012; Finkelstein 2013).[2] The presence of these texts in the Judean Scriptures is most easily explained through a large-scale immigration of scribes from the north into Judah after the Assyrian campaign in 733–32 and the subsequent fall of the Northern Kingdom. The intermingling of texts of different origins suggests active interaction between northern and southern scribes in seventh-century Judea and Jerusalem. Such an interaction between scribes from Jerusalem and their colleagues in Samaria between 800 and 732 is certainly possible, but less likely.

Some texts bear clear traces of censoring by Judahite scribes to adapt their message to Judahite theology. After the fall of Samaria, a negative

---

2. As one example, see p. 81 on the use of Gideon traditions in Isa 9:1–6 [9:2–7].

perspective on northern history can be perceived among Deuteronomistic scribes.[3]

The integration of northern refugees in Judah would pave the way for an all-Israelite identity and ideology: with time the people of Judah incorporated the remnants of "all Israel" and could therefore make the textual heritage of the northerners their own. Subsequently "Israel" could commonly be used as a designation for the nation that was centered in Judea in the early sixth century and then dispersed.

The Dynasties of the North

The history of the Northern Kingdom and its ruling dynasties demonstrates the continuous power struggle between clans from the highlands and the lowlands. The struggle for power between these families and the alliances between them resulted in the formation of the kingdom of Israel, which appeared on the international scene under the Omrides. For Sergi (2019, 45–50), the Omride state was the first organized polity known as Israel.

This Israelite state, however, should be regarded as a continuation of the earlier rule of Saul and his son Ishbaal (see pp. 17–19). From the end of the tenth century, Saul's "Little Israel" in the highlands expanded into a "Greater Israel" under Baasha and Omri.

The tribal union of the north had kept an identity of their own throughout the alliance with Judah under David and Solomon. Subsequently, "all Israel" acclaimed Jeroboam of the house of Joseph as their king—still without any dynastic covenant (1 Kgs 12:1–24). While Jeroboam's tribe is not specified, his clan was Ephrathite (also said about David, 1 Sam 17:12), and his rise to power is connected with the house of Joseph (1 Kgs 11:26–28). Jeroboam (927–907) ruled from Ephraimite territory: "Jeroboam fortified Shechem in the hill country of Ephraim and resided there; he moved out from there and fortified Penuel" (12:25 NJPS). Ephraim had been prominent among the northern tribes—it was listed first in the early battle account in Judg 5:12–22.

---

3. A prominent example is the proclamation of Jeroboam connected to the Bethel sanctuary: "Here are your gods, Israel, who brought [plural] you up from the land of Egypt" (1 Kgs 12:28, my translation), likely adapted from an original "Here is your god, Israel, who brought [singular] you up."

The biblical accounts exaggerate the dimensions of Jeroboam's rule. Shechem remained sparsely settled during Iron Age IIA (Finkelstein 2006). And there was no Israelite sanctuary from his time at Dan, which was included in the kingdom only under Jeroboam II (cf. 1 Kgs 12:29–30; Arie 2008; Finkelstein 2013, 74–75, 128–29). A memory of Jeroboam II building a Dan sanctuary for Yhwh may in DtrH have been moved back to Jeroboam I and the foundational period of the Northern Kingdom. For DtrH, such a break with the Deuteronomic principle of cult centralization from the beginning would explain the troubled history of the kingdom of Israel.

Clearer archaeological traces can be found from Jeroboam's successors Baasha (906–883) and Omri (882–871), also ruling from the territory of Ephraim:

> In the third year of King Asa of Judah, Baasha son of Ahijah began to reign over all Israel at Tirzah; he reigned twenty-four years. (1 Kgs 15:33)

> In the thirty-first year of King Asa of Judah, Omri began to reign over Israel; he reigned for twelve years, six of them in Tirzah. He bought the hill of Samaria from Shemer for two talents of silver; he fortified the hill, and called the city that he built, Samaria. (1 Kgs 16:23–24)

Around 900, Tirzah (= Tell el-Far'ah, 8 km north of Shechem) rapidly developed from a small settlement into a rich urban center, exhibiting social hierarchy, cultic activity, and long-distance trade. It was, however, destroyed after some decades and abandoned (Kleiman 2018; Sergi 2020, 61). The building of Tirzah may be the first archaeological sign of the emerging Northern Kingdom.

Then, in the early ninth century, Samaria (12 km northwest of Shechem) was transformed from an agricultural estate to a lavishly built city with a royal palace. The site had no previous urban tradition, and it was located close to the region's traditional ruling center, Shechem: "The Omride palace manifests the power and wealth of newly emerged political elite that chose to reside in an entirely newly built political center and not in the former, traditional one" (Sergi and de Hulster 2016, 3). The Omrides, with their power base in the Ephraim highlands, extended their hegemony over vast territories, and the Northern Kingdom expanded, possibly to its largest extension ever. Royal compounds of the Omride dynasty (882–845) have been identified in Megiddo and Jezreel. Guarding the northern border, Hazor and Yokneam were built and fortified. In the east, Gilead was securely annexed to the kingdom. In the southeast, Omride power extended to the high plains of Moab, maintained through a network of fortifications and alliances with local tribes (cf. 2 Kgs 3:4; Finkelstein 2013, 83–112; Sergi 2019, 45–47; for the extension of the kingdom, see figure 2, p. 25).

The appearance of Tirzah and Samaria exemplifies the development of statehood in the Levant. The construction of national identities such as Israel, Aram, Moab, Edom, and Judah is intimately connected with state formation. It reflects the need to form a politically and socially unified structure under centralized rule and at the same time legitimize and manifest the power of this centralized rule (Sergi and de Hulster 2016, 6). Under the Omrides, Judah was practically a vassal kingdom under the hegemony of Israel.

"Israel" was the kinship group with which the highland Omrides were affiliated and by which they identified themselves. By calling their kingdom "Israel," a conscious connection was drawn back to the old tribal union attested in Judg 5. An "Israel identity" was applied to the entire entity they ruled—in 852 the Kurkh Monolith referred to "the forces of Ahab the Israelite" (Sergi 2019, 47, 49).

Around 840, the Mesha Stela demonstrated that the kingdom, with a powerful history east of the Jordan, continued to be known as "Israel" after the downfall of the Omrides in 845.[4] Indeed, the name "Israel" or "house of Israel" would cling to the Northern Kingdom until its destruction in 722.

The house of Jehu took over from the Omrides, and this dynasty ruled 845–745. The tribe of Jehu is not specified, but he appears to have his home in Ramoth-gilead (2 Kgs 9:1). The name of Jehu's grandfather Nimshi (1 Kgs 19:16) appears on two or three ninth-century ostraca found in excavations at the powerful Israelite city of Rehov, south of Beth-shan (Mazar and Aḥituv 2011, 302–4).[5] Thus, while Omri and the tribe of Ephraim had their core supporters among the highlanders, the forces behind Jehu's revolt were likely from Gilead and the Jezreel Valley.

The last two kings of this dynasty, Joash (801–787) and his son Jeroboam II (787–747), dominated Judah to the south (cf. 2 Kgs 14:11–13;

4. Cf. the following words: "Omri was king of Israel, and oppressed Moab during many days. . . . In my days . . . Israel said, 'I shall destroy it forever' . . . the king of Israel fortified Ataroth. . . . And Chemosh said to me, 'Go take Nebo from Israel!'. . . . And the king of Israel fortified Jahaz and occupied it." For a fuller text of the inscription, see p. 15.

5. In Rehov, Mazar observes a peaceful transition from Canaanite to Israelite identity in the early ninth century. Being the hometown and power base of Jehu, the city was violently destroyed toward the end of the next century, likely by Hazael around 830; cf. 2 Kgs 10:32–33 (Mazar 2016, 107–12).

Finkelstein 2020, 47). Through his campaigns Joash pushed the Arameans eastward, a triumph that DtrH ascribes to Yhwh's faithfulness and his covenant with the fathers (2 Kgs 13:22–25). Under Jeroboam, Israel conquered large territories and expanded to the north, Dan and Abel-beth-maacah were incorporated into the kingdom—through successful campaigns and victories that both Amos and DtrH attribute to Yhwh's intervention (2 Kgs 14:25–27; Amos 6:13). DtrH preserves a memory of these powerful states and the eighth-century extension of Israel and Judah together in the reference to "all Israel, from Dan to Beer-sheba" (Judg 20:1; 1 Sam 3:20; 2 Sam 17:11; 24:2; Finkelstein 2013, 129).[6]

The strength of the Northern Kingdom under the house of Jehu is reflected in the fortified caravanserai at Kuntillet ʿAjrud in the Negev, operating for some decades during the period 830–750. The site, 50 km south of Kadesh-barnea, was built under the auspices of the Northern Kingdom and related to Samaria, not Jerusalem, as authority. A number of features show the northern affiliation of the site: the theophoric suffix *yw* in the personal names (as opposed to the Judean *yahu*), the reference to "Yhwh of Samaria and his ashera" ("his sacred pole" rather than "his spouse"), and pottery made in the northern hill country (in addition to pottery from the southern coastal region).[7]

Meshel (2012, 69) connects the construction of the site with King Joash, who captured the Judean King Amaziah in the battle of Beth-shemesh, de-

6. Finkelstein (2019, 13–15) sees the historical core of the united monarchy tradition in the state of the Omrides and Jeroboam II (787–747). The tradition of the large northern state was subsequently ideologically transformed by Judean theologians after 722 and included in DtrH. Finkelstein recently (2020, 43–47) suggested an alternative hypothesis: Saul's kingdom extended from Qeiyafa and Hebron in the south to the Jezreel Valley in the north. The memory of a northerner ruling from a southern hub with a kingdom that covered both the north and the south was brought to Judah by northern scribes after 722 and subsequently Davidized by Judean scribes.

7. On Kuntillet ʿAjrud, see Meshel 2012, esp. 3, 61–69, 286–87, 327–36. Zeʾev Meshel, leader of the excavations, stresses the cultic nature of the site and suggests that priests offered religious services and blessings to desert travelers, caravan drivers, and pilgrims to Sinai and Mount Horeb. The understanding of the site as a desert way station, perhaps with rooms with a cultic function, seems better founded (thus Horwitz et al. in Meshel 2012, 336). The site was located at a road junction and had access to local water wells. The interpretation of the inscriptions and drawings is updated in Aḥituv and Eshel 2015. The reference to "Yhwh of Samaria and his ashera" alongside "Yhwh of Teman and his ashera" suggests the existence of a temple for Yhwh in the city of Samaria. The site was abandoned after some decades and thereafter suffered earthquake destruction—possibly the earthquake during Uzziah's reign, ca. 760 (cf. Amos 1:1; 2:13; Zech 14:5).

stroyed the walls of Jerusalem, and seized the treasures of the temple and palace (2 Kgs 14:7–16; 2 Chr 25:5–24). Joash dominated Judah and controlled the travel routes in the Negev that connected Elat, Sinai, and the Gaza region. According to Meshel, Joash expelled the Judeans from Kadesh-barnea, abandoned its fortress, and built the site of ʿAjrud to demonstrate Israel's control over the Judean border region and its road system.

With the Syro-Ephraimite war in 734–732, Israel was reduced to a rump state covering only the territory of Ephraim and Benjamin. Most of the land was included in Assyrian provinces. With the fall of Samaria to the Assyrians in 722, Hezekiah was able to (or allowed to) incorporate most of Benjamin into the kingdom of Judah.

Yhwh and the Kings of the North

The biblical text notes that Saul, David, and Jeroboam I were acclaimed as "king of Israel" by the tribal union. These covenants were not dynastic, they were valid only for the lifetime of the king. During the two centuries after Solomon, the kingdom would repeatedly see revolts and new kings or dynasties taking over. The Benjaminite Saul was followed by his short-lived son Ishbaal and Jeroboam by his son Nadab, who ruled only a year.

Only once is there recorded a divinely given dynastic promise similar to the Nathan oracle. A prophetic word through Ahijah of Shiloh acclaimed Jeroboam I as king over the ten tribes, to take them away from the house of David: "If you will listen to all that I command you, . . . as David my servant did, I will be with you, and will build you an enduring house, as I built for David, and I will give Israel to you" (1 Kgs 11:29–39 at 11:38).[8]

In spite of the Deuteronomists' critical reflection on the history of the Northern Kingdom about the people's worship on the high places and in the Bethel and Dan sanctuaries, DtrH does give expression to Yhwh's continuous goodwill vis-à-vis the house of Israel through its history (Schniedewind 1999, 59). The institution of kingship is never questioned per se, while kings failing to live up to the (Deuteronomic) ideals of true faith in Yhwh are heavily criticized.

---

8. The words "enduring house" (*bayit-neʾĕmān*) echo *neʾĕman bêtkā* ("your house is made firm") in 2 Sam 7:16. Jeroboam II is thus promised a lasting dynasty. The text connects Ahijah or his family with Shiloh, a town that had been lying in ruins for more than a century; it was destroyed around 1050, likely by the Philistines (note, however, that 1 Sam 14:3, 18–19 mentions Ahijah, belonging to a Shilonite priestly family, in the service of Saul).

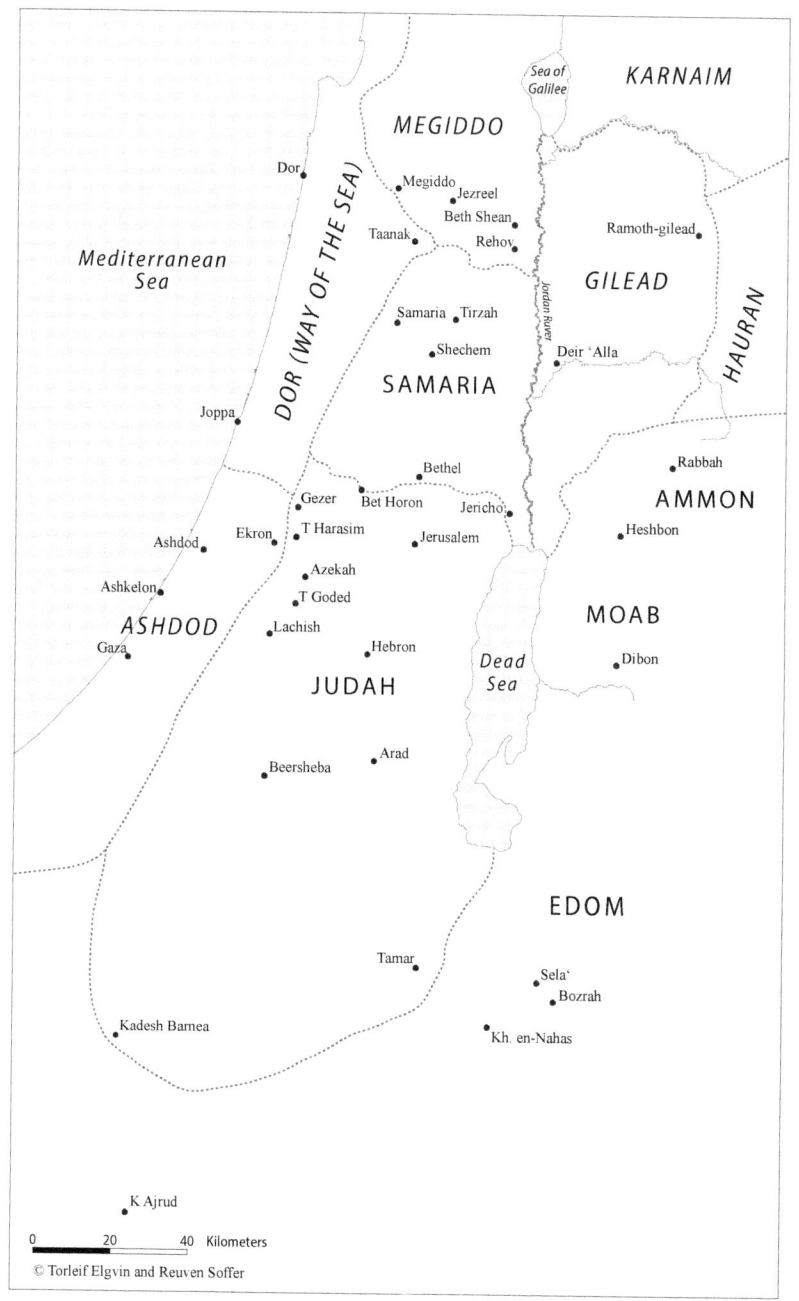

Figure 4. Judea in the late eighth century BCE among Assyrian provinces after the 733 and 715 campaigns.

Prophetic oracles express Yhwh's goodwill toward the house of Israel and proclaim that Yhwh elected and commissioned a number of the northern kings.

Toward the end of his rule, Basha (who replaced the house of Jeroboam I) received a divine oracle: "I lifted you up from the dust and made you a ruler over my people Israel, but you followed the way of Jeroboam and caused my people Israel to sin, vexing me with their sins. Therefore, I am going to sweep away Baasha and his house" (1 Kgs 16:2–3 NJPS adapted). Later, a disciple of Elisha anointed Jehu king to remove the house of Omri and Ahab: "Thus says Yhwh the God of Israel: 'I anoint you king over the people of Yhwh, over Israel. You shall strike down the house of your master Ahab'" (2 Kgs 9:1–10 at 9:6–7 NRSV adapted).

From the end of the ninth century, DtrH preserves the following statement: "King Hazael of Aram oppressed Israel all the days of Jehoahaz [ruled 808–802]. But Yhwh was gracious to them and had compassion on them; and he turned back to them for the sake of his covenant with Abraham, Isaac, and Jacob, and would not destroy them; nor has he banished them from his presence *until now*" (2 Kgs 13:22–23, my translation).

Northern kings are generally praised for their military strength, whereas southern kings rarely are (1 Kgs 16:5, 27; 22:46 [22:45]; 2 Kgs 10:34; 13:8, 12; 14:28; cf. Schniedewind 1999, 59). DtrH criticizes Jeroboam II (787–747) for not living up to Deuteronomic ideals but keeps a statement of praise: "He restored the territory of Israel from Lebo-hamath to the Sea of the Arabah, in accordance with the promise that Yhwh, the God of Israel, had made through his servant, the prophet Jonah son of Amittai from Gath-hepher. For Yhwh saw the bitter plight of Israel, with neither bond nor freed left, and with none to help Israel. And Yhwh resolved not to blot out the name of Israel from under heaven; and he delivered them through Jeroboam son of Joash" (2 Kgs 14:25–27, my translation).

These oracles were likely preserved by northern scribes who had migrated to Judah and may have strengthened their confidence in Yhwh's lasting goodwill toward the remnant of Israel.

The ninth-century Northern Kingdom is the arena of the Elijah-Elisha narratives, interspersed in 1 Kgs 17–2 Kgs 13. The narratives reflect a positive attitude to the northern state and its continued existence under royal leadership. Elijah is critical of Ahab and Jezebel for their support of non-Yahwist cult but (in contrast to the eighth-century Amos) never calls for an end to the kingdom. In 2 Kgs 6–7, Elisha is portrayed as a guarantee for the survival of Samaria. Elisha's exclamation when Elijah was taken away, "Oh, father, father! Israel's chariots and horsemen!" (2:12, my translation), expresses that

Elijah had been the spiritual defender of the house of Israel. And at Elisha's deathbed, King Joash of Israel laments him with the same words (13:14).

Ten km north of Elisha's hometown, Abel-meholah, was the powerful city of Rehov. During the Rehov excavations, a mid-ninth-century ostracon was unearthed, inscribed "for Elisha." It was found in a separated section of a large domestic house. A hallway where two horned ceramic alters were found led into a room with two benches. These findings may suggest a historical kernel in the Elisha narratives (in particular 2 Kgs 4:8–37; Mazar and Aḥituv 2011, 306–7; Mazar 2016, 111–14).

Balaam: A Star of Jacob

Among the Balaam oracles in Num 22–24, the royal oracle 24:15–19 (my translation) has a prominent place:

> [5]How fair are your tents, Jacob, your dwellings, Israel!
> [7b]. . . his king shall be higher than Agag, and his kingdom exalted.
>
> . . .
>
> [15]An oracle of Balaam son of Beor,
> words of the man whose eye is true,
> [16]words of him who hears the speech of El,
> who obtains knowledge from the Most High
> and sees the vision of Shaddai,
> who falls down, but with eyes unveiled:
> [17]What I see is not yet,
> what I behold is not near:
> A star shall come out of Jacob,
> a scepter shall rise out of Israel,
> he shall crush the borderlands of Moab,
> and the territory of all the Shethites.
> [18]Edom will become a possession,
> Seir a possession of his enemies,
> while Israel performs valiantly.
> [19]One out of Jacob shall rule,
> and destroy the survivors of the city.

Preserved and transmitted by later Judean scribes, this oracle retains a remarkable north-Israelite color (Carr [2011, 481–82] notes echoes of the oracle in Deut 23:5–6 [23:4–5] and Josh 13:22). The nation is twice called Israel and twice Jacob—in early tradition the ancestor of the Israel tribes. Balaam envisions a future king coming out of the northern tribes: "A star shall come out of Jacob, a scepter shall rise out of Israel . . . one out of Jacob shall rule" (vv. 17–19).

In exilic and postexilic times, "Israel" and "Jacob" had been transformed to designations for the full nation that had survived the upheavals of the eighth–sixth centuries. As the most prominent royal prophecy in the Tetrateuch alongside Gen 49:8–12, this oracle would easily be interpreted on a future Judean ruler, likely of Davidic origin.

However, in an original ninth-century context, the oracle would be read as a prophetic support of the expansion of the Omride kingdom to the east and south, toward Gilead, Moab, Edom, and the mountain region Seir.[9] Subsequently remembered all through the eighth century—parallel to the rise of the Assyrian superpower and the careers of Amos and Hosea with their critical perspective on royal house and society—the oracle would retain the hope of a future renaissance for the house of Israel: a rebirth of the nation headed by one of their own, who would subdue their enemies around. While Hosea refrains from using the term "king" (but rather *rō's*, "head") for the future joint head of the sister nations (2:2 [1:11]), the term "scepter" (Num 24:17) belongs to royal terminology. Further, "star" would traditionally be connected to kingship in the ancient Near East (with eighteenth-century Mari texts on King Zimri-Lim as one example).

A book scroll that included the Balaam oracles ended up in scribal workshops in seventh-century Judea. It is notable that the north-Israelite color was not camouflaged or neutralized. In this time period, the oracle betrays the hope of scribes coming from the north of a future mighty ruler coming out of the northern tribes.

Until 1967, the seer Balaam son of Beor was known only from the biblical text. At that time, two fragmentary eighth-century inscriptions written on plaster and ascribed to Balaam were excavated at Deir 'Alla, where the river Zarqa (biblical Jabbok) flows into the Jordan River from the east, midway between the Sea of Galilee and the Dead Sea. Tel Deir 'Alla is identified by many with the biblical town of Succoth (Judg 8:16). The plaster inscriptions were found in debris caused by an earthquake and had likely been written on a wall of a building identified as a sanctuary. Pottery found in this stratum,

---

9. It remains possible that the oracle was polished and updated after Hasmonean conquests of Moab and Edom in the period 128–85 (see pp. 223–24).

C[14] tests, and paleographical analysis all suggest a dating around the eighth century, ± one century (Levine 1981; Hackett 1992).

The language of the inscriptions is enigmatic, as it represents a Northwest Semitic dialect or language not known from other sites.[10] Prominently placed in a sanctuary, the inscriptions are written by a professional scribe and represent copies of an earlier text. In this region, the seer Balaam was clearly celebrated as a divinely inspired prophet from some time in the past.

There are close parallels between the inscriptions and the Balaam oracles in Numbers, which suggest some traditio-historical links between the texts.[11] The inscriptions presuppose a polytheistic setting. The first part of the first inscription runs:

> [The inscrip]tion of [Bala]am, [son of Be]or, a divine seer.
> The gods came to him at night [and spoke to] him on the vision
>   of El,
> speaking to [Bala]am, son of Beor: "This will [the gods] do in the
>   future,
> and no man has s[een what you have he]ard."
> ... and Balaam arose in the morning ... weeping thoroughly.
> And his people came to him, asking, "Why do you fast and weep?"
> He answered, "... I will show you what the Sha[dday-gods are up
>   to,]
> the gods have joined forces,
> their council have said to (the goddess) Sha[gar],
> 'Cover up the heavens with dense clouds
> so that darkness, and no brilliance will be there.
> Concealment, and no bristling light.
> ... dread ... darkness ... voice of vultures ... distress and trou-
>   ble!'" (Levine 1981, 196–97)

10. According to Michael Langlois (personal communication), the inscriptions represent either another local dialect from the early centuries of the first millennium or a wider but earlier Northwest Semitic language from the late second millennium. He further notes that they are written by a professional scribe and perhaps served as a model for students learning to write.

11. Compare "and the gods [*'elwh*] came to him at night" (I 3) and "at night Elohim came to Balaam and said to him" (Num 22:20); "and Balaam arose in the morning" (I 8) and "in the morning Balaam rose" (Num 22:21); "and his people came to him" (I 12) and "I now return to my own people" (Num 22:34). Further compare "Sha[dday-gods]" (I 16) with the biblical designation El Shaddai.

In the continuation there is reference to diviners and a ritual that includes incantations and a role for a priestess, to prevent the predicted evils.

The biblical version of the Balaam oracles should likely be dated to the time of the Omride dynasty, 882–845, since "Israel" and "Jacob" recur in the oracles, and the Omrides ruled Gilead (to the north of the Jabbok) and the region east of the Dead Sea. At this time, a tradition of the divinely inspired seer Balaam, son of Beor, was alive in the region. Scribes of the Northern Kingdom likely contextualized and Israelized texts ascribed to Balaam, adopted and transformed them into a Yahwistic setting, writing in Classical Biblical Hebrew. In their hermeneutical circle, ninth-century northern scribes would locate Balaam in the foundational period of their nation, in the generation of Moses: a prophet in Moses's time did foresee the glory of the Omride kingdom! Subsequently, seventh-century scribes working on the growing tradition of the Tetrateuch-to-be would faithfully include the text of the "Balaam scroll" from the north almost "as is," as an inspired text giving hope for the future.

The Balaam oracle became a foundational text for the Bar Kokhba Revolt (132–36 CE) (my paraphrase).

> Because of his great deeds, Rabbi Akiva said, "The star rising from Jacob"—that is Kosiba rising from the people of Jacob. He is the King Messiah! (Jerusalem Talmud, tractate Ta'anit 4.5 || *Lamentations Rabbah* 2.4)

Some decades before Bar Kokhba, Balaam's oracle was echoed in Matthew: "The king of the Judeans, we have seen his star at its rising/in the east" (2:2, my translation). The Matthean story (2:1–12) is presented as a sequel to a finished hypotext.

Joseph and Judah in Jacob's Blessings

The collection of tribal blessings of Gen 49 has origins in the Northern Kingdom—the divine epithets appearing in the Joseph oracle: *'ăbîr ya'ăqōb* ("the Mighty One of Jacob") and *'eben yiśrā'ēl* ("the Rock of Israel") belong to the northern heritage. Different from the archaic tribal list in Judg 5 and the list of Solomon's twelve administrative districts (see pp. 16–17, 22), the tradition of twelve tribes is clearly established: Judah and eleven tribes of the northern union, identical with the sons of Jacob as listed in Genesis. The Judah and Ephraim oracles run as follows (NRSV adapted):

[8]Judah, your brothers shall praise you,
your hand shall be on the neck of your enemies,
your father's sons shall bow down before you.
[9]Judah is a lion's whelp; from the prey, my son, you have gone up.
He crouches down, he stretches out like a lion,
like a lioness—who dares rouse him up?
[10]The scepter shall not depart from Judah,
nor the ruler's staff from his divisions,[12]
until what is due will come to him,[13]
and the obedience of nations is his.
[11]Binding his foal to the vine
and his donkey's colt to the choice vine,
he washes his garments in wine
and his robe in the blood of grapes;
[12]his eyes are darker than wine,
and his teeth whiter than milk. . . .
[22]Joseph is a fruitful bough,
a fruitful bough by a spring;
his branches run over the wall.
[23]The archers fiercely attacked him;
they shot at him and pressed him hard.
[24]Yet his bow remained taut,
and his arms were made agile
by the hands of the Mighty One of Jacob,
by the name of the Shepherd, the Rock of Israel,
[25]by the God of your father, who will help you,
by Shaddai who will bless you
with blessings of heaven above,
blessings of the deep that lies beneath,
blessings of the breasts and of the womb.
[26]The blessings of your father
are stronger than the blessings of the eternal mountains,

---

12. Reading with the Samaritan text *degalāyw* ("his standards/divisions") not *raglāyw* ("his feet"; NRSV) with M. Graphically, the two readings are nearly identical, with *dalet* and *resh* being formed very similarly.

13. I choose not to elaborate on the enigmatic sentence *'ad kî-yābō' šîlōh*. There are numerous interpretations of these words, with "until Shiloh comes" as one alternative translation (cf. a Talmudic interpretation; see p. 295).

may the bounties of the everlasting hills be on the head of
    Joseph,
on the forehead of him who was set apart from his brothers.

From its inception, the Northern Kingdom overshadowed Judah in size and power. This changed only with the Assyrian invasion during the Syro-Ephraimite war in 734–732.

An oracle giving Judah royal power over the other tribes hardly makes sense in a collection from the north. In an earlier recension, the words "your father's sons shall bow down before you" (Gen 49:8) would have referred to Joseph (cf. Gen 37:5–11). Thus, the Judah oracle reflects editing in the south after the fall of Samaria—scepter and ruler's staff have been transferred to Judah (scepter is a prerogative of the Davidic king in Ps 110:2 and of the promised northern king in Num 24:17). According to the oracle, the present royal power "shall not depart from Judah" until "the obedience of nations is his"—that is, the time when neighboring nations will submit to Judah or its king (the subject of this sentence is either the king or Judah as a tribe), as envisaged in Ps 2:8–10. The confidence that "the scepter shall not depart from Judah" remains rooted in the Davidic tradition of 2 Sam 7, Ps 2, and Ps 110.

If the Judah oracle with its royal color had been inserted from scratch after 722, we would have expected it first in the sequence. Judah's fourth place in the collection is likely original and testifies to an early tradition of a union between Judah and the northern tribes (Weingart 2019, 29). The present text reworked an earlier version that contained a shorter oracle on Judah and a royal oracle on Joseph.

In this tribal list, "Joseph" appears where we might have expected separate oracles for Ephraim and Manasseh (in Judg 5:14–18, Machir and Gilead represent Manasseh). Joseph and Benjamin (only a short oracle on the latter) appear at the end of the list, as the sons of Rachel.[14]

The Joseph oracle is slightly longer than that of Judah and concludes that Yhwh's blessings shall "be on the head of Joseph, on the forehead of him who was set apart from his brothers" (Gen 49:26). The description of Joseph as set apart from his brothers and standing firm against enemies by the name and power of the God of Jacob/Israel preserves elements of an earlier royal oracle, when kingship belonged to the house of Joseph and

---

14. Benjamin is here associated with Joseph, not with Judah, while the district of Benjamin was connected to Judah in the early tenth century and the post-722 period (Weingart 2019, 29).

the words "your father's sons shall bow down before you" were directed to Joseph, not Judah.

Such a form of Jacob's blessings should be dated to the time of the Omrides, when kingship belonged to the tribe of Ephraim of the house of Joseph. The Jacob and Joseph narratives in Genesis, with Joseph in the first place, are painted in colors reflecting the same time period.

Concluding, it is clear that the royal oracle on the "Lion of Judah" in the biblical text transforms earlier traditions from the house of Israel, including the Balaam oracle, to which "scepter" and "the obedience of nations" may be indebted (cf. Num 24:17–18).

With a hermeneutical framework of salvation history, one could reflect on the dynamic ways of God, who may change his plans for a nation dependent on the people's interaction with him and his ways. At one point in history, Joseph/Ephraim was chosen to rule one of the sister nations in parallel with the house of David in Judah (cf. the prophetic words to Jeroboam I in 1 Kgs 11:38). With the fall of Samaria, only the kingdom of Judah with its royal house remained, and remnants of the northern tribes with their texts and traditions were in time integrated into the larger nation of Judah.

As hypotext, the blessing on Joseph that singles him out as a warrior would receive a sequel in rabbinic tradition with the idea of the messiah son of Joseph/Ephraim, who will rise as leader of Israel, lead the fight against the enemies, and die in battle—thus preparing the way for the Davidic messiah.

Hosea: One Head for Israel and Judah

The blessings on the northern tribes in Gen 49 and the Balaam oracle in Num 24:5–19 reflect the heyday of the Northern Kingdom, likely under the Omrides. In contrast, Ps 80 and the prophet Hosea belong to the troubled years after the downfall of the house of Jehu in 745.

Psalm 80 provides a window into the troublesome last decade of the kingdom, between the devastating Assyrian campaigns in 733–732 and the fall of Samaria in 722. The psalm is a lament of war and destruction, appealing to the shepherd of Israel and Joseph to appear before the tribes of Ephraim, Benjamin, and Manasseh, the core tribes of the highlands (my translation):

> [2][1]Give ear, Shepherd of Israel,
> you who lead Joseph like a flock!

³⁽²⁾Appear, you who are enthroned on the cherubim,
before Ephraim, Benjamin, and Manasseh!
Stir up your might and come to our help!

Following Eissfeldt, Zenger notes that only between 732 and 722 did these three tribes converge in a political unit. Tiglath-pileser's campaign led to the establishment of the provinces of Dor, Gilead, and Megiddo (= "the way of the sea," "the land beyond Jordan," "Galilee of the nations"; Isa 8:23 [9:1]; cf. figure 4, p. 63), which effectively left only the tribes of the highlands around Samaria as a "rump state" of Israel (Hossfeld and Zenger 2005, 311). The psalm was composed by learned singers for services of lament—probably celebrated both in the north and among refugees to Judah (my translation):

⁵⁽⁴⁾Yhwh, God of hosts, how long will you be wrathful
toward the prayers of your people?
⁶⁽⁵⁾You have fed them tears as their daily bread,
made them drink great measures of tears.
⁷⁽⁶⁾You set us at strife with our neighbors,
our enemies mock us at will.
⁸⁽⁷⁾O God of hosts, restore us,
show your favor that we may be delivered.
⁹⁽⁸⁾You plucked up a vine from Egypt,
you expelled nations and planted it.
¹⁰⁽⁹⁾You cleared a place for it,
it took deep root and filled the land.
¹¹⁽¹⁰⁾The mountains were covered by its shade,
mighty cedars by its boughs.
¹²⁽¹¹⁾Its branches reached the sea,
its shoots, the river.
¹³⁽¹²⁾Why did you breach its wall
so that every passerby plucks its fruit,
¹⁴⁽¹³⁾wild boars gnaw at it,
and creatures of the field feed on it?
¹⁵⁽¹⁴⁾O God of hosts, turn again,
look down from heaven and see,
take note of that vine,
¹⁶⁽¹⁵⁾the stock planted by your right hand,
the stem you have taken as your own.

17[16]For it is burned by fire and cut down,
perishing before your angry blast.

The psalm is a heartfelt cry about the destruction of the land, calling upon Yhwh to show mercy toward the people he had called out from Egypt and planted in the land—the vine that now is cut down and given to the fire.

With time, the Judahites also learned to put their soul into these words. At the time of Josiah, a plea for the king was added, a plea that echoes the royal/Zion Ps 110: "Let your hand be upon the one at your right hand, the one whom you made strong for yourself!" (80:18 [80:17]; see p. 44).

Hosea's prophetic career can be dated from the mid-eighth century to the early years after the fall of Samaria in 722. The book bears traces of a Judean redaction under Josiah (Sweeney 2001, 259–61) or Hezekiah (my view). The prophet may himself have been among the survivors who fled to the south. In 2:1–3 [1:10–2:1] the prophet foresees a unification of the remnants of Israel and Judah under one leader (*rō'š 'eḥād*, "one head"):

> ¹Yet the number of the people of Israel shall be like the sand of
>   the sea,
> which can be neither measured nor numbered.
> Instead of being told, "you are 'Not My People,'"
> they shall be called "Children of the Living God."
> ²The people of Judah and the people of Israel shall be gathered
>   together
> and appoint for themselves one leader,
> and they shall go up from the land,
> great shall the day of Jezreel be.
> ³Oh, call your brothers "My People,"
> and your sisters "Beloved."
> (Hos 2:1–3 [1:10–2:1], my translation)

Hosea 2:1–3 [1:10–2:1] is closely linked to 1:2–9, and its terminology is typical for the prophet (Stuart 1987, 36–37). I see no reason to doubt that a core of 1:2–2:3 goes back to Hosea himself.

During the Syro-Ephraimite war in 734–732, Israel and Judah were actively fighting each other. This oracle may be dated only a few years later—a tough background for speaking about a coming unification of the sister nations. Thus, the previous enemies will be reconciled with one another and with Yhwh their God. "Three dramatic reversals will constitute Jezreel's great new day. These are the unification of Israel and Judah under a single leader, their return from exile, and their revival" (Stuart 1987, 38).

The prophet avoids the term "king" for the future leader of united Israel, likely due to his disappointment over the kings he had experienced in the north—with six short-lived kings between the death of the powerful Jeroboam II in 747 and the fall of Samaria in 722. In their present form, these verses are addressed to the people of Judah, and it remains noteworthy that the Judean redaction does not change the term *rōʾš* to "king," but keeps the terminology of the prophet.

The words "they shall go up from the land" are enigmatic in the context. For Stewart (1987, 39), they mean either returning from exile or being resurrected "from the earth," that is, from death, thus comparing the deliverance of the nation of Israel with bodily resurrection. In my view, these words foresee that people from the north shall "go up" (make pilgrimage) to Jerusalem from their own land. At that stage, the Judahites will receive their brethren from the north with their new names expressing the grace of Yhwh.

The conclusion of 3:1–5, "the Israelites will turn back and seek Yhwh their God *and David their king*," bears the stamp of post-Hosea redaction in Judea—there is no evidence elsewhere in the book that Hosea promoted Judean royal ideology. While the theme of redemption in 3:5 is integral to 3:1–5, the words "and David their king" are a later addition (cf. the prophet's avoidance of the term "king" in 2:2 [1:11].

Hosea 2:1–3 [1:10–2:1] has a substantial posthistory: the hope for a future union between Israel and Judah, or the remnant of "Israel" returning to Yhwh, was maintained after the breakdown of the Northern Kingdom in 733–722, which ended with the deportation of large parts of the population eastward (2 Kgs 17:6). In addition to northerners fleeing to the south, some texts suggest that northerners also remained in their own land: Jeremiah's appeal to "Israel" to come back to Yhwh (Jer 2:4–4:2), the exilic postscripts to the book of Amos (9:11–12 and 9:13–15; see pp. 112–14), the exilic oracle of a coming king for "Jacob" and the "remnant of Israel" in Mic 2:12–13, and the later addition of Mic 5:2 [5:3] into 5:1–8 [5:2–9] (see pp. 98–101). At least parts of the group that in the fifth century appeared as the Samaritan community that built the Gerizim temple would be among these northerners who stayed in the land (Kartveit 2009, esp. 351–70). The family of Sanballat of Beth-horon, postexilic governor of Samaria, was likely Israelite, since he was father-in-law of a Judean priest (Neh 13:28).

Hosea's avoidance of the term "king" for the future leader, rather using *rōʾš* ("head"), might be echoed in later oracles that would find terms other than "king" for a future or end-time leader.

Early exilic times saw the growing together of an early four-prophet scroll consisting of Hosea, Amos, Micah, and Zephaniah (Nogalski 1993, 278–80; Albertz 2004, 207–11). In this scroll, the early text Hos 2:1–3 [1:10–2:1] set the tone for exilic hopes for the future and may have inspired the composition and inclusion of Davidic oracles into the books of Amos and Micah (Amos 9:11–12, 13–15; Mic 2:12–13; 5:1, 3–5 [5:2, 4–6]; see pp. 98–103, 112–14).[15]

15. Messianic/eschatological sequels to Hos 1:6–2:2 [1:6–11] as hypotext appear with two first-century Jewish exegetes, Paul and Matthew. In Rom 9:25–26, Paul foresees an end-time inclusion of Israel in the messianic community, when they will be called "My People" and "Beloved"; this happens "instead of it being said/where it was said [*en tō topō*]" to them "Not My People" and "Not Beloved." In Matt 16:16, Hosea's "sons of the living God" and "one head for Judah and Israel" are transformed into Peter's confession: "You are the messiah, son of the living God!" If this passage reflects early gospel tradition (cf. par. Mark 8:27–30; Luke 9:18–21; John 6:67–69), the saying could express a Davidic messianism rather than a reflected high Christology.

CHAPTER 3

From Isaiah to Josiah

Two Isaianic oracles on the birth of a Davidide set a lasting mark in biblical tradition. My discussion of the oracles in Isa 7 and Isa 9 will focus on their meaning in the sociopolitical context of the eighth and seventh centuries. Following the editorial growth of the book of Isaiah, a reinterpretation of these oracles and the role of Isaiah's contemporary, the righteous King Hezekiah, is evident. With another righteous king, Josiah, and his Deuteronomy-inspired reform in the late seventh century, hopes for a new Davidic king were accentuated. Josiah's death in battle crushed this hope and was an omen of the soon-to-come end of a ruling house of David.

Isaiah 7 and 9: A New Prince

Immanuel: Survival through War and Devastation

I regard Isa 7:14–17 and possibly 8:23b–9:6 [9:1b–7] as authentic oracles from the mouth of Isaiah, both related to the son of David tradition, while 11:1–5 is exilic (see pp. 114–17). The same goes for 4:2–6, where *ṣemaḥ* ("sprout") refers to the nation and not to the Davidide as in Zechariah (Wildberger 1972, 154).

Isaiah 7 and 9 contain two prophetic oracles about a coming prince. Isaiah 7:14–17 foretells the birth of a new prince in the house of David (see Collins 2010a for an updated discussion). Isaiah 7:1–17 bears clear traces of later editing—in contrast to Isa 6, this narrative is formulated in the third person. The core oracle should be dated to the Syro-Ephraimite war in 734, thus deriving from Isaiah's early career. With the words of testing or judgment to King Ahaz as background, the son to be born is likely intended to replace Ahaz. The expression "your land, Immanuel" (8:8) points to the lad being a royal figure. This verse and the last words of the passage, *kî 'immānû 'ēl* ("for God is with us"; 8:10), suggest that the lad was already born when 8:6–10 was spoken.

The narrative 7:1–17 betrays close links to the Davidic tradition and the Nathan oracle: Isaiah addresses Ahaz with the words "house of David" (cf. "your house" in the address to David in 2 Sam 7:16). In the proverbial saying "if you do not stand firm in faith, you shall not stand," the words *ta'ămînû* ("stand in faith") and *tē'āmēnû* ("stand") allude to *ne'ĕman bêtkā* ("your house will stand"; 2 Sam 7:16):

> [14]Therefore the Lord himself will give you a sign. Look, the young woman is with child and shall bear a son, and shall name him Immanuel. [15]He shall eat curds and honey by the time he learns to choose between good and evil. [16]For before the lad learns to choose between good and evil, the land of the two kings you fear will be deserted. [17]Yhwh will cause to come upon you and your people and your ancestral house such days as never have come since Ephraim turned away from Judah—through the king of Assyria.[1] (Isa 7:14–17, my translation)

As the narrative in general, the name Immanuel is rooted in the son of David tradition; compare 2 Sam 7:9 and 7:14–15: "I will be a father to him . . . my steadfast love will not depart from him." The name also plays on the Zion tradition; compare the refrain of the Zion-centered Ps 46:8, 11 [46:7, 10]: "Yhwh of hosts is with us." In spite of the narrative's explicit criticism of the present house of David, Yhwh's earlier promises to David and Zion warrant a continuation: in the midst of the coming turmoil, Yhwh will bring forth a prince as a sign of Yhwh's continued presence in his people. At the same time, the oracle foresees war and destruction in the near future not only for Aram and Israel (Isa 7:16) but also for Judah (7:17). According to 7:21–25, "eating curds and honey" (7:15) is a sign of a ravaged land; no cultivated yields of the land are available (Collins 2010a, 233–35). Collins concludes:

> The original prophecy of Isaiah to Ahaz was one of reassurance.[2] The sign of Immanuel was offered to induce the king to have faith in the promise.

1. The words "(through) the king of Assyria" were added to 7:17 after Sennacherib's invasion of Judah in 701.
2. Collins follows Høgenhaven 1987, while others see the oracle as expressing judgment on Ahaz. For example, Williamson (1998, 244–54) reads 7:9, 17 as a threat of judgment,

The prophecy was not necessarily one of simple deliverance. The symbolism of the curds and honey may have been deliberately ambiguous: there would be hardship for a few years, but the food provided by the uncultivated land would still have an idyllic quality. The promise to David is not revoked.

Eventually, of course, it became clear that the king would not heed the prophet's advice.... Immanuel is not introduced in opposition to Ahaz, but as a sign of hope for the continuity of the Davidic line. (Collins 2010a, 237, 239)

In my view, Collins underplays the harshness of the oracle, which signals survival solely for a remnant through war and devastation—a theme known from 6:11–13 and 10:20 and evinced in the names of Isaiah's sons: "Soon booty, rapid plunder," and "only a remnant will return" (7:3; 8:1–4).

There is no distant messianic flavor in this oracle; it foresees the birth of an earthly prince in a time of political upheaval. Scholars have proposed that the oracle aims at Hezekiah, an option held by some early rabbis: "There will not be any future messiah for Israel, as they enjoyed messianic times already in the days of Hezekiah" (Babylonian Talmud, tractate *Sanhedrin* 98b); as the Immanuel child is connected to Davidic promises, so is Hezekiah. A problem with this suggestion is Hezekiah's time of birth. Based on the biblical sources, his time of ascending the throne can be dated to either 727 or 715, and he is noted to be twenty-five when he became king (2 Kgs 18:1, 9, 13), so another son of Ahaz may be more likely.

In the collection Isa 1–38, when seventh-century editors reflected on the role of Hezekiah, the Immanuel oracle was likely reread with Hezekiah in focus, who would again be a type for the coming king (see pp. 91–92).

A Son Born to Us: A Judean Countermonarch

As hypotext, 7:1–17 would receive a continuation in 8:23–9:6 [9:1–7].[3] The Assyrian flavor of 8:23–9:6 [9:1–7] suggests an eighth- or seventh-century

---

not only against Ahaz, but against all the house of David ("your ancestral house"); cf. the plural "you" in 7:9, 13, 14. The prophet warns Ahaz that he can forfeit the continuation of the Davidic dynasty. Williamson sees Immanuel as a divinely ordained, non-Davidic leader who should replace the house of Ahaz. I cannot see this as consistent with Williamson's openness to Isaianic authorship of the pro-Davidic oracle 8:23–9:6 [9:1–7] (1998, 257–58).

3. For the following, see Alt 1950; Wildberger 1972, 363–89; Carlson 1974; Barth 1977, 141–77; Høgenhaven 1987; Roberts 1997; Childs 2001, 77–81; Williamson 1998, 255–57.

date for this text. Building upon groundbreaking contributions by Alt and von Rad, some scholars date these verses to 732–722, the last decade of the remnants of the Northern Kingdom.[4] Other voices see 9:1–6 [9:2–7], with or without the preamble in 8:23 [9:1], as a relecture of the Immanuel oracle from the second half of the seventh century.

Isaiah 8:23aα [9:1aα] closes the preceding section 8:16–22 (thus G), while the prosaic 8:23aβb [9:1aβb] functions as an introitus to the hymnic oracle 9:1–6 [9:2–7], which celebrates Yhwh's acts of salvation.[5] The hymn celebrates the events envisaged as already taken place, thus creating a kind of literary fiction within which the future is anticipated (Høgenhaven 1987, 220):

> [8:22b]Behold: distress and darkness, only the gloom of anguish and banishment of shadowiness,
> [8:23 [9:1]]yes, there will be no gloom for her who was in anguish.
> [23aβb]In the former time he humiliated the lands of Zebulun and Naphtali,
> while in a later time he will glorify the Way of the Sea, the Land beyond Jordan,
> and Galilee of the Nations. (my translation)[6]

4. E.g., Wildberger, Høgenhaven, Childs, Sweeney. Childs dates the oracle around 730 and sees the four names as intended for a coming prince: "The Assyrian conquest forms the background of desolation and gloom against which the ensuing prophetic note of light and hope is sounded" (2001, 79–81 at 79). He warns, however, against a highly historizing interpretation of the oracle and suggests an eschatological edge in this oracle on a Davidic messiah. The qualities of the divinely selected ruler are hard to attach to a ruler taking the place of Ahaz: "Each name brings out some extraordinary quality for the divinely selected ruler: a counsellor of unique wisdom and abundant power, endowed with enduring life, and bringer of eternal peace. The description of his reign makes it absolutely clear that his role is messianic" (2001, 81). Sweeney (1996, 182) interprets 9:1–6 [9:2–7] as a coronation psalm of thanksgiving that is likely older than its present use, a psalm inspired by Egyptian custom. In its present context of 8:16–9:6 [8:1–7], closely connected with the Syro-Ephraimite war, the new king would be understood as Hezekiah.

5. Isa 8:23–9:6 [9:1–7] may have been editorially added to 8:16–22 due to a *Stichwort* connection: darkness–darkness, gloom–light. For stylistic reasons I write 8:23 [9:1] instead of 8:23aβb [9:1aβb].

6. Grammatically, 8:23 [9:1] is difficult (see Childs 2001, 79). Alt (1950) and Barth (1977, 142–44;160–61) suggest different emendations to make easier sense of the text. The verbs "humiliate" and "glorify" appear in *hiphil* perfect. Nevertheless, "glorify" is commonly interpreted as referring to the future, while Emerton (1969) insists that both verbs must refer to the past: "First, he humiliated . . . later he glorified." Balogh (2014) suggests that the geographical regions of the north were added by a later editor, leaving the

Isaiah 8:23 [9:1] describes agony in three locales of the north, anguish that shall be changed to honor and joy. The three locales are "the Way of the Sea," "the Land beyond Jordan," and "Galilee of the Nations," which designate the three provinces established in the region by Tiglath-pileser after his 732 conquest, the coastal province of Dor, Gilead, and Megiddo (see figure 4, p. 63).

Following Alt (1950), scholars commonly see 8:23 [9:1] as a description of the Assyrian devastation of the north in 733–732 and the partition of the region into Assyrian provinces. Some still follow Alt in seeing all of 8:23–9:6 [9:1–7] as a literary unit from the period 732–722 that prophesies a soon-to-come redemption for the people of the north, now trampled and subdued by the Assyrian military.[7]

In 7:14–17 there is no distant messianic flavor. Does this change when 9:1–6 [9:2–7] was added to an early Isaiah scroll? There is a hypertextual relation between these two oracles, so that they together appear as a messianic pair, probably already from the proclamation of 9:1–6 [9:2–7], which presents itself as a continuation to 7:1–17 in a time of turmoil. The hymnic oracle ends with jubilation for a new Davidic king. While 7:14–17 foresees the soon-to-come birth of a prince, 9:1–6 [9:2–7] is formulated as a celebration of a prince already born or a king coronated (my translation):

> [1[2]]The nation who walked in darkness has seen a great light,
> those who lived in a land of deep darkness—on them light has
>   shined.
> [2[3]]You have magnified the nation, you have increased its joy,
> they rejoice before you as with joy at the harvest,

---

original text as follows: [8:23 [9:1]]"Nevertheless, there will be no gloom for the one who was in anguish. As the first time he humiliated, but finally he glorified—[9:1](thus) the people walking in darkness will see a great light, those living in the land of deep darkness, a light will shine upon them." This solution would give 8:23 [9:1] a poetic form and connect all of 8:23 [9:1] or 8:23b [9:1b] smoothly with the continuation. Without mention of the northern regions, the oracle would be read about Judah (as Isa 8) trampled by the Assyrians in 701 (Balogh 2014, 533). The proposal is ingenious, but it is not easy to see why a pure Judean oracle from around 701 would attract a seventh-century extension transforming 8:23–9:4 [9:1–5] to a passage with the northern tribes in focus. As the complete text stands, *with* the geographical regions, it remains difficult to interpret "glorify" in the past tense.

7. Alt argues that the oracle was composed for Hezekiah's enthronement, that 9:5 [9:6] refers not to the birth of a prince but to the coronation of the new king and that the names were enthronement names parallel to the fivefold titulary of the Egyptian king. In contrast, a postexilic date is argued by Karl Marti and Otto Kaiser.

as people exult when dividing plunder.

3[4]For the yoke of their burden and the stick on their shoulder,
the rod of their oppressor,
you have broken as on the day of Midian.

4[5]For all the boots of the tramping warriors
and all the garments rolled in blood
have been fed to the flames and devoured by fire.

5[6]For a child has been born for us, a son given to us,
authority rests upon his shoulders,
and he is named Counselor of Wonders, Mighty God,
Father Forever, Prince of Peace,

6[7]so that there will be no end to mighty government and peace
for the throne of David and his kingdom,
and it will be firmly established
with justice and righteousness now and evermore.

Harrelson (1962, 153) notes parallels with the Gideon narrative, a feature that places the promised son in the line of deliverers of the nation. "The day of Midian" (9:3 [9:4]) connects with Gideon's victory over the Midianites in Judg 7–8. The name Immanuel alludes to *Yhwh ʿimmĕkā* (Judg 6:12, 16), and three of the throne names allude to the Gideon story: *pele' yôʿēṣ* alludes to *kol-niplĕ'ōtaw* (6:13), *'ēl gibbôr* to *gibbôr heḥāyîl* (6:12), and *śar-šālôm* to *Yhwh šālôm* (6:24). The use of Judg 6–8, a narrative from the northern tribes, demonstrates that the Gideon story was known in Judah, which again may suggest a post-722 date for the oracle. It further bolsters the view that the oracle envisaged the promised son of David as a hope for the northern tribes that had been downtrodden during the Assyrian campaigns between 734 and 722.

The darkness of Isa 9:1 [9:2] and the yoke of 9:3 [9:4] signify the Assyrian oppression of the northern tribes. Isaiah 9:1–4 [9:2–5] proclaims the coming liberation from the Assyrian war machine, singing as if the liberation already has happened. In 9:4 [9:5], the prophet adopts the Akkadian term *šēnu* for "trampling of soldier boots," a term not used elsewhere in the Bible. The use of this term demonstrate that the speaker had thorough knowledge of Assyrian ideology.

Who are the speakers in the oracle? Von Rad (1947) sees the deity as the speaker—similar to the decree handed to the new pharaoh during the coronation, while the "we" of 9:5 [9:6] is the people. Slightly in contrast, Alt (1950) sees 9:5 [9:6] as the message of royal heralds sent to the former territories of the Northern Kingdom to call their residents to accept the recently crowned Hezekiah as their king. Building on these two scholars, Roberts (1997, 128–29) attributes the "we-voice" of 9:2–3, 5 [9:3–4, 6] to the heavenly council in analogy with the council of the gods in the Egyptian ritual. He notes that members of the heavenly council are speaking in 6:3 and 40:3: "In short, one may read Isa 9:5 as reflecting the joyous assent of the divine council to the new king, Yahweh's son" (1997, 129). I see no difficulty in identifying the speaker with the prophet, who in 9:5 [9:6] would include shouts of jubilation from the Judean people.

Name giving was an essential part of the Egyptian coronation ritual; the new king would receive five names that expressed qualities desired of the new monarch. Name giving had likely been a traditional element also in Judean coronation liturgies, originally inspired by Egyptian custom.

The four throne names in 9:5 [9:6] give rise to two questions: (1) Are these names given to a newborn crown prince at his birth, or are they coronation names, to be given when the new ruler is installed (as in Egypt)? (2) Should the names be understood as theophoric names, names that denote what Yhwh means to the prince (Wegner 1992; Williamson 1998, 255–56), or rather (with most scholars) as names that ideally reveal the nature and function of the prince, similar to Egyptian tradition?

Biblical personal names can connote (expected) qualities or characteristics by the bearer of the name, such as *mənaḥēm* ("comforter"). Names can also be theophoric, expressing divine characteristics or the relation between God and the child or his parents; *'immānû 'ēl*, *yərubba'al* ("Baal/the Lord will fight"; Judg 6:32), *yəša'yāhû* ("Yahu will save"; Isa 1:1), *šəmû'ēl* ("God has heard"; 1 Sam 1:20) are examples of the latter. Judahite royal names were commonly theophoric: *'uzziyāhû* ("Yahu is my might"), *yəhôšāpāṭ* ("Yahu judges"), *ḥizqîyāhû* ("Yahu is my strength").[8]

Names could also carry a symbolic meaning—such as the names of the children of Hosea and Isaiah (Hos 1:4–9; Isa 7:3; 8:1–4), *'ādām* ("man of earth"; Gen 2:7), *ḥawwâ* ("life"; 3:20), *hebel* ("futility"; 4:2–8), *maḥlôn* ("sick"), and *kilyôn* ("ruined"; Ruth 1:5).[9] Thus, we should ask if the throne

---

8. Schniedewind (1999, 27) notes that Yahwistic names begin to appear only in the late tenth century, suggesting that the entrenchment of Yhwh could not have begun before the late tenth century. By the eighth century, the Judean onomasticon points to almost exclusive Yahwistic allegiances.

9. Names with a negative symbolic value appear in Isa 8:1–4, Hos 1:6, 9, Gen 4:2–8, Ruth 1:5. A late seventh-century seal from the City of David carries the name *mā'aśyāhû* ("Yahu has rejected") (Mendel-Geberovich, Chalaf, and Uziel 2020, 163–65).

names should be interpreted as referring to the identity and qualities of the prince (as per Egyptian custom), or if they carry symbolic or theophoric connotations, more commonly expected in Judah.

Wildberger (1972, 377–78) interprets the joyful words that "a child has been born for us, a son given to us," as describing cheering in court circles at the actual birth of a crown prince, shouts of joy soon echoed in the nation at large. If the proclamation was followed by throne names, it would show that elements of oriental royal ideology were connected not only with coronation in Jerusalem but also with the birth of a crown prince.

Is the prophet describing a recent birth in the royal family, envisaging a birth of a prince soon to happen or far into the future, or symbolically describing a royal coronation?[10] In my view, Isa 9:5–6 [9:6–7] may consciously merge cheering at the court and in the people at the birth of a prince with elements connected with the act of coronation in Judean royal ideology. For the prophet, cheering and royal-name giving known from Jerusalem tradition would be a fitting conclusion to an oracle of salvation that celebrates the military defeat of the enemy.

The last of the four names is *śar-šālôm*. The term signifies an earthly ruler who will bring welfare and peace, and could only with difficulty refer to God. In contrast to the first three throne names, the meaning of this name is explicated in the subsequent verse: the prince will implement a mighty government with lasting character. The use of the preposition *lə* to open the two stichs of 9:6 [9:7], *ləmarbēh hammiśrâ* ("to mighty government") and *ləhākîn 'ōtâ* ("to establish it"), rather than making the prince the active subject, indicates that Yhwh is the real instigator of the new era. *Mišpāṭ* and *ṣədāqâ* ("justice and righteousness") is a pair that signals Yhwh's good will and ethical norms that the king shall implement, as in Ps 72:2. The new era of peace and justice follows a military breakdown of the Assyrian army (Isa 9:2–4 [9:3–5]).

The prince is profiled as a countermonarch to the Assyrian "great king," *šarru rābû*.[11] Also in the more or less contemporary Ps 72:7, *šālôm* is con-

---

10. Roberts (1997, 128) goes for the latter: "While the Egyptian texts may identify the onset of the king's divine sonship with the physical birth of the king, the actual public announcement of that divine birth comes only at his accession and coronation.... That a Judean adaptation of this ceremony should take the form of a traditional birth announcement and accordingly should use vocabulary referring to a young child is not at all surprising. It does not suggest a recent birth of a new royal baby any more than the parallel birth narratives in the Egyptian enthronement texts do."

11. Carlson (1974, 133) notes that the Assyrian king was denoted "king of the four quarters" (of the world), a designation upheld by Tiglath-pileser III (745–727), and then

nected with the Davidic king: "Righteousness shall flourish in his time, and *šālôm* shall abound till the moon is no more" (my translation). And the exilic Mic 5:4 [5:5] describes the future son of David or his rule with the words *wəhāyâ ze šālôm* ("he shall be peace" or "such shall the peace be").

Pele' yôʿēṣ may be interpreted "counselor of wondrous deeds"—elsewhere the plural *niplā'ōt* signifies the great deeds of Yhwh for his people. The term "counselor" could match designations of the Assyrian king as "king of counsel and discernment," "the possessor of judgment and counsel." If the prince is described as *pele' yôʿēṣ*, it would indicate that he will take over the role as divinely endowed ruler. If the counselor is God who will advise his king, these words imply judgment on the Assyrian king for his hybris.

The term *qarrādu* ("hero") was frequently used in laudation of Mesopotamian kings, and the next great ruler, Sargon II (722–705), placed the determinative *ilu* ("god") before his name. This usage is echoed in *'ēl gibbôr*, which could be translated "Mighty God" or "Divine Hero." If *'ēl gibbôr* is a designation of the prince, it would signal the superiority of the coming Davidic king compared to the present Assyrian overlord. An inherent difficulty with this interpretation is that elsewhere in the Bible, only one verse possibly addresses the king as *'ĕlōhîm* (the difficult verse Ps 45:7 [45:6]).[12] The biblical tradition does not ascribe any kind of divine nature to the Davidic king. If the term, in contrast, refers to the heavenly Lord who will install the prince, it shows the might of God in contrast to earthly rulers.

Akkadian rulers regularly denoted themselves as *abu* ("father"), explicated as "the lord who is as a real father to his people." If *'ăbî'ad* is a designation of the prince, the Assyrian is overshadowed also in this function by the coming Davidic ruler, who shall be *'ăbî'ad* ("Always Father" or "Father Forever") with a lasting fatherly care for his people. The term *'ad* refers to the foundational promise for the Davidic line: "I will establish the throne of

---

suggests that this titulary influenced the choice of *four* throne names in Isaiah (not five as in Egypt): "In 9:5 there is a play upon that symbolic number four with the intent of denoting the Messiah-child with legitimate, universal, lordship." Roberts (1997, 117–18) sees this proposal as somewhat farfetched.

12. Barth (1977, 169–70) finds support for attributing *'ēl gibbôr* to a present king (namely Josiah) at his coronation in Pss 45:7 [45:6]; 21:5 [21:4]; 72:5; 89:37–38 [89:36–37]. References to the success of his plans and Yhwh's blessing being experienced in his rule would be found in Ps 20:5 [20:4] and 2 Sam 23:5. However, 2 Sam 23:5 should not be used as background for preexilic oracles, as David's last words (23:1–7) are a late Davidic/messianic text that should be dated to the third or early second century (Elgvin 2020b, 295–97; see pp. 168–70). Further, if preexilic, Ps 45:7 [45:6] would likely be read as *kis'ăkā yihyeh 'ôlām wā'ed* ("your throne will last [*yihyeh*] forever and ever") (see pp. 163–65).

his kingdom forever" (2 Sam 7:13).[13] A view to the Judean royal tradition, consequently describing Yhwh as the father who adopts/gives birth to the king as his son in the act of coronation (2 Sam 7:14; Pss 2:7; 110:3 [G, Syr]) would strongly suggest that the reference of *'ăbî'ad* is to God and how he will relate to the prince.

Most interpreters see all four names as referring to qualities of the son to be born. In such a scenario, the oracle would describe the coming prince in a symbolic, hyperbolic way, making clear that the son of David and his reign will overshadow the Assyrian king and superpower. And the oracle would rhetorically describe the prince with terms drawn from Assyrian royal ideology.[14] If spoken by Isaiah himself, the oracle would concur with his viewing Ahaz's alliance with Assyria as disobedience to Yhwh (cf. Isa 7:4–17).

In my view, "Prince of Peace" and perhaps "Counselor of Wonders" refer to the prince, while "Mighty God" and "Father Forever" naturally describe Yhwh's role vis-à-vis the prince and king. If "Counselor of Wonders" also refers to God, the first three throne names would have a heavenly reference, leading to the fourth name *śar-šālôm* as characterizing the earthly king, immediately explicated with "mighty government and peace" and "be firmly established with justice and righteousness now and evermore."

If spoken by Isaiah, the prophet likely imagined a prince that should replace Ahaz and bring hope to both Judah and the north. The shouts of joy about "the child born to us" may merge the joyous celebration at the birth of a prince and his later coronation, bringing hope for a renewal of the Davidic dynasty, envisaged to be "firmly established with justice and righteousness now and evermore." It "seems to announce that its readers are living at a turning point in the dynasty's fortunes and the long-hoped-for rule of justice and righteousness is about to begin" (Williamson 1998, 257). The full oracle foresees a longed-for peace for the northern tribes, inviting them to unite with their brethren under a new Davidic monarch.

At the same time, the prophet might imagine a full realization of the promises of wonders/wondrous deeds, mighty government, and peace further into the future. In my view, however, an eighth- or seventh-century

---

13. Barth (1977, 170) understands *'ăbî'ad* as "always father" in the meaning "father of the whole land" ("Vater für immer," "Landesvater").

14. "Isaiah has passionately proclaimed his belief, without regard to how absurd it might seem in his historical-political situation. The intervention made by Tiglath-pileser in the territories of the kingdom of David is an infringement upon Messianic sovereignty and ultimately an offence against the Almighty on Zion" (Carlson 1974, 135).

prophet would still envision the coming king as a thoroughly earthly figure without any supernatural messianic traits.[15]

Alternatively, the oracle could find a meaningful setting at the time of Josiah. Barth (1977, 141–77) dates the full text of 8:23–9:6 [9:1–7] to Josiah's time.[16] Isaiah's view of the present house of David is evinced in 7:9b, 17; 10:33a; 11:1–5 and contrasts with the elevated view of a present king in 9:5–6 [9:6–7]. Isaiah would never see the contemporary Davidic king as embodying Yhwh's salvific presence, being instrumental in turning the fate of the northern regions and introducing a time of lasting peace. Further, never during Isaiah's career could the nation look back on liberation from the usurper's yoke as well as the birth, enthronement, and righteous rule of a new king. The demise of the Assyrian Empire and its withdrawal from the north during the early years of Josiah would provide a fitting context for the hope for the northern provinces (8:23 [9:1]) and the Assyrian defeat (9:2–4 [9:3–5]). The hope for a reestablishment of a Davidic rule over "all Israel" was indeed vibrant in Josiah's time (Barth 1977, 171).

In Barth's view, 9:5 [9:6] looks back on Josiah's birth and his coronation when he was eight years old (1977, 176–77). The four throne names are those actually used during his coronation. That only the last of the four names is explicated in the subsequent verse shows that the combination of these four names was given before the oracle was spoken.

In my view, both a Hezekiah and a Josiah dating are possible, but I tend to side with Barth's reading: the flavor of 9:1–6 [9:2–7] is so different from the Immanuel oracle that it would make more sense as a sequel to or relecture of the Immanuel oracle, a post-Isaiah reinterpretation of the son of David tradition. A seventh-century dating of 9:1–6 [9:2–7] (with or without 8:23 [9:1]) would demonstrate the lasting confidence in (the divine promise to)

---

15. Childs (2001, 101) roots 7:10–14 and 9:1–6 [9:2–7] in the eighth century but adds that "the messianic promise far transcends the initial eighth-century setting." Both Carlson and Childs anachronistically import Second Temple messianic connotations into 9:1–6 [9:2–7]. When Isa 36–38 later would connect 7:14 and 9:1–6 [9:2–7] with Hezekiah, these oracles were clearly read about a pious, earthly king. If 9:1–6 [9:2–7] later would be connected with Josiah, this would presuppose an earthly reading of the oracle in the late seventh century. As argument for an eighth-century date of 11:1–5, Williamson (1998, 264) remarks that "the new David remains, apparently, within the historical continuum, and has not yet been cast as an eschatological figure." But the terms used in 9:1–6 [9:2–7] would open for more transcending interpretations by later readers.

16. Williamson (1998, 254–55) is open to both a Hezekiah and Josiah date: "The hopes vested in the early Hezekiah or in the early Josiah would seem to be historically possible."

the house of David and evince how the Immanuel oracle would be read anew in a later generation, as is the case in Mic 5:2 [5:3].

From the Syro-Ephraimite war (734–732), Judah was more or less a vassal state under Assyria, and Judah remained in the shadow of Assyria until the 630s.[17] The sociopolitical context of Josiah's time is another than that of Isaiah's time in the 720s. However, the anti-Assyrian thrust of the oracle and the hope for a new Davidide would nevertheless be similar in these two different historical contexts.

Isaiah 1–38: Hezekiah Reconsidered

Following a revolt by Hezekiah, the Assyrian King Sennacherib invaded the southern Levant in 701. The Judean Shephelah was devastated and partly given over to Philistine rule. In annalistic style, 2 Kgs 18:13–16 describes the invasion and the large tribute imposed on Hezekiah by the Assyrians—this early source was later included in the subsequent narrative. These verses can be compared to two Assyrian inscriptions, a short account and a detailed report of the campaign:

I laid waste the large district of Judah and made the overbearing and proud Hezekiah, its king, bow in submission. (following Pritchard 1969, 288)

As to Hezekiah the Judean who did not submit to my yoke, I besieged forty-six of his strong cities and the forts and villages in their vicinity, and conquered them with ramps, battering rams, and foot soldiers. . . . I drove out 200,150 people . . . and made them my booty. Himself I made a prisoner in Jerusalem, his royal residence, like a bird in a cage. . . . His towns which I had plundered I took away from his country and gave them to the kings of Ashdod, Ekron, and Gaza. Thus I reduced his country, still I increased his annual dues and the tribute which he sent to Nineveh, my royal city: elite troops, . . . thirty talents of gold, eight hundred talents

17. Around 700, a magnificent compound was built at Ramat Rachel, 4 km south of Jerusalem. A main purpose of the site was to serve as collection center for agricultural products produced from royal estates. The excavators suggest that, during the seventh century, Ramat Rachel served as residence for the Assyrian representative in Judea (Lipschits et al. 2017, 52). The site was not destroyed in 587 and survived into Hasmonean times. In Persian times it functioned as the governor's seat and displayed a luxurious Persian-style royal garden.

of silver, precious stones, antimony, jewels, large carnelians, ivory-inlaid couches, ivory-inlaid chairs, elephant hides, ebonywood, boxwood, all kinds of valuable treasures, as well as his daughters, his harem, his male and female musicians. (following Pritchard 1969, 288)

Sennacherib's account should not be taken at face value. The number of 200,000 war prisoners is definitively exaggerated, as are details of the tribute imposed on Hezekiah.

The biblical text attributes the retreat to divine intervention, decreed by an oracle of Isaiah, where the core may go back to the prophet (Isa 37:22–25, 28–29, 33–35). The oracle concludes with Yhwh confirming his lasting election of Zion and the Davidic line: "For I will defend this city to save it, for my own sake and for the sake of my servant David."

Two chronicle-like verses on Sennacherib's retreat and later assassination in Nineveh (in fact happening in 681) see the cause of the retreat in the angel of the Lord's slaughter of 185,000 Assyrian soldiers (2 Kgs 19:35–37 ‖ Isa 37:36–38).

Scholars seek to discern the historical cause behind what the biblical author explains supernaturally. Why did Sennacherib refrain from conquering Jerusalem, the seat of the rebellious king, retreating to Assyria with a tribute only? Bolstering suggestions by early scholars and the comprehensive arguments of Aubin (2002/2003), a group of recent scholars sees the military invention of the Nubian army as a main cause of Sennacherib's retreat from Jerusalem (Bellis 2019, 2021).

According to the record of 2 Kings, Judea trusted its alliance with Egypt (18:19–24), and Sennacherib was told that "King Tirhakah of Kush has set out in war against you" (19:9, my translation). At a time of strong Kushite rule in Egypt (the Twenty-fifth Dynasty), Prince Taharqo (Tirhakah, pharaoh from 690) was leading a Nubian military campaign against the Assyrians. Sennacherib's annals confirm that he was confronted by the Egyptian-Nubian army at Eltekeh in the Shephelah.

Historical and textual elements noted by Aubin and the scholars assembled by Bellis include the following: positive relations existed between Judah and the Nubian dynasty even before 701, and biblical texts portray the Nubians in highly positive terms. With the term "covenant with death," Isaiah refers to his countrymen's covenant with the Kushites who had Mut (*mūt* = "death" in Hebrew) as their national god, celebrated at the main sanctuary in Thebes (28:1–15); suckling this mother goddess and drinking in her presence belonged to Mut imagery and cult (cf. 28:7–9). Nubia-Egypt was the only contemporary power with military capacity to confront Assyria, and it became politically and commercially very active in the Levant in the subsequent years. The Kushites enjoyed a strong military reputation (Isa 18; Nah 3:9; Ezek 38:5). Texts from Isaiah confirm that the Assyrians withdrew with heavy military losses (31:8–9; 14:24–25), and Herodotus says the same. The Assyrian punishment of Jerusalem was much milder than that of contemporaneous Ekron and Ashkelon, or Samaria two decades earlier.

The battle at Eltekeh happened late in the Assyrian campaign when Sennacherib's resources were exhausted—perhaps leading to a political-military draw between the two superpowers. Thus, the Egyptian intervention and Hezekiah's defensive maneuvers may have led to a three-party agreement between Assyria, Egypt, and Judah, which led to Assyrian withdrawal and the tribute paid by the Judeans, as well as opening the way for active Egyptian commercial involvement in the region. Aubin comments (2003, 275), "later generations would see Jerusalem's miraculous survival as the Deliverance through which Yahweh had demonstrated his commitment to them." The earliest narrative would give the Nubians the credit of being Yhwh's tool for the survival of Jerusalem, while a later midrashic reading would magnify the role of Yhwh through the story of the punishing angel.

A modern reader who would like to uphold the idea of divine intervention may see Isaiah's oracle fulfilled through Assyria's enemy from the west, while the later midrash would downplay the role of the Nubians and stress Yhwh's intervention. As I read Aubin (2003, 272–85), both Egypt and the God of Israel may be credited for the survival of Jerusalem—an event that proved crucial for Israelite faith in Yhwh's commitment to the nation, to Zion, and to the house of David.

The Immanuel oracle, which concludes "I will cause to come upon you and your people and your ancestral house such days as never have come since Ephraim turned away from Judah" (7:17, my translation), was soon after 701 supplemented with the short note: "(this happened through) the king of Assyria." In concourse with 2 Kgs 18:13–16, this scribal addition views Sennacherib's invasion as a devastating event for Judah, foretold by Isaiah. With some distance in time from the invasion, a new interpretation would gain prominence.

The literary growth of the Isaiah tradition through the seventh and early sixth centuries led to the collection Isa 1–39. In Isa 36–39 ‖ 2 Kgs 18–20 Hezekiah appears as a counterfigure to King Sennacherib, who is portrayed as a kind of antichrist, mocking Hezekiah, the Judahites, and Yhwh. With his confidence in Yhwh alone as the source of salvation, Hezekiah appears as a paradigmatic Judean. The royal narrative Isa 7:1–17 undergoes a literary transformation when central motifs are reused in the royal narrative in Isa 36–38. In contrast to Ahaz, Hezekiah is portrayed as a king who turns to Yhwh and listens to the prophet (37:2–7; 38:3–5), which leads to Yhwh's deliverance of his people and city.

EXCURSUS: THE HEZEKIAH NARRATIVES IN ISAIAH 36–39

Panov (2019, 2021) delivers a thorough analysis of the Hezekiah-Isaiah narratives in Isa 36–39 ∥ 2 Kgs 18–20 and their transtextual or midrashic reuse of earlier texts. The chapters can be divided into three narratives: (1) the Assyrian siege and messages to Hezekiah followed by Yhwh's miraculous intervention (Isa 36–37); (2) Hezekiah's sickness, healing, and thanksgiving psalm (Isa 38); and (3) Hezekiah showing the envoys of the Babylonian king all his treasures (Isa 39).

Standing at some distance from the events of 701, narratives 1 and 2 interpret Jerusalem's survival solely as Yhwh's act of deliverance—with the insertion of the verse detailing the angelic slaughter of the Assyrian soldiers.

According to Panov, the taunt song on the king of Assyria (37:22–35) is the earliest text in the collection of Isa 36–39 (early seventh century?). It closely follows up Isaiah's oracle against Assyria in 10:5–19, 24–26, mixes the genres of song and prophetic oracle, and was secondarily inserted into the first narrative of Isa 36–37. This narrative is a composite text (as one example, 37:9b–14 reuses material from 36:14–20) that likely existed as an independent source, with its salvation-theological interpretation of the 701 siege and Jerusalem's survival. It was subsequently included into the growing books of Isaiah and Kings.

Panov dates narrative 1 with its story of the miraculous deliverance of Jerusalem to midway between Sennacherib's 701 siege and the fall of Jerusalem in 587 (cf. Sweeney 2001, 52–76). The narrative reflects some distance from the siege, while its trust in Yhwh's promise to guard and defend Jerusalem places it well before the first Babylonian conquest of Jerusalem in 597. The narrative interacts with 22:15–25 (the figures Shebna and Eliakim appear in both texts). In Isa 22, Shebna is demoted from his position as steward of the palace and substituted by Eliakim, while in Isa 37, Eliakim is steward of the palace and Shebna only a scribe. While Isa 10 is directed against Assyria and its (unnamed) king, in narrative 1 with the song of taunt, Sennacherib is named as the antagonist of Hezekiah and object of ridicule.

Narrative 2 (Isa 38), the story about the king's sickness and healing through the prophet's intervention, reuses material from narrative 1. Text-critical and compositional observations indicate that this story was first included in Kings and thereafter in Isaiah. Only the Isaiah version includes Hezekiah's thanksgiving psalm, which occupies a prominent place in Isa 38. According to Panov, the psalm testifies to the adoption of epithets connected to El into the image of Yhwh and appears as a witness of a reflected mono-theistic faith, even before Deutero-Isaiah. The psalm uses the El epithet "the living God" for Yhwh and proclaims Yhwh's oneness and majesty and the nonexistence of other gods.

The latest stratum in 2 Kgs 18–20 is represented by 18:1–12, which extends the earlier royal chronicle in 18:1–2, 13–16; 20:20–21. While narratives 1 and 2 can describe Hezekiah as weak and hesitant, this editorial introduction hails the king in a unique way: "He trusted only in Yhwh the God of Israel; there was none like him among all the kings of Judah after him, nor among those before him" (my translation).[18]

In Isa 29–31, the prophet castigates the Judahites for their stubbornness, trusting in Egyptian power and lacking trust in Yhwh. In Isa 36–38, however, this stubbornness is dissolved, with Judah and its king recognizing Yhwh as their only hope. As the representative of the nation, Hezekiah appears as the righteous king who trusts in Yhwh only, in spite of the powerful enemy who taunts Judah and its god. Thus, Hezekiah demonstrates that Yhwh will open a future for his people. These texts would likely give hope for Jerusalem when it was besieged by the next superpower, the Babylonians.

At a yet later stage, Isa 39 (= 2 Kgs 20:12–19) would be inserted as a literary precursor and prophetic warning of the Babylonian exile, paving the way for Deutero-Isaiah's message of redemption in Isa 40–55.[19] In Isa 39, Hezekiah is much less a hero than in Isa 36–38. By the early fifth century, Isa 33–35 and Isa 36–39 would form a bridge between the two major parts of the (still growing) book of Isaiah (cf. Williamson 1994, 212–17; Panov 2019, 109–11).

When reading Isa 36–38 together with 7:1–17 and 8:23–9:6 [9:1–7], Hezekiah would appear as a model king and type for a future son of David

18. Sweeney (2001, 64–75, 177) dates narratives 1 and 2 to the decades following Sennacherib's assassination in 681 and included in a mid-seventh-century recension of DtrH.

19. Thus Panov, who suggests an early postexilic date for Isa 39. In contrast, Clements (1983) and Sweeney (2001, 70–71) argue that this story was composed between 597 and 587 to come to terms with the deportation of Jehoiachin by the Babylonians, since the narrative refers to deportation of Davidic sons and not the destruction of Jerusalem or the temple.

(Laato 1998, 31, 118–21; Panov 2019, 162–64). The statement in 2 Kgs 18:7 about Hezekiah that "Yhwh was with him" (*wəhāyâ yhwh ʿimmô*) alludes to *ʿimmānû ʾēl* of Isa 7:14 and suggests that the last version of the narratives in Isa 36–38 ‖ 2 Kgs 18–20 identified Hezekiah as Immanuel and possibly connected Isa 9:1–6 [9:2–7] with him.

The laudation of Hezekiah in 2 Kgs 18:3–7 would be echoed by words on Josiah in 22:2 and 23:3, 5, indicating that both were viewed as paradigmatic kings (Panov 2019, 138). The main thrust of Isa 36–38 ‖ 2 Kgs 18–20 would be particularly meaningful during the days of Josiah, when Hezekiah would be portrayed as a forebearer of Josiah's reform and attempted Davidic restoration.

With the inclusion of the Hezekiah-Isaiah narrative in 2 Kgs 18–20, Hezekiah would in exilic times serve as an antitype to the ungodly Zedekiah who symbolizes Judah's way toward destruction (2 Kgs 24:17–25:21). As Assyria was destroyed according to the prophecies of Isa 10 and 37, so will Judah's enemies be destroyed under a future Davidic king. In its later portrait of the spirit-filled prince from the family of Jesse, the early-exilic oracle 11:1–5 would develop Davidic themes, likely with Hezekiah as one of its models.

Josiah and Davidic Restoration

Josiah, great-grandson of Hezekiah, was put on the throne at the age of eight and ruled from 640 until he fell in battle against Pharaoh Necho at Megiddo in 609. The historicity of the reform that 2 Kgs 22–23 ascribes to Josiah in 622 and its connection with Deut 12–26 is contested. I follow those scholars who find a historical core in the description of the reform (e.g., Naʾaman 1991; Laato 1998, 131–42; Sweeney 2001, 40–51).[20] The time that passes from 622, first to the deportation of the elite, including Deuteronomistic scribes, from Jerusalem in 596 and then to an exilic recension of DtrH around 561 (2 Kgs 25:27–30; cf. Sweeney 2001, 33–39, 319; Carr 2011, 245) is rather short and suggests a historical memory of Josiah and his deeds.

---

20. For a skeptical voice, see Pakkala 2010, whose article is entitled "Why the Cult Reforms in Judah Probably Did Not Happen."

We could add to this that Deuteronomistic scribes clearly were active in Josiah's time, so that the Deuteronomistic School should be expected to preserve a true memory of his acts. DtrH bear traces of substantial editing in the time of Josiah, and its critique of the many cult sites in the north is based on the Deuteronomic principle of cult centralization—Deut 12 was a foundational text for these scribes, as it was for the Josianic reform.[21]

For Deuteronomistic thinkers, Josiah's death in battle (2 Kgs 23:29) would be problematic and painful. The righteous king who had put his confidence in Yhwh had been killed. The record of his death suggests a trustworthy historical memory in these chapters, as do the close echoes of Assyrian covenant treaties. The anti-Assyrian cultic measures reported in 23:5, 11–12 belong to the basic stratum of 2 Kgs 22–23 and hardly make sense without some kind of cult reform having taken place (Kratz 2010, 127–30). Cross (1973, 274–89), Laato (1992; 1998, 138–50), and Sweeney (2001) stress the role of Josiah both in and behind the texts.

Josiah received the highest marks by DtrH: "There was no king like him before who turned back to Yhwh with all his heart and soul and might, in full accord with the teaching [tôrâ] of Moses; nor did any like him arise after him" (2 Kgs 23:25 NJPS adapted). As his precursor Hezekiah, Josiah fulfilled a Davidic role: "He did what was pleasing to Yhwh and he followed all the ways of his ancestor David" (22:2 NJPS adapted; cf. 18:3). The reference to the tôrâ of Moses shows Josiah's compliance with Deuteronomic laws. Thus, Josiah walked in the ways of Moses as well as David.

With the demise of the Assyrian Empire in the 630s, Josiah could extend the borders of Judah northward to the Bethel-Jericho line and reconquer the Shephelah (Lipschits 2020, 173–77). The moves of Josiah during his last years indicate that he parted with the rising power, the Babylonians, against an Egyptian-Assyrian alliance. His fate was sealed when he tried to hold back the Egyptians from supporting the faltering Assyrian army (Laato 1998, 134–38; Sweeney 2001, 210).

Josiah's territorial expansion to the north was an essential part of his walking in "the ways of his ancestor David," who had ruled both the north and the south. According to 23:15–20, the king acted in northern territories, demolishing the altar in Bethel and the high places in Samaria, actions that received scribal support: the verses referring to Bethel are closely related to 1 Kgs 12–13, whose anti-Bethel profile suggests editing in Josiah's time.

---

21. A Josianic editing of DtrH is argued by Frank Moore Cross, Richard Nelson, Steven McKenzie, William Schniedewind, Marvin Sweeney, and Gary Knoppers.

Also 2 Kgs 17 reflects Josianic editing: 17:24–41 notes that following the fall of Samaria, three generations had continued their syncretistic cult until "today"—a passage making more sense during the time of Josiah than during the exile (Laato 1998, 139–40; Sweeney 2001, 77–92, 175–77).

Texts outside 2 Kgs 22–23 function as support for Josiah's campaigns to the north (Laato 1998, 134–50; Sweeney 2001, 14–15). The anti-Bethel attitude of Amos (4:4; 5:5–6; 7:10–17; 8:12; 9:1), a book edited and transmitted in the south, would strengthen Josiah's campaign in the Benjamin region. Texts in Jeremiah on a reunification of the houses of Judah and Israel and the return of the northern tribes to Zion (3:11–25; 31:6, 10–14) suggest that the prophet supported the king's attempt to include northerners in his restored kingdom.

Josiah's program involved purification of the Yahwistic cult in Jerusalem, destroying offensive objects and constructions introduced by Ahaz, Manasseh, and Solomon, as well as shattering the stone pillars and cutting down the sacred poles (2 Kgs 23:12–15). By destroying the Bethel sanctuary, which was "made by Jeroboam son of Nebat who caused Israel to sin" (23:15 NJPS), Josiah complied with the Deuteronomic ideal of one central sanctuary only.

During the reign of Josiah or his sons, the northern lament of Ps 80 was brought forward and supplemented by a plea for the Judean king: "Let your hand be upon the man at your right hand, the son of humankind you made strong for yourself!" (80:18 [80:17], my translation). The "man at God's right hand" is the king (110:1), the one being upheld by Yhwh's right hand (18:36 [18:35]; 20:7 [20:6]; Hossfeld and Zenger 2005, 312, 316). In this way, the Jerusalem community would in their prayers remind God about the divine promises of Pss 2, 72, and 110.

For Deuteronomistic scribes in exilic times, Josiah's death demonstrated that the sins of Manasseh were the cause for Yhwh's judgment on Judah, a judgment that could not be recalled (2 Kgs 23:24–27). Even the righteous king could not withhold the wrath of Yhwh. Thus, the defeat at Megiddo became a final blow to the confidence in Yhwh's continued protection of Zion and the house of David. The "eternal dynasty" promised in 2 Sam 7 had come to an end.

The final form of the oracle from Huldah the prophetess (2 Kgs 22:15–20) is hard to understand: even before Josiah begins his reforms, Huldah foresees that the repentant king will die in peace (at odds with the report about his violent death in 23:29). But she also proclaims Yhwh's decision to bring the kingdom of Judah to an end after the death of the pious king. Sweeney (2001,

40–51) reconstructs an early recension of 2 Kgs 22–23, where the last part of the oracle (22:18–20a) would form the conclusion of the Josiah narrative in a recension of DtrH from the days of the king. The oracle would then function as a prophetic support of Josiah's reform program. The present form of the oracle bears the mark of exilic reworking of these chapters.

The stance of Jeremiah vis-à-vis Josiah and his reform is contested (cf. Sweeney 2001, 208–33). He was called to be a prophet five years before the reform (Jer 1:2; 2 Kgs 22:3). Some texts suggest a critical edge toward the king and the reform: the condemnation of Judah and Jerusalem in oracles dated to Josiah's time (Jer 3:6–6:30), the speech against the cult in the temple (7:1–8:3),[22] the condemnation of sages pretending to follow Yhwh's Torah while they are writing in vain with a pen without purpose (8:8–9),[23] harsh words on violation of the covenant, and Yhwh's proscribing the prophet from interceding for the nation (17:1–17).

However, some factors also suggest positive links between Jeremiah's and Josiah's reforms. Jeremiah had close associates in the family of Shaphan the counselor, an elite family with a central role in Josiah's reforms (2 Kgs 22:3–11; Jer 36:10–12, 25; 40:5–6). The prophet advocated alliance with or submission to Babylon, an ally of Judah in Josiah's days. Jeremiah 22 criticizes Josiah's sons and successors to the throne, possibly in contrast to their father, and displays a closeness to Deuteronomy and the reform:

> [3]This is what the Lord says: Do justice and righteousness,
> deliver one seized from the hand of the wrongdoer!
> Do not oppress, and do not act impiously against guest, orphan,
>   and widow,
> do not shed innocent blood in this place! . . .
> [10]Do not weep for him who is dead, nor bemoan him!
> Weep rather for the one who goes away,
> for he shall never come back to see the land of his birth. . . .
> [13]Woe to him who builds his house by unrighteousness,
> and his upper rooms by injustice,
> who makes his fellow man work without pay,

22. Jeremiah's temple speech (7:1–8:3) is not dated. The reworked Deuteronomistic version of the speech dates it to the beginning of Josiah's son and successor Jehoiakim (26:1).

23. Jer 8:8 does not denote the torah of the scribes (perhaps Deuteronomic) as false, as often argued. Weinfeld (1972, 160) notes that *laššeqer* here does not mean "lie" or "forgery," but rather "in vain" or "to no purpose," as in 1 Sam 25:21 and Jer 3:23.

and does not give him his wages. . . .

[16]Lacking knowledge, they did not judge the cause for the lowly
nor the cause of the needy.

Is not this so, because you do not know me? Says the Lord.

[17]Behold, are not your eyes and your heart on nothing but your
greed

and on innocent blood to shed it

and on wrongdoing and on committing murder? (GJer 22:3, 10,
13, 16–17, my translation)

The oracle advocates welfare for the poor; righteousness to the resident
alien, widow, and orphan; and proper payment to workers—all essentials
of the Deuteronomic ethos and likely proclaimed by the Torah scroll that
inspired Josiah's reforms (Weinfeld 1972, 158–64; Sweeney 2001, 210–11).
Sweeney concludes (2001, 233) that Jeremiah supported Josiah's reforms
and called for the return of the northerners to the temple and the house of
David. Similarly, Weinfeld argues (1972, 158–61) that Jeremiah identified with
the ideology of Deuteronomy and appears to have supported the Josianic
reforms, as is evident in his defense of "this covenant" in 11:1–8.[24]

Sweeney (2001, 185–233) finds prophetic voices supporting Josiah and his
reforms in Zephaniah, Nahum, and Jeremiah and "Josianic editing" in many
other scrolls: Isa 1–38, Hosea, Amos, and Micah.[25] To squeeze all this editorial
activity into the last twenty years before Josiah's death seems exaggerated.
However, a wide array of different texts appears to support the anti-Assyrian
and pro-Babylonian stance of Josiah's later years or concur with Deuteronomic ideals, ideals brought to the forefront through Josiah's reforms; some
of these texts were likely edited in Josiah's time, others might be later.

Is Sweeney right that a kind of Davidic image was attached to Josiah,
during his life and possibly thereafter (cf. the title of his 2001 book: *King*

24. A caveat: 11:1–8 (in both M and the shorter G version) are among the speeches in
Jeremiah that reflect Deuteronomistic editing, so we do not necessarily find the voice of
the prophet in all the terms used here.

25. "Prophets and prophetic literature play a substantial role in relation to the reign
of King Josiah and his reform. Prophets who were contemporary with Josiah actively
addressed various aspects of his reform program and frequently point to aspects that are
not evident in the DtrH account of his reign"; "Josiah apparently saw himself as the king
or messiah of a reunited and restored kingdom of Israel centered around Jerusalem and
the temple, but his unexpected death at Megiddo by the hand of Pharaoh Necho of Egypt
resulted in the loss of that grandiose vision" (Sweeney 2001, 311, 315).

Josiah of Judah: The Lost Messiah of Israel)? Was the prophecy of Isa 9:1–6 [9:2–7] connected with him, as probably had been done with Hezekiah either before Sennacherib's 701 invasion or a generation or two thereafter?

Josiah's death at Megiddo and failure to succeed in a Davidic restoration of the Judean kingdom set a lasting mark on Israelite tradition, which could reflect that he indeed had been hailed as the promised son of David (Laato 1998, 143–50). According to Jer 22:10–12, the nation continued to mourn for Josiah four years after his death, so Jeremiah exhorts the people not to mourn any more for Josiah, but rather for his defeated son Shallum, exiled in 605.

While the Greek Jeremiah text quoted above consistently castigates Josiah's son Shallum (Jehoiahaz), the M recension (early third century; see p. 110) would transform this passage to a praise of Josiah as a righteous king who enjoyed Yhwh's favor (22:6, 15–16). Chronicles, also a third-century text, recounts that mourning songs for Josiah still were sung in its time (2 Chr 35:24–25).

Another third-century text, Zech 12:10–13:9, may preserve themes connected with Josiah. In 13:7–9, Josiah may be a type for Yhwh's close friend and shepherd who shall fall for the sword, leading to the dispersal of the nation (see p. 156 n. 13). According to 2 Chr 35:23, Josiah was fatally wounded by Egyptian archers, and Zech 12:10–14 foresees the mourning over the pierced one, leading to Megiddo-like mourning, as one mourns a firstborn or only son—terms alluding to Yhwh's election of the Davidic king (2 Sam 7:14; Ps 89:27–28 [89:26–27]; Laato 1998, 146–47, 216–17).

Thus, there are reasons to agree with Laato and Sweeney to a certain degree. Because of his reforms, Josiah would be hailed by many as a true son of David who would realize Davidic promises and implement the Mosaic Torah (as understood by Deuteronomists) (similarly Williamson 1998, 257). Davidic oracles such as Isa 7:14–17 and Jer 23:5–6 and the Balaam oracle of Num 24 would easily have been connected to him. But the term "messiah" may be anachronistic with regard to royal ideology of the preexilic period.

Josiah's premature death at the age of thirty-nine meant that the Davidic restoration failed, as his sons did not live up to the ideals of their father, and that the nation rather headed toward destruction and exile. GJer 22 reflects the ethical failure of his sons and demonstrates the deep mourning for the dead Josiah.

With the Babylonian razing of the countryside, the conquests of Jerusalem in 596 and 587, and the deportation of the city's elite and large parts of the nation, Davidic hopes were shattered. The time of the exile would see the beginnings of a transformation of Davidic promises.

Micah 5: The Birth of the Davidide Postponed

Micah 5:1–8 [5:2–9] presents a relecture of the Davidic oracles in Isa 7 and 9.

There are different views on the growth and composition of the book of Micah. Ben-Zvi (2000) understands the book as a product of learned postexilic scribes who artificially built their book around their image of the eighth-century prophet Micah from the Shephelah.[26]

More commonly, the first part of the book is ascribed to the historical prophet (Mic 1–3 with the exception of 2:12–13), while passages on the restoration of Judah are dated to exilic or postexilic times (Carr 2011, 248–49, 329–31). It is difficult to recognize the voice of the prophet of doom of Mic 1–3 in the oracles of future salvation. The promonarchic voice in 5:1–8 [5:2–9] contrasts with the words of judgment on Zion and the leaders of the sister nations in Mic 1–3 (cf. 1:9, 12–14; 3:1–4, 9–12). Thus, I regard Mic 4–7 as exilic and postexilic additions to the Micah section of an early scroll from exilic times that contained Hosea, Amos, Micah, and Zephaniah (Nogalski 1993, 278–80; Albertz 2004, 207–11; Carr 2011, 248).

Sweeney (2001, 293–300) is a "maximalist voice" who finds more eighth-century material in the book than most of his colleagues: he identifies the voice of Micah also in 5:1–8 [5:2–9], which expects a restored remnant of the sister nations in Zion. The restoration will be headed by a Davidic king who will defeat the Assyrian invaders of the land. Texts referring to an Assyrian threat against Judah should be dated to the eighth century, and a meaningful historical setting of 5:1–8 [5:2–9] would be Hezekiah's revolt against Assyria toward the end of the century.

Some passages in Mic 4–7 interact with an early Isaiah scroll. In analogy with the repetition of Isa 5 in Mic 4:1–5, Mic 5:1, 3–8 [5:2, 4–9] should be read as an exilic sequel and relecture of the oracles on a new Davidide in Isa 7:14–17 and 9:1–6 [9:2–7]:[27]

> [1][2]But you, Bethlehem of Ephrathah,
> one of the small clans of Judah,
> from you shall come forth for me

26. Suggestions to identify Micah's hometown Moresheth-gath on the ground include Tel Harasim, a Judahite settlement established around 900, and Tel Goded, a large Judahite city in Iron Age II (see figures 1, 2, 4 on pp. 8, 25, 63).

27. "The eighth-century oracle has been reworked later in an exilic situation" (Hillers 1984, 65). According to Carr (2011, 248–49), Mic 4–5 should be dated to the Babylonian period at the earliest; he finds an exilic date most likely.

one who will be ruler in Israel,
whose origin is from of old, from ancient days.
   2[3]Truly, he will leave them until she who is to bear has borne,
    then the remainder of his kindred shall return to the children
      of Israel.
3[4]He shall rise as shepherd in the strength of Yhwh,
in the power of the name of Yhwh his God.
Then they will live secure,
for great shall he be unto the far corners of the land.
4[5]Such shall the peace be:
if the Assyrians come into our land and tread upon our soil,
we will raise against them seven shepherds and eight princes.
5[6]They shall tend the land of Assyria with the sword,
the land of Nimrod with the drawn sword.
He will deliver us from the Assyrians
if they invade our land and surpass our borders.[28]
6[7]Then the remnant of Jacob, surrounded by many peoples,
shall be like dew from Yhwh, like showers on the grass,
which do not depend upon people or wait for any mortal.
7[8]Then the remnant of Jacob among the nations, surrounded by
    many peoples,
shall be like a lion among the animals of the forest,
like a young lion among the flocks of sheep,
which, when it goes through, treads down
and tears in pieces, with no one to deliver.
8[9]Your hand shall be raised up over your adversaries
and all your enemies be cut off. (Mic 5:1–8 [5:2–9], my
    translation)

In exilic and especially postexilic texts, "Israel" may be used of the surviving nation of Judah that had incorporated remnants of the northern tribes. In

---

28. M has a section divider after Mic 5:5 [5:6], which may suggest that 5:6–8 [5:7–9] on the remnant of Jacob could be a separate oracle, an explicative addition to the earlier one. Some interpreters see "he shall be the One of Peace" in 5:4 [5:5] as the conclusion of the Davidic oracle—thus Hillers 1984, 64–69, who contrasts the individual figure in 5:1–4a [5:2–5a] with the collective leadership in 5:4b–5 [5:5b–6]. Hillers's division into three separate oracles (5:1–4a [5:2–5a]; 5:4b–5 [5:5b–6]; 5:6–8 [5:7–9]) is an artificial solution—at most, 5:6–8 [5:7–9] could represent a postexilic addition, as 5:2 [5:3]. The opening phrase "on that day" marks 5:9 [5:10] as the beginning of a subsequent oracle.

this oracle, however, "Israel" seems to be used of the land and people of the north; see the use of "Judah" and "Israel" in 5:1 [5:2] and the promised extension of the rule of the Bethlehemite "until the far corners of the land" (5:3 [5:4]).

If exilic or postexilic, "Assyria" has become a symbolic name for mighty enemy nations (as in the second century it would symbolize the Seleucid Empire, the enemy to the north—in the direction of ancient Assyria). Assyria is the great enemy in Isa 1–39. And the gloss appended to the hypotext 7:14–17, "the king of Assyria," may have further inspired the use of "Assyria" in Mic 5:1–8 [5:2–9]. The active memory of (the house of) Israel and Assyrian oppression suggests an exilic rather than a postexilic date for 5:1, 3–8 [5:2, 4–9].

Micah 5:1 [5:2] describes a God-sent leader, born in the south and ruling Israel and Judah. David is not mentioned in the oracle, but coming from Bethlehem, the foreseen ruler would be a Davidide. His origin "from ancient days" connects him with David who ruled both nations; the same will be true for the future leader. He shall be a true shepherd, a classic designation for the Davidic ruler (2 Sam 5:2). Similar to the "head" of the sister nations in Hos 2:2 [1:11] (from the opening column of the four-prophet scroll), he is not called king but "ruler" (*môšēl*).

In Mic 5:3–8 [5:4–9], the land is threatened by the mighty enemy. The forthcoming ruler and his army will defend the land against the Assyrians and inflict on the invaders a blowing defeat. According to 5:4 [5:5], this Davidic ruler will introduce a time of peace for the nation in the land. *Wəhāyâ zeh šālôm* can be interpreted either "he shall be one of peace" (related to the preceding) or "this/such shall the peace be" (related to the following). I am not convinced by the proposal that *šālôm* here is a royal, quasi-divine title, "the One of Peace"—for which cf. *śar-šālôm* in Isa 9:5 (thus Hillers 1984, 65, 67).

This peace is achieved by military means, and the arena is the land of Israel and Judah. In Mic 5:3 [5:4], I interpret *'apsê-'āreṣ* as "the far corners of the land," not "the ends of the earth"; cf. the description of the invaders in the subsequent verse: "coming into our land and treading upon our soil."

Micah 5:4b–5 [5:5b–6] and 5:6–8 [5:7–9] conclude the Davidic oracle. A collective leadership will stand at the side of the ruler to come and guard the land against the Assyrian invader. The words "tend [lit., shepherd] the land of Assyria with the sword" should be interpreted as military victory, not a continued Israelite rule over Assyria. In 5:6–8 [5:7–9] there is a change of focus: the remnant of Jacob, that is, the northerners, will be victorious among the hostile nations around.

In the context, 5:2 [5:3] appears as a literary addition, while 5:1 [5:2] has its natural continuation in 5:3–5 [5:4–6]. In 5:1 [5:2], God is the speaker, while in 5:2 [5:3], "he will leave them" refers to God in the third person. Thus, in 5:2 [5:3] we have a later qualification added to 5:1, 3–8 [5:2, 4–9]. Micah 5:2 [5:3] is "yet another (enigmatic, exilic-sounding) oracle" (Carr 2011, 248). Carr interprets "she who is to bear" as Lady Zion, who will give birth to the promised son of David. Whether the pregnant one is Lady Zion or a woman of Zion, this verse looks back on Isa 7:14 and 9:5–6 [9:6–7] as words from the past—and 9:5–6 [9:6–7] is clearly read on the birth of the Davidide, not as words of coronation. An interpreter writing after the disappearance of the Davidic Zerubbabel would be painfully aware that the nation had not experienced peace; the Davidic ruler promised in 7:14–17 and 9:1–6 [9:2–7] had not appeared. In hindsight this scribe would add Mic 5:2 [5:3]: from the eighth-century perspective of Isaiah and Micah, God would temporarily abandon his people and send them into deportation and exile; only thereafter should the nation expect the birth of a new Davidide.[29]

The last part of this verse, "then the remainder of his kindred [lit., his brothers] shall return to the children of Israel," is enigmatic. The easiest meaning of "remainder" (*yeter*) is those not gone into exile but remaining in the land. The literal meaning would be that the Judeans still left in the land shall be united with the remnants of the northern tribes.

Yeter 'eḥāyw could alternatively mean "he who surpasses his brothers," for which compare the words of Reuben in Gen 49:3 (Hillers 1984, 66–67, following Ernst Sellin). Emending the verb from plural of *šûb* ("to return") to singular of *yāšab* ("to dwell") would make the Davidide the subject: "He who surpasses his brothers will preside over the children of Israel."

In the scroll, the Davidic promise in Mic 5:1, 3–8 [5:2, 4–9] would resound with another exilic oracle characterized by shepherd imagery, 2:12–13 (my translation):[30]

> [12]I will surely gather all of you, Jacob,
> I will gather the survivors of Israel.
> I will set them together like sheep in a fold,

29. Another relecture would be apparent in the mid-second-century translation of Isaiah into Greek in Heliopolis and Alexandria (see pp. 193–94), where "the young woman shall bear" (7:14) was rendered "the virgin shall bear." In its turn, GIsa 7:14 would, as hypotext, receive a sequel in Matt 1:18–23.

30. Carr (2011, 249) notes the shepherd imagery in other exilic texts: Pss 44:12 [44:11]; 74:1; 79:13; Isa 40:9–11; Ezek 34:23–31.

like a flock in its pasture, it will resound with people.
¹³The one who breaks through will go up before them,
(and then,) they will break through, pass the gate and go out
through it.
Their king will walk before them, and Yhwh be at their head.

In this oracle, only the remnant of the northern tribes is addressed: "Jacob ... the survivors of Israel." In contrast to 5:1 [5:2], the future ruler is here designated "king"—so the scribe or scribal circle is not the same as in Mic 5.

This king of Israel is painted as a shepherd lodging with his flock far out in the fields. Such a distant fold has an open gate, being blocked during the night with branches and thorns. In the morning the shepherd will move the blockade aside, he will "break through" and lead his flock out and into the pastures.

The king will "go up" from the sheepfold. The use of the verb √ʿālâ instead of √yāṣ'â ("to go out") is likely intended. Elsewhere, √ʿālâ may designate "going up" to the land and to Jerusalem, in pilgrimage or return from exile. Thus, this oracle with pastoral colors promises a return to the land, and remnants of the northern tribes (whether still residing in their homeland or exiled) will recognize Jerusalem as their spiritual capital. This "going up" echoes the first salvation oracle in the four-prophet scroll (Hos 2:2 [1:11]): "The people of Judah and the people of Israel shall be gathered together and appoint for themselves one leader, and they shall *go up* from the land" (my translation).

Micah 4:6–14 [4:6–5:1] contains two oracles of salvation, likely from exilic times. According to 4:6–7, Yhwh will gather his dispersed people and restore the nation. However, in contrast to the two Davidic oracles discussed above, here the king is God himself: "Yhwh will reign over them in Mount Zion, now and forever."

The Masoretic text marks a section break before 4:8, which promises the return of kingship to Zion:

And you, watchtower of the flock, the ridge of daughter Zion,
to you it shall come, the dominion of former times shall return,
the kingship of daughter Jerusalem. (my translation)

Micah 4:8 changes the focus from "Mount Zion" (4:7) to "daughter Zion," the addressee of the subsequent oracle (4:9–14 [4:9–5:1]). Thus, this verse functions as a bridge between the Yhwh-king oracle in 4:6–7 and the subsequent oracle. Micah 4:9–14 [4:9–5:1] observes the end of the Judahite kingdom and the exile of daughter Zion. However, through her trials Yhwh will save daughter Zion and give her victory over her enemies. Likely inspired by the Davidic oracles in 2:12–13 and 5:1–8 [5:2–9], the editorially added 4:8 would make it clear that the surrounding two oracles would be fulfilled through a renewed earthly kingship in Zion.

CHAPTER 4

The End of the Kingdom

The biblical writers in the exilic period provide different responses to the fall of the temple, the loss of the land, and the abolition of the house of David. The Servant Songs in Deutero-Isaiah have their beginnings with this exilic prophet, although some of the songs likely postdate Deutero-Isaiah and the exile.

The Trauma of the Exile and the Fall of the House of David

The fall of the temple and the end of the Judean kingdom is the deepest trauma in Hebrew Bible history. Two exilic texts that express this trauma are Lamentations and the royal Ps 89 (esp. 89:4–5, 19–52 [89:3–4, 18–51]).[1] Lamentations phrases the feelings of the survivors in the following way (my translation):

> 2:5The Lord has become like an enemy; he has destroyed Israel,
> he has destroyed all its palaces, and laid in ruins its strongholds.
> . . .
> 2:6He has broken down his booth like a garden, he has destroyed his tabernacle,
> Yhwh has abolished in Zion festival and Sabbath,
> in his fierce indignation he has spurned king and priest.
> 2:7The Lord has scorned his altar, disowned his sanctuary,
> he has delivered into the hand of the enemy the walls of her palaces. . . .

1. Other exilic psalms express this trauma; see Pss 44:10–17, 20, 23 [44:9–16, 19, 22]; 74:3–9; 79:1–4.

> [4:20]Yhwh's anointed, the breath of our life, was taken in the enemy's pits—
>
> the one of whom we said, "Under his shadow we shall live among the nations." . . .
>
> [5:11]Women are raped in Zion, virgins in the towns of Judah.
>
> [5:12]Princes are hung up by their hands; no respect is shown to the elders. . . .
>
> [5:16]The crown has fallen from our head; woe to us, for we have sinned!
>
> [5:17]Because of this our hearts are sick, because of these things our eyes have grown dim,
>
> [5:18]because of Mount Zion, which lies desolate, jackals prowl over it.
>
> [5:19]But you, Yhwh, reign forever; your throne endures to all generations.
>
> [5:20] Why have you forgotten us completely? Why have you forsaken us these many days?

Scribes and laity alike felt that the God of Judah and Israel had broken his promises to his people, to Jerusalem, and to the Davidic dynasty. He had "destroyed Israel," "broken down his booth," "destroyed his tabernacle," "scorned his altar," and "disowned his sanctuary."

The loss of kingship is mentioned twice. God "has spurned king and priest" and allowed "Yhwh's anointed, the breath of our life, [to be] taken in the enemy's pits."

Lamentations 4:20 is the only verse where "Yhwh's anointed" is used as a fixed term for the king outside 1–2 Samuel, where the phrase is used eight times of Saul (1 Sam 24:7, 11 [24:6, 10]; 26:9, 11, 16, 23; 2 Sam 1:14, 16) and once of David (2 Sam 19:22 [19:21]). In both 1–2 Samuel and Lam 4:20, the thematic context is the question of hurting or not hurting "Yhwh's anointed"; this usage is echoed in Ps 89:39 [89:38]. In contrast, in the contemporary Isa 45:1 ("thus says Yhwh to his anointed [məšîḥô], to Cyrus") and the later Ps 132:17 ("a lamp for my anointed one [məšîḥî]"), "my/his anointed" is a designation of honor.

With the words "Yhwh's anointed, the breath of our life, . . . the one of whom we said, 'Under his shadow we shall live among the nations,'" the deep communion between king and nation is expressed in a way we have not seen in earlier texts—the closest is the description of the king's duties in Ps 72:1–7, 12–14, 16–17a. Here we may encounter an idealized image of the king, still conceived in earthly categories, perhaps combined with a memory of the righteous King Josiah.

These laments proclaim that Yhwh does reign from his throne, but his ways are not transparent for his people. The cry "Why have you forgotten us completely?" is lifted to the heavens without any answer.

Psalm 89 is one of the clearest biblical expressions of the Davidic promises as well as the trauma of the fall of the house of David. The psalm can be subdivided as follows (cf. Hossfeld and Zenger 2005, 402–7):[2]

2–3 [1–2]	hymnic introitus
4–5 [3–4]	introduction to Yhwh's covenant and oath to David
6–19 [5–18]	hymn on creation, ending in three verses on God's people and king
20–38 [19–37]	divine speech on election of David
39–52 [38–51]	exilic communal lament (48–49 [47–48] added later)

I quote the most relevant verses (NRSV adapted):

4[3]You said, "I have made a *covenant* with my chosen one,
I have *sworn* to my servant David:
5[4]I will establish your descendants forever
and build your throne for all generations." . . .
20[19]Then you spoke in a vision to your faithful ones:
21[20]". . . I have found my servant David;
with my holy oil I have anointed him;
22[21]my hand shall always remain with him;
my arm shall strengthen him. . . .
24[23]I will crush his foes before him
and strike down those who hate him.
25[24]My faithfulness and steadfast love shall be with him;
in my name his horn shall be exalted.
26[25]I make him rule with one arm unto the sea,

2. Following Veijola 1982, Spieckermann regards "David" in Ps 89 as a cipher for the postexilic "David people," perhaps taking up a motif from the exilic period (Feldmeier and Spieckermann 2011, 58–62, 409). I stay with the traditional interpretation as a royal psalm and exilic lament, as do Schniedewind 1999, 111–14; Fried 2002, 382–83; Carr 2011, 391–92.

and his right hand unto all the rivers.
27[26]He shall cry to me, "You are my Father,
my God, and the Rock of my salvation!"
28[27]I will make him the firstborn,
the highest of the kings of the earth.
29[28]Lasting I will keep my steadfast love for him,
my covenant with him will stand firm.
30[29]I will establish his line for time enduring,
and his throne as long as the heavens last. . . .
35[34]I will not violate *my covenant*
or alter the word that went forth from my lips.
36[35]Once and for all *I have sworn* by my holiness:
"I will not lie to David.
37[36]His line shall continue for times lasting,
and his throne endure before me like the sun.
38[37]It shall be established forever like the moon,
an enduring witness in the skies."
39[38]But now you have spurned and rejected him;
you are full of wrath against your anointed.
40[39]You have renounced the *covenant* with your servant;
you have defiled his crown in the dust.
41[40]You have broken through all his walls
and have laid his strongholds in ruins.
42[41]All who pass by plunder him;
he has become the scorn of his neighbors.
43[42]You have exalted the right hand of his foes
and made all his enemies rejoice.
44[43]You have turned back the edge of his sword,
and you have not supported him in battle.
45[44]You have removed the scepter from his hand
and hurled his throne to the ground.
46[45]You have cut short the days of his youth
and have covered him with shame.
47[46]How long, Yhwh? Will you forever hide yourself?
How long will your wrath burn like fire? . . .
50[49]Lord, where is your steadfast love of old,
which by your faithfulness you swore to David?
51[50]Remember, O Lord, how your servants are taunted,
how I bear in my bosom the insults of the nations,

52[51]with which your enemies taunt, Yhwh,

with which they taunt the footsteps of your anointed.

The psalm echoes the adoption or sonship motif from 2 Sam 7: the Davidide can call upon Yhwh as his father for protection, authority, and guidance. In Hossfeld's words, the psalmist undertakes a scribal relecture of 2 Sam 7, focusing on David as dynastic founder. The relecture also relates to Ps 2:7 and Ps 72. According to Glessner and Carr, 89:20–28 [89:19–27] preserves essential elements of an early royal oracle.[3]

Compared to earlier royal psalms, Yhwh's "covenant" with David and "swearing his oath" to him (89:4, 35, 36, 40 [89:3, 34, 35, 39]) are new elements; this terminology was likely coined after the fall of Jerusalem, when the continuation of the house of David was put into question. This Davidic covenant theology is inspired by Deuteronomistic covenant theology: elements of the Sinai covenant are here transformed into a Davidic covenant.[4] Further, the exilic text Isa 55:3 alludes to a Davidic covenant; there the covenant is with the nation and possibly not any more with David. The psalm's covenant theology will find echoes in Ps 132:11–12 and the late text 110:4. Psalm 89:39 [89:38] ("spurned and despised him . . . against your anointed") may echo Lam 2:6 and 4:20 ("spurned king and priest," "Yhwh's anointed . . . was taken in the enemy's pits").

The declarative character of 89:36–38 [89:35–37], which quotes Yhwh's oath to David, may be compared with 2:7–9. This divine declaration elaborates the lasting election of the house of David. These verses fall outside the movement of 89:29–35 [89:28–34] and seem to have been added together with 89:4–5 [89:3–4].

Psalm 89:27–28 [89:26–27] describes an intimate relation between the king and his God in a way that stands out from earlier royal texts: "He shall cry to me, 'You are my Father, my God, and the Rock of my salvation!' I will make him the firstborn, the highest of the kings of the earth." These words would later be democratized and used on the individual's relation to God and in his petition to his heavenly father:[5]

3. This is clearer in the independent textual version of Ps 89 preserved in 4QPs[x]. 4QPs[x] seems to preserve an earlier version of this oracle (Glessner 1992; Carr 2011, 391–92).

4. "In its emphasis on God's reliability and faithful love in connection with a mention of the covenant, the Davidic covenant theology of Psalm 89 has a close parallel in the interpretation of the Sinai covenant as formulated in Deut 7:9, and expands it with the element of the oath in interpreting the covenant with the patriarchs in Deut 7:12" (Hossfeld and Zenger 2005, 405).

5. In the Bible divine fatherhood relates either to Israel as God's son (Exod 4:22; Hos

> [9]I raised my voice from the dust, my plea from the gates of the
> netherworld,
> [10]I extolled the Lord, "You are my father, for you are my mighty
> savior!
> Do not leave me in a time of crisis, on a day of ruin and desola-
> tion!" (Sir 51:9–10, Hebrew manuscript B, my translation)

For Hossfeld, the scribal relecture of 2 Sam 7 and the conscious transformation of Deuteronomistic covenant thinking point to the postexilic milieu that coined the Korah and Asaph psalms (Hossfeld and Zenger 2005, 405–6). With such a dating, it remains a crux that the psalm does not refer to Zion or the temple. To me, Ps 89:40–46 [89:39–45] conveys an expression of fresh memories of the catastrophes of 596 and 587. The king who was covered with shame and whose days of youth were cut short likely refers to Jehoiachin, who in 596 was exiled at the age of eighteen and with his family put in Babylonian custody (2 Kgs 24:8, 12; 25:27). The closeness to Egyptian and Neo-Assyrian royal ideology is easier to understand in an exilic setting than in postexilic Judah. If, however, Hossfeld hits the mark in his postexilic dating of the final form of Ps 89, the psalm would anyway preserve memories of the early exilic community in Babylon.

While focusing on Yhwh's promise to David, the psalm is colored by the same deep anguish as Lamentations: God burns with wrath and has re-nounced his covenant with the house of David. Yhwh is the God who hides himself. The petition of lamentation psalms recurs: "Will you forever hide yourself? How long will your wrath burn like fire?"

These texts do not dare to proclaim a confidence in the validity of the Da-vidic promises and can be compared with the Deuteronomistic aphorism that concludes the reflection on judgment and exile in Deut 29: "The secret things belong to Yhwh our God, but the revealed things are for us and our children for-ever, to observe all the words of this torah" (29:28 [29:29], my translation).

A New Davidide and a Paradisiac Land

In contrast to the anguish of Lamentations and Ps 89, three contemporary texts did not give up the Davidic line. Similar to preexilic Judean texts, they

---

11:1; Jer 31:9, 20) or to the Davidic king. Sirach 51 is the first text where an individual prays to God as "my father." The same usage is found in the fragmentary 4Q460 (4QNarrative Work and Prayer) 5 I 5.

express the hope of restoration and a coming earthly king, although only one of them uses the term "king" (which may reflect the correcting hand of a later scribe).

The book of Jeremiah has a complex editorial history, beginning with Baruch and sixth-century Deuteronomistic editors; "the bulk of the shaping of the book probably was complete already in the exilic period" (Carr 2011, 247). The book continued to develop in two textual families that may have reached their final form in the third century: one ended as the *Vorlage* to the Greek translation (of the mid-second century), the other as the proto-Masoretic Text. The latter is around 15 percent longer than the former.[6] The shorter shape of the Greek recension indicates that its *Vorlage* underwent less substantial reworking than its proto-Masoretic cousin and to a large extent preserves the earlier tradition.[7]

The Greek text of Jer 23:5–6, spoken during or just after the reign of Zedekiah (598–587), runs as follows (my translation):

6. The arrangement of Jer 25–52 is substantially different in these two recensions. MJeremiah shows knowledge of political development in Egypt in the period 315–290 (Bogaert 2005; Lange 2010a, 77–82). It remains an open question whether these scribes resided in Egypt or Judea.

7. The Qumran Jeremiah scrolls provide a window into the growth and processing of the book. The skins of 4QJer^a (4Q70, late third century) and 4QJer^e (4Q72b, ca. 100) were recently identified as cowskin, while 4QJer^b (4Q71) and 4QJer^d (4Q72a) were written on sheepskin, the most common medium in Qumran scrolls (Anava et al. 2020). 4QJer^b and 4QJer^d (both copied ca. 50, around a century after the translation into Greek) are cousins of the shorter recension of the Septuagint, while 4QJer^c (ca. 100) and 4QJer^c (4Q72, mid- or late first century) match the long text of M. 2QJer (2Q13, ca. 50) is an independent scroll, closer to M, with which it may have a common ancestor (dating of the scrolls according to Langlois 2019b). 4QJer^a is an independent witness relatively close to M and may testify to the growth of the proto-Masoretic recension throughout the third century. A slightly later scribe (early second century) inserted 7:30–8:3 (a prophetic admonition) in a section break and the margin. This paragraph was likely lacking in the *Vorlage* of 4QJer^a and may not have existed at that time (Langlois 2019b, 24–25). Only the two small fragments of 4QJer^b and 4QJer^d evince the short proto-Greek recension. Langlois characterizes them as indirect witnesses of G, preserving variant readings of their own. Langlois considers 4Q71 and 4Q72a as written by the same scribe and probably deriving from the same scroll (2019b, 15–20). However, recent analysis of the skins shows that the genetic relatedness of these two scrolls in sheepskin is relatively low (Anava et al. 2020). For Langlois, the dating of the scrolls may question the common view that proto-G is earlier than proto-M. In contrast, most scholars hold that literary analysis strongly suggests that the shorter proto-G is the earlier recension (Tov 2012, 137, 286–93). The six Jeremiah scrolls from Qumran demonstrate that active redactional work continued in both textual families until the turn of the era.

Behold, days are coming, says the Lord, when I will raise up for David a righteous dawn. This king shall reign, he will have insight and execute justice and righteousness in the land. In his days Judah will be saved and Israel encamp in confidence. And this is the name by which he will be called: "The Lord Yhwh is righteousness."[8]

In the eyes of Jeremiah, Zedekiah had not lived up to his name, ṣidqiyāhû ("Yahu is my righteousness"). The prophet envisions a restoration by the hand of Yhwh who will raise up a new king. The prophet includes both Judah and Israel in the foreseen restoration. The scene is the land, while Zion, Jerusalem, or temple is not mentioned. The use of the term "king" in this oracle is exceptional among exilic texts; a term such as "ruler" or "prince" may have been changed by a postexilic editor.

Also in 30:18–22, the Greek text of Jeremiah carries a Davidic hope. This will be radically changed in the proto-Masoretic recension of the early-third century, where the leader of the people is a priest who risks his life in a sacrificial act in God's presence (see pp. 150–52):

> [18]Thus says Yhwh:
> Behold, I will bring back the exiled Jacob and have mercy on his
> captivity.
> The city shall be rebuilt upon its mound and the sanctuary set on
> its rightful site.
> [19]. . . I will make them many . . . [20]their sons shall go in as
> formerly,
> their testimonies shall be rectified before me,
> and I will punish those who oppressed them.
> [21]His own strong men shall be set over them,
> his ruler shall come from his midst.
> I will gather them, and they shall return to me,
> because who is this one who dedicates his heart to me?
> Says Yhwh. (GJer 37:18–21 ≈ MJer 30:18–22, my translation)

With the phrase "exiled Jacob," Jeremiah brings the exiled ones from the Northern Kingdom into focus; Judah is not explicitly mentioned. Similar to Hos 2:2 [1:11], the prophet foresees a future ruler but does not use the

---

8. GJer 23:6b closes with the words *ho kalesei auton kyrios iôsedek*. The words *kyrios iôsedek* probably renders *'ădōnāy yh ṣedeq*.

term "king" or other terms with Davidic connotations, such as "shepherd" of the nation. However, "rebuilding the city upon its mound and setting the sanctuary on its rightful site" points to a restoration of Jerusalem, where one would expect a new ruler to be a Davidide. This ruler will have his heart dedicated to the Lord (literally, the Greek runs "he has given his heart to return to me").

Two composite Davidic passages were added to Amos and Isaiah after the fall of the kingdom. Amos 9:11–15 is easier to date than Isa 11:1–10. The historical Amos never talked about a Davidic restoration of Judah. In Amos's time Judah lived safely, his prophetic warnings aimed solely at the Northern Kingdom (Amos 2:4–5 is a later addition with Deuteronomistic flavor). After 587, a prophetic writer, perhaps one who had read the promise of Jer 23:5–6, added a conclusion to the Amos scroll, a book he wanted to convey a lasting message to the exiled nations of Israel and Judah. This author knew from fresh memory that "the booth of David" had fallen down, with only breaches and ruins left (cf. Lam 2:6: the Lord "has broken down his booth").

Evidence from excavations of ancient Edom during the last two decades makes an eighth-century dating of Amos 9:11–15 unlikely.[9] The expression "the remnant of Edom" (9:12) hardly fits the well-functioning Edomite kingdom of the eighth to sixth centuries with Bozrah/Busayra as capital but rather points to the chaotic mid-sixth century when the kingdom fell apart. Eighth-to sixth-century Edom was an organized kingdom with a well-built capital and forts controlling the countryside. In Busayra, archaeologists can observe a social stratification with an elite class and a dynastic ruler and ample evidence of the state's administrative system (Levy, Najjar, and Ben-Yosef 2014a, 251–52, 287–90; 2014b, 993). Edom did not support its "brother nation" when Judah was attacked by Nebuchadnezzar, and Edomite tribes subsequently extended their territory westward into Judahite Negev (Am 1:11 [a post-587 verse]; Obad 9–12; Ps 137:7; Ezek 35:5, 14). A royal relief with an inscription recently identified in Sela (close to Busayra) confirms that the state broke down with the invasion in 551 by the Babylonian king Nabonidus, who purposely destroyed the temple and palace in Busayra (Crowell 2007).[10]

---

9. Schniedewind (1999, 63–65) ascribes Amos 9:11–15 to a Judahite redaction under Hezekiah. For him, "the fallen booth of David" is the broken united kingdom, which shall be restored with King Hezekiah. Similarly, Sweeney (2001, 279–81) argues that 9:11–15 preserves Amos's vision of reestablishment of Davidic rule over the north. He understands 5:4–6 as the prophet's call on northerners to seek Zion, not Bethel and other shrines of the north. In contrast, Carr (2011, 249) dates these verses to the exile.

10. For a recent history of the Edomite state, see Crowell 2021.

> [11]On that day I will raise up
> the booth of David that is fallen,
> repair its breaches,
> raise up its ruins,
> and rebuild it as in the days of old,
> [12]so that they may possess the remnant of Edom
> and all the nations who are called by my name,
> the word of Yhwh will bring this to pass. (Amos 9:11–12, my
> translation)

According to a plain reading of the text, the booth of David has fallen down, and it is still not raised up. Thus, Amos 9:11–12 should be dated after the end of the Judahite kingdom (587) and the downfall of Edom (551), possibly before the Cyrus edict of 538, and certainly before the rebuilding of the temple in 520–515. According to this text, the Davidic dynasty will again come to power, and Jerusalem and Judea—destroyed by the Babylonians—will be rebuilt. Then the Judeans will subdue the surrounding lands and nations, including the tribes of Edom that recently have been crushed. Any violent or military takeover of these nations is not mentioned, dominion is probably achieved by peaceful means. And the other nations would be called by Yhwh's name, that is, be blessed by the God of Israel. This oracle would later receive a sequel that provides new, supplementing information. A double introductory formula, "see, days will come / the word of Yhwh," evince a literary seam in the text (my translation):

> [13]See, the days will come, so is the word of Yhwh,
> when the one who plows shall overtake the one who reaps,
> and the treader of grapes the one who sows the seed,
> the mountains shall drip sweet wine and all the hills shall flow
> with it.
> [14]I will restore the fortunes of my people Israel,
> they shall rebuild the ruined cities and inhabit them,
> they shall plant vineyards and drink their wine,
> they shall make gardens and eat their fruit.
> [15]I will plant them in their land,
> and they shall never again be plucked up
> out of the land that I have given them,
> says Yhwh your God.

Where the hypotext talked about repairing and rebuilding the ruins and has the booth of David in focus, the sequel describes the restoration of the land in pastoral and paradisiac terms. The earlier text had the booth of David in focus, here "my people Israel" is the active subject in cultivating the land and building the cities.

The structure and thematic lines of this composite post-587 addition to Amos should be compared to Isa 11:1–5 and 11:6–9, where a passage on a new Davidide is followed by paradisiac conditions in the land. There are contrasting opinions whether 11:1–9 (alternatively 11:1–5) is an authentic Isaiah oracle from the late eighth century. Arguments for an eighth-century date include the following:

- The vocabulary is typical for Isaiah: root, spirit, wisdom and understanding, counsel, might, poor, lowly, strike with a rod, faithfulness—but this could also be explained as conscious coloring of the text by a later editor.
- Isaiah 11:1–5 interacts with the royal or messianic vision in 9:1–6 [9:2–7]. However, there is a marked contrast between these two texts: 9:2–6 [9:3–7] celebrates the arrival of a just king (by birth or coronation), while 11:1–5 anticipates the coming of a just king from the cutoff stump of the dynasty.
- After the purging of the nation anticipated in the preceding verses (10:32–34), a Davidide will head the restoration. Referring to Jesse (Isai) does not mean that the house of David has fallen; rather than negatively dwell on the purging of the nation, it stresses that the new ruler will be a second David, still conceived within the historical continuum (Williamson 1998, 262–64).
- Isaiah 11:1–10 reworks motifs from Assyrian royal ideology to present the image of a king whose power rivals that of Assyria, but whose royal ideology is diametrically opposed to that of Assyria. Isaiah 11:1–8 describes how a local Judahite king will replace Assyria's king as the one on whom Judah relies. The king has an intimate relation to Yhwh, not the god Assur. He does not revel about himself but recognizes divine sovereignty. In contrast to the well-armed Assyrian king, he rules peacefully by virtue without weapons. The paradisiac animal imagery contrasts the motif of animal hunting associated with the king and his campaigns. "The nations seeking him" mirrors the Assyrian concept *šubat neḥti* used to describe the king's care for his people (Aster 2018).
- While Barth dates 8:23–9:6 [9:1–7] to the Josianic period, he reads 11:1–5 closely with 10:27b–33a as words of Proto-Isaiah (1977, 62–73). Isaiah 10:27b–32 is an unfinished oracle of doom against Jerusalem; its continu-

ation is found in 10:33a as well as 11:1–5. According to 10:33a, in his wrath Yhwh will cut down the crown of a tree, which prepares the field for the shoot to grow from the stump; through judgment and doom God will open a new future for the remnant.

Scholars who see 11:1–5 as words from Isaiah tend to date it late in his career: the oracle would then reflect the traumatic experience of Sennacherib's 701 invasion or Sargon II's campaign in the Levant in 713–711 (cf. Isa 20). The oracle would betray a deep disappointment over Hezekiah's foreign policies, his alliance with Egypt and support of Ashdod in its revolt against Assyria. This would lead the prophet to anchor the hope for a new king in David's family roots, not the present king, therefore using "Jesse" and not "David" as in 9:6 [9:7]. One proposal would see the birth of Manasseh around 710 as a catalyst for the oracle, which would then reflect the prophet's hope for Manasseh to become an ideal king (Koh 2018).[11]

In my view, substantial factors point to composition during the exile. Thematic features indicate that 11:6–9 is a later interpretation of 11:1–5. In contrast to 7:14 and 9:1–6 [9:2–7], 11:6–9 abounds in images from nature and adds paradisiac motifs to the vision of a new Davidide. Before 587, the expected Davidide is consistently described as an earthly ruler. Thus, 11:6–9 can hardly be dated earlier than exilic times. The latest addition (11:10) is postexilic and foresees the inclusion of gentiles in the messianic kingdom.

The question that remains is, Does 11:1–5 date to the eighth or the sixth century? The parallels with Ps 72, a seventh-century royal psalm (see pp. 49–52), pull the evidence toward a post-587 date for Isa 11:1–5, and not to the eighth century. The structural and thematic similarity with Amos 9:11–12 and 9:13–15 is a strong argument for dating Isa 11:1–5 and 11:6–9 to post-587 times.

When the text talks about the "stump of Jesse" (David's father), the plain meaning is that the Davidic tree has been cut down—only a stump is left, as indeed happened in 587, not in 701. Echoes of Mesopotamian royal tradition would carry equal meaning in the first decades after the destruction of Jerusalem (my translation):

¹A rod shall come out from the stump of Jesse,
a shoot will grow from his roots.

11. Zenger characterizes 11:1–9 as an early postexilic text (Hossfeld and Zenger 1993, 279). However, if the "shoot" (ṣemaḥ) of Zech 3:8 echoes "rod" and "sprout" in Isa 11:1, a postexilic dating would be questionable.

> [2]The spirit of Yhwh shall rest on him,
> the spirit of wisdom and understanding,
> the spirit of counsel and might,
> the spirit of knowledge and the fear of Yhwh.
> [3]His delight shall be in the fear of Yhwh.
> He shall not judge by what his eyes see,
> or pass sentence by what his ears hear,
> [4]but with righteousness he shall judge the poor,
> and decide with equity for the lowly of the land.
> He shall strike the land with the rod of his mouth,
> and with the breath of his lips, he shall kill the wicked.
> [5]Righteousness shall be the belt around his waist,
> and faithfulness the belt around his loins.

This vision confirms that even after the catastrophe of 587, a son of David can be called to lead his people. An anonymous prophet added his words to the Isaiah scroll, subsequent to the Davidic passage 9:1–6 [9:2–7] (whether from the late eighth or the late seventh century) and the long oracle in Isa 10 on the downfall of the superpower Assyria—the latter was likely reread as prefiguring the downfall of Assyria's successor Babylon.

The Davidic tree is broken, but God will open for a new beginning and give life to another shoot from David's larger family: a ruler who has his heart dedicated to God and will execute righteousness in the land as a fair and non-partisan judge and leader of his people. The oracle should be dated between the fall of the kingdom and the appearance of (the Davidic) Zerubbabel—parallel to Jeremiah's oracle of the coming ruler, "the one who dedicates his heart to Yhwh" (GJer 37:18–21 ≈ MJer 30:18–22). There is no sign in the text about the turning of Judah's destiny that came with Cyrus's edict in 538. I thus date the oracle to early exilic times, before Cyrus appeared mightily on the scene in the 540s.

This oracle in poetic style likely plays on images of the wise Solomon, the righteous Josiah, and Hezekiah as described in Isa 36–38 as types for the coming spirit-filled king. The son of David will implement the description of the righteous king in the royal Ps 72 (with 72:1–7, 12–14, 16–17a as an original core). In contrast to the words "the throne of David and his kingdom" (Isa 9:6 [9:7]), but similar to Hos 2:2 [1:11], the oracle consciously avoids the phrase "king."

Isaiah 11:1–5 describes a righteous ruler in ordinary earthly terms. In 11:4, however, the ruler "puts on God's sandals": "striking the land with the rod of his mouth, and with the breath of his lips killing the wicked" recalls scriptures that describe the might of God's voice that causes fear and destruction (such as 30:30, 31; 66:6; Jer 25:30; Amos 1:2; Ps 29:5–8). I struggle to see that the first Isaiah would give the Davidide a voice as powerful as God's own.

While Isa 11:1–5 has only the ruler in view, he is not mentioned in 11:6–9 (nor in Amos 9:13–15), which introduces the theme of renewed nature without any bridging element. These verses appear as a sequel to Isa 11:1–5, a sequel that adds new information about the reign of the shoot of Jesse. While 11:1–5 foresees an earthly ruler, the limits of human existence are transcended in the words of 11:6–9.

Further, the theme of the paradisiac garden typically colors the texts of other biblical writers in the sixth century. In some of these we encounter a man with royal qualities set in the garden by God, as in the Eden story. Ezekiel uses this image to convey God's judgment on the kings of Tyre and Egypt (Ezek 28 and 31): since the kings of these overflowing gardens had exalted themselves in pride, God will cause their downfall.

There is no consensus on the dating of the Eden story of Gen 2:4–3:23, which possibly could be another paradise story from the time of the exile.[12] With a tentative dating to exilic times, I imagine a Yahwistic thinker struggling with the trauma of 587 and asking why the creation story, written by wisdom-influenced scribes in preexilic Jerusalem, does not hold true anymore. God cannot any more look upon his land and conclude that "it is good."

Without the Jerusalem temple as counterpart to the universe created by Israel's God, there is a stunning disharmony in the world. Through his strug-

---

12. Many European scholars ascribe Gen 1 to the Priestly Source, which they date to exilic or postexilic times. In contrast, with Israeli scholars I date central parts of P to preexilic times (e.g., Faust 2019). Whether Gen 1 derives from priestly or sapiential circles, the harmony of creation proclaimed here presupposes a standing temple in a well-functioning land, not the trauma of the exile or the poor and tiny temple community of postexilic Jerusalem. The concluding words in 2:1–3 echo the building of the tabernacle (Exod 39:32, 41–43): as microcosm, the tabernacle and subsequently the (still standing) temple are a reflection of the universe, the macrocosm. In my view, the Eden story is intended to be read as a contrasting commentary on Gen 1:1–2:3. With a dating of Gen 1 to preexilic Jerusalem, the Eden story is better understood as an exilic relecture. If the text had been postexilic, we would have expected *pardēs*, not *ʿēden* for "garden" (Hendel and Joosten 2018, 27). Carr (2020, 17–26, 229–45) argues that 1:1–2:3 is dependent on the (earlier) Eden story and that the former should not be dated later than the early Neo-Assyrian period—and both belong to pre-P material in Gen 1–11. If such an early dating of the Eden story holds true, both Amos 9:13–15 and Isa 11:6–9 would consciously echo central themes of this classical story from the authors' heritage.

gle this theologian came to write one of the greatest symbolic stories ever told: God had planted Judah and Israel in his land, his garden. In this beautiful garden they communicated with their creator through priests, temple, and prophets. But the people were disobedient to God and took the staff in their own hands. And in the end God had no other choice than casting them out of the garden and exiling them to other lands. But he did not ultimately disown them: as Adam and Eve outside the garden received clothing and guidance from God, Yhwh will still follow his people in their exilic wanderings. In this way the Eden story answers the existential question of Israelites reflecting on the fate of their nation: Why it is not true anymore that "it is good"? For the author, the story also has a universal meaning: Israel's history with Yhwh symbolizes and reflects the history of humankind with its creator.

Back to Isa 11:1–5, which describes a new ruler in the land in ordinary human terms. He has his heart with God, is a bearer of God's spirit and acts as a righteous judge and leader of his people. In contrast, 11:6–9 describes the time of the coming shoot of Jesse in paradisiac terms. This radical change of perspective suggests two prophetic authors with some time between them. Isaiah 11:1–5 is an early-exilic text from the first decades after 587. The "new revelation" of 11:6–9 was later added as a sequel to the first passage, perhaps by a Yahwist thinker who had digested aspects of the Eden story: there should be a reflection of Eden when God restores the land and sends the shoot of Jesse to his people (my translation):

> ⁶The wolf shall live with the lamb,
> the leopard lie down with the kid,
> the calf and the lion and the fatling together,
> and a little child shall lead them.
> ⁷The cow and the bear shall graze,
> their young shall lie down together,
> and the lion shall eat straw like the ox.
> ⁸The nursing child shall play over the hole of the asp,
> and the weaned child put its hand on the adder's den.
> ⁹They will not hurt or destroy
> on all my holy mountain,
> for the earth will be full of the knowledge of Yhwh
> as the waters cover the sea.

Did the author of this text foresee a transformation of creation with the coming of the shoot of Jesse? Or is this rather a symbolic description of the future restoration of Judah in the land? The same questions can be raised vis-à-vis Amos 9:13–15.

In the continuation, 11:1–9 would be read in both ways, either on an earthly kingdom or a radically changed messianic era. By the early fifth century, Isa 65–66 would talk about a new creation, a new heaven and a new earth. Large parts of the Isaiah apocalypse (Isa 24–27) were shaped during the Babylonian exile, and here also we find texts on cosmic changes initiated by Yhwh (24:17–23; 25:6–9; 26:21–27:1; 27:12–13).[13]

In postexilic times, the Davidic/messianic collage in 11:1–5 and 11:6–9 would receive a conclusion that adds yet another perspective. Other prophecies or royal psalms describe the son of David as a military ruler who will subdue the enemies of the people (Pss 2:8–12; 110; Mic 5:3–5 [5:4–6]). In contrast, Isa 11:10 belongs to the few passages that describe the coming restoration and the God-sent ruler as a blessing to the gentile nations, who without any armed conflict will acknowledge the king/ messiah of Israel. Isaiah 11:10 opens with the words "And it shall be on that day that the root of Jesse. . . ." The formula *wəhāyâ bayyôm hahû'* ("and it shall be on that day") betrays a literary seam in a prophetic text, signifying that here comes information added by another writer (my translation):

> [10]And it shall be on that day that the root of Jesse shall stand as a
> banner to the peoples,
> the nations shall seek him, and his dwelling shall be glorious.

Similar to Amos 9:11–12, in the time following the restoration of the booth of David, the gentile nations will be peacefully included in the restored kingdom. We also note the messianic edge in this verse: in contrast to the nations' pilgrimage in 2:2–4, the nations shall seek the messiah, not Yhwh, and it is the messiah's dwelling that is described as glorious, not the temple or Zion as God's dwelling.

---

13. Hays (2019a, 2019b) argues for a dating of the Isaiah apocalypse to Josiah's time: this text celebrates the receding of Assyrian power from Judah and especially from the citadel at Ramat Rachel, in the late seventh century. Josiah and his scribes used this historical window as a political opportunity for an overture to the inhabitants of the former Northern Kingdom.

Ezekiel: Restoration without a Son of David

When Nebuchadnezzar in 598 conquered Jerusalem for the first time, he exiled the Judean elite: King Jehoiachin and his house, scribes, priests, and officials. Among the exiled was Ezekiel, son of a priestly family. Four years later, this young priest had a groundbreaking experience: "I was among the exiled by the Chebar river, the heavens opened, and I saw visions of God" (1:1, my translation). In the last decades, cuneiform tablets stemming from or relating to the exiled Judeans have come to our knowledge. Some of them refer to "the Judean City"; one mentions Al-nar-Kabara, the Chebar river.[14]

Ezekiel's prophecies and visions became the core of the book of Ezekiel, transmitted and edited by Yahwist priests in Babylon. Early on, Ezekiel was a prophet of doom who saw Yhwh's presence leaving Zion and the temple. After the fall of the temple, he foresaw a coming restoration of the remnant of the people, as did his contemporary Jeremiah.

Ezekiel 34 is the great "shepherd chapter" of the Hebrew Bible. Here Yhwh pronounces his judgment on the shepherds of Judah, who had failed in their ministry and not taken care of the sheep, the people (34:1–10). In 34:11–22 and 34:25–31, the Lord is the single actor who intervenes for his people. He is the good shepherd who takes care of the flock, renews his relation to his people, brings back the exiled, and makes the land fruitful. In the mouth of Ezekiel, no subshepherds will be needed, the job description is for Yhwh alone.

With the introduction of a supporting actor, 34:23–24 (my translation) appears as a later insert inspired by Jer 23:

> [23]And I will appoint over them one shepherd, and he shall tend them—my servant David. He shall tend them and be a shepherd to them. [24]I, Yhwh, will be their God, and my servant David shall be the prince [*nāśî'*] in their midst. I, Yhwh, have spoken.

Ezekiel 34:23 rephrases GJer 23:4–5: "I will appoint shepherds over them, and they shall tend them . . . and I will raise up for David a righteous dawn" (my translation). The insertion in Ezekiel closes with the words "I, Yhwh, have spoken"—a formula that closes a prophetic oracle, not regularly used

---

14. Joannès and Lemaire 1996, 50–52 (text 7:5). The earliest text mentioning the Judean City (Al-Yahudu, also called Al-Yahudaia, City of the Judeans) is from 572 (Pearce and Wunsch 2014, 98–99 [text 1]).

in the middle of a prophetic speech. Thus, the scribe who inserted these two verses made transparent that these words are an addition; to say it theologically, new revelation supplemented the previous one (Zimmerli 1969, 844).[15] The original oracle underlines that Yhwh always is the central actor in the promises about the future—in some of them there is a secondary actor too, such as king, messiah, Cyrus, or the servant of Yhwh.

The description of the future restoration in Ezek 36:16–38 is void of a Davidide. It is therefore pertinent to ask if the prophet foresaw a role for the Davidide in the coming restoration. Ezekiel criticized the last kings of Judah harshly, and the book proclaims Yhwh's lordship. Would there then be room for a future earthly king?

Ezekiel 37:15–28 is another passage of restoration, where the main point is the future unification of Israel and Judah in the land. The original oracle ended in v. 23, "I will save them from all the apostasies into which they have fallen, and will cleanse them. Then they shall be my people, and I will be their God." Does the term "king" of v. 22 go back to the prophet?

> I will make them one nation in the land, on the mountains of Israel; and one *king* shall be king over them all. Never again shall they be two nations, and never again shall they be divided into two kingdoms. (MEzek 37:22)

Joyce (1998, 335) notes that "the most natural reading of 37.22 is probably a reference to a human king." However, he overlooks the Greek version of this verse. Greek Ezekiel preserves an earlier recension of the book. Many small details and additions evince that the Hebrew text was reworked, resulting in a slightly longer text than the *Vorlage* represented by the Greek (see, e.g., Tov 1999, 397–410; Lust 1986; Bogaert 1986). And in GEzek 37:22 there is a "ruler," not a "king": "I will give them into one nation in my land and on the mountains of Israel, and they shall have one *ruler*, and they shall no longer be as two nations, nor shall they be divided into two kingdoms" (NETS). In the earlier text, Israel and Judah shall be one nation under one ruler (likely a translation of *môšēl*). The prophet consciously avoids the terms "king" or "prince." And nothing is said of any Davidic pedigree for the future ruler.

Ezekiel 37:24–28 is a later explicating sequel to 37:15–23. First, 37:24–25 appears as yet another Davidic insert into a salvation oracle where Yhwh is the central actor.

---

15. Rofé (2015, 96) regards 34:1–16, 31 as the original oracle and 34:17–30 as a post-Ezekiel addition. This difference does not affect my argument above.

²⁴My servant David shall be king over them; and they shall all have one shepherd. They shall follow my ordinances and be careful to observe my statutes. ²⁵They shall live in the land that I gave to my servant Jacob, in which your ancestors lived; they and their children and their children's children shall live there forever; and my servant David shall be their prince [*nāśî'*] forever.

As in 34:23–24, the term "my servant David" is repeated, betraying the same (post-Ezekiel) editorial hand. The continuation runs,

²⁶I will make a covenant of peace with them, it shall be an everlasting covenant with them, and I will multiply them and set my sanctuary among them forevermore. ²⁷My dwelling shall be with them, and I will be their God, and they shall be my people. ²⁸Then the nations shall know that I, Yhwh, sanctify Israel, when my sanctuary is among them forevermore. (NRSV adapted)

These verses represent post-Ezekiel editing by temple priests (Weyde 2021, 64–70). The term *miškān* ("dwelling") is not used elsewhere in Ezekiel—it is an import from the Priestly Source. And within Ezek 1–39, only these verses foresee a sanctuary (*miqdāš*) as center of the restored nation—and it is the *sanctuary* that will make the gentiles recognize Yhwh (≠ 36:36).

The last passage in Ezek 1–39 that may foresee a Davidide appears at the end of the allegorical chapter Ezek 17. Ezekiel 17:3–10 is a poetic allegory followed by an explanation in 17:11–21: 17:3–4 symbolizes the deportation of King Jehoiachin; the topmost shoot (*yənîqâ*) of a cedar was taken by the eagle (the king of Babylon) and exiled to another country. In 17:5–10, the subsequent king (Zedekiah) is described as a flowering vine, planted by the Babylonians. But this vine would move its branches toward another eagle (Egypt) and forsake his earlier covenant with the gardener who planted it. In the end the vine will dry out—this king will be judged in Babylon for breaking his covenant with the king of the East.

At the end of the chapter follows a poetic vision for the future (17:22–24): Yhwh will take a shoot (*yôneqet*) from the top of a cedar and plant it in the land of Israel. It will grow into a great tree that will give shelter to the birds of heaven. Levenson (1976, 77–84) notes the parallel between the shoot taken from the crown of the cedar in 17:4, a symbol for Jehoiachin who was exiled, and the shoot of 17:22–24 and concludes that Ezekiel in these verses foresees a future Davidide. For Joyce (1998, 329), this poem "forms a hopeful appendix to an otherwise judgmental chapter; moreover, its presence in the first half of the book could also point to redactional origin." I concur, these verses could not have been spoken by the prophet before the fall of Jerusalem. They were editorially added at a later stage, more probably by an editor than by the prophet himself.

I conclude that Ezekiel the prophet did not include a Davidic king in his visions of the restoration, where Yhwh's lordship will be recognized by all (Joyce 1998, 332–35). The prophet advocated no individual messianism. The creation of a new heart and a new spirit within the Israelites as part of the restoration (36:22–38)—can this be denoted a collective messianism, where redemption will come through the action of the people of God (Monti 2004, 28; Sayyad Bach 2020, 238–39)? However, for the prophet, the people will be a passive recipient and Yhwh the sole actor in restoring the fortunes of Zion. There is no room for a Davidic shepherd as Yhwh's assistant actor in this scenario of the future.

The book of Ezekiel closes with a symbolic blueprint for the new temple province in Ezek 40–48. In this section, 45:7–8 and 46:1–18 foresee a prince (*nāśîʾ*) leading the people, whose office is connected to the sacrifices: "The *nāśîʾ* is essentially the chief patron of the liturgy, responsible for supplying the materials elsewhere required for the sacrificial system of worship" (Joyce 1998, 331).

Scholars disagree on whether there is continuity between the *nāśîʾ* of 34:24 and 37:25 and the *nāśîʾ* of Ezek 40–48. Joyce (1998, 331–32) tends to follow Levenson (1976, 57–99) in a middle way. There is a certain continuity between these *nāśîʾ* passages, as Ezekiel foresees a Davidic prince with limited authority to avoid abuse of power: Judah will be ruled by an apolitically anointed Davidide. Since I ascribe both 34:24 and 37:25 to postexilic editors, I do not see any royal or Davidic office in the *nāśîʾ* of Ezek 40–48. Any Davidic pedigree is not mentioned for this overseer of the temple. The *nāśîʾ* of Ezek 40–48 is an agent of a different kind than the prince and shepherd addressed as "my servant David" in the later versions of Ezek 34 and 37.

Thus, Ezekiel's vision of the future did not include a Davidic king (Rofé 2015, 95–97). For the prophet, the passionate cry of Ps 89 to God to show mercy on the imprisoned king has not been answered. God has other ways for the future.

For postexilic editors of Ezekiel's book, the picture is different. Since Jeremiah had foreseen a future king of Judah, a royal *nāśîʾ* would appear in the editorial additions in Ezek 34:24 and 37:25, and the *ruler* (*môšēl*) of 37:22 would be rephrased as "king" in the longer reworked M recension of

Ezekiel. In this editorial process, it would follow that the allegorical Ezek 17 should include a poem on a new Davidide providing protection for his people (17:22–24).

Deuteronomistic Perspectives

Scribes of the Deuteronomistic school were among the exiled Jerusalem elite in 598. The dating and origins of Deuteronomy has been a matter of dispute the last decades. I belong to "the old school" that finds a preexilic core in the Deuteronomic law book (Deut 12–25), a core that includes Levitical traditions from the Northern Kingdom, transformed in the south after 722. Deuteronomy 1–11 and 26–31 belong to the exilic, Deuteronomistic framework of Deuteronomy, a book that also would receive postexilic polishing and be supplemented with the poems of Deut 32–33.[16] For these exilic scribes, Deuteronomy is the preamble to the DtrH. Second Kings concludes with the rehabilitation of King Jehoiachin and his house at the court of the Babylonian King Amel-Marduk in 561, which suggests that a major recension of the DtrH was finalized at this time:[17]

> [27]In the thirty-seventh year of the exile of King Jehoiachin of Judah, in the twelfth month, on the twenty-seventh day of the month, King Evil-merodach of Babylon, in the year that he began to reign, released King Jehoiachin of Judah from prison; [28]he spoke kindly to him, and gave him a seat above the other seats of the kings who were with him in Babylon. [29]So Jehoiachin put aside his prison clothes. Every day of his life he dined regularly in the king's presence. [30]For his allowance, a regular allowance was given him by the king, a portion every day, as long as he lived. (2 Kgs 25:27–30)

These scribes were not prophets and did not dare to prophesy about a future restoration. But they consciously concluded their long epic with this passage of hope. In the meantime, one should heed the admonition

16. Cf. Weinfeld 1972, 158–71. Otto bolstered this view in 2012 and 2013.

17. DtrH would undergo further editing. Compared to M, the three Samuel scrolls from Qumran and G often preserve earlier and better texts. 2 Sam 21–24 contains late literary additions, only some of these were included in the early-Herodian 1QSamuel scroll (see p. 168). G3 Kingdoms translates a reworked Hebrew version of 1 Kings.

they added to the book of Deuteronomy: "The secret things [i.e., also the future] belong to Yhwh our God, but the revealed things are for us and our children forever, to observe all the words of this torah" (29:28 [29:29], my translation).

A Babylonian cuneiform tablet from the court of Nebuchadnezzar from the year 593 puts the conclusion of 2 Kings into profile. This text prescribes the monthly portions of olive oil to be distributed to Jehoiachin and his house, still in confinement (Weidner 1939, 925–27 [my translation]):

> 15 liters for Jehoiachin, the king of the land of Judah
> 2.1 liters for the five sons of the king of the land of Judah
> 3.4 liters for eight officials of the land of Judah, 0.4 liter each

Another text repeats the same portions of oil for Jehoiachin and his five sons but adds "as given by the hands of (the official) Qanama." The mention of payment for prison wards in one text underlines that in 593 Jehoiachin was still a prisoner.

Deutero-Isaiah: Anointed Emperor and Anointed Prophet

Isaiah 40–55, the book of Deutero-Isaiah, gives meaning in Babylon only when the Persian King Cyrus marched forth and subdued the Middle East. After his victory over the Lydian King Croesus in 547, Cyrus emerges as the leader of the new superpower. In 539 he marched peacefully into the city of Babylon and was hailed as the new ruler in the name of its god Marduk, as evidenced by the Cyrus Cylinder:

> Marduk . . . [12]sought a just ruler to suit his heart, he took him by the hand: Cyrus, king of Anshan, he called, for dominion over the totality he named his name. . . . [14]Marduk, the great lord, who cares for his people, looked with pleasure at his good deeds and his righteous heart. [15]He ordered him to go to Babylon. . . . Like a friend and companion, he went by his side. [17]Without battle and fighting he let him enter his city Babylon. . . . [25]The city of Babylon and all its cult-centres I maintained in well-being. The inhabitants of Babylon . . . [26]I allowed them to find rest from their exhaustion, their servitude I relieved. . . . [30]From Ashur and Susa, [31]Agade, Eshnunna, Zamban, Meturnu and Der as far as the territory of Gutium, . . . whose dwelling-places had of old fallen into ruin [32]—the gods who dwelt

there I returned to their home and let them move into an eternal dwelling. All their people I collected and brought them back to their homes. [33]And the gods of Sumer and Akkad . . . [34]I caused them to move into a dwelling-place pleasing to their hearts in their sanctuaries. . . . [36]The lands in their totality I caused to dwell in a peaceful abode. (Kuhrt 2007, 71–72)

The following year, Cyrus permitted Judean exiles to return and build their temple anew (cf. Cyrus Cylinder, lines 25–36, and Ezra 6:3–5; Ezra 1:2–4 is a more polished Yahwist edition).

According to Ezra 1–2, there were two waves of returnees, first led by Sheshbazzar around 538 and then by Zerubbabel around 520 (cf. 1 Esdr 5:6; Hag 1:1). In the edited version of Ezra, Sheshbazzar is entitled *nāśîʾ* ("prince"; 1:8), possibly a Davidic designation. Ezra 4:4–5 suggests that Sheshbazzar's attempts to rebuild the temple were halted and then launched anew by Zerubbabel in 520. Two different sons of Jehoiachin are named as father of Zerubbabel—Pedaiah (1 Chr 3:19) and Shealtiel (Ezra 3:2–8; 5:2; Hag 1:1, 12, 14; 2:2, 23). The identification of Sheshbazzar with Shenazzar, another son of Jehoiachin, is linguistically problematic. Laato (1998, 186–95) suggests that his mission failed because he was not a Davidide.

According to archaeologists, only a small number returned to the province of Yehud and a few hundred to Jerusalem. The returnees were few; resources were sparse. The great majority of Judeans in Babylon and Persia remained there, building their lives and integrating into society, as admonished by Jer 29:1–7 and evidenced by a large number of texts from the Judean diaspora in the east, from both the sixth and fifth centuries (Pearce 2006; Pearce and Wunsch 2014; Wunsch 2018).

Since Bernard Duhm in 1892, Deutero-Isaiah has commonly been regarded as an individual prophet from around 540 whose book would be seen as a contrasting sequence to Isa 1–39 (Duhm 1914, xxi–xxii). Berges (2008, 38–43) suggests that the originators of the book were a group of Levitical singers with prophetic self-understanding, dating their "oratorium of hope" to 550–515, while Schmid notes: "The form-critical shaping of the material in Isa 40–55 . . . makes the thesis of a prophet 'Deutero-Isaiah' as plausible as ever" (2012, 131).

Deutero-Isaiah demonstrates how Judean scribes were integrated into Babylonian society. His comforting words interact with divine oracles to Assyrian kings, for example, this oracle to Esarhaddon [680–669]:

Fear not, I am Bel, I have shown you mercy!

Fear not, Esarhaddon! I am Bel, speaking to you. I guard the
veins of your heart. . . . Sixty great gods still stand around
you, they have girded the belt around you.

Lift your eyes and look upon me! I am Ishtar of Arbela. . . . I carried you when you were a suckling child. Fear not, praise
me! (Oracles to Esarhaddon 9.1.4 [Cole and Machinist
1998, 139])

Kratz dates Isa 40–48 around 539. He asserts that the titles the prophet attributes to Cyrus—Yhwh's shepherd and messiah, friend of the Lord—make
sense only in retrospect, as interpretation of history.[18] Indeed, that Yhwh
has "grasped his right hand" and "called upon your name" (45:1, 3) is easier to understand if the final version of this text is subsequent to the Cyrus
Cylinder.[19]

The appearance of the prophet antedated Cyrus's seizure of the city of
Babylon. Isaiah 45:1–2 originally anticipated a violent conquest of the city
("I will break in pieces the doors of bronze") and was subsequently edited
to match the historical events, the capture of Babylon without a fight, "to
open doors before him" (Kratz 1991, 26; Blum 2009, 143). Similarly, Schmid
(2012, 131–32) notes that the truth of the prophet's message is to be seen in it
being proclaimed beforehand, which is a strong argument that the prophet
indeed appeared before the fall of Babylon.

In the concluding chapter, the prophet proclaims the nation heir to the
Davidic promises. Other prophetic passages describe the gentile nations
coming to pay homage to the son of David; in this text they come to the
people of Zion. The first line, 55:3, is phrased as an address in the plural:

³Incline your ear, and come to me;
listen, so that you may live. [second-person plural]
I will make with you an everlasting covenant—
my faithfulness to David.

18. Kratz 1991; 2017; cf. Cyrus Cylinder, line 15: "Like a friend and companion, he
(Marduk) went by his side."

19. Cf. Sparks 2005, 398: "In the Cyrus cylinder . . . Cyrus claims divine sanction for his
conquest of Babylon by citing the blessing of Marduk, the chief deity of his new subjects.
. . . In this light, one wonders how much the Hebrew view of Cyrus as Yhwh's 'messiah'
was influenced by Persian propaganda."

> [4]Him I made a witness to the peoples,
> a leader and commander for the nations.
> [5]See, you shall call on a nation that you do not know [second-
>   person singular],
> a nation that do not know you shall run to you,
> for the sake of Yhwh your God, the Holy One of Israel,
> for he has glorified you. (Isa 55:3–5, my translation)

For this prophet, there is no role for the son of David in the restoration of Israel.[20] The anointed leader is not the son of David, but Cyrus—the present ruler of the empire and redeemer of nations. Cyrus has replaced David as anointed king and temple builder. Yhwh calls him *rēʿî* ("my close friend") and *məšîḥô* ("his anointed"). Yhwh calls Cyrus by name and gives him a name of honor:

> [44:28]He who says to Cyrus, "my close friend"[21]—
> he shall carry out all my purpose;
> and who says of Jerusalem, "It shall be rebuilt,"
> and of the temple, "Your foundation shall be laid."
> [45:1]Thus says Yhwh to his anointed, to Cyrus,
> whose right hand I have grasped
> to subdue nations before him
> and strip kings of their robes,
> to open doors before him,
> and the gates shall not be closed.
> [2]"I will go before you
> and level the mountains,
> I will break in pieces the doors of bronze
> and cut through the bars of iron,
> [3]I will give you the treasures of darkness
> and riches hidden in secret places,
> so that you may know that it is I, Yhwh,
> the God of Israel, who call you by name.

20. Laato (1998, 195) disagrees, suggesting that 55:3–5 makes the nation's return to Judah a premessianic act, without abolishing the Davidic hope.

21. Following a suggestion by Moshe Weinfeld (personal communication), I read *rēʿî* ("my close friend"). M vocalizes *rōʿî* ("my shepherd"), a common epithet for the son of David (G has a different text); cf. my note on Zech 13:7 (see p. 155 n. 11).

⁴For the sake of Jacob my servant
and Israel my chosen,
I have called you by name
and given you a name of honor,
even though you do not know me." (Isa 44:28–45:4, my
translation)

¹⁴Yhwh loves him;
he shall perform his purpose on Babylon
and his arm shall be against the Chaldeans.
¹⁵I, even I have spoken, I have called him,
I have brought him, and he will prosper in his way. (Isa 48:14–15,
my translation)

Cyrus allied himself with priests and temple officials of the conquered nations, as did his successors. Fried (2002, 383–89) notes that priests of powerful temples delivered up to their Persian conquerors the titles and ideologies of their earlier local kings. The Cyrus Cylinder presents the emperor as the chosen one of Marduk, the chief god of Babylon. As crown prince, his son Cambyses (559–530) participated in the New Year Akitu festival and was taken by hand by the god Nabu. When Cambyses later conquered Egypt, he was hailed as pharaoh, King of Upper and Lower Egypt, offspring of (the god) Re. A Susa inscription hails Darius the Great (521–486) as chosen by the supreme god Re and being the god Atum in effigy.

Deutero-Isaiah evinces a similar application of Davidic theology to Cyrus. Cyrus is Yhwh's anointed, his beloved, his close friend (or shepherd), the one who fulfills his purposes, the initiator of the rebuilding of the temple. Titles and characteristics of the Davidic monarch were now applied to Cyrus—although I would not say with Fried that the prophet saw Cyrus as "in actuality the genuine Judean king":

Deutero-Isaiah was convinced that Cyrus was in actuality the genuine Judean king, i.e., YHWH's anointed, his Messiah, because Cyrus was able to do what a legitimate king must do. . . . He rebuilt the temple, ordered the temple vessels replaced in it, and permitted the Jews to return to worship their God in Zion restored. (Fried 2002, 392–93)

Babylonian and Egyptian inscriptions enroll Cyrus and his successors into a polytheistic thought-world. Egyptians could hail Cambyses as a representative of God on earth. In contrast, Deutero-Isaiah integrates Cyrus into a strict monotheism: Yhwh is the only living god, he is the one able to foresee future history and reveal it to his prophet. He is the sovereign creator who now recasts Davidic theology when he shapes history and opens a new window for his people, with Cyrus as chosen king and temple builder. What God once did through David and Solomon, he now does through Cyrus.

The Servant Songs: Cyrus and the Prophet Reinterpreted?

Duhm was the first to identify the four Servant Songs: Isa 42:1–7; 49:1–9a; 50:4–11; 52:13–53:12. Since there are good arguments to date the first two songs around 540, I discuss these four songs here without going into a comprehensive discussion (for a survey of early scholarship, see Rowley 1965, 3–93; more recently, Blum 2009).

The songs of the suffering servant color the lament of the individual singer in the Teacher Hymns of the Qumran Thanksgiving Hymns (Elgvin 2005, 30–32; Collins 2010c, 145–47), as well as two Qumran songs on the end-time priest (see pp. 241–48). New Testament writings evince an individual interpretation of these songs (Brooke 2005, 148–57), as do a few messiah texts of the Talmud (see pp. 294–96).[22]

From the exegetes Ibn Ezra and Rashi (eleventh and twelfth centuries),[23] Jewish interpreters have remained with a collective reading—Israel suffering for the nations, an interpretation shared by many modern scholars.[24] First some initial observations:

22. Jesus's understanding of his ministry was substantially formed by the Servant Songs combined with the Son of Man passage in Dan 7:9–14 (cf. Moule 1982, 83–87). New Testament references may be classified as sequels to or transformation of the Servant Songs (their hypotexts) in a new textual and historical context.

23. According to Origen (*Contra Celsum* 1.55), Jewish exegetes of his time argued for a collective reading. However, rabbinic writings do not preserve any traces of such an interpretation.

24. I follow the "Duhm tradition," which sees the Servant Songs as a particular transtextual strand within Isa 40–66. Some scholars who identify the servant with Israel would disagree. But they tend to ignore that subsequent biblical (MJer 30:18–22; Zech 12:10), Qumran, New Testament, and early Jewish traditions relate the Servant Songs and the suffering servant to the fate and odyssey of individual figures, so these scholars effectively disconnect the songs from their close interpretation history. Thus, one should not take a *Farewell to the Servant Songs* (the title of Mettinger's 1983 booklet). Mettinger recognizes

- It cannot be ascertained that all the songs originate with Deutero-Isaiah.
- The descriptions of the servant in the four songs do not necessarily refer to the same figure, and ancient readers did not necessarily read these four texts together as a group.
- "Servant" is a favorite term in Deutero-Isaiah, a book that has undergone thorough editing—the text uses this term on different figures, including Israel.
- The first three songs are divided into two parts. Isaiah 42:5 and 49:7 separate the second part with "thus says Yhwh," preceding words of Yhwh addressed to the servant. In all three cases, the second part could have been added by the same prophetic author or a later scribe.
- Isaiah 61:1–4 is transtextually linked to the other songs, in particular 42:5–7 and 49:8–9a. If at least one Servant Song is original within Isa 40–55, we can confidently identify a process of textual growth.
- Isaiah 49:3 identifies the servant with Israel. "Israel" may here be an explanatory addition (although it is present in all textual witnesses). Isaiah 49:5 gives the servant the task to "bring Jacob back to God so that Israel is gathered to him"—clearly portraying the servant as an individual with a ministry toward the nation Israel.
- The servant in the fourth song is portrayed with both individual and collective traits, and prophetic, royal, and cultic terminology is used.

Isaiah 42:1–4, 5–7 has parallels in Persian royal ideology as outlined in Achaemenid inscriptions, such as the Cyrus Cylinder and the inscriptions of Darius I (522–486):

> By the favor of Ahuramazda I am king; Ahuramazda bestowed kingship upon me. These are the peoples who obey me . . . in all twenty-three peoples. These are the peoples who obeyed me; by the favor of Ahuramazda they became my faithful subjects, they brought me tribute. (Darius's Bisitun Inscription, explaining how he accessed the throne)

> A great god is Ahuramazda, who created earth and heaven, created humankind, and gave well-being to man. He made Darius king and bestowed upon Darius the king kingship over this wide earth, in which there are many lands.

---

only *one* servant throughout Isa 40–55, viz. Israel, and saw the songs fully integrated in their textual contexts. For a critical response to Mettinger, see Hermisson 1984 and Blum 2009.

Ahuramazda, when he saw this earth in commotion, bestowed it upon me and made me king—I am king. By the favor of Ahuramazda I put it down in its place. They did what I said to them, as was my desire.

I am a friend of what is right, not of what is wrong. It is not my wish that the strong should inflict harm on the weak, neither that the strong should have harm done to him by the weak. . . . To the man who is a follower of the lie I am no friend. I am not hot-tempered. I hold my anger firmly under control by my thinking power and rule over my impulses. (Darius's tomb inscription in Naqsh-i Rustam)[25]

If 42:1–7 was the only Servant Song we had, seeing the song as yet another Deutero-Isaianic oracle on Cyrus would make sense. As one who "will bring forth justice to the nations" and not "be crushed until he has established justice on the earth," while "the coastlands wait for his teaching"—this description could suit the imperial ruler who "collected all their people and brought them back to their homes" (Cyrus Cylinder, line 32). Kratz (1991; 2017), who delimits the Deutero-Isaianic book to Isa 40–48, identifies the servant of 42:1–7 with Cyrus, a proposal that has not received wide acceptance.

Blum (2009) has a brilliant analysis of Isa 40–55 with the Servant Songs in focus. He separates a carefully arranged early core in 42:1–49:12, designed by the prophet. This *Grundkomposition* is chiastically formatted around the Cyrus oracle in 44:24–45:7 and is flanked by the two Servant Songs, each is separated from the Cyrus text by two short hymnic passages (42:8–13 and 44:23; 45:8 and 48:20–21). In both cases the two hymnic passages are interspersed by long intermediate texts (42:14–44:22; 45:9–48:16). In both songs, the servant is called to be "a covenant for the people" and "light for the nations." He is called to liberate prisoners and has a role vis-à-vis Israel (49:5–6). "Go out" is the servant's call to those in darkness, the same words used by the prophet in the preceding passage: "Go out from Babylon, flee from Chaldea!" (48:20)—a proclamation that Blum dates after Cyrus's calling to the Judeans to return to their land and restore their sanctuary, followed by an asserted weak response from Judeans, who were happily residing in a foreign land. The prophet's exhortation in 48:20 to his people to make their exodus from Babylon is a direct response to Yhwh's call to the servant (49:8–9, my translation):

25. livius.org/articles/person/darius-the-great/9-death/.

[8]Thus says Yhwh:
I created you and appointed you a covenant for the people
restoring the land,
allotting anew the desolate holdings,
[9]saying to the prisoners, "Go free,"
to those who are in darkness, "Show yourselves!"
They shall pasture along the roads
and feed on the bare hills.

Elsewhere in the *Grundkomposition*, Yhwh complains that another servant of his, that is, Israel, is blind and unable to fulfill its calling to proclaim Yhwh to the nations (42:18–20; 43:10–12). Consequently, Blum identifies the servant of the first two songs as the prophet himself, whose calling is to realize Israel's mission.[26] In 49:4, we encounter him lamenting the lack of headway among his people for his prophetic ministry: "I have labored in vain, I have spent my strength for nothing and vanity; yet surely my cause is with Yhwh, and my reward with my God" (NRSV adapted)—an echo of "he will not grow faint or be crushed" (42:4).

The prophet has remarkable self-confidence: the calling of Cyrus (44:24–45:7) is surrounded by two songs on Yhwh's servant-prophet, whose mission will reflect the ministry of a righteous king and surpass even that of Cyrus himself. The word of Yhwh—through the prophet—will fulfill God's purpose and implement his will among the nations.

In 50:4–9 we again hear the lament of the prophet, still being haunted by his fellow Judeans but trusting in God's guidance and protection. The *Grundkomposition* was subsequently extended, opening with a prologue (40:1–5, 9–11) and closing with an epilogue (52:7–10). The final stratum of Isa 40–55 would include the song of the suffering servant, which led to a relecture of the earlier songs. At this stage the servant of all four songs was reinterpreted as the people Israel, having suffered among the nations, now forgiven by its God (40:1–2) and given the mission to expiate for the nations, suffer as into death, and experience a spiritual resurrection. At the same time, two additions in the second song make clear who the servant now is: "You are my servant" would be supplemented by "Israel" (49:3), and 49:7 would describe him as despised by nations and rulers. Thus, Isa 40–55 (except for a few additions) can now be read as "the Servant-Israel-book." Blum finds this relecture so embedded

---

26. Here Blum follows earlier scholars who identify the servant of all four songs as Deutero-Isaiah himself (Hermisson, Steck, Janowski).

in the message of the prophet that it remains possible that the two last stages of literary growth were implemented by Deutero-Isaiah himself.

Blum finds no traces in Isa 48–53 of founding the temple or building the sanctuary, of the perspectives of Haggai and Zechariah, or of allusions to the two anointed ones of Zech 4. Thus, these chapters and the relecture of the Servant Songs should be dated between Cyrus's edict of 538 and 520.

I can easily follow Blum's analysis up to the second song in Isa 49. He presents convincing arguments for seeing the first two songs (without 49:7 on the despised one and "Israel" in 49:3) as integral in the book of Deutero-Isaiah, as songs reflecting the calling and mission of the prophet. In the first song, the mission of the prophetic servant mirrors and surpasses that of Cyrus vis-à-vis the nations. And the addition in 49:7 represents a later pasting of colors from the suffering painted in the last two songs, into the second one.

However, there is no similar "repainting" of the righteous and victorious servant in 42:1–9. Thus, Blum's suggested relecture is not fully implemented. I prefer to see another author behind the suffering servant portrayed in the last two songs. They indeed represent a relecture of the first two songs, but this second author did not enforce his understanding of a servant of another kind into Isa 42 and 49. He consciously painted a servant different from that of the first two songs. The last two songs represent sequels to the first two hypotexts; they offer new episodes following a complete hypotext. The insertion in the second song of a figure "despised by nations and slave under rulers" (49:7) represents a yet later addition. If this third scribal hand indeed identified the servant with (suffering) Israel, the contrast with the servant of 49:5 who is given a ministry vis-à-vis Israel/Jacob was not resolved.

Isaiah 50:4–9 is a song in the first person of a prophetic figure who listens to the Lord Yhwh. With his word he sustains the weary (50:4–5a). In 50:5b–7 the speaker complains of trials and torments, in 50:8–9 he is confident that Yhwh will rescue and vindicate him. Subsequently there is a change of speaker in 50:10–11; only here is "servant" used about the suffering prophetic figure. The term *'ădōnāy yhwh* ("the Lord Yhwh") is used four times in 50:4–9, while it is used only twice in Isa 40–49 (40:10; 49:22).[27] This is one of many indications that the third and fourth Servant Songs should be seen as later inserts into the Deutero-Isaianic book.[28] The suffering prophet

---

27. Isa 48:16b is difficult to read; cf. the BHK apparatus. *'ădōnāy* ("the Lord") is not rendered in G and is likely secondary here.

28. Schmid (2012, 136) comments: "In the course of time the basic Deutero-Isaiah writ-

of 50:4–9 does not see his trials as expiation for others, and 50:10–11 has a different perspective. Thus, 50:4–9 can be read as a bridging passage that "prepares the way" for the fourth song.

The literature on 52:13–53:12 is seemingly without end. Here the servant is portrayed with traits that could fit the exiled people but also as an individual, a member of the people, with a ministry vis-à-vis the "we-group" in front of "the many." If the servant is an individual who suffers for his nations, the "we-group" represents Israel, and "the many" represents the nations with their kings; if the servant is Israel, the "we-group" should be identified with the nations and their kings (Blum 2009, 149).

Blum's reading of the last song as a "Servant-Israel-song" is a viable reading; less convincing is his reading of Isa 40–55 as "the Servant-Israel-book." For the understanding of the suffering servant, I prefer to keep both options open—there are good arguments both for a collective and an individual interpretation of the servant (I have a slight preference for the latter). With an individual reading, the "many" may signify the Judean people at large, the small population in Judah as well as the majority residing in the diaspora. And the servant would take upon himself God's judgment on the errant people and carry their transgressions as an offering for sin. Some scholars interpret ’āšām in 53:10 in a legal way as a secular notion of guilt reparation. In light of the many references to sin, guilt, and transgressions in this chapter, the term should more likely be understood in a cultic way as a reparation for sin (Blenkinsopp 2016).

The close parallels between Isa 53:7–8 and Jer 11:19 may assist in dating the fourth song. In both texts God's elect is led as a lamb to the slaughter (although different terms are used for lamb), and the servant will be cut off from the land of the living (my translation):

Isa 53:7–8	Jer 11:19
like a lamb [śeh] led to the slaughter	but I was like a lamb [kebeś] led to the slaughter
for he was cut off from the land of the living	let us cut him off from the land of the living

ing was expanded repeatedly. . . . Thus within chapters 40–55 we can identify with some certainty the polemic against other gods . . . as a particular kind of addition. Likewise, the Zion texts in chapters 42–55 . . . seem to have entered the book in succession. Finally, we should also mention the Servant Songs, which in the traditional view were first created independently but now are more frequently thought also to be redactions added to the main text."

Jeremiah 11:19 is probably the earlier text that influenced the other. The verse is nearly identical in M and the G *Vorlage* and was likely present in an early Jeremiah scroll in the late sixth century. The use of an already recognized Jeremiah scroll suggests a postexilic date for Isa 53. The image of Jeremiah as the suffering prophet is one of many colors used to paint the image of the servant in postexilic times. While royal, prophetic, and cultic terms are used in the portrayal of the servant, the combined evidence of Jer 11:19, Isa 50:4–11, and Isa 52:13–53:12 emphasizes the servant of the last two songs as a prophetic figure—which in itself should not exclude a collective reading.

There are also Mosaic colors in the song. Von Rad (1965, 260–62) points to the Deuteronomic image of Moses who goes into God's presence on behalf of the people (Exod 32:30–34; Deut 3:23–26; 4:21; 5:20–24 [5:23–27]; 9:18–29), emphasizing that the servant is portrayed as a prophet like Moses.

As argued by Blum, the first two Servant Songs set in motion an interpretative process where another figure was designated "my servant." However, this relecture should rather be dated after Deutero-Isaiah. If one goes for the individual interpretation of the servant, the last two songs may be intended either as foreseeing a future or end-time figure or as a description of a servant God already had sent to his people—or a combination of these two options.

I imagine an early fifth-century scribe who struggled to see the Deutero-Isaianic predictions realized in Zion, a small temple village in a poor and powerless province. The images of Moses as a prophet interceding for his people and Jeremiah as the suffering prophet persecuted by some of his own gave colors to the songs he composed about a suffering servant.

Could there be yet another figure from Israel's long odyssey through history that was perceived as a model for this servant? An early proposal by Sellin may be reconsidered: in addition to the interplay with the figures of Moses and Jeremiah, the servant of the last two songs could have Zerubbabel as a model.[29] Perhaps meditating on the Persians' violent removal of Zerubbabel (commonly assumed by many scholars; see pp. 148–49) and Isa 40:2 ("that her iniquity [*ʾăwōnāh*] is expiated;[30] for she has received at

---

29. In consecutive publications, Sellin suggests a number of biblical figures as type for the suffering servant: Zerubbabel (Sellin 1898), Jehoiachin (Sellin 1930), and Moses (Sellin 1937).

30. The word *ʾāwōn* ("misdeed, iniquity") recurs in Isa 53:5 with reference to the "we-group" and in 53:11 to "the many."

the hand of Yhwh double for all her sins"; NRSV adapted), he saw the need for a servant of Yhwh of a different kind, who through trials would take upon himself God's judgment on the errant Judean people and carry their trespasses as a sin offering.

With Zerubbabel as a model, 49:8–9a could be reread as referring to the Judean leader sent by the Persians to "restore the land, allocate portions (of land) to the desolate, and call out to those who are in bonds, 'Come out!'" If Zerubbabel's fate plays in the background, this can explain the royal features in the last Servant Song.[31]

Summing up, both a collective and individual interpretation of the suffering servant are viable readings of the biblical text. However, up to the end of the rabbinic period, Jewish interpreters would see the two texts of the suffering servant as prefiguring the innocent suffering of righteous individuals.

In the fifth-century Isaiah scroll, the Cyrus oracle of Isa 44–45 and the four Servant Songs would resonate with another song. Isaiah 61, in particular 61:1–4, is related to the first two songs, with a close intertextual link to 42:5–7 and 49:8–9a. The song is a programmatic self-presentation by a prophetic figure, anointed to proclaim freedom to captives and prepare God's planting his people anew in the land. This text may preserve the self-presentation of the prophetic voice called Trito-Isaiah.[32] The text alludes to Elijah's anointing of Elisha to be prophet in his place (1 Kgs 19:16) and thus demonstrates the importance the prophet ascribes to himself and his ministry of interpreting and creating history for Judah on the scene of nations. In the full Isaiah scroll, both Cyrus and the prophetic voice of Isa 61 would be denoted as "anointed" for related but different tasks—and 1QIsa[a] denotes the suffering servant in the same way (52:14; see below).

There is no distant hope for the house of David in Isa 40–66. In 55:1–5, God's love toward David is transformed into a covenant with the nation, which is exhorted to listen to the prophet. The description of redemption and new creation expected by Trito-Isaiah (Isa 65–66) contains no job description for a Davidide.

---

31. In Laato's view (1998, 184), the task of Deutero-Isaiah's messiah (i.e., the servant) is to complete the actions of Cyrus in leading the people back to Judah and reorganize the cult, a task the "son of oil" Zerubbabel took upon himself.

32. Duhm sees Isa 61 as Trito-Isaiah's programmatic presentation and suggests that Isa 61–66 originally opened the Trito-Isaiah scroll (1914, xx, 423–24). In contrast, Paul here finds the voice of Deutero-Isaiah: "In the first three verses . . . Deutero-Isaiah's appointment to prophecy is described (in the first-person) and his mission delineated" (Paul 2012, 536–42 at 536).

When various scrolls were combined into Isa 1–66, would the message of Isa 40–66 remain as the main proclamation? Or would the few Davidic promises from the first part of the book (7:14–17; 9:5–6 [9:6–7]; 11:1–10) still have a lasting meaning for the readers? Isaiah 11:10, a postexilic addition to the Davidic promise in 11:1–9, would affirm the future son of David as a banner for the nations. Thus, the message of redemption in the full Isaiah scroll is not one-dimensional.

The Great Isaiah Scroll: The Servant Is Anointed

The three Qumran scrolls preserving text from Isa 53 contain some important textual variants; they include a messianic reading in the Great Isaiah Scroll.

53:3b—"sickness being known and as hiding face for him/us" (M); the reading "knowing sickness and as hiding his face from us" (1QIsaᵃ,ᵇ ≈ G) is preferable.

53:11a—"he shall see, be satisfied" (M); "he shall *see light* and be satisfied" (1QIsaᵃ,ᵇ, 4QIsaᵈ ≈ G) is preferable. With 1QIsaᵃ, this stich concludes with "be satisfied," as indicated in 1QIsaᵃ with a long word space and the verbal form "and be satisfied" (imperfect with *waw* copulative). The verbal form of 4QIsaᵈ and 1QIsaᵇ carries the same meaning, which suggests the same division of 53:11a as in 1QIsaᵃ.

53:11b—"through his knowledge, the righteous, *my servant*, shall justify the many" (M); "through his knowledge, the righteous, *his servant*, shall justify the many" (1QIsaᵃ, 4QIsaᵈ) is preferable. 1QIsaᵃ and 4QIsaᵈ (contra the DJD editors) clearly read ʿabdô ("his servant"). The Masoretic ʿabdî ("my servant") is the minority reading, and ʿabdô runs easier in the context. The verse is made up by three stichs: (a) through the anguish of his soul he shall see light and be satisfied; (b) through his knowledge, the righteous, his servant, shall justify the many; (c) and he shall bear their iniquities.

53:12b—"he carried the sin of many and interceded for transgressors" (M); "he carried the sins of many and interceded for their transgressions" (1QIsaᵃ,ᵇ, 4QIsaᵈ) is preferable; "he carried the sins of many, and because of their sins he was given over" (G). In all these cases, M represents the minority reading, one textual witness against a plurality of two, three, or four textual witnesses.

1QIsa^b is a quality M-like scroll from 50–25. 4QIsa^d (which preserves Isa 53:8–12) is a quality scroll dated to 30–68 CE.

Isaiah was translated into Greek around 145 (Seeligmann 2003, 50, 233–51). GIsa 53 is slightly targumic in style and should be used only with caution as a text-critical witness. Two tendencies can be identified: (1) God is not depicted as willingly causing the servant's suffering, but as wanting to save and vindicate him (53:4b, 5bα, 6b, 9a, 10aα, 10b–11a); (2) the "we-group" is depicted as siding with God and the servant throughout the text (53:1a, 2b–3, 4b, 8aα).

1QIsa^a 52:14 reads "so I anointed [*māšaḥtî*] his appearance above any man, and his form above any sons of man," for M's "so marred [*mišḥat*] was his appearance, beyond that of men, and his form beyond that of any sons of man." The Masoretic pointing *mišḥat* hardly makes sense and is usually corrected to *mōšḥāt* ("blemished").

The text-critical value of 1QIsa^a is a subject of controversy.[33] It has often been brushed aside as a "vulgar" scroll or as a scroll written by creative, independent scribes. It remains, however, the oldest of the well-preserved and carefully written Isaiah scrolls. Further, recent material analysis of small margin pieces of 1QIsa^a and 1QS demonstrates that these two scrolls from around 100 are written on parchment of a remarkable quality (Rabin 2016, 66–67). In this respect, these two scrolls (and the Temple Scroll as well) stand out from the large majority of the scrolls found in the Judean Desert. 1QIsa^a should therefore not be classified as a vulgar scroll. While the two scribes at times handled the text in a creative way, the scroll was highly valued by the sectarian community behind the scroll—as was its "cousin" 1QS, written on parchment prepared in the same professional workshop.

For the creative scribe of 1QIsa^a, the servant is anointed, and 52:13–15 is consistently read on the elevation of the servant.[34] 1QIsa^a clearly

---

33. Blum (2009, 148–49) often prefers readings evinced by 1QIsa^a. Thus, in 53:10, he reads with 1QIsa^a: "It was the will of Yhwh to crush him, and he pierced him," reading *wəyəhalleluhû* (*polal*) for the problematic *heḥĕlî*, referring to the same two verbs used in 53:5: "pierced for our transgressions and crushed for our misdeeds." The pierced one in Zech 12:10 likely alludes to Isa 53:5, 10 (different verbs are used for "pierce").

34. One could compare the creative targumist behind Pseudo-Jonathan to Isa 52:13–53:12, who opens with "see my servant the messiah will prosper." This targumist attributes all the suffering to the nations and makes the messiah the vindicator throughout the text. This chapter may belong to the earliest strata of Targum Pseudo-Jonathan (around 100 CE; see pp. 270–75).

contains a *lectio facilior* (easier reading) that makes better sense in the context of 52:13–15—but it is the minority reading (against M, 1QIsa^b, G, Syriac). It remains, however, the only reading that makes 52:14 a logical bridge between 52:13 and 52:15, so that this reading should not easily be brushed aside as secondary. *Māšaḥtî* may either be the original reading or represent a conscious messianic interpretative rereading around 100: the suffering servant is an anointed minister of God, as Cyrus was in his time and his way, and as the anonymous prophet proclaimed about himself in 61:1.

Late-Exilic Perspectives

What were the perspectives when the Israelites approached the end of seventy years of exile as numbered in Jer 29:10? Cyrus had commissioned Sheshbazzar governor of Judea to rebuild the temple, but the plans to rebuild the sanctuary had been halted (Ezra 4). Excavations and surveys of the settlements that archaeologists are able to identify suggest that the return to the land was small in scale. A few thousand lived in Judea and a couple hundred in Jerusalem. To find the local power center one had to look to the provincial governor's seat in Mizpah.

The majority of the Israelites made their lives in the eastern diaspora, and a substantial number resided in Egypt. Cuneiform texts show Judeans well integrated into Babylonian society and in no need of returning to the land.

The prophecies and expectations for the future were pluriform and do not paint a single picture. GJer 30:18–22 promises a future "ruler" in the land (similar to Hos 2:2 [1:11]); while GJer 23:5–6; Isa 11:1–5; and Amos 9:11–12 foresee a new Davidic leader. The two latter passages received additions that painted the coming Davidic kingdom in paradisiac colors.

In contrast, the "crazy prophet" Ezekiel expected a restoration without a Davidic ruler. The book's symbolic blueprint for a new temple province within the Persian Empire sketches sacrificial tasks for a priestly ruler or prince. The Deuteronomists concluded their epic with an optimistic sign for the future, the rehabilitation of King Jehoiachin at the Babylonian court in the year 561. But they could say no more than that the hidden future is in God's hands.

The rise of Cyrus caused Deutero-Isaiah to draw a new picture: the people as a collective are heirs to the Davidic promises (55:1–5). Yhwh's anointed, close friend, and elect servant is Cyrus (44:24–45:7), the present redeemer and temple builder. Yhwh's presence will return to Zion, and his flock will follow. The restoration was foreseen within the framework of the Persian Empire.

There was no established biblical collection at this time. Deuteronomy and the Tetrateuch were growing into shape. Deuteronomistic circles in Babylon attributed authority to Deuteronomy and secondarily to DtrH, but we do not know how many of the exiles in the east shared this view. Prophetic scrolls were around and were steadily being edited and extended. But who is a true and who is a false prophet?

Some prophetic scrolls were recognized as having been important at junctures in the past, but could Proto-Isaiah and Amos contain any inspired words to the post-587 communities? Deuteronomistic editing of Jeremiah and Amos shows that these two prophets were highly regarded by the Deuteronomistic circles. An authoritative collection of prophetic writings, as reflected in Sirach, is still far into the future.

The texts discussed above should be seen as some of the voices competing for attention and authority among the Judeans in the east and the small community in Judah. A monotheistic and exclusive Yahwism was held by some, but certainly not all, Judeans. The cuneiform texts in the Sofer Collection show a pluriform and tolerant Yahwism held by many in Babylon. And the Elephantine archives show a similar picture among Judeans in late fifth-century Egypt (Pearce and Wunsch 2014; Granerød 2016, 244–58, 324–40).

Thus, we do now know to which extent and by whom the scrolls discussed here were accepted as inspired or authoritative. Different Yahwist voices outlined a variety of views on the future of the Israelites and their leaders, and some of these voices claimed prophetic authority. The future is open, and only time will show which prophecies would be vindicated—in the short term or further into the future.

In a theological perspective one could say that Yhwh "kept the cards close to his chest." As history would be rolling its way, he would face different choices and only in time put the cards on the table and show the trump. In a biblical perspective, God's way is not predetermined but is being crystallized during his co-wandering with his people through history. One could compare a later rabbinic dictum:

Rabbi Joshua ben Levi opposed two verses, as it is written, *See, one like a Son of Man came with the clouds of heaven* (Dan 7:13), while elsewhere it is written, *See, your king comes to you, humble and riding upon an ass*

(Zech 9:7). This means, if they are meritorious, he will come with the clouds of heaven; if not, humble and riding on an ass. (Babylonian Talmud, tractate Sanhedrin 98a, part of a long collage of messiah texts in Sanhedrin 97–99; see pp. 294–95)

Some of the scribes involved would have knowledge of texts with perspectives and expectations different from their own. They may have thought along lines like this: "We do not know what kind of a future the Lord will create for his people and what kind of leaders he will install. But we have to take care of the old texts with different testimonies from our fathers. Then it remains in Yhwh's hands how he will fulfill and implement the promises we and our predecessors faithfully have written down."

CHAPTER 5

The Return to Judah and Messianic Hopes

In 538, Cyrus gave orders for Judeans to return and rebuild the temple, implementing the policy reflected in the Cyrus Cylinder. In Ezra 1:2–4 we find an Israelite, polished version of Cyrus's decree in Hebrew, while 6:3–4 seems to preserve the Aramaic original, more generally formulated and less Yahwistic in tone.

The prophecies of Deutero-Isaiah were only partly fulfilled, the return being small in scale, and Jerusalem far from shining of Yhwh's glory between the nations. Ezra 4:4–5 suggests that Sheshbazzar's attempts to rebuild the temple were halted and later launched anew by Zerubbabel in 520 (cf. Ezra 4:24; 6:13–22; Hag 1:1–2:4; Zech 4:6–9). If Sheshbazzar indeed was a Davidide cannot be determined. And the texts do not reveal how Sheshbazzar and Zerubbabel fared and ended their lives. But Zech 6:9–15 suggests that Zerubbabel was taken out of leadership while Joshua still held the office of high priest.

After the disappearance of Zerubbabel, the governors of the fifth and fourth centuries were secular officials of the Persian Empire, not connected to the Davidic line. While Mizpah, 12 km north of Jerusalem, was the Babylonians' administrative center in exilic times, the Persians relocated the governor's seat and his administration to Ramat Rachel, 4 km south of Jerusalem. The site, which had survived the destructions of 587, was thoroughly rebuilt. The Persian-era compound comprised a high-standard residence with an exclusive garden in royal style as well as rooms for scribes and administrative officers (Lipschits et al. 2017, 95–116). In comparison, Jerusalem remained a poor temple village throughout the fifth, fourth, and third centuries. One could speculate if the high priest would choose to live in Ramat Rachel rather than Jerusalem, either on his own initiative or at the behest of the Persian governor, to secure governmental control of the temple leadership.

In 331, the province of Yehud was integrated into the empire of Alexander the Great. After his death in 323, the empire was divided. Alexander's commander Ptolemy founded a new pharaonic dynasty in Egypt, while Seleucus ruled the Levant from Damascus. During the third century, Yehud remained under Ptolemaic rule, while the two dynasties fought each other for generations. In this time period the high priest functioned both as civil and religious leader of Yehud—there was no governor at his side (VanderKam 2004, 122–23).

Daniel 11 is a description of the wars between Egypt and Syria following the death of Alexander the Great ("the wars of the Diadochi") hidden in a symbolic, prophetic veil, presented as prophecy given by the legendary hero Daniel, but in fact being some kind of a chronicle written after these wars, a *vaticinium ex eventu* text.

In the Ptolemaic period, Ramat Rachel would lose its central role in the province. The early Hasmonean rulers would again use it as a collection center for agricultural products, before the large compound was purposely and thoroughly leveled to the ground by the Hasmoneans in the late second century (Lipschits et al. 2017, 113–18).

Settlement and History of Postexilic Judah:
An Archaeological View

What is the social context of postexilic messianism? Messianic hopes focus on a restoration and renewal of Judah and Jerusalem. An understanding of social realities in Judah and Jerusalem during the centuries following the exile will set the expectations into profile. And there seems to be a clash between the description of postexilic Judah and Jerusalem in the books of Ezra and Nehemiah and the remains that archaeologists have unearthed in their excavations and surveys. Recent archaeological findings suggest a sparsely inhabited Judah, with Jerusalem being a tiny temple village until the early second century—in noted contrast to Ezra's description of a large wave of returnees and Nehemiah's story of the building of Jerusalem's walls under the leadership of regional officers.

According to archaeologists, before the Maccabean period the province of Yehud was sparsely populated and Jerusalem a village only.[1] Faust and

---

1. Faust characterizes Yehud during the entire Persian period as a post-collapse society (2012, 125).

Finkelstein give lower estimates than their predecessors on the population of Persian-period Yehud. For Faust, the population slowly grew from around 10,000 up to 20,000 or 30,000 (2012, 119–25), while Finkelstein estimates the population of Yehud at around 12,000 (2018, 57–59, 76, 137).[2]

In Persian times, the settled part of Jerusalem was concentrated in the City of David. Based on the inhabited area (2.0–2.5 hectares), it housed only a few hundred people. Finkelstein estimates the population of Jerusalem in 200 at approximately 500—and it was lower in Persian times (2018, 13; cf. Faust 2012; Geva 2007, 2015). Jerusalem was no more than a temple village. The scribal milieu connected to the temple would be small, even though there likely were scribes competent in Hebrew literature in Mizpah (until the mid-fourth century)[3] and in the administrative center Ramat Rachel.

The town did not grow much during the third century. According to Dan 11:14–16, 20, neither Judea nor Jerusalem escaped the trials of the wars of the Diadochi, Josephus noting that Antiochus III ordered the restoration of "their city which had been destroyed by the hazards of war" and its repopulation by "bringing back to it those who have been dispersed abroad" (*Antiquities* 12.138). A scribal flowering in the third century is therefore unlikely.

Remarkably few remains from Ptolemaic and Seleucid Jerusalem have been discovered (Finkelstein 2012, 55–57). However, the 2018–19 Givati excavations (in the upper western part of the City of David ridge) identified traces of Persian-era squatters (fifth–third centuries) in the ruins of a large eighth-century public building. In the early second century, a large public building measuring 70 m × 12 m was built on top of these ruins (dated by Hellenistic, pre-Hasmonean pottery). Two or three contemporary buildings have been identified at the western slopes of the City of David, suggesting expansion westward in the early second century under Antiochus III (Gadot and Shalev 2019, Yuval Gadot in personal communication).

Following his conquest of Judea in 198 (*Antiquities* 12.133–44), Antiochus III gave Jerusalem privileges as a temple city, spurring the growth of the

---

2. Finkelstein counts 118 settled sites covering around 61 hectares. With 200 inhabitants per hectare, he calculates 12,000 people.

3. Renewed examination of the Tel en-Nasbeh excavations shows no settlement break between exilic and Persian-era Mizpah, which remained a significant settlement during the early- and mid-Persian period. The site was largely abandoned in the second half of the fourth century and remained small and insignificant until the second century (personal communication from Aharon Tavger of Tel Aviv University and Dvir Raviv of Bar Ilan University).

city and Ramat Rachel (he gave similar privileges to the Samaritan temple city and sanctuary on Mount Gerizim). The combined evidence of Josephus, archaeology, and Sir 50:1–4, which lauds the temple renovations and fortifications done by the high priest Simon II, demonstrate that the town experienced a small renaissance under Antiochus III:[4]

> [1]Simon the high priest, the son of Onias, who in his life repaired the house again, and in his days fortified the temple: [2]and by him was built from the foundation the double height, the high fortress of the wall about the temple: [3]in his days the cistern to receive water, being in compass as the sea, was covered with plates of brass: [4]he took care of the temple that it should not fall and fortified the city against besieging. (Sir 50:1–4, my translation)

Based on the distribution of Yehud seal impressions, Finkelstein traces a slight third-century expansion of Yehud to the north with the highlands of Mizpah. A further expansion under the Seleucids is reflected by the location of Judah the Maccabee's battles with the Seleucids and the fortresses built by Bacchides after the death of Judah (1 Macc 9:50–52). Finkelstein estimates a population of Judah including the Shephelah in the 160s to around 42,000.[5] Only Hasmonean times (160–63 BCE) would see a transformation of the small province to a large state and a rapid growth of Jerusalem.

Haggai and Zechariah: A Davidide and a Priest

The books of Haggai and Zechariah reflect Judean restoration and hopes under the leadership of Zerubbabel—grandson of King Jehoiachin and Persian governor in the province of Yehud, responsible for rebuilding the temple together with the high priest Joshua during the years 520–515.

Messianic hopes would easily be connected to Zerubbabel, a Davidide of the royal family. The book of Haggai ends with a kind of messianic dec-

4. Sir 50:1–4 depicts the building projects initiated by the high priest Simon II (218–192). VanderKam (2004, 137–54) maintains that Ben Sira refers to Simon I (high priest ca. 300). In light of Finkelstein's analysis, it is difficult to imagine large renovations being carried out in Jerusalem during this period. Simon II's restoration of the temple fits Josephus's account of Antiochus's decree: "I would also have the work about the temple finished, and the cloisters, and if there be anything else that ought to be rebuilt" (*Antiquities* 12.141).

5. 180 settled hectares in Judea, 30 in the Shephelah (Finkelstein 2018, 64).

laration to Zerubbabel: "On that day, says Yhwh of hosts, I will take you, Zerubbabel my servant, son of Shealtiel, and make you like a signet ring, for I have chosen you, says Yhwh of hosts" (Hag 2:23 NRSV adapted). Mason (1998, 340–42) notes messianic features in this oracle: "my servant" (a Davidic designation), "I will take you" (terms of election), "I have chosen you," "a signet ring" (a sign of authority) (cf. the oracle on his grandfather Jehoiachin in Jer 22:24):

> His Davidic descent, and especially the fact that Jehoiachin was the last Davidic king, the reversal of whose banishment as expressed by Jeremiah is here suggested by the use of the rare word "signet ring," seem more than a coincidence . . . however, there is no reason to see in Hag. 2.23 anything other than a belief that the Davidic dynastic line would be renewed in Jerusalem and would be a feature of the new, postexilic age of God's rule as it was of the earlier, preexilic one. (Mason 1998, 342)

For Zechariah, Zerubbabel is the promised Davidide, the elect Shoot, ṣemaḥ (3:8; 6:12). Zechariah 3:8 relates transtextually to Isa 4:2, which uses ṣemaḥ of the nation, and to the sprout (neṣer) in 11:1.

In Zech 4, the prophet is given a vision of two olive trees flanking the menorah, the lampstand with seven branches. In 4:11–14, the interpreting angel explains to the prophet the meaning of the vision. The seven-branched oil lamp symbolizes the presence of Yhwh, while the two olive trees are "the two sons of oil who stand by the Lord of the whole earth" (4:14). The "two sons of oil" must refer to Zerubbabel and Joshua, the Davidide and the priest, both with essential roles in establishing the temple and the temple service.

The text consciously uses "sons of oil" (bǝnê-hayyišhār) and not "anointed ones." A term such as "Yhwh's anointed ones" might have been perceived as a provocative proclamation in the political context of the Persian Empire. At the same time, "sons of oil" clearly refers to the custom of anointing king and priest to their office.[6]

---

6. Anointing Saul, David, and Solomon: 1 Sam 9:16; 10:1; 15:1, 17; 16:12; 2 Sam 2:4 ‖ 1 Chr 11:3; 2 Sam 2:7 ‖ 1 Chr 14:8; 2 Sam 3:39; 5:3, 17; 12:7; 19:11 [19:10]; 23:1; 1 Kgs 1:34, 39, 45; 5:15 [5:1]; 1 Chr 29:22; Ps 151:4. Anointing the priest: Exod 28:41; 29:7; 30:30; 40:13, 15; Num 3:3. Anointing the king of Israel: 1 Kgs 19:16; 2 Kgs 9:3 ‖ 2 Chr 22:7; 2 Kgs 9:6, 12. Anointing the king of Judah: 2 Kgs 11:12 ‖ 2 Chr 23:11; 2 Kgs 23:30; Pss 45:8 [45:7]; 89:21 [89:20]; 132:10; Lam 4:20. Anointing foreign kings: Hazael anointed

Zechariah 4 is a landmark in the development of messianism. It will be constitutive for the dual messianism of the Qumran community—their end-time expectation included both an anointed priest and a son of David. In the centuries after Zechariah, some scribes would stress the expectation of the anointed ruler, others that of the anointed priest. The notion of the sons of oil standing in the presence of the Lord of the whole earth could pave the way for the idea of a messiah present in the heavenly realms or a messiah with a universal task (see pp. 198–202, 206–7). In late rabbinic times, another dual messianism would develop with the messiah son of Joseph as forerunner of the messiah son of David.

Zechariah 6:10–14 describes a ceremony where crowns are given to the high priest: 6:11 and 6:14 refer to crowns in the plural, 6:12–13 talk about the Shoot who shall build the temple and rule from his throne alongside the priest on his throne, while 6:11 reports the crowns (plural) being set only on the head of Joshua the priest. An earlier version of the text clearly had crowns being set on both of them (cf. the hypothetic addition in italic below). The text seems to have been slightly edited to conform with reality after the disappearance of Zerubbabel. An earlier version with crowns equally for the priest and the Davidide may reflect a theological ideal more than historic reality—in Persian times the priest would always be subordinate to the governor:

> [11]Take the silver and gold and make crowns, which you shall set on the heads of [*Zerubbabel son of Shealtiel and*] the high priest Joshua son of Jehozadak, [12]and say to him: Thus says Yhwh of hosts: Here is a man whose name is Shoot: below him it shall shoot forth, he shall build the temple of Yhwh. [13]He is the one that shall build the temple of Yhwh, he shall bear royal honor and sit and rule on his throne. There shall be a priest by his throne, with peaceful understanding between the two of them. [14]And the crowns shall be in the custody of Heldai, Tobijah, Jedaiah, and Josiah, son of Zephaniah, as a memorial in the temple of Yhwh. (NRSV adapted)

This text is the clearest evidence that Zerubbabel indeed was regarded as the promised Davidide and that he later on would be removed from the

by Yhwh's prophet in 1 Kgs 19:15 and Cyrus in Isa 45:1. Anointing a prophet: 1 Kgs 19:16; Isa 61:1.

governor's seat. Subsequently, an editor of Zechariah had to take this into account and project the expected Davidide far into the future. Zerubbabel faded out of history; there are no further records about his fate.

To have a Davidide as governor could be problematic for the Persians—the messianic hopes reflected in Haggai and Zechariah could indeed be interpreted by the Persian authorities as enticement to revolt. Zerubbabel was likely removed by the Persians. If he was imprisoned, exiled, and executed, Zerubbabel's fate could have colored the description of the suffering servant in Isa 50 and 53, texts likely written in the early fifth century when his memory was still vividly present. If this indeed was the case, these two texts could indicate that this Davidic servant of Yhwh suffered persecution, torture, and a violent death at the hand of the Persians.

With his death or removal, messianic hopes connected to Zerubbabel and his house would be crushed for generations. To cope with historical reality, the final version of the book of Zechariah would postpone the Shoot to the future. The appearance of the two sons of oil would also be considered a future event, foreshadowed by Joshua and Zerubbabel (Laato 1998, 200–202).

On the political scene there would be no room for a Judean kingdom, not to say a Davidic ruler. If there were Davidic hopes in the Persian period (and there were), they would reflect some kind of a utopian worldview without any sense for *Realpolitik*.

In the book of Ruth—a book of another genre—we encounter a brilliant novelist with a particular interest in the Davidic line. The language of this short story is Transitional Biblical Hebrew from around 500 (Zevit 2005; Hendel and Joosten 2018, 133). David's family tree (4:18–22) is an early source. The tradition that David had a Moabite great-grandmother carries the traits of authenticity—in postexilic times one would not invent a story that traced David's origins to the enemy people of Moab. In the subsequent century Ezra and Nehemiah would forbid intermarriage with neighboring peoples (perhaps including Israelites who had remained in the land during the exile and lacked genealogies; Ezra 9–10; Neh 10:31 [10:30]). In contrast, the author of Ruth gave another perspective on gentile women, on the role of women in general, and reminded his people not to forget David and the Davidic line.

Can we speculate about the authorial milieu of this short story? I can hardly imagine temple scribes behind this novel, so void of purity concerns. We should rather look to the high-class governor residence at Ramat Rachel. Recent excavations reveal that the site, probably identified with biblical Beth-haccherem (Jer 6:1; Neh 3:14), was an important administrative center from the seventh century until Hasmonean times (Lipschits et al. 2017, 95–118). Ramat Rachel, overlooking the Bethlehem region (the scene of Ruth), was a center where Judean and non-Judean scribes were working together, some of whom were overseeing the trade routes eastward through Moab, the place of sojourn of Ruth and her mother-in-law. Archival documents such as Cyrus's edict (Ezra 6:3–12) and genealogies would naturally be stored at Ramat Rachel. But a scribe of this imperial center could have produced a work within a totally different genre, the book of Ruth.

Different from oracles in Haggai and Zechariah, Ruth could not be read as enticement to revolt against the Persian authorities. On the surface it reads as a short story about the historical origins of the kingdom of Judah. Possibly written shortly after the removal of Zerubbabel as governor, we may sense between the lines a particular interest in the Davidic line. The novelistic form of this short story may reflect the scribe's knowledge of narrative traditions from other nations (the scribal milieu at Ramat Rachel had to be multilingual).

Prophetic Oracles from Late Persian and Hellenistic Times

During the Persian and Ptolemaic periods, any hope for a new David would be far removed from political realities on the ground. The hope for seeing a Davidic ruler on the throne had likely been crushed with the disappearance of Zerubbabel. A Davidic hope would have to be postponed to a utopic future. With the high priest as political leader of the province in Hellenistic times, we might expect that hopes centered around the temple or a priestly messiah would more easily come to the surface than Davidic expectations.

The composite chapters Jer 30 and 33 thematize the future time of salvation for the nation. According to MJer 30:20–22, a future breakthrough to times of redemption will be performed by a priestly leader in a risking act in Yhwh's presence. MJer 30:18–22 (≈ GJer 37:18–21) is a text from early Hellenistic times that casts light on the development of a twofold messianism. As outlined above (see pp. 111–12), the earlier G version (likely from the sixth century) foresees a future ruler with his heart dedicated to the Lord (lit., "he who has set his heart to return to me"), a text that could be recast in different directions (my translations):

GJer 37:18, 20–21	MJer 30:18, 20–22
[18]Thus says the Lord:	[18]Thus says Yhwh:
Behold, I will bring back the exiled Jacob and have mercy on his captivity.	I will restore the fortunes of the tents of Jacob, and have compassion on his dwellings.
The city shall be rebuilt upon its mound,	The city shall be rebuilt upon its mound,
and the sanctuary set on its rightful site.	and the citadel set on its rightful site.
[20]Their children shall go in as formerly,	[20]Their children shall be as of old,
their testimonies shall be rectified before me,	their congregation shall be established before me,
and I will punish those who oppressed them.	and I will punish all who oppress them.
[21]Its strong ones shall be set over them,	[21]Its chieftain shall be one of its own,
its ruler shall come from its midst.	its ruler shall come from its midst,
I will gather them, and they shall return to me,	I will bring him near, so that he can approach me,
for who is this one, who dedicates his heart to me? Says the Lord.	for who is this one, who stakes his life coming near to me? Says Yhwh.
[no 37:22]	[22]And then you shall be my people, and I will be your God.

With the words "I will bring him near," the term $\sqrt{q\bar{a}rab}$ in *hiphil* ("to bring near") brings us into the priestly, sacrificial realm (M 30:21b).[7] Coming into Yhwh's presence, the leader will pledge his life. HALOT renders ʿārab ʾet-libbô as "to pawn one's heart, meaning to stake one's life" (Koehler, Baumgartner, and Stamm 1995–2000, 877). These terms suggest that MJer 30:21 refers to a priestly figure.

Verses 23–24 are the same in G and M. But M adds a new verse (30:22) containing the covenant formula "and then you shall be my people, and I will

---

7. Of thirteen biblical occurrences, Isa 5:8; 26:17; Ezek 22:4; Mal 1:8 have the general meaning "come near." The other cases in Ezekiel and Haggai all refer to bringing sacrifices before the Lord.

be your God." The ruler's daring act in God's presence is done for the sake of the people and will lead to a renewed covenantal relation.

The leader comes out of the people: he is "its chieftain" (*'addîr*) and "its ruler" (*môšēl*). Perhaps for the first time in Scripture, *môšēl* is used for the priest—probably a reflection of present political reality in the province of Yehud, in Hellenistic times the high priest was civil leader of the Judean community.

The extended Masoretic version betrays knowledge of political development in Egypt around 300 (see p. 110 n. 6). Thus, Judean scribes in Egypt may have been involved in polishing a Jeremiah scroll at this late stage. And Judeans in Egypt did relate to the situation in Yehud and the small temple village of Jerusalem.[8] MJer 30:20–24 uses the present priestly ruler in Jerusalem as a type for a future priestly figure who in the end times (cf. 30:24) would risk his life in a sacrificial act before God. Whether he will die in Yhwh's presence is left open, but Isa 53:10–11 may play in the background.

This text goes alongside other passages in the longer proto-Masoretic recension of Jeremiah that foresee a future son of David. But it is the noble priestly ruler (MJer 30:21) who will be the tool for the renewal of the covenant people, when God by his wrath fulfills his will toward the nations (30:23–24).

Zechariah's "two sons of oil" would find an echo in MJer 33:17–22, absent in the earlier Greek recension. This text is a strong (fourth- or third-century) affirmation of Yhwh's covenant both with his servant David and the ministering Levites (NRSV adapted):

> [17]For thus says Yhwh: David shall never lack a man to sit on the throne of the house of Israel, [18]and the Levitical priests shall never lack a man in my presence to offer burnt offerings, to make grain offerings, and to make sacrifices for all time. [19]The word of Yhwh came to Jeremiah: [20]Thus says Yhwh: If any of you could break my covenant with the day and my covenant with the night, so that day and night would not come at their appointed time, [21]only then could *my covenant with my servant David* be broken, so that he would not have a son to reign on his throne, and *my covenant with my ministers the Levites.* [22]Just as the host of heaven cannot be

---

8. Cf. the communication between the Judeans of Elephantine and Jerusalem in an earlier period. Josephus reports a migration of Judeans, including a leading priest named Hezekiah, to Egypt following the conquest of Gaza by Ptolemy I in 312 (*Against Apion* 1.186–87).

numbered and the sands of the sea cannot be measured, so I will increase the offspring of my servant David and the Levites who minister to me.

Are the royal and the priestly ministries here going side by side, as in Zech 3–6? The text expects a future Davidide—his tasks are not explicated—while the anointed priestly line is represented by the ongoing priestly/Levitical ministry in the temple.

A similar vague description of the role of the future son of David appears in the combination of oracles in Jer 30 (the last part of the chapter, 30:20–24, is discussed above). Jeremiah 30:5–7 and 30:16–17 preserve an authentic oracle from the prophet: through war and distress Jacob will ultimately see salvation, God will heal their wounds and crush those who plundered them. Here, Yhwh is the only redemptive actor. Another (possibly authentic) oracle would soon be added. Jeremiah 30:12–14 (introduced by "thus says Yhwh") explicates the trials God allowed when he struck the nation by the hand of enemy armies. At a late stage, the oracle would receive an explicating addition (30:8–9), introduced by the formula "on that day." Here, the nation "will serve Yhwh their God and David their king"—but any job description for "David their king" is not provided (see pp. 157–58 on nearly identical additions in three prophetic books). These oracles appear both in the G and M recensions.[9]

Only the early Jeremiah oracle 23:5–6 keeps a job description for the coming Davidide: he will reign as king and execute justice and righteousness in the land (see p. 111). But inspired by other prophetic books, the reworked M recension would introduce a new messianic term into the book of Jeremiah. The earlier "I will raise up for David a righteous dawn" (G) now appears as "I will raise up for David a righteous *Shoot*"—a term echoing Zech 3:8 and 6:12 and likely alluding to Isa 11:1.

In a close to identical form, this oracle was subsequently pasted into MJer 33:14–16 (not in G), introducing 33:19–22 on the ongoing temple ministry and a future Davidide. A final editor would see the need for a bridging passage and added 33:17–18.

A different perspective with a new image of the Davidic king surfaces in Zech 9, a text from the early Hellenistic period (NRSV adapted):

9. In 30:10–11, the M recension added a salvation oracle inspired by Deutero-Isaianic texts (Isa 44:1; 41:10; 43:5). The same goes for Jer 30:15, which echoes Isa 40:2; cf. the terms 'āwōn ("guilt") and ḥaṭṭā't ("sin").

> ⁹Rejoice greatly, O daughter Zion!
> Shout aloud, O daughter Jerusalem!
> Lo, your king comes to you,
> triumphant and victorious is he,
> humble and riding on a donkey,
> on a colt, the foal of a donkey.
> ¹⁰I will cut off the war chariot from Ephraim
> and the war horse from Jerusalem,
> and the battle bow shall be cut off.
> He shall command peace to the nations,
> his dominion shall be from sea to sea,
> from the Great River to the ends of the earth.

Zechariah 9–11 and Zech 12–14 comprise collections of texts from the Persian and Ptolemaic periods. As the text unrolls, the role of the king in the restoration of Judah and Jerusalem is weakened in favor of the temple and its cult. Zechariah 9:9–10 transforms the traditional royal ideology. Against all current forms of leadership, these verses expect a future king radically different from the David of DtrH and the king of the royal psalms. The king has no military role; it is his humility and piety that is underlined. In the process of restoration, God will demolish the nation's military in a way reminiscent of the end-time vision of Isa 2:1–5. He will enable the humble king to rule an empire in peace, an empire reaching "to the ends of the earth" (the context makes it clear that the words ʿad-ʾapsê-ʾāreṣ do not mean "to the borders of the land" as it could in earlier Davidic promises). This description of a non-military king appears as a contrast to most Hellenistic rulers. It transcends the nature of earthly kings and relates transtextually to the postexilic stratum of Ps 72:8–11, 15, 17b; the phrase "dominion from sea to sea, from the Great River to the ends of the earth" recur word for word in 72:8. One of these texts consciously repeats the other.

The last section of the book of Zechariah opens with an eschatological vision of God making an end to the nations' attack on Judah and Jerusalem (12:1–13:1). The house of David has a prominent role, but any kingship is not mentioned, only a cultic role in prayer, lament, and supplication. The nation will lament over an enigmatic figure who has been pierced (12:10 NRSV adapted):

> I will pour out a spirit of compassion and supplication on the house of
> David and the inhabitants of Jerusalem, so that, when they look upon

me/the one whom they have pierced,[10] they shall mourn for him, as one mourns for one's only son, and weep bitterly over him, as one weeps over a firstborn.

The end-time figure that will be pierced may contain an echo of Isa 53:5, 10 (the servant was crushed and pierced; see p. 139 n. 33) and was possibly inspired by the death of the righteous King Josiah (thus Laato; see pp. 97, 156 n. 13).

The oracle Zech 13:7–9 is usually dated to the Ptolemaic period (my translation):

> [7]Sword, awake against my close friend,[11]
> the man who is my associate, says Yhwh of hosts.
> Smite the shepherd, so that the flock will be scattered
> when I turn my hand against the small ones.
> [8]In the whole land, says Yhwh,
> two-thirds shall be cut off and perish,
> one-third shall be left alive.
> [9]I will put this third into the fire,
> refine them as one refines silver,
> test them as one tests gold.
> He will call on my name,
> and I will answer him.
> I will say, "He is my people,"
> and he will say, "Yhwh is my God."

Zechariah 13:7 foresees the death of God's close associate, but no sacrificial death. Is this figure, who in a time of turmoil gives his life, a priestly or a royal

10. M reads "they shall look *upon me* whom they pierced"—in a literal reading God would be the pierced one. Due to the graphical similarity between *yod* and *waw*, one may suggest an original *ʾēlēyw* ("upon him") for *ʾēlay* ("upon me") (cf. the subsequent "mourn for him"). However, all textual witnesses read "upon me," and the Hebrew tradition continues to transmit this daring text.

11. Preferably read *rēʿî* ("my close friend") for the Masoretic pointing *rōʿî* ("my shepherd")—*rēʿî* constitutes a better parallel to the subsequent *geber ʿămîtî* ("the man who is my associate"). This reading gives a wordplay between *rēaʿ* in 13:7a and *rōʿeh* in 13:7b. Isa 44:28 is another example of the Masoretic pointing *rōʿî*, thus changing "my close friend" to "my shepherd" (see p. 128 n. 21). Alluding to Isa 44:28, the singer of the Qumran Self-Glorification Hymn declares that he is "the King's beloved and companion of the holy ones" (see p. 245).

figure? The concluding "I will say, 'He is my people' and he will say, 'Yhwh is my God'" closely echoes "and then you shall be my people, and I will be your God" of Jer 30:22. And the terms "my close friend" and "the man who is my associate" bring to mind "I will bring him near, so that he can approach me, for who is this one who stakes his life coming near to me" of Jer 30:21.

These parallels may suggest that the death of this associate of God represents a reinterpretation of the priest of Jer 30:21 who risks his life in a sacrificial act, although Zech 13:7 contains no priestly, sacrificial terminology. The nation's shepherd who is close to God could be a priest—analogous to the ruling priest in Jerusalem. In contrast to Jer 30, the term "sword" suggests a violent death by the hand of enemies, not risking one's life in temple precincts and God's presence.

"Shepherd" may elsewhere designate the Davidide (2 Sam 5:2; Mic 5:3–5 [5:4–6]), but in Zech 13:7b it may be used with reference to a priestly figure. The text describes the violent death of the shepherd and the annihilation of two-thirds of the people.[12] The wars of the Diadochi that led to devastation in Jerusalem during the third century (cf. Dan 11:14–20; see p. 145) may provide some background for this scenario of the end times. The fate of King Josiah could also play in the background (see p. 97).[13] Another option would be to date these verses to the 170s and see in this text a reflection of the violent removal of the high priest Onias III (see pp. 194–95).

In referring to Ezek 34:23–24; 37:24–25; Jer 30:8–9; and Hos 3:5—all of which mention "David their king" or "David their prince" and Yhwh being "their God," Rofé (2015, 97) asks: "Who is this David who will be brought back for Israel?" For Rofé, other oracles use collective terms with the entire dynasty and each of its members in view ("house of David," "the booth of

12. A later sequel to Zech 12:10 and 13:7 would appear with the rabbinic tradition on the slaying of the messiah son of Joseph.

13. For Laato (1998, 146–47, 209–18), Zech 9–13 is filled with texts on the Davidic messiah: King Josiah is the type for Yhwh's close friend and shepherd who shall fall for the sword, leading to the dispersal of the nation, as indeed happened two decades after Josiah's death. Laato notes that a preceding passage, 12:10–14, foresees Megiddo-like mourning over the pierced one, as one mourns a firstborn or only son—terms alluding to Yhwh's election of the Davidic king—and according to the contemporary text 2 Chr 35:23, Josiah was fatally wounded by Egyptian archers (see p. 97): "13:7–9 . . . describing the symbolic death of the Messiah based on the model of the King Josiah's death in Megiddo" (Laato 1998, 216). Thus, the pierced one in 12:10–14 "should be identified with the good shepherd of the messianic programme" (1998, 217). Laato's messianic interpretation of these chapters almost has New Testament colors. He does not note that there is no sacrificial death in Zech 13:7–9, only killing by the sword.

David," "a lamp for David," "the stock/shoot of Jesse," "the seed of my servant David," "men of David's line"). In contrast, these four clarifying additions belong to the same fifth-century editorial layer and share a belief in the resurrection of the dead and look forward to an individual *David redivivus*, David himself brought back to life, at a time when the image of David grew to legendary proportions, as evidenced by the fourth-century composition of 1 Sam 16–18 (Rofé 2015, 86–87, 95–98).[14]

I struggle to find evidence of a resurrected David in these texts. But these four oracles do evince a Davidic hope in late Persian-era Judea. In contrast to Isa 11:1–5 and Mic 5:1–5 [5:2–6], their job description for the Davidic prince or king is remarkably vague. Perhaps we may sense a reflection of the removal of Zerubbabel—these Davidic hopes were not formulated in terms that would be provocative to the Persian rulers.

As argued above, Ezekiel did not include David in his visions for God's restoration. With the term *nāśî'* ("prince"), his blueprint for a new temple referred to a leader with a sacrificial office. His book was transmitted by priestly circles, in Babylon and later in Judea. Thus, it may be a priestly scribe who inserted passages on a Davidic shepherd and "viceroy" alongside Yhwh in the salvation oracles of Ezek 34 and 37, to conform the book of Ezekiel with other Scriptures. The earlier Greek text refrains from using the term "prince" (David is only their "ruler"), so this scribe acknowledges that the prophet used *nāśî'* for a priestly office (45:7–8; 46:1–18). In contrast, M's "prince" evinces a yet later redaction. For the first scribe, the viceroy is ruler only, while his successor shared an expressed royal Davidic hope, using the terms "prince" and "king" in MEzek 37:24–25 (my translation):

GEzek 34:23–24	MEzek 34:23–24
[23]And I will appoint over them another shepherd [*rō'eh 'aḥēr*], and he shall tend them—my servant David, and he shall be their shepherd. [24]I, Yhwh, will be their God, and David shall be *ruler* in their midst; I, Yhwh, have spoken.	[23]And I will appoint over them one shepherd [*rō'eh 'eḥād*],[15] and he shall tend them—my servant David, and he shall be their shepherd. [24]I, Yhwh, will be their God, and my servant David shall be the *prince* [*nāśî'*] in their midst. I, Yhwh, have spoken.

14. Since both these Ezekiel oracles and Nehemiah (5:1–13) speak about local leaders selling their poor brothers, Rofé dates these oracles to the time of Nehemiah.

15. There is only a minute graphical difference between *resh* and *dalet*, leading to the different readings *rō'eh 'aḥēr* and *rō'eh 'eḥād* (I tend toward the former as the more original).

GEzek 37:24–25	MEzek 37:24–25
[24]My servant David shall be *ruler* in their midst, and they shall all have one shepherd . . . [25]. . . My servant David shall be their *ruler* forever.	[24]My servant David shall be *king* over them, and they shall all have one shepherd . . . [25]. . . My servant David shall be their *prince* [*nāśîʾ*] for all time.

It must have been another postexilic scribe who specified the royal hope in the Judean people with his inserts in the books of Jeremiah and Hosea. Instead of using the terms "ruler" or "prince," both texts declare that the nation shall seek (or serve) "Yhwh their God and David their king":

> [8]In that day, declares Yhwh, will I break the yoke from off their neck and burst their bonds, they shall not be bondservants for foreigners. [9]But they shall serve Yhwh their God, and I will raise up David their *king* for them. (GJer 37:8–9, my translation ‖ MJer 30:8–9)

> Afterward, the Israelites will turn back and will seek Yhwh their God and David their *king*, and they shall come in awe to Yhwh and his bounty in the days to come. (Hos 3:5, my translation)

David in the Psalms

Royal Psalms

The royal psalms 2, 72, and 110 have their roots in preexilic times. During the time of the Judean kingdom, they presented an ideal of the Davidic king, ruling in the land and dominating the neighboring countries. This ideal would be in marked contrast to political reality in the early Levant, where Judah remained a tiny kingdom in the shadow of the empires.

When these psalms were reread and edited during the Second Temple period, they presented a utopic ideal. In the shadow of the Persian and Hellenistic empires, any vision of the son of David's rule would have to be postponed to an indefinite future.

Psalm 72, in particular, would easily be read as depicting a messiah transcending the nature of an earthly king. With Zenger, I separate 72:8–11,

15, 17b as postexilic additions with new perspectives (italicized below, my translation):[16]

> [1]O God, endow the king with your judgments,
> he who is a king's son with your loyal justness,
> [2]that he may judge your people with righteousness,
> your lowly ones with justice.
> [3]Let the mountains produce well-being for the people,
> the hills, the reward of justice.
> [4]Let him champion the lowly among the people,
> deliver the needy folk and crush the oppressor.
> [5]May his days be long as the sun shines,
> while the moon lasts, generations on end.
> [6]He shall be like rain falling on a mown field,
> a downpour of rain in the land.
> [7]Righteousness shall flourish in his time,
> Peace and welfare abound till the moon is no more.
> [8]*Let him rule from sea to sea,*
> *from the Great River to the ends of the earth.*
> [9]*Let desert dwellers kneel before him,*
> *and his enemies lick the dust.*
> [10]*Let kings of Tarshish and the islands pay tribute,*
> *kings of Sheba and Seba offer gifts.*
> [11]*Let all kings fall down before him,*
> *and all nations serve him.*
> [12]For he saves the needy who cry out,
> the lowly who have no helper.
> [13]He cares about the poor and needy,
> he brings the needy deliverance.
> [14]He redeems them from oppression and violence,
> the shedding of their blood touches his heart.
> [15]*So let him live, and receive gold of Sheba,*
> *let prayers for him be said always,*
> *blessings on him invoked at all times.*
> [16]May there be abundant grain in the land,

---

16. Hossfeld and Zenger 2005, 207–8. In contrast, Carr (2011, 393–94) finds preexilic royal motifs all through Ps 72.

to the tops of the mountains,
the crops thrive like the forest of Lebanon,
and men sprout up in towns like the grass of the field.
^{17a}May his name endure forever
and get offspring as long as the sun lasts.
^{17b}Let men invoke his blessedness upon themselves,
let all nations pronounce him blessed.

Here the messiah has worldwide dominion and is honored as an ancient Near Eastern emperor by his subordinate vassal kings. While Ps 2 and Ps 110 and prophetic oracles such as Mic 5:4–8 [5:5–9] describe the king as a conquering warlord, the reign of this king is peaceful and characterized by abundance in the fields and happiness among men.

Preexilic and exilic texts evince the idea of a great Davidic state, where the son of David is portrayed as ruling over a large territory with peoples paying homage to him (Ps 2:8–11; Mic 5:3 [5:4]; Ps 89:26 [89:25]). In postexilic texts, such an earthly Davidic kingdom seems to be transformed into a world empire (Sæbø 1978):

- *'ad-'apsê-'āreṣ*, originally read as "to the borders of the land" (Mic 5:3 [5:4]), would now be read "to the ends of the earth" (Ps 72:8–11; Zech 9:10).
- *Kol-hā'āreṣ*, originally read as "all the land," is interpreted as "all the earth."
- "From the sea to the sea" and "from the Great River to the sea," originally read as "from the Mediterranean to the Dead Sea/the Gulf of Aqaba" and "from the Euphrates to the Mediterranean" (Amos 8:12; Ps 72:8; Zech 9:10; cf. Ps 89:26 [89:25]), would become terms for a Davidic empire.

Such an understanding could be inspired by Isa 11:6–9 and Amos 9:11–15, texts that describe a restored Davidic kingdom with terminology that could bring the thoughts to some kind of new creation, even if these passages originally were coined in symbolic language.

In its canonical form, Ps 72 reflects this ideological development. The preexilic core was a prayer for the king who is ruling the land on God's behalf. In the full text, the earthly Judean king has been transformed into a messianic king with worldwide dominion, a source of blessing for the nations.

With its description of a luxurious wedding of Solomon, Ps 45 stands out among the royal psalms (my translation):

[1b]For learning, a song of love.
[2[1]]My heart is astir with gracious words,
I speak my poem to a king,
my tongue is the pen of an expert scribe.
[3[2]]You are fairer than all men,
Grace is poured upon your lips,
rightly has God blessed you forever.
[4[3]]Gird your sword upon your thigh, O hero,
in your splendor and glory!
[5[4]]Ride on victoriously in your glory,
in the cause of truth and meekness and right,
and let your right hand lead you to awesome deeds.
[6[5]]When nations prostrate before you,
your arrows, sharpened,
will hit the breast of the king's enemies;
[7[6]]Your throne will stand forever and ever,
your royal scepter is a scepter of equity.
[8[7]]You love righteousness and hate wickedness,
rightly has Elohim, your God, anointed you
with oil of gladness beyond your companions.
[9[8]]Your robes are all fragrant with
myrrh and aloes and cassia;
from palaces adorned with ivory, flutes entertain you.
[10[9]]Royal princesses are your favorites,
the queen stands at your right hand,
adorned with the purest gold.
[11[10]]Take heed, maiden, and note, incline your ear:
forget your people and your father's house!
[12[11]]Let the king desire your beauty,
since he is your lord, fall down before him!
[13[12]]O Tyrian maiden, the wealthiest people
will court your favor with [14[13]]luxurious gifts;
The royal princess, her dress embroidered with gold and pearls,[17]
[15[14]]is led to the king,
behind her the virgins, her companions, are presented to you.
[16[15]]They are led in with joy and gladness
as they enter the palace of the king.

---

17. Emending *panîmâ* ("inside, into") to *panînîm* ("pearls, corals").

¹⁷⁽¹⁶⁾Your sons will succeed your ancestors,
you will appoint them as rulers throughout the land.
¹⁸⁽¹⁷⁾I commemorate your fame for all generations,
so peoples will praise you forever and ever.

The dating of Ps 45 is contested. For Hurwitz, Hendel, and Joosten, linguistic criteria most likely suggest a postexilic time of origin (Hendel and Joosten 2018, 132). I follow scholars who see 45:11–16 [45:10–15] as a postexilic addition to an earlier royal hymn, represented by 45:2–10 [45:1–9] and likely also 45:17–18 [45:16–17], which would flow easily if they followed directly on 45:10 [45:9].¹⁸ Zion or the temple is not thematized in the psalm.

Psalm 45:11–16 [45:10–15], which describes a royal wedding in hyperbolic terms, was inspired by the splendid court scene of 45:2–10 [45:1–9] as well as the wider legacy of Solomon. The superscript "for learning, a song of love," fits the full form of Ps 45, which includes the wedding section. *Yədîdōt* ("love") could just as well be interpreted "lovemaking" (cf. the use of *dōdîm* in Ezek 16:8; 23:17; Prov 7:18; and the later use of *dôdî* ["my lover"] in Canticles; Ehrlich 1914, 11; Fox 1985, 97, 313).

In contrast to the last sections of the psalm, the poem of Ps 45:2–10 [45:1–9] addresses the king in the second person. If preexilic, 45:2–10 [45:1–9] does not celebrate a concrete king, but praises the king's divinely given office, with the relation between God and the king in focus (Hossfeld and Zenger 1993, 279), as is the case with 21:2–10 [21:1–9]. These verses could be characterized as a court poet's praise of the king's beauty and qualities. Taking the words of the hymn at face value, an actual court setting during the time of the monarchy would provide a meaningful *Sitz im Leben*. It would be more difficult to imagine a postmonarchic poet formulating such a praise, fitting the regent of a kingdom long gone. Thus, a preexilic date for the poem of 45:2–10 [45:1–9] is preferable.

This hymn for the king can be read in consort with the royal psalms 72 and 21, in particular the latter. In Ps 21, God is crowning the king and clothing him with glory, topics reappearing in more elaborate form in Ps 45.

The nations prostrating before the Judean king in 45:6 [45:5] recur in 72:8–11, with one of these texts echoing the other. The final section (45:17–18

---

18. Zenger dates 45:2–10, 17–18 [45:1–9, 16–17] to preexilic times (Hossfeld and Zenger 1993, 278–79). For Carr, "parallels to ancient royal psalms suggest that Psalm 45 likewise contains much ancient material as well. It is probably another text from the early monarchic period" (2011, 390–91 at 391).

[45:16–17]) focuses on the king's lasting fame and nations praising him—a theme recurring in the postexilic 72:15, 17b.

In late postexilic times, the psalm would be read on the messianic king, in consort with Pss 2, 21, 72, and 110.

EXCURSUS: A DIVINE KING/MESSIAH OR A DIVINE THRONE IN PS 45:7 [45:6]?

One verse needs particular attention: Ps 45:2–10 [45:1–9] addresses the king in words of praise, before the psalm continues with the description of a royal wedding. Psalm 45:7 [45:6] has been a crux for interpreters: *kis'ăkā 'ĕlōhîm 'ôlām wā'ed, šēbeṭ mîšōr šēbeṭ malkûtekā* ("your throne, *'ĕlōhîm*, (is) forever and ever, your royal scepter is a scepter of equity" [my translation]). Is the Israelite king here described as divine?

King (1959, 73–84) discusses the various interpretations of 45:7 [45:6]. The most important are summed up in the following (with post-1959 bibliography added):

1. Most scholars (e.g., Kittel, Gressmann, Gunkel, Fitzmyer, Carr) explain the vocative addressed to the king as elevated oriental court style. For Hossfeld and Zenger (1993, 279), the core of the psalm is a preexilic royal song. The king is a living representative of God, he has a "divine" office and is to implement God's righteousness on earth. Psalm 45:11–16 [45:10–15] is a postexilic addition at a time when the king is reinterpreted as the messiah who receives Zion as his bride. Mowinckel and de Vaux note that *'ĕlōhîm* can be used of supernatural beings (82:1, 6) and metaphorically of human charismatic figures such as Moses (Exod 4:16; 7:1) and the house of David (Zech 12:8). In a similar vein *'ĕlōhîm* can designate an earthly king without making him divine.

2. Throughout history Jewish exegetes read the psalm as the wedding between the messiah and the chosen people. The same goes for church fathers such as Jerome.

3. Süssenbach (2005, 366) sees 45:7 [45:6] as a late editorial addition at a stage when the psalm was read allegorically of Yhwh as bridegroom and Zion as bride, similar to the allegorical reading of the Song of Songs.[19]

4. *'ĕlōhîm* can be read as predicate of the sentence "your throne is divine(ly

---

19. The analogy with the Song of Songs is anachronistic, as the compilation of Canticles should be dated to the first century (Elgvin 2018, 2020c).

given) forever and ever" (Ibn Ezra [twelfth century]). For Ehrlich (1905, 101–2), the king cannot be a king of Judah, but more likely a postexilic high priest with royal power.

5. *Kissē'* can be understood elliptically: "Your throne is (a throne) of God forever and ever" (Kirkpatrick, Nötscher). For this solution, cf. 1 Chr 29:23: "So Solomon sat on the throne, the one of Yhwh, being king in the place of David his father" (my translation).

6. Dahood (1965, 273) has an ingenious suggestion. Keeping the consonants, he vocalizes *kissē'ªkā*, reading the word as a *piel* verb, "enthrone." He then reads "the eternal and everlasting God has enthroned you"—a suggestion seconded by Craigie (2004, 336–37), who sees this as the easiest solution to the crux. With Dahood's vocalizing one could also read "God has enthroned you forever and ever." This reading is questionable, for nowhere else is *kissē'* used as a verb.

King subscribes to the first view and concludes that Solomon is the king of Ps 45: "The king who is an *elohim*, a charismatic figure, a manifestation of Yhwh inasmuch as in him the power of Yhwh appears, is rightly a type or figure of the Messiah, the antitype" (1959, 73–84, 103–30 at 129).

Options 4, 5, and 6 remain artificial readings of the Hebrew. With only 45:7a [45:6a] in view, the first option flows linguistically easy and is attractive. But it remains odd that nowhere else is the king addressed or designated *'ĕlōhîm*. Further, this solution does not flow easily with the subsequent verse that affirms "rightly has Elohim, your God, anointed you" (polished from the pre-Elohistic version: "rightly has Yhwh your God anointed you"). Both the earlier and the Elohistic version of 45:8 [45:7] regards the heavenly Lord as the king's *'ĕlōhîm*.

In the end I subscribe to a solution suggested independently by Charles Bruston in 1865 and F. Giesebrecht in 1887 (see King 1959, 76–77 for bibliography): the original text read *kis'ăkā yihyeh 'ôlām wā'ed* ("your throne will last [*yihyeh*] forever and ever"). The letters *yod* and *waw* are graphically similar and were sometimes confused by scribes, so *yhwh* could reasonably be misread *yhyh* or vice versa. With this original text, 45:7a [45:6a] would constitute a more direct parallelism with 45:7b [45:6b]. Subsequently, when Levitical editors of the Elohistic Psalter (Pss 42–83) in the fourth or third century replaced most cases of Yhwh with Elohim, they erroneously read *yhyh* as *Yhwh* and replaced it with *Elohim*, as they did with *yhwh* also in 45:8 [45:7].

In my view, Ps 45:7a [45:6a] originally read "your throne will stand forever and ever." A scribal misreading of *yod* as *waw* led to reading *yhwh* for *yihyeh*. When Elohistic editors changed *yhwh* to *ʾĕlōhîm*, the text ended up with a vocative phrase addressing the king as *ʾĕlōhîm*. It is still remarkable that scribes continued to transmit the text with the king or messiah addressed as *ʾĕlōhîm*, and the ancient versions presuppose *ʾĕlōhîm* read as a vocative. Scribes would likely see an analogy between the enthroned messiah addressed as *ʾĕlōhîm* in Ps 45 and the king/messiah in Ps 110, enthroned in heaven at the right hand of the Lord, as well as the later enthroned Son of Man in Dan 7:14. With time, the psalm would be read metaphorically on the wedding between God or a heavenly messiah and Zion/the people/the church.

Ps 132 is prominent among postexilic Zion and David psalms (my translation):

> ¹A song of ascent.
> Yhwh, remember in David's favor all the hardships he endured,
> ²how he swore to Yhwh and vowed to the Mighty One of Jacob,
> ³"I will not enter my house or get into my bed,
> ⁴I will not give sleep to my eyes or slumber to my eyelids,
> ⁵until I find a place for Yhwh, a dwelling place for the Mighty
>   One of Jacob."
> ⁶We heard of it in Ephrathah; we found it in the fields of Jaar.
> ⁷"Let us go to his dwelling place; let us worship at his footstool."
> ⁸Rise up, Yhwh, and go to your resting place, you and the ark of
>   your power!
> ⁹Let your priests be clothed with righteousness, and your faithful
>   shout for joy.
> ¹⁰For your servant David's sake, do not turn away your anointed
>   one!
> ¹¹Yhwh swore to David a firm oath that he will not renounce:
> "One of the sons of your body I will set on your throne.
> ¹²If your sons keep my covenant and my decrees that I teach
>   them,
> then their sons also shall sit forever on your throne."
> ¹³For Yhwh has chosen Zion, he has desired it for his habitation:
> ¹⁴"This is my resting place forever; here I will dwell, thus I desire.
> ¹⁵I will abundantly bless its provisions; I will satisfy its poor with
>   bread.

> [16]Its priests I will clothe with salvation, its faithful will shout for joy.
> [17]There I will make a horn sprout for David and set up a lamp for
> my anointed.
> [18]His enemies I will clothe with disgrace, while on him his crown
> shall sparkle."

In Ps 132 the election of David and the election of Zion go together, and the David theology is subordinate to the cultic theology of the temple. Similar to Chronicles, David primarily appears as originator of the temple cult. He is the founding hero who brought the ark of the covenant from Kiriath-jearim to Zion and paved the way for the building of the temple (2 Sam 6:1–19). Slightly in contrast to 2 Sam 7, the election of David is here intimately connected with David's transfer of the ark to Zion. The two sections of the psalm (132:1–10 and 132:11–18) are interrelated and stand side by side from the beginning.[20]

Part of the psalm is quoted in the Chronicler's version of Solomon's prayer at the dedication of the temple (2 Chr 6:40–42). The composers of the psalm used 2 Sam 6–7 and Ps 89 as sources. Psalm 132:11–12 refers to Yhwh's covenant with David and the divine oath to the king—themes that first came to the surface in Ps 89. Psalm 132:17–18 is formulated as a promise for the future: Yhwh will let a horn *sprout* for David in Zion, an echo of Isa 4:2; 11:1–5; Zech 3:8; 6:12.[21] Together this evidence points to an origin in the fourth or early third century.

David's oath to Yhwh to provide him with a dwelling place (132:2–5) corresponds to Yhwh's oath to provide a dynasty for David and protect it against enemies (132:11–12). The first oath leads to the second. Yhwh vows to dwell in the temple of Zion, walk with its priests, and feed the people. The psalm is celebrated in the temple, with priests ministering and faithful ones around—they are actors in the present, while the Davidic promise is set in the future. The late passage Jer 33:17–22 conveys the same message (see pp. 152–53). The psalm was likely used in the temple liturgy before it was included in the songs of ascent, Ps 120–32.

---

20. The psalm can be divided into two sections, with a seam either before or after 132:10. Those who find a seam between 132:9 and 132:10 see the psalm as a petitionary prayer for the king with two sections. Locating the seam between 132:10 and 132:11 would mean that the full psalm is read as a divine promise to Zion, an interpretation that is followed here. In my understanding of this psalm, I follow Hossfeld and Zenger 2011, 454–68, even though Cross (1973, 97n24) notes that the psalm contains archaic language.

21. Ps 132:17 uses a verbal form of √ṣmḥ ("to sprout, shoot"). A nominal form is used for the nation in Isa 4:2 and for the Davidic ruler in Zech 3:8 and 6:12. Isa 11:1 uses ḥōṭer ("rod") and nēṣer ("shoot").

The psalm concurs with the M version of 2 Sam 7:16 (the promise is to David), not the (perhaps earlier) G phrasing, where the promise refers to Solomon, his throne, his house and kingdom (see pp. 33–34).

Psalm 132:12 reflects on the behavior of preexilic kings and the experience of the exile: "If your sons keep my covenant and my decrees that I teach them, then their sons also shall sit forever on your throne" (NRSV adapted). In 2 Sam 7, the divine pledge to David on a lasting dynasty is unconditional, while this psalm makes the pledge conditional. Recognizing that the failure of Davidic kings led to the exile and end of the kingdom, the psalm upholds the promise of a future for the house of David: "There I will make a horn sprout for David and set up a lamp for my anointed" (Ps 132:17, my translation). The horn is a symbol of power and specifically of royal power (1 Sam 2:10; Pss 18:3 [18:2]; 75:5–6 [75:4–5]; 89:18, 25 [89:17, 24]; 92:11 [92:10]; 112:9). Thus, the future Davidide is not the peaceful ruler of Zech 9:9–10 and the postexilic stratum in Ps 72:8–11, 15, 17b, but a monarch with political and military might. The "lamp to be set up for my anointed" quotes the promise of 1 Kgs 11:36: "Yet to his [Solomon's] son I will give one tribe, so that there always will be a lamp for my servant David in my presence in Jerusalem, the city I elected for myself to set my name" (my translation).

Responding to the passionate cry of Ps 89 and Lam 4:20, the promise of a future Davidide is confirmed. In the present, the nation continues to celebrate its liturgies in the temple—which again point to a successor to David, the temple's founding father, far into the future.

Davidic-Messianic Editing of 11QPs^a and 2 Samuel

David was a central figure when the books 1–2 Samuel received their final form in the late third and second centuries—which demonstrates that there was an expressed hope for a future son of David in Ptolemaic, Seleucid, and Hasmonean times.

Rofé (2015, 78) argues that the story of Samuel's anointing of David (1 Sam 16:1–13) is unknown to the rest of 1–2 Samuel and not alluded to in Chronicles, only to be referred to in Ps 151 in the Septuagint and Qumran texts. He thus regards it as "a final layer in the saga of David's rise to power." I do not concur. But if Rofé is right and this story is roughly contemporary with the Chronicler, it would be a remarkable testimony to Davidic messianism in the late third century, where the prospects of a renewed Davidic reign seemed far from reality in the poor and war-ridden Jerusalem.

In 2 Sam 20:23–24:25 we find eight appendices to the Deuteronomistic History, all connected to David, the last seven thematically arranged in a chiastic pattern.[22] I have created a material reconstruction of the last columns of 1QSamuel (1Q7), an early-Herodian scroll of 1–2 Samuel where most of the preserved fragments are from the end of 2 Samuel (Elgvin 2020b, 2021a). The material evidence suggests that this scroll contains only three of these eight appendices: the record of the Philistine wars and their heroes (2 Sam 21:15–22), David's last words (23:1–7), and one of the lists of David's warriors (23:8–23). These three appendices were arranged in a chiastic pattern, with the two lists flanking the poetic unit 23:1–7.

In my view, the scroll evinces a specific stage in the literary growth of 2 Samuel (a recension still transmitted in the late first century), a growth continuing into Hellenistic times. Thus, 1QSamuel preserves a precanonical recension, which has frozen one specific stage of the literary growth of 2 Samuel.

Compared with the canonical recension, we lack the list of David's officials (20:23–26), the two stories on royal guilt and expiation (21:1–14; 24:1–25), Ps 18 (= 2 Sam 22), and the second list of David's warriors (23:24–39). These five appendices were likely attached to 1–2 Samuel in the last stage of editorial growth in Hasmonean times.[23]

A comparison with the recension of M demonstrates that Davidic appendices were added to 2 Samuel in stages. Post-Deuteronomistic scribes wanted to bring to the forefront the figure and image of David—a reflection of a vivid Davidic hope in Hellenistic times. "David's last words" (23:1–7) is one of the earlier of these additions and particularly instructive:

> ¹The oracle of David, son of Jesse,
> the oracle of the man whom God exalted,
> the anointed of the God of Jacob,
> the pleasant one among the singers of Israel:

22. (A) offense of Saul and expiation, (B) list of heroes, (C) David's hymn of praise, (C') David's last words, (B') combined list of heroes, (A') offense of David and expiation.

23. It is problematic to trace a substantial influence from the inserted Ps 18 throughout 1–2 Samuel, as suggested by Gosse (2010, 199; 2015, 42, 47): "We have seen that in the books of *Samuel* in the continuity of the insertion of Ps 18 in 2 Sam 22, we have a new reading of the history of David in relation to the Davidic titles of the *Psalter*." Parallels between 1–2 Samuel and the "variants" in the inserted psalm in 2 Sam 22 should be explained by the later 2 Sam 22 echoing 1–2 Samuel rather than the other way around. Further, the editorial processes reflected in 1QSamuel suggest that the insertion of 2 Sam 24 postdates the Chronicler, even though some of the idiosyncrasies of 2 Sam 24 vis-à-vis 1 Chr 21 may go back to an early source.

²The spirit of Yhwh speaks through me,
his word is upon my tongue.
³The God of Israel has spoken,
the Rock of Israel has said to me:
One who rules over people justly,
ruling in the fear of God,
⁴is like the light of morning,
like the sun rising on a cloudless morning,
gleaming from the rain on the grassy land.
⁵Is not my house like this with God?
For he has made with me an everlasting covenant,
ordered in all things and secure.
Will he not cause to prosper
all my help and my desire? (2 Sam 23:1b–5 NRSV adapted)

"David's last words" underlines central features of an ideal image of David: he is Yhwh's elect and anointed, he rules justly in the fear of God, he is the founder of the "house of David." Different from earlier Davidic oracles or royal psalms, he is "the pleasant one among the singers of Israel"—a reference to Davidic psalms and psalm scrolls circulating at this time. Another new feature is the portrayal of David as *prophet*: Yhwh speaks through him, and the poem is stylized as a prophetic oracle. The text echoes a number of biblical texts, such as 2 Sam 7:11–16; Deut 32:4 (the Rock); Isa 11:2 (ruling in the fear of God); 50:4 (tongue of disciples); 61:1 (spirit of Yhwh); Ps 89:29 [89:28]; 132:12 (covenant with David). These intertextual connections demonstrate that "David's last words" were authored in late postexilic times.[24]

A large scroll from Cave 11 contains both biblical and nonbiblical psalms.[25] The last section of 11QPsᵃ contains "David's last words"—the last six words of 2 Sam 21:7 appear in the top line of the penultimate column of 11QPsᵃ (11Q5) (the lower part of the scroll is not preserved). In this scroll, "David's last words" are followed by "David's compositions"

24. I contest Carr's dating of 2 Sam 23:1–7 to the early monarchic period (2011, 400, 481). The poem alludes to the exilic Ps 89 and the postexilic texts Ps 132 and Deut 32 (the Song of Moses is one of the last additions to Deuteronomy).

25. 11QPsᵃ was copied in the first century CE but contains much earlier nonbiblical psalms. Schuller (2006) sees a pre-Maccabean date for all the nonbiblical psalms in 11QPsᵃ as probable. Lange (2009, 39–40) suggests an early date for 11QPsᵃPlea, since "let not any 'satan' have power over me" is repeated in Hebrew form in a prayer in the third-century Aramaic Levi (11QPsᵃ XIX 15; Aramaic Levi 3:9 = 4Q213a 1 17).

(XXVII 2–11) and Ps 140, with the last column containing 134:1–3 and the biographical David Pss 151A (XXVIII 3–12) and 151B (opening in XXVIII 13–14).

There are thematic links between the messianic poem 2 Sam 23:1–7 and the three subsequent texts related to David in the scroll: "David's compositions" and Pss 151A, 151B, which together comprised a Davidic-messianic ending of 11QPsᵃ. The three David psalms that conclude 11QPsᵃ may be related when it comes to time and milieu of origin, being authored in the late third or early second century. Psalms 151A/B were likely included in some scrolls of the Psalter during the second century, before the early first-century translation into Greek.

The prosaic "David's compositions" is plainly a CV-like "list of publications" for David the songster, "the pleasant one among the singers of Israel," seen through the eyes of a Qumran scribe:

> David the son of Jesse was wise and shone like the light of the sun. He was a scribe ³and man of discernment, blameless in all his ways before God and humankind. Yhwh gave ⁴him a brilliant and discerning spirit, so that he wrote: psalms, 3,600; ⁵songs to sing before the altar accompanying the daily ⁶perpetual burnt offering for all the days of the year, 364; ⁷for the Sabbath offerings, 52 songs; and for the new moon offerings, ⁸all the festival days, and the Day of Atonement, 30 songs. ⁹The total of all the songs that he composed was 446, not including ¹⁰4 songs for the odd calendar days.²⁶ The sum total of everything, psalms and songs, was 4,050. ¹¹All these he composed through prophecy given him by the Most High. (11QPsᵃ XXVII 2–11, my translation)

This list-style text presupposes the 364-day calendar of the Yahad (the so-called Qumran community) and related circles, and it attributes to David the composition of 364 songs to accompany the daily offerings. This composition is likely younger than the three David psalms.

In the scroll, David's list of publications was followed by two biographical psalms. The first is preserved in full, but less than two lines of the second. The Septuagint conflated the first psalm and the beginning of the second into

---

26. The words *ʿal happəguʾim* ("on the afflicted") are commonly interpreted "(songs) for the demon possessed." Following a suggestion by Shemaryahu Talmon (oral communication), I see this as a reference to the odd calendar days that appears four times in a calendar of 364 days, with months numbering 30, 30, 31 (four times).

one composition, placed at the end of the Psalter. Some Syriac Bibles include Ps 151 as well as four other nonbiblical psalms from 11QPs[a]. The Hebrew text of Ps 151A/B is different from the Greek:[27]

GPs 151A	11QPs[a] (11Q5)
This psalm is outside the numbering and autographical by David, when he fought Goliath.	Hallelujah! Of David, son of Jesse.
Hallelujah! A psalm of David, son of Jesse.	I was smaller than my brothers, youngest of my father's sons.
I was small among my brothers, the youngest in the house of my father,	He made me [4]shepherd of his sheep and ruler over his goats.
I would shepherd the sheep of my father.	My hands fashioned a pipe, my fingers a lyre,
[2]My hands made an instrument; my fingers tuned a harp.	[5]and I glorified Yhwh.
[3]And who will report to my lord? Yhwh himself, it is he who listens.	I said to myself, the mountains do not testify
[4]It was he who sent his messenger, took me from the sheep of my father and anointed me with the oil of his anointing.	[6]and the hills do not talk about him.
[5]My brothers were handsome and tall, Yhwh did not take delight in them.	Trees, echo my words! Sheep, echo my deeds!
[6]I went out to meet the allophyle, and he cursed me by his idols.	[7]Who can proclaim and who can declare the deeds of the Lord?
[7]But I, having drawn the dagger from him,	God has seen all, [8]he has heard all, and he listens to all.
I beheaded him and removed reproach from the children of Israel.	He sent his prophet to anoint me, Samuel, [9]to magnify me.
	My brothers went out to meet him: beautiful of figure, beautiful of appearance.
	They were tall of stature [10]with beautiful hair,
	yet Yhwh God did not choose them.
	No, he sent and took me [11]who followed the flock and anointed me with holy oil.
	He set me as prince of his people and ruler over the children of [12]his covenant.

27. GPs 151A is adapted from NETS, 11Q5 XXVIII adapted from Accordance.

Ps 151B

[13][Dav]id's first mighty d[ee]d after the prophet of God had anointed him.
"Then I s[a]w the Philistine, [14]throwing out taunts from the [enemy] r[anks]. I [beheaded] the [Philistine]

The liturgical scroll 11QPs[a], copied by a sectarian scribe, was carefully formatted with a Davidic-messianic ending. The placement of "David's last words" together with Ps 151A/B may be more original than its late canonical setting with the appendices to DtrH in 2 Sam 21–24.[28]

I tentatively date the 1Q7 recension of 2 Samuel to the late third or early second century (post-Chronicles) and date further growth in the M recension of 2 Samuel to the second century. However, whenever we date the process of editorial growth of 2 Sam 21–24, it clearly has a Davidic edge throughout. With "David's last words," a messianic message shines through already in the 1Q7 recension.

Psalm 18, belonging to the early Davidic collection Pss 3–41, was pasted into 2 Samuel in the second century. In the final editorial stage, the chiastic pattern was extended to seven appendices. The inclusion of Ps 18 in 2 Samuel was a good choice. In contrast to other psalms that were editorially connected to events in David's life, Ps 18 concludes: "Great triumphs he gives to his king, / he shows steadfast love to his anointed, / to David and his descendants forever" (NRSV adapted).

David the Songster

In Chronicles, David is primarily the founding father of the temple cult, conducted by priests and Levites. Writing in the third century, the Chronicler presents a positively polished image of David and Solomon compared to the Deuteronomistic History. The Chronicler is silent about David's affair

28. Edenburg (2014, 177–80) suggests that David's last words originally belonged to a psalm scroll similar to 11QPs[a], to which it gave Davidic authority, and subsequently was duplicated into 2 Samuel.

with Bathsheba and the death of Uriah. David is presented as initiator of the temple (1 Chr 22, 28–29) and the one who initiated the temple ministry with priests and Levites (1 Chr 23–26).

First Chr 17 closely parallels 2 Sam 7, and David is promised a lasting dynasty. According to David's speech of exhortation for building the temple, the reason for the divine choice of David is that his son Solomon shall build the sanctuary (1 Chr 28:6, 10). And he assures Solomon that God is with him: "he will not let you down or desert you until all the work in the service of Yhwh's sanctuary is complete" (28:20, my translation):

> The Chronicler does not end his history where the Deuteronomistic historians ended theirs, with the restoration of the Davidic line to some kind of favour in Babylon. It ends with the decree of Cyrus which speaks of the restoration, not of the Davidic line, but of the Temple.
>
> On this view, then, the Davidic dynasty for the Chronicler was not an end in itself but God's choice of agent to prepare for the postexilic Temple theocracy which has now replaced and fulfilled it. It is in this sense that the promises of an "eternal" covenant with David find expression. (Mason 1998, 363)

Chronicles is also silent about Solomon's many foreign wives and their idols. Solomon is described as the great temple builder and officiating priest at the dedication of the sanctuary. With Chronicles being edited well into Hasmonean times (see p. 221), Solomon may be interpreted (between the lines) as a precursor of the Hasmonean priestly rulers, builders of Jerusalem who gave new splendor to the temple (1 Macc 14:15).

As founding figures for the temple and its cult, the presence of David and Solomon could still be felt at a time without any political power for the Davidic line. The Chronicler's image of David as instigator of the Levitical ministry in the temple drew on the hymnic tradition, where a growing number of psalms carried David's name in the superscription, thus cultivating the image of David as poet and musician.[29]

29. *Mizmôr ləðāwîd* can be interpreted as "a psalm [written] by David," "a psalm for David," "a David psalm," or "belonging to the David collection" (Hossfeld and Zenger 1993, 16). Many psalms initiated by *ləðāwîd* express piety connected to the temple; in these cases *ləðāwîd* cannot be read "written by David." Where the superscription connects a psalm to a specific incident in David's life (e.g., 18:1; 51:1), it may still be read "a psalm *for* David, when the prophet Nathan came to him after he had been with Bathsheba." After his reading of 2 Sam 12 (in particular 12:13–14), the Levite author of Ps 51

The tradition of David as musician, being brought into Saul's service and soothing Saul's spirit with his harp, appears in 1 Sam 16:14–23 and again in 18:10–11, the latter passage not being part of the shorter recension preserved by the Septuagint.

EXCURSUS: DAVID THE SONGSTER AND FIGHTER— IN TWO RECENSIONS

The Greek text of 1 Sam 16:14–18:30 (LXX[B]) is substantially shorter than M. In the latter, we find the following additions to the text common for both: 17:12–31, 41, 48b, 50, 55–58; 18:1–6a, 10–11, 17–19, 29b–30. The Greek text is a fairly faithful translation of a Hebrew *Vorlage*. It is "less repetitive, less apparently contradictory, and contains a simpler and more straightforward story-line" (Johnson 2015, 7). Here the young and harp-playing David is enlisted into Saul's entourage (16:14–23) and—already being close to Saul— volunteers to fight Goliath.

The longer M text includes an alternative and more contradictive story: David comes to the battlefield with provisions for his brothers, he is unknown to Saul, runs toward Goliath without being commissioned by the king, and is subsequently introduced to Saul after the killing of Goliath. A number of scholars regard G as the earlier recension, to which M added another tradition of how David was introduced to Saul (McCarter, Lust, Tov, Hendel). However, recent scholars argue convincingly that the composite M text represents the earlier version, while the G *Vorlage* represents a harmonizing and shorter recension (Barthélemy, Gooding, Pisano, van der Kooij, Wesselius, Rofé).

There are tensions also in the shorter story: David is designated "a man of war" (16:21) but comes to the battlefield with a shepherd's equipment and is unable to wear Saul's armor (17:38–40). G lacks the initial interaction between David and Jonathan, without which the progression of their relationship makes less sense. The story sets the stage for Saul's displacement by David as king: Saul, the warrior king, refrains from encountering the enemy himself. David appears as Israel's deliverer, and Yhwh will save the nation by David's hand.

---

wrote a text that would have been fitting in David's mouth and at the same time function as a paradigmatic cultic text for the confession of sin, a penitential prayer (Gerstenberger 1988, 211–15).

Editorial stages can be noted also in the earlier, longer M version. The text of M includes editorial comments trying to smooth out contradictions (17:15, 16, 31, 50), and the pluses display intertextual links with other parts of 1 Samuel. The pluses vis-à-vis G underline David's character as a young shepherd and include the motif of tension between David and his older brothers. Here Saul appears as a confused leader who does not recognize David his servant. He is an unstable person hardly able to lead his people anymore; he cancels his promise to give his eldest daughter Merab to David in marriage. In contrast, in G, Saul is a jealous king, but not unfit to lead his people (Johnson 2015, 6–7, 219–20, 226; Hendel 2007, 102–4, 109–13). The M version recalls the genre of the folktale, with a young shepherd happening to be at the battlefield at the right time to slay a giant and subsequently receiving the king's daughter as reward.

According to Rofé (2015, 77), the story is not integral to the Deuteronomistic History. It was shaped in the Persian period when the tradition of David the legendary king was well established: "The portrayal differs entirely from that found in most of the other, earlier stories concerning the rise of David (1 Sam 16–2 Sam 6). A complete idealization of David has been performed by presenting him as an exemplary figure, the personification of faith and courage." In Rofé's view, a folktale-like story formed in preexilic times was subsequently theologically reworked in the fourth century.[30]

The passage in 1 Sam 16–18 is not the earliest text that portrays David as musician. Around 760, Amos refers to such a tradition without paying much respect to the king: "Those who sing idle songs to the sound of the harp, and like David improvise on instruments of music" (6:5). Elsewhere in DtrH we encounter David the songster in his laments over Saul and Jonathan (2 Sam 1:19–27) and his mourning song over Abner (3:33–34)—texts older than the David-Goliath story in Rofé's dating.

Some hymnists of the Psalter may have seen David as an ideological father, and Levite editors of psalm scrolls surely did. The number of Davidic superscriptions differs substantively between the Hebrew and the Greek manuscripts, as at this point the textual tradition remained fluid.

---

30. For Rofé, the bulk of the material in 1–2 Samuel is preexilic, while the features of 1 Sam 16–18 set it apart from the rest of the book.

The superscriptions display David in a role different from king, ruler, and prototype for a future king or messiah. Here David appears as instigator of the temple cult and ideological type for Levite temple singers and praying Judeans.

Thus, with the disappearance of Davidic rulers, the figure of David remained important for the temple community as cultic fellowship. We encounter David in the way a later appendix to 1–2 Samuel phrases it: "David, son of Jesse, . . . the pleasant one among the singers of Israel," singing prophetically, guided by God's spirit (2 Sam 23:1; see p. 168). Gosse finds this motif most clearly expressed in the last book of the Psalter, Pss 107–50. He concludes that in the final editing of the Psalter, the Davidic dynasty was rehabilitated as founders of the temple and the temple cult and the role of the king was subsumed into the Levite idea of David as prototype for the temple singers (2015, 43, 47, 124–27).

These two images of David existed side by side in third- and second-century Jerusalem (cf. the early third-century Jer 30:8–9; see p. 158), while some circles would stress one more than the other. The evidence of 1QSam and 11QPs[a] shows that Samuel editors around 200 found it pertinent to close 1–2 Samuel with three Davidic appendices, and their successors brought in four more; in both cases the appendices were structured in a chiastic pattern. Second Sam 24 (pasted from 1 Chr 21 and an earlier source) would underline David as founder of the temple cult; the others would point to David as type for the coming messiah.

Editing and Growing Together of Psalm Scrolls

The book of Psalms reflects a process of editing and growing together of smaller psalm scrolls during the postexilic period.[31] A "Davidization" with a messianic edge is transparent throughout the process.

The translation of 151 psalms into Greek in Egypt in the early first century[32] evinces that the collection had reached its full size at this time.[33] At

---

31. See Hossfeld and Zenger 1993, 8–16; and Willgren's comprehensive analysis (2016).

32. Van der Kooij (1983) argues for an early first-century date of the translation. The reference to Moab and Idumea in GPs 59:9–10 [= M 60:9–10 = 60:7–8 English] and 107:9–10 [= M 108:9–10 = 108:8–9 English] suggests a time after the Hasmonean conquest of Idumea in 107 (cf. Schaper 1995, 42–45).

33. The forty-two psalm scrolls from the Judean Desert have led some scholars to suggest that the content of Pss 1–89 was stabilized relatively early (first half of the second

the same time, the translation itself testifies to the book's importance for the Judean nation. The book would be divided into two major scrolls (1–72, 73–150) since one scroll would be too large to handle easily.[34] Psalm 72:20 marks the conclusion of the first scroll, which programmatically ended with the royal/messianic Ps 72, with words of the everlasting name and fame of the messiah and a messianic age where God's glory will fill the whole world. At the time the colophon of 72:20 was added, the second scroll included 73–119 or 73–136 (Willgren 2016, 196–201, 237–41, 379).

The growth of the Psalter was no linear process. Willgren (2016, 387) concludes his comprehensive analysis: "The process is better conceptualized as a growing body of psalms that was increasingly valued in the exilic and postexilic community. Only after a long period of time would the psalms be juxtaposed and fixed in sequences that overlap with what is now known as the MT/LXX 'Book' of Psalms." The early scroll of Pss 3–41 was combined with Pss 42–50 and Pss 51–72 into a collection opening and closing with two Davidic/messianic psalms, Ps 2 and Ps 72.[35] The collection grew with the addition of Pss 73–83 and Pss 84–89. A particular theological edge is

century), while the content of the rest of the Psalter remained fluid, so that different recensions were circulating until the late first century CE (thus Wilson, Sanders, and Flint; cf. Flint 2014). I follow scholars who regard the "deviating" 11QPs[a] as a liturgical, not a biblical scroll (Talmon, Goshen-Gottstein, Skehan, Tov). That Qumran has commentaries only on canonical psalms bolsters this view. With the Greek translation, the Psalter had reached its full form; cf. Flint's observation (2014, 222) that the early Herodian scroll MasPs[b] concludes with Ps 150. This would not prevent different collections of psalm scrolls from circulating for liturgical or devotional purposes (including scrolls comprising biblical and nonbiblical psalms, such as 11QPs[a,b]).

34. Scholars who discern three parallel recensions of Psalms until the first century CE have not taken this material aspect into consideration (cf. Willgren 2016b, 199). No single scroll would have been produced that included more than eighty-nine psalms. Smaller psalm scrolls would continue to circulate, as is evidenced by Qumran scrolls.

35. Hossfeld and Zenger (1993, 14–16; 2005, 6) see the core of Pss 3–41 as a late preexilic collection that was extended and Davidized in exilic and postexilic times. At this early stage, the contents and internal sequence within these three scrolls could be somewhat different from the later Psalter. Ps 2 could later have been taken from a Davidic scroll and relocated as a messianic preamble to the larger collection. Psalms 2–89 have been characterized as an early Davidic psalter with messianic overtones (e.g., Hossfeld and Zenger 2005, 5–6). Burnett comments: "The bracketing of the dual psalm book thus achieved by the royal psalms in Pss 2 and 89 accentuates its Messianic and Davidic character as emphasized by Christoph Rösel and as identified by others" (2007, 99n19). However, Ps 72 is a better postlude to an early messianic psalter than the lament of Ps 89 (thus Spieckermann in personal communication). In the continued growth of the soon-authoritative psalter, Ps 89 and Ps 110 may have provided temporary messianic closures.

represented by Levite editors who worked through Pss 42–72 and Pss 73–83, producing the so-called Elohistic Psalter (Pss 42–83).[36]

Around 200, other editors would extend the frame with the wisdom Ps 1 and Ps 119, presenting the Psalter as a book to be read and meditated upon in dialogue with the Mosaic Torah (cf. Ps 1:2), not only being a collection of psalms to be sung in the temple:[37] "Used in the Second Temple cult and in relation to, among others, the public reading of the torah of Moses, they were also to become authoritative for the community, eventually becoming scripture themselves" (Willgren 2016b, 136–71, 379–81, 386–88, 396 at 386). As part of the programmatic beginning of the Psalter, Ps 2 would remain a lasting testimony to singers and readers about the Davidic hope of the people of Judah.[38]

Psalm 18:1 and 36:1 designate David "the servant of Yhwh"—echoing God's calling David "my servant" in DtrH (2 Sam 3:18; 1 Kgs 11:13, 32, 34; 14:8), as does the lamenting Ps 89:4, 21 [89:3, 20].[39] These two superscriptions may be related—in time and (Levite) milieu—to the two Davidic inserts in the book of Ezekiel (34:23–24 and 37:24–25), which use "my servant David" four times (see pp. 157–58).[40]

36. When late second-century editors compiled the book of 150/151 psalms into a two-scroll collection, the *Vorlage* they chose for Pss 42–83 was an Elohistic one. "The Elohistic Psalter reunited at the same time the second book of Psalms (Pss 42–72) and a particular part of the third book (Pss 73–83)" (Gosse 2015, 137). There is a clear theological reflection behind this redaction, which retains *yhwh* for certain purposes. The use of *'ĕlōhîm* emphasizes God's distance and transcendence, accentuating the dark, remote mysterious God. *'ĕlōhîm* is used where God's universality is underscored, *yhwh* where a close personal relation is in sight, as well as in the defined phrase *yhwh ṣəbā'ôt* (Hossfeld and Zenger 2005, 4–5).

37. According to Hossfeld and Zenger (1993, 8–9), Ben Sira programmatically refers to Ps 1 in Sir 14:20–15:10—which is possible, but far from certain.

38. According to Gosse, who at times overplays the evidence, "the messianic question [i.e., the David tradition] played a fundamental role in the structuring of the Book of Psalms" (2015, 137). He sees the Davidization of the Psalter as a reaction to the crushing of the Davidic line after 587, so deeply expressed in Ps 89 (2010, 73–118, 195–99; 2015, 31–48). Gosse notes different Davidic images represented in the various psalm scrolls: Pss 3–42 comprise the first Davidic collection, Pss 51–72 the second, and these two books are interspersed by the Levite Korah/Asaph Pss 43–50. In the first collection, every psalm programmatically carries David's name (Pss 9–10 is in fact one psalm, as evidenced by the Septuagint, which also opens Ps 33 with "by/for David"). The superscriptions in 3:1; 7:1; 18:1; and 34:1 connect existing psalms with particular events in David's life and career, and 3:1 represents the opening of the first Davidic scroll. This feature appears more frequently in the second Davidic collection (Pss 51, 52, 54, 56, 57, 60, 63).

39. 2 Sam 3:18 and 1 Kgs 11:13, 32, 34 may be the only preexilic verses using the designation "my servant David." 1 Kgs 14:8 belongs to 14:1–20, a long section absent from the Septuagint.

40. The term "servant of Yhwh" is a late addition to these superscriptions; it is not found in the duplicate of Ps 18 in 2 Sam 22.

In Ps 18, the editors framed an existing psalm with a biographical David introduction and a messianic closure (18:51 [18:50]). The added "postlude" changes a royal hymn (cf. vv. 36–49 [35–48]) to a messianic psalm. It proclaims a future hope for the Davidic line: "Great triumphs he gives to his king, and shows steadfast love to *his anointed*, to David and his *descendants* forever." It is in this later form it was appended into 2 Sam 22.

Psalm 20:7–10 [20:6–9] expresses a similar hope (NRSV adapted):

> [7][6]Now I know that Yhwh will help *his anointed*,
> he will answer him from his holy heaven
> with mighty victories by his right hand.
> [8][7]Some take pride in chariots, some in horses,
> but our pride is in the name of Yhwh our God.
> [9][8]They will collapse and fall,
> but we shall rise and stand upright.
> [10][9]Yhwh, give victory to the king,
> hear us on the day we call upon you!

The use of "his [Yhwh's] anointed" in these two psalms evinces a Davidic messianism alive in fifth-century Judea, a tiny, powerless province within the great Persian Empire—an empire that relied on horses and chariots. The Levite singers had not given up their hope in a turn of history and a renaissance for the Davidic line.

Psalms 18–21 appear as four related "David messianic psalms." In 19:12–14 [19:11–13], the singer calls himself "your servant," which may identify this singer with David. It would be read together with the preexilic royal Ps 21, which expresses Yhwh's lasting blessing and protection of the king. Following the lamenting Ps 22 (which nevertheless concludes with redemption and praise in 22:23–32 [22:22–31]), Ps 23 may also be read as another "David psalm" with its "you anoint my head with oil."[41] Another Davidic reference is found in Ps 28: "Yhwh is the strength of his people; the saving stronghold of *his anointed* is he" (28:8, my translation). Thus, a Davidic hope is transparent in the first Davidic collection (Pss 3–41).[42]

41. Gosse stretches the textual evidence when he sees Pss 18–25 as a "David collection" (2015, 36–38). His Davidic reading of the Psalter is not always convincing. And interpreting Pss 3–41 in light of Chronicles (2015, 39–41, 46–47) remains problematic, as Chronicles should be dated after this collection of psalms.

42. In Gosse's analysis of the five books of the Psalter, the second Davidic collection (51–72) is more uncertain about a future son of David—the opening Ps 51 stresses David's shortcomings and concludes with a prayer for the sanctuary (2015, 53–55). In my view, the

The final formation of the Psalter includes the addition of Pss 120–36, 137–44, 145, 146–50, and a stabilization of the internal sequence of the psalms. I date this process to second-century Hasmonean Jerusalem. It should not be interpreted as an expression of anti-Hasmonean sentiments—the Hasmonean priestly rulers considered themselves legitimate successors of David and Solomon (see pp. 215–19), and Levite psalms editors were part of the temple echelon controlled by the Hasmoneans. Thus (contra Gosse 2010, 73–118, 195–99; 2015, 31–48), a Davidic messianism was not given up by temple circles, even though temple singers would primarily point to David as their ideological father and instigator of the cult. The full collection was seen as a David collection and read as some kind of a prophetic book, as evinced in Qumran writings and Acts 2:30.[43] In late Second Temple times, Judeans would read and pray in communion with David as part of the tradition instigated by their first king and legendary songster.

concluding Ps 72 underscores the Davidic-messianic hope that may be questioned in Ps 51. Further, Gosse is far too optimistic when he presupposes the exact same contents in the early psalms scrolls as in the subsections of the later canonical Psalter. The collection Ps 51–72 was framed by the (fourth- or third-century) Levite editors of the Elohistic Psalter (42–83), who avoided the phrase "anointed" and focused on the temple (Gosse 2015, 49–75)—the anointed in 84:10 [84:9] is the anointed priest, not the anointed king (2015, 54). The addition to the third book, Pss 84–89, concludes with the bitter lament over the crushing of the Davidic line (2015, 77–81), still a reality in third-century Jerusalem. The fourth book (90–106) stresses the kingship of Yhwh and is silent about an anointed king. David recurs in the fifth book, which includes the royal psalms 110 and 132, but this book primarily sees David as the ideal type of the cultic singers. According to Gosse, the final editors of the Psalter framed the Elohistic Psalter and the "Yhwh-king psalter" (90–106) with two Davidic collections, the early 3–41 and the later 107–50 (2015, 43, 47). For Gosse (2015, 140–46), the singer of the psalms of ascent (120–34) identifies with David, and the same is true for the concluding psalms 138–50. In his view, in the final Davidization of the Psalter we see the singer's identification with the figure of David: there is a Davidization of the singers, not any more a specific hope for a Davidic king. The temple and the praying Levites represent the lasting legacy of David.

43. Later, the Davidic Psalter would programmatically open the Ketuvim. The early first-century translation into Greek reflects its growing authority. Around the same time the conclusion of the halakhic letter from Qumran (4QMMT C 10–11; DJD 10:58–59) refers to "the book of Moses [and] the books [of the p]rophets and Davi[d and the books of events] of ages past" (the last group may refer to Joshua–Kings). The DJD editors dated MMT to the mid-second century (DJD 10:109–21); I prefer a first-century dating for the following reasons: (1) the manuscripts are early or mid-Herodian; (2) the language of MMT is the closest we come to Mishnaic Hebrew among Qumran writings (Morag 1996); (3) "sacrifice for the gentiles" in the temple (B 8) primarily makes sense in the Roman period.

The Upheavals of
the Second Century BCE

Great changes occurred in Judea throughout the second century BCE. In 198, Antiochus III tore Judea out of the hands of the Ptolemies and gave privileges to the temple cities and temples of Jerusalem and Gerizim. In the 170s and 160s, Hellenists and traditionalists strove in Jerusalem, and newcomers repeatedly usurped the high-priestly office (Jason 175, Menelaus 172, Alcimus 162).

The sources differ on whether the high priest Onias III, deposed in 175, thereafter was killed in Antioch. Either Onias III or his son Onias IV fled to Egypt and got pharaoh's permission to build a temple for Yhwh in Heliopolis. Scribes connected this Egyptian exile for the true heir of the high-priestly office with prophecies in the Scriptures. In its turn, the flight of Onias and his group to Egypt set their own traces in the Scriptures, in Dan 9–12, the Greek translation of Isaiah, and (suggested here) Zech 12–14.

The 170s and 160s was a time of *intifada* (trembling, shivering) in Judea. In particular, the Seleucid King Antiochus IV Epiphanes (175–164) set deep footprints in Judean history and the development of Judean apocalyptic literature. His use of oriental royal ideology conflicted with the Yahwistic faith of the Judeans. In 169–168, Antiochus twice sacked Jerusalem and instigated harsh anti-Jewish measures. This led to the Maccabean Revolt and the liberation of the temple in 164, which was followed by a gradual growth of the entity that evolved into the Hasmonean state.

The persecutions under Antiochus sharpened apocalyptic trends in some Judean circles. A wide array of texts evinces a periodical view of history, with trials and persecutions ultimately leading to the rebirth of the elect nation: Enochic writings, Dan 7–12, and Qumran texts such as 4Q246 (the "Son of God text").

When was a Hasmonean state a political reality in the Levant? It may be a fact on the ground with the Seleucid recognition of Jonathan as ruling high priest in 152. Judea certainly has the characteristics of a state when John Hyrcanus, soon after the death of Antiochus VII in 129, struck Judean coins with the legend "Yohanan the high priest and the community of the Judeans," a coin used only by Judeans (its distribution shows the geography of Judean settlement throughout the land; Syon 2015, 59–60, 149–65).[1] The Hasmonean state expanded greatly under John Hyrcanus (135–105) and his son Alexander Jannaeus (104–76), and Jerusalem developed into a real *polis* (see figures 7 and 8, pp. 213 and 214).

The growth of the Hasmonean state would lead to messianic fervor in some circles and to radical skepticism toward the new dynasty in others. Some voices were critical of the Hasmoneans' occupying both the office of ruler (from 104 on: king) and that of high priest.

The second century saw a renaissance of Judean literature written in Hebrew. Perhaps by the 120s, there would be a state-sponsored library in Jerusalem, with scribes handling literature in Hebrew, Aramaic, and Greek.[2] Hasmonean-time scribes were actively editing scrolls of their fathers and played a major role in editing and enlarging many of the books that became "biblical" (Elgvin 2021b).

With many scholars, I date the beginnings of the Yahad, the "Qumran community," to the mid-second century. Scribes of this community would compose and copy numerous new texts and be caretakers of scrolls written by others. And by the chances of history, the work of these scribes would lead to the finding of the Dead Sea Scrolls, which have given us many new windows into the history, culture, and literature of Judea in the last three centuries of the Second Temple period (see chap. 7).

1. Hyrcanus's earliest coinage is the "Basileus Antiochou Euergetou" coins from 131, minted under Antiochus's patronage immediately after his three-year successful siege of Jerusalem (Josephus, *Antiquities* 13.236–48). The siege started in 135/134 and ended in 132/131. A large number of amphoras from a Seleucid army camp were unearthed in 2017 in a salvage excavation in Mea Shearim; seventeen of them can be dated to 132/131 (personal communication from Gerald Finkielsztejn, Israel Antiquities Authority).

2. 2 Macc 2:13–15 portrays Nehemiah and Judah the Maccabee as library founders in Hellenistic style: "In the same way Judas [Judah] also collected all the books that had been lost on account of the war that had come upon us, and they are in our possession. So, if you have need of them, send people to get them for you." This section of the fictive letter of 2 Macc 1:10b–2:18 suggests the existence of a Hellenistic-style royal library. While the letter purports to be from the time of Judah the Maccabee, it presupposes a stable state seeking to enlarge its Jewish population, hardly fitting the days of Judah, Jonathan, or Simon. The early years of Hyrcanus's rule seems preferable, with the major expansion of the state occurring during his later years (Doran 2012, 52; Lange 2010b, 164–67; Schorch 2010, 180).

Figure 5. Coin of John Hyrcanus from the 120s: "Yohanan the high priest and (head of) the community of the Judeans."

Figure 6. Coin of Alexander Jannaeus, around 90 BCE, anchor encircled by "King Alexander" (*Alexandrou basileos*). Reverse: wheel or star of Jacob within a diadem.

The expectations of a personal messiah need to be placed in the context of wider eschatological hopes in the second and first centuries. End-time hopes do not necessarily stress a personal messiah as God's special agent.

A Restored Zion without a Son of David

In their scenarios for the future, some early second-century texts envisage a glorious temple in a restored Jerusalem without paying attention to prophecies about the future son of David.

Around 190, Yeshua ben Sira led an elite school in Jerusalem, called a *bêt-midrāš* (Sir 51:23; Genizah manuscript B). Ben Sira belonged to the upper echelon in society and was close to the temple leadership—he gives a glorious description of the high priest Simon II (218–192) celebrating the liturgy

(50:5–21) and portrays Simon acting as civil leader of the people (50:1–4; Horbury 2003, 43–50). A later rabbinic dictum is put in the mouth of Simon the Just (= Simon II): "Simon the Just was among the last of the men of the Great Assembly. He used to say, 'On three things the world stands: on the Torah, on the temple service, and on acts of loving-kindness'" (*Avot of Rabbi Nathan* 4.1). The temple and its service uphold the world, at least as tannaitic rabbis formulate it. Around the time of Simon II, there are indeed texts that focus on the restored temple and its service, while a Davidic leadership is not in focus.

What is the profile of Ben Sira's eschatological hope? Is there room for a restored house of David in the end time, or only a glorified temple with anointed priests? Sirach 45:24–26 makes the covenant with Aaron greater than that with David. The Hebrew version of 45:25 limits the Davidic promise to Solomon, while the covenant with Aaron is lasting: "And there is also a covenant with David, son of Isai [Jesse], from the tribe of Judah; the inheritance of a man [i.e., David] is to his son alone, the inheritance of Aaron is also to his seed" (Genizah manuscript B, translation Horbury).

The panegyric praise of Simon in Sir 50 hardly allows for a Davidic ruler at the side of the priest in the close future. However, the section on David and Solomon in Ben Sira's praise of the fathers could suggest a possible fulfillment of Davidic promises far into the future:[3] "The Lord . . . exalted his [i.e., David's] horn forever, he gave him a royal covenant and a glorious throne in Israel. . . . But the Lord would not go back on his mercy, or undo any of his words. He would not obliterate the issue of his elect, nor destroy the stock of the man who loved him; and he granted a remnant to Jacob, and to David a root springing from him" (47:11, 22, my translation).

In Ben Sira's time, the high priest was the religious and civil leader of the Judeans, a situation that may have influenced his eschatology. His main hope is an ingathering of the exiles and a glorious restoration of Zion and the temple, without any mention of a Davidic ruler:

---

3. Genizah manuscript B inserts a hymn of praise between 51:12 and 51:13, which includes these lines: "Give thanks to him who makes a horn to sprout for the house of David, give thanks to him who has chosen the sons of Zadok as his priests." The hymn includes features that indicate a date of composition after the Second Temple period. The above benediction is inspired by the fifteenth benediction in the *Amidah* (a prayer that in its complete form should be dated post-70): "Speedily cause the sprout of your servant, David, to flourish! Let his horn be exalted by your salvation . . . you, O Lord, who causes the horn of salvation to flourish" (Beentjes 2003, 92–93; Skehan and Di Lella 1987, 568–71).

[13]Gather all the tribes of Jacob,
and give them an inheritance, as from the beginning!
[14]Have mercy, O Lord, on the people called by your name,
on Israel, whom you named your firstborn!
[15]Have pity on the city of your sanctuary,
Jerusalem, the place of your dwelling!
[16]Fill Zion with your majesty,
and your temple with your glory!
[17]Bear witness to those whom you created in the beginning,
and fulfill the prophecies spoken in your name!
[18]Reward those who wait for you
and let your prophets be found trustworthy!
[19]Hear, O Lord, the prayer of your servants,
according to your goodwill toward your people,
and all who are on the earth will know
that you are Lord, the God of the ages. (Sir 36:13–19 [= 36:13–22
          in NRSV numbering]

According to Skehan and Di Lella (1987, 416–22), this prayer is part of the last psalm in a sequence of poems composed by Ben Sira himself (34:21–31; 35:1–13, 14–22a, 22b–26; 36:1–22). In theme and form, 36:1–22 contrasts with the preceding poems that are permeated by wisdom instruction. Thus, Ben Sira may here have inserted an earlier psalm.

Another of the so-called Old Testament Apocrypha is the book of Tobit, a short story written in Aramaic, likely between 225 and 175.[4] Most interpreters suggest a place of origin in the eastern diaspora. In the penultimate chapter, the author or editor includes two hymns (13:1–8, 9–18). The second hymn addresses Zion in the second person, a psalmic literary form breaking through around 200, likely inspired by Deutero-Isaianic oracles addressed to Zion:[5]

---

4. Tobit exists in two main recensions, a longer one preserved in Sinaiticus (followed here) and a shorter one, represented by Alexandrinus and Vaticanus. A third, hybrid version, mixes the two main recensions. A comparison with the five Qumran manuscripts (four in Aramaic, one in Hebrew) suggests that the longer recension is the more original (Fitzmyer in DJD 19:2–4).

5. The hymn was likely composed in Hebrew. Centuries later, the Spanish poet Judah Halevi (ca. 1075–1141) would cultivate and refine this form. His "Ode to Zion" would, in turn, be an inspiration for Naomi Shemer's song "Jerusalem of Gold." She would turn around Judah's words to Zion: "Dreaming of the end of your exile, I will be a harp for your songs [ʾanî kinôr ləšîrāyīk]."

⁹Jerusalem, Holy City,
God scourged you for your handiwork
yet still will take pity on the sons of the upright.
¹⁰Thank the Lord as he deserves
and bless the King of the ages,
that your Temple may be rebuilt with joy within you
and within you he may comfort every exile,
and within you he may love all those who have been distressed,
for all generations to come.
¹¹A bright light shall shine
over all the regions of the earth;
many nations shall come from far away,
from all the ends of the earth,
to dwell close to the holy name of the Lord God,
with gifts in their hands for the King of heaven.
Within you, generation after generation,
shall proclaim their joy,
and the name of her who is Elect shall endure
through the generations to come.
¹²Cursed be any who affront you,
cursed be any who destroy you,
who throw down your walls,
who raze your towers,
who burn your houses!
Blessed for ever be all who build you!
¹³Then you will exult, and rejoice
over the sons of the upright,
for they will all have been gathered in
and will bless the Lord of the ages.
¹⁴Happy are those who love you,
happy those who rejoice over your peace,
happy those who have mourned
over all your punishment!
For they will soon rejoice within you,
witnessing all your blessedness in days to come.
¹⁵My soul blesses the Lord, the great King,
¹⁶because Jerusalem shall be built anew
and his house for ever and ever.
What bliss if one of my blood is left

to see your glory and praise the King of heaven!
The gates of Jerusalem shall be built
of sapphire and of emerald,
and all your walls of precious stone;
the towers of Jerusalem shall be built of gold
and their battlements of pure gold.
[17]The streets of Jerusalem shall be paved
with ruby and with stones from Ophir,
the gates of Jerusalem will resound
with songs of exultation,
and all her houses will say,
"Alleluia! Blessed be the God of Israel."
Within you they will bless the holy name
for ever and for ever. (Tob 13:9–17 Jerusalem Bible)

As in Sirach, the hope for the end time focuses on a restoration of Zion without any mention of a Davidide. In only two stanzas is attention given to the temple: "That your temple may be rebuilt with joy within you" and "Jerusalem shall be built anew and his house for ever and ever." The focus is the glorious redemption of Jerusalem, which will include the nations making pilgrimage to Zion, as in Isa 2:2–4.

Daniel 11:14–16, 20 indicates that Judea and Jerusalem did not escape the turmoil of the third-century wars of the Diadochi, and Josephus notes that Antiochus III by 198 ordered the restoration of "their city that had been destroyed by the hazards of war," and its repopulation by "bringing back to it those who have been dispersed abroad" (*Antiquities* 12.138). Sirach 50:1–4 reports renovations of the temple and its walls under Simon II, likely being done in the 190s under Seleucid sovereignty:[6]

6. Simon's renovations may be identified archaeologically: 32 m north of the southeastern corner of Herod's temple mount there is a visible seam in the wall. South of the seam, the masonry is Herodian, the stones north of the seam are mounted in typical Hellenistic fashion. Tsafrir (1975, 517–20) identifies the lower stone courses north of the seam as pre-Hasmonean, the upper ones as Hasmonean. From the seam at the southeastern corner, an artificial platform can be reconstructed, measuring 500 cubits square (262.5 m × 262.5 m) (Mazar 1985). Its western edge, indicated by steps and ancient paving stones, runs parallel to the eastern rather than the western wall (for the square, cf. Ezek 42:16–20; 45:2; Mishnah, tractate *Middot* 2.1). Such a monumental project would have required a strong state with significant economic resources. If preexilic, the platform should be assigned to the strong Judean state of Hezekiah or the seventh-century monarchy. With a square of this size being referred to for the first time in Ezekiel, a seventh-century construction

[1]The leader of his brothers and the pride of his people
was the high priest, Simon son of Onias,
who in his lifetime repaired the house,
and in his time fortified the temple.
[2]He laid the foundations for the high double walls,
the high retaining walls for the temple enclosure.
[3]In his days a water cistern was dug,
a reservoir like the sea in circumference.
[4]He considered how to save his people from ruin,
and fortified the city against siege.

The psalms of Sir 36 and Tob 13, longing for a restoration of Jerusalem
and the temple, suggest that the state of the Second Temple was far from
glorious (Sir 36:15–16; Tob 13:10; cf. Ezra 4:12–13). These two psalms may
have been written before the renovations of the 190s, and the psalm in Sir
36:1–22 may be earlier than the bulk of Ben Sira's book.

The same Zion-centered eschatology permeates one of the nonbiblical
psalms in the great psalm scroll from Qumran Cave 11, 11QPs[a]Zion (column
XXII; see p. 169 n. 25 on this scroll). As in Tob 13, Zion is addressed in the
second person. The temple is not specifically mentioned:

I will remember you, O Zion, for a blessing,
with all my might do I love you.
May your memory be blessed forever!
Great is your hope, O Zion:
the peace and salvation you await shall come.
Generation after generation shall dwell in you,
and generations of the pious be your ornament.
They who desire the day of your salvation
shall rejoice in the greatness of your glory.
At your glorious bosom they will suckle,
in your beautiful streets rattle their bangles.
You shall remember the pious deeds of your prophets,
and glorify yourself in the deeds of your pious ones.
Purge wrongdoing from your midst,

would make sense (cf. Elgvin 2018, 125–26). Alternatively, cf. Patrich's suggestion (2020,
267) that the large platform was constructed by the Hasmoneans, who extended an earlier
square constructed by Simon II (190 m × 190 m) toward the south and east.

lying and iniquity be cut off from you.
Your children shall rejoice within you,
your loved ones be joined to you.
How much they have hoped in your salvation,
how much your perfect ones have mourned for you!
Your hope, O Zion, shall not perish,
your expectation will not be forgotten.
Is there a righteous man who has perished?
Is there a man who has escaped his iniquity?
Man is tested according to his way,
each one repaid according to his deeds.
Your oppressors shall be cut off from around you, O Zion,
and all who hate you shall be dispersed.
Your praise is pleasing, O Zion,
it rises up all over the world.
Time and again I will remember you for a blessing,
I will bless you with all my heart.
You shall attain to eternal righteousness,
and shall receive blessings from the noble.
Take the vision which speaks of you,
and the dreams of prophets requested for you.
Be exalted and increase, O Zion—
give praise to the Most High, your redeemer!
May my soul rejoice in your glory![7]

Sirach 36:13–17 is a heartfelt petition to God to heed the prayers of many for the restoration of Jerusalem and the sanctuary. Somewhat in contrast, the Tobit psalm and 11QPs^aZion display an expressed confidence in Jerusalem's promised glory indeed to become reality.

The temple has a central place in Ben Sira's petitionary prayer. A future anointed priest is not specifically mentioned, but in light of Ben Sira's confirmation of the lasting covenant with Aaron, the praise of the contemporary high priest, and the mention of God's dwelling in the sanctuary and a future temple filled with his glory (36:15–16), there would without doubt be

---

7. For translation of Qumran texts, I consulted Accordance; Vermes 1997; Wise, Abegg, and Cook 1996; García Martínez and Tigchelaar 1997, 1998; and often provide my own translation. When it comes to English style, Vermes's translation is by far the best of the published translations.

a central role for the anointed priests in a restored Zion with its temple. The Tobit psalm trusts that the Lord's house shall be "built anew forever." The Apostrophe to Zion does not mention the temple; the focus is the glorious restoration of Zion.

None of these psalms speak about the anointed end-time high priest, so, in contrast to many Qumran texts, there is no expressed priestly messianism here.

The psalms discussed above can be compared with Aramaic Levi, a third-century priestly composition that elevates the patriarch Levi and portrays him as the ideal priest (Kugler 1996, 130–38; Greenfield, Stone, and Eshel 2004). Aramaic Levi stresses the purity of the priest and the community and attaches the roles of sage and scribe to the priesthood. The author is engaged in polemic against some form of the priesthood and in promotion of his own notion of the office's proper character. Aramaic Levi's elevation of Levi and the priesthood hardly allows for a dual leadership with priest and Davidide alongside each other, as in Zech 4 and later Qumran messianism. At the same time, the Yahad preserved Aramaic Levi as an expression of their self-definition and negative assessment of the Hasmonean high priesthood (Kugler 1996, 225).[8]

Aramaic Levi is an early example of the literary genre of the patriarchal testament, where a patriarch on his deathbed gives instructions to his sons, including prophecies about the future and the end time. The Levi testament tradition is dynamic and fluid from the third century BCE to the second century CE (see chap. 7 for discussion of two Qumran texts that likely focus on the eschatological high priest).

Aramaic Levi is the great-grandfather of the Testament of Levi, part of the Testaments of the Twelve Patriarchs that received its final form in the late second century CE. Here, a descendant of Levi will be the end-time priestly messiah. The Testament of Levi contains Christian (perhaps Jewish-Christian) interpolations, but most of the text goes back to a Jewish *Vorlage*. Different from Aramaic Levi, the patriarch Levi is commissioned as priest *and* warrior. This *Tendenz* suggests that, with Aramaic Levi as a main source, this *Vorlage* was coined as an apology for the dual offices of Hasmonean rulers, perhaps in the time of Hyrcanus (135–105; Kugler 1996, 201–25).

8. Aramaic Levi is represented by two Qumran manuscripts, 4Q213 and 4Q214, and Hebrew fragments from the Cairo Genizah. The text is further reconstructed with the help of Greek manuscripts.

Yhwh in Egypt: Onias, Greek Isaiah, and Zechariah 12–14

In the mid-second century, a particular messianism focused on an anointed high priest who built a purified temple for Yhwh in Egypt—an Israelite city of refuge in times of turmoil, times perceived as birth pangs of the last days.

The fate of King Josiah may have been formative for the oracles in Zech 12:9–14 and 13:7–9 (see p. 156 n. 13). In 13:7–10, Josiah could be a type for Yhwh's close friend and shepherd who shall fall for the sword, leading to the dispersal of the nation (Laato 1998, 216). The mourning over the pierced one in 12:10–14 could also have Josiah in mind. Below I will propose an alternative, second-century date for these oracles.

In the 160s, a group of Judeans exiles led by Onias the priest built a temple for Yhwh in Heliopolis, a temple functioning until Vespasian in 74 gave orders to close it down.[9] Josephus gives two contrasting versions of the fate of the high priest Onias III, ousted from his office by the Hellenizing Jason in 175. According to *Jewish War* (1.31–33; 7.421–36), Onias III, well and alive, led a group of Judeans to Egypt and became the temple builder in Heliopolis. In *Antiquities*, however, Onias III was killed in Antioch around 171, and it is his son, Onias IV, who leads his group into the Egyptian exile (*Antiquities* 12.237–38, 387; 20.235–36). The latter version concurs with 2 Macc 4:32–35.[10]

According to Josephus, Onias got permission from pharaoh to build his temple, and the exiles saw themselves as fulfilling an Isaianic prophecy about a Yhwh presence in Egypt:

[18]On that day there will be five cities in Egypt speaking the Canaanite language and swearing in the name of the Lord, one city will be called City of Righteousness/City of the Sun.[11] [19]On that day *there will be an altar to the*

9. For a survey of the history of the Oniad temple, see Bohak 1996, 19–40. The temple was destroyed in the 70s CE.

10. For discussion of the Onias texts of Josephus, see Piotrkowski 2019, 32–122. He prefers the relevant texts in *Jewish War* over those in *Antiquities* and argues that Onias III, rather than being killed in Antioch, was the one who built the Heliopolis temple after Antiochus put an end to Judean temple ministry in 168. My interpretation of Zech 13–14 would bolster the version of 2 Maccabees and *Antiquities*, also preferred by Bohak (1996, 20–22, 32–33).

11. The Hebrew reads *'ir haheres* ("City of the Sun" = Heliopolis) per a number of witnesses (1QIsaᵃ, Symmachus, Vulgate, Hebrew mss). In post-70 times the Masoretic text was changed into the tendentious *'ir haheres* ("city of destruction"). G reads *'ir haṣṣedeq* (*polis-asedek* = "City of Righteousness") (= Isa 1:26), surely the name the Onias group

Lord in the land of the Egyptians and a stele to the Lord at its border. ²⁰And it will be a sign forever to the Lord in the country of Egypt, because they will cry to the Lord on account of those who oppress them, and *the Lord will send them a man who will save them*—judging he will save them. ²¹And the Lord will be known to the Egyptians, and the Egyptians will know the Lord on that day and will offer sacrifices and make vows to the Lord and repay them. ²²And the Lord will strike the Egyptians with a great blow and heal them with healing, and they will return to the Lord, and he will listen to them and heal them. (GIsa 19:18–22 NETS adapted, emphasis added)

According to the Greek, "the Lord will send them a *man* who will save them"—this man must be Onias the priest (M reads: "He will send them a redeemer who will fight and save them").

The community of Onias enjoyed great respect in Egyptian society. Two sons of Onias IV were serving in prominent positions in the Egyptian army toward the end of the second century (*Antiquities* 13.285, 348–51; *Against Apion* 2.49).

Bohak (1996) convincingly argues that the fascinating novel Joseph and Aseneth has its origin in the priestly milieu of Heliopolis. Chapters 16–17 are an allegory on priests leaving their dwelling and source of life to find refuge with Aseneth, the future wife of the patriarch Joseph (Gen 41:50). Aseneth is shown a honeycomb and is given from it to eat, from "the comb of light," a comb with the scent of paradise. Then, a swarm of bees with the color of priestly robes rises from the comb and makes a new one on her lips. The first comb is subsequently devoured by fire, so that only her honeycomb remains (Bohak 1996, 4–18, 81–82). She is then told (my translation):

Happy are all who attach themselves to the Lord God in repentance, because they will eat from this comb, which is the spirit of life. . . . This is a comb of life, and everyone who eats of it will not die forever and ever. . . .

Behold, you have eaten bread of life, and drunk a cup of immortality, and been anointed with ointment of incorruptibility. . . . And you shall be like a walled mother-city of all those who seek refuge in the name of the Lord God. (Joseph and Aseneth 16:14, 16)

---

gave to their settlement. Targum Pseudo-Jonathan combines the two Hebrew renderings—"The city, the House of the Sun, which is destined for destruction, of it will be said, 'That is one of them'"—demonstrating that the targumist knew that the text read *haḥeres* but was interpreted as *haheres* ("the destruction").

According to the allegory, the Jerusalem temple of Jason and Menelaus is spiritually corrupt and destined for destruction, while the true priests will settle with Aseneth, who will be a City of Refuge, pointing to a future city of God in Egypt:

> And you shall be seven pillars of the City of Refuge, and all the fellow inhabitants of the chosen of that city will rest upon you forever and ever. (Joseph and Aseneth 17:6)

> The Lord God founded your walls in the highest,[12] and your walls are adamantine walls of life, because the sons of the Living God will dwell in your City of Refuge, and the Lord God will reign as king over them forever and ever. (Joseph and Aseneth 19:8–9)

With its temple, Aseneth's City of Refuge will be the only true Jerusalem in the coming eschaton, "the City of Righteousness" about which the prophets had spoken.

In the moderate messianism of Joseph and Aseneth, the anointed high priest will, with his colleagues, establish a city that will be the end-time Jerusalem. Its temple will be the dwelling of God and a source of life and immortality for Judeans and Egyptian converts. The true sons of the Living God will be "called from darkness to light . . . from death to life . . . be renewed by God's spirit . . . and the chosen ones will live in God's eternal life forever and ever" (8:10–11).

According to Seeligmann (2004, 50, 233–51), Heliopolis traditions were included in the Greek translation of Isaiah, made in Alexandria in the 140s. In addition to GIsa 19:18–22 (above), Seeligmann finds a reference to the flight of Onias IV to Egypt in GIsa 8:7–8: "The Lord is bringing up against you . . . the king of the Assyrians and his glory, and he will take away from Judea a man who can lift his head and accomplish things; his camp will fill the breadth of your country—God is with us." Also in GIsa 10:24, Antiochus Epiphanes appears in the role of the Assyrian king, and the text is rewritten to relate to Judeans fleeing to Egypt: "Oh, my people, who live in Zion, do

---

12. According to Josephus (*Jewish War* 7.427), the Heliopolis temple "resembled a tower of large stones, sixty cubits high." Before Herod, the Jerusalem temple was formed as a cube (60 cubits × 60 cubits, as decreed in Ezra 6:3). During Herod's reconstruction, the tower was raised to 100 cubits, and "shoulders" were added on each side (Mishnah, tractate *Middot* 4.6–7; Bohak 1996, 29).

not be afraid of the Assyrians, because he will beat you with a rod, for I bring a stroke upon you so that you will see the way of Egypt."

Isaiah's repeated references to "the king of Assyria" are either read directly as prophecies of the ungodly king ruling from Damascus or consciously given a secondary meaning in a new historical context (Isa 7:17, 20; 8:4, 7; 10:12; 20:4, 6). In 8:8 and 10:24, the M hypotext is *transformed* into a prophecy of Antiochus beating Jerusalem and causing the righteous and legitimate high priest into an Egyptian exile.

Another window into the hopes of Judeans residing in Egypt is found in book 3 of the Sibylline Oracles, which contains future prophecies of Egyptian Jews (Collins 2010c, 46–49). Collins dates the earliest section to the mid-second century. The oracles are concerned with the rise and fall of kingdoms and attach great hope for change to "the young seventh king of Egypt . . . numbered from the line of the Greeks" (Sibylline Oracles 3.608–9)—to be identified either with Ptolemy VI (180–145), the king who allowed the building of the Heliopolis temple, or Ptolemy VII (145–144). One prophecy speaks concretely of a future king: "Then God will send a king from the sun, who will stop the entire earth from evil war, killing some, imposing oaths of loyalty on others; and he will not do all these things by his own plans but in obedience to the noble teachings of the great God" (Sibylline Oracles 3.652–56). The term "king from the sun" resounds with Egyptian mythology—pharaoh was considered son of the sun-god Re. Thus, this oracle attaches messianic hopes to a coming king of Egypt. "The Sibyl, then, resembles Deutero-Isaiah in endorsing a Gentile king as the agent of deliverance" (Collins 2010c, 49, referring to the prophet's hailing Cyrus as Yhwh's anointed deliverer).

Daniel 7–12 is commonly dated to the 170s and 160s, reflecting the third-century wars of the Diadochi, the campaigns of Antiochus IV, and the Maccabean uprising. These upheavals should also be considered as background for the completion of the book of Zechariah. Zechariah 13:7–9 may retell in a symbolic way the story of the killing of Onias III in Antioch in 171 (2 Macc 4:34–36; Josephus, *Antiquities* 12.237–38; 20.235–36) and the subsequent trials under Antiochus IV, and thus represents a second-century addition to Zechariah:

> [7]Sword, awake against my close friend,[13]
> the man who is my associate, says Yhwh of hosts.
> Smite the shepherd, so that the flock will be scattered

13. On reading *rēʿî* ("my close friend") for the Masoretic pointing *rōʿî* ("my shepherd"), see p. 155 n. 11.

when I turn my hand against the small ones.
[8]In the whole land, says Yhwh,
two-thirds shall be cut off and perish,
one-third shall be left alive.
[9]I will put this third into the fire,
refine them as one refines silver,
and test them as one tests gold.
He will call on my name,
and I will answer him.
I will say, "He is my people,"
And he will say, "Yhwh is my God." (Zech 13:7–9, my translation)

Is it feasible that a prophetic book could receive such an addition as late as the second century? Ben Sira knows the prophetic books, including the Twelve, as authoritative writings (Sir 49:7–10). This does not mean that the Twelve necessarily was a closed literary entity or that the individual books had grown to their canonical state. The Septuagint evinces a different order of the individual books, closer to their historical composition and growth, with Hosea, Amos, Michah, and Joel as the first four, likely representing a more original sequence (Jones 2020, 295–97)—an early scroll from exilic times likely contained Hosea, Amos, Micah, and Zephaniah. A reconstruction of the earliest Qumran copy, 4QXII[a] (4Q76), dated to 150–125, suggests that this scroll ended with Zechariah, Malachi, and Jonah—only fragments of these three were preserved. 4QXII[f] (4Q81) may have contained only Jonah (or Jonah + Micah), and 5QXII only Amos. The earliest Hebrew scroll that seems to have contained all the Twelve in the canonical order is the early-Herodian 4QXII[g] (4Q82) (DJD 3:173; DJD 15:221–22, 268, 271–317). With such a large variation as to which books were included in scrolls of the Twelve and to their sequence in a given scroll, literary additions during the second century should not surprise us.

Scholars struggle to interpret this enigmatic passage and suggest a fitting historical setting in the fourth or third century.[14] However, if prophetic books could be updated during the second century, an Oniad-Epiphanes dating of this passage could solve the crux. Rē'î ("my close friend") would be a fitting designation for the high priest, who could be considered in line with the heavenly temple in his sacrificial service (cf. 1QSb [1Q28b] III 25–26; IV

---

14. As noted on p. 156 n. 13, Laato (1998, 216) reads Zech 13:7–9 as a third-century prophecy about the Davidic messiah, modeled on King Josiah and his fate.

22–26). Since the high priest in the Hellenistic period functioned as civil leader of the Judeans, the term "shepherd" (for his flock) in the third stich would also be fitting.

A catastrophic fallout for the nation would follow the death of the shepherd, when only a third of the people will survive. Such a decimation of the people would be difficult to imagine between the destruction of the First Temple and the persecutions of Antiochus IV, although the persecutions of the latter hardly led to such a gruesome slaughter. The concluding stichs envisage that, through trials and refinement, the nation will be led to a renewed covenant relation with God, centered around Jerusalem or Heliopolis, or perhaps both of these temple communities.

The text closely parallels Daniel passages that symbolically recast the history of the 160s: thousands shall be slayed during times of trials (7:21, 23; 11:41; 12:1), an anointed one is being cut off (commonly identified with Onias III; 9:26),[15] and the trials will ultimately lead to a renewed relation of the nation with God (7:18, 27).

My interpretation of Zech 13:7–9 suggests that scribes in Judea or Heliopolis saw the need to update and actualize Zech 12–14 in light of the murder of Onias III and the upheavals of the 160s. In their eyes, the hypotext was unfinished and in need of a continuation. The subsequent 14:2–5 may have been polished in the same editorial stage (my translation):

> ²For I will gather all the nations against Jerusalem to battle,
> the city shall be taken, the houses looted, the women raped,
> half the city shall go into exile,
> but the rest of the people shall not be cut off from the city.
> ³Then Yhwh will go forth and fight against those nations
> as he fights on a day of battle. . . .
> ⁵And you shall flee by the valley of my mountains,
> for the valley between the mountains shall reach to Azal,
> and you shall flee as you fled from the earthquake in the days of
> King Uzziah of Judah.
> Then Yhwh my God will come, and all the holy ones with him.

Zechariah 14:2–3 may refer to Antiochus's twofold sacking of Jerusalem in 169–168. Those fleeing from the city and going into exile may refer to those

---

15. *Yikkārēt māšîaḥ* ("an anointed will be cut off") may indicate the death of the anointed or his being taken away from the priestly office.

who followed Onias IV to Egypt. Daniel 12:1 ("the many who will escape from the trials") may have the same reference. The concluding stich parallels the Ancient of Days taking the throne and the thousands of angels prostrating before him (7:9–10). The oracle concludes with the only occurrence in Zechariah of the term *qədōšîm* ("holy ones")—a term well known from Dan 7, where it refers to both the angels and the earthly "people of the holy ones" (i.e., the community in alliance with the angels; Collins 1993, 313–19). In the early second-century poetic preamble to the Book of Watchers (1 En 1:3–9), "the Great Holy One will appear with his heavenly armies, he comes with myriads of *holy ones*." These parallels with Dan 7:9–10 and 1 En 1:3–9 bolster my theory of an early-second-century date for parts of Zech 13–14.

A comparison of Zech 13–14 with Dan 7, 9, 11, 12 suggests that all these chapters in different ways contain symbolic reflections of the bloody history of Judah and Jerusalem in the decade following the murder of Onias III.

How did the scribal editor of Zech 13:7–9 intend his text to be read? The text could have been written (a) after the murder of Onias and reflect the first experience of Antiochus's persecutions, expecting worse to come, or (b) after the persecutions as a *vaticinium ex eventu* text or using the events typologically in a foretelling on the future or the end times.

A Mighty Messiah with Heavenly Powers

The Son of Man in Daniel 7

Daniel 7 is a composite chapter that grew to its final form during the Maccabean Revolt. In a manner typical of apocalyptic writings, 7:2–8, 11–12 is a historic allegory of the empires ruling the Middle East, culminating in the last horn to grow forth at the head of the beast, a horn that pushes other horns aside and is boasting with arrogant words (i.e., Antiochus Epiphanes). At the end, the beast with the horn is being killed, the beasts that symbolize the empires are deposed, and the time of their termination is decided. This part of the vision does not reveal what will come thereafter.

Daniel 7:15–27 follows the interpretation of the allegory, also specifying the sins of the arrogant last horn. At the end, his power will be broken and the people of God will receive ultimate power; their kingdom will last forever.

Interspersed here is the throne vision of 7:9–10, 13–14. In this judgment scene, heavenly thrones are set for the Ancient of Days and the Son of Man—

after the latter has arrived with the clouds of heaven. Then, the Ancient of Days gives the Son of Man ultimate power over all the earth:

> ⁹Thrones were set in place,
> and the Ancient of Days took his seat.
> His garment was like white snow,
> and the hair of his head was like lamb's wool.
> His throne was tongues of flame,
> and its wheels blazing fire.
> ¹⁰A river of fire streamed forth before him,
> thousands upon thousands worshiped him,
> myriads upon myriads attended him.
> The court sat and the books were opened. . . .
> ¹³One like a human being
> came with the clouds of heaven,
> he reached the Ancient of Days
> and was presented to him.
> ¹⁴Dominion, glory, and kingship were given to him,
> all peoples and nations of every language must serve him.
> His dominion is an everlasting dominion that shall not pass away,
> and his kingdom shall not be destroyed. (Dan 7:9–10, 13–14
> NJPS adapted)

A postexilic reading of two early royal psalms may provide some background for the Son of Man in Dan 7. In Ps 110, the earthly Davidic king is enthroned alongside God's heavenly throne. In the postexilic addition of 110:4, he is bestowed with a priestly office and ministry. The full postexilic version of Ps 110 may be compared with texts from the second and first century, where the earthly priest or high priest appears with some kind of an "online" connection with the heavenly sanctuary.

Psalm 2 describes a close union between Yhwh and the king: "The rulers take counsel together, against Yhwh and his anointed" (2:2). And the divine proclamation to the king, "You are my son; today I have begotten you" (2:7), would have potential to inspire reflections on a godlike or heavenly status of the messiah.[16]

---

16. Another relevant royal text is the plea for the king in Ps 80:18 [80:17]: "Let your hand be upon the man at your right hand, the son of humankind you made strong for yourself!" In the second colon, the king is designated "son of humankind" (*ben-'ādām*), the Hebrew equivalent of Aramaic *bar 'ĕnāš*.

Collins (1993, 304–10) lists three main lines of interpretation for the Son of Man: (a) an exalted human being (*bar 'ĕnāš* would normally mean "a son of humankind"), (b) a collective symbol (cf. 7:15–27, where the reign is given to the people of God), and (c) a heavenly being. Collins sympathizes with the third option.

The first option should be given more attention in light of Ps 2 and Ps 110 as well as texts from the scrolls and Enochic writings that refer to humans exalted to or being "online" with the heavenly realms. I sympathize with the minority of scholars who see the Son of Man as an exalted messianic figure (e.g., Noth 1926; Gese 1977, 152–59; 1983, 152–60). The authority he is given over peoples and nations is easiest read in light of biblical texts on the future or universal rule of the Davidic king. We should note the royal terminology of 7:14: "kingship" (*malkû*) is given to the Son of Man, his "kingdom" (*malkût*) shall not be destroyed.

Further, biblical texts before Dan 7 do not afford angelic figures with universal rule or a large empire. And we should keep in mind that the earliest interpretative traditions—4Q521 (second half of second century) and the Enochic Similitudes (second half of first century; see below)—read the Son of Man as a messiah.

Isaiah 11:6–10 and Amos 9:11–15 describe a restored Davidic kingdom with terminology easily connected to some kind of new creation, even if these passages originally were coined in symbolic language. Further, a Davidic figure with a heavenly role and universal rule could find support in Ps 45:7 [45:6], easiest read as a vocative where the Davidic king is addressed as *'ĕlōhîm* ("God/heavenly being"), and Ps 72, which asserts that all nations shall serve him and his name endure forever (72:11, 17).

An earthly Davidic kingdom that breaks through old patterns would need some kind of heavenly support. I would interpret the Son of Man in Dan 7 on this background. If the Son of Man is some kind of Davidic figure, one can perceive three alternative options:

a. an end-time, earthly Davidic king being "online" with heaven while he still rules on earth, in line with the king/messiah of Ps 11
b. a heavenly figure who at a certain point in history is given a messianic office, in the image of a son of David on earth
c. the earthly messianic king being elevated to heaven and enthroned

I tend toward option (a) as the text's original intention. The interpretation history goes more toward (b) and (c). Both New Testament tradition and some Jewish texts refer to a heavenly or preexistent messiah, who at a certain point in salvation history is being sent to earth to perform his ordained ministry (see pp. 295–96, 311–13). As for option (c), already 1 En 12–16 and 17–36, texts from the third and early second century, portray Enoch, a human figure, being moved to the heavenly realms. This line of thought would receive a radical reinterpretation during the next century, in the Parables of 1 En 37–71.

Both before and after the Hasmonean takeover, the power in Jerusalem would belong to the high priest. With a powerful anointed priest, one does not necessarily need a son of David at his side. How then should Davidic promises from the Bible be interpreted? One could either transfer the Davidic figure to the end times or elevate him to the heavens.

The Heavenly Messiah in 4QMessianic Apocalypse

A much-discussed Qumran text casts light on early understanding of the Danielic vision:

> [For hea]ven and earth will obey his anointed,
> [and nothing th]at is in them will turn away from the commandments of the holy ones.
> Be strong, you who seek the Lord, when you serve him!
> Indeed, in this you will find the Lord, all you who hope in your hearts
> that the Lord will attend to the pious and call the righteous by name.
> Over the poor his spirit will hover, with his strength he will restore the faithful,
> on the throne of the eternal kingdom, he will honor the pious,
> he who sets prisoners free, opens the eyes of the blind, and raises up those who are bo[wed down.
> [ ].. I shall hold fast [to the Lord
> [ ].. and by his loving kindness .. [ ][17]
> the fru[it of good dee]ds(?) to a neighbor shall not tarry.

17. Examination of the original fragment in the lab shows that line 9 as reconstructed by the editor Émile Puech in fact represents line 9 *and* 10 in the fragment; cf. Justnes 2009, 189–94.

[12]The Lord shall do glorious things that have never been done,
just as he said.
[13]For he shall heal the badly wounded, revive the dead, and proclaim good news to the afflicted.
[14]He shall satis[fy the poo]r, guide the uprooted, and enrich the
hungry. (4Q521 2 II + 4 1–14, my translation)

4Q521 (4QMessianic Apocalypse) was copied around 100 (DJD 25:36) and
likely authored sometime during the second half of the second century. The
text does not bear features characteristic of the Yahad and is heavily dependent on biblical passages (Justnes 2009, 179–277; Elgvin 2016a).

The passage above should be read as a midrash on Dan 7, Ps 146, and
1 Sam 2. In my view, line 1 makes the text a clear sequel to Dan 7:13–14, as
it attributes universal lordship to "his anointed one" (məšîḥô), that is, *the*
messiah. Whatever the original meaning of "son of humankind" in Daniel,
here this figure is read as the end-time messiah. Daniel 7:13–14 is read as a
heavenly inauguration of Israel's Davidic messiah.[18]

The term "commandments of the holy ones" (line 2) indicates that
the angels are mediators of the commandments that have their source
in God and/or the messiah.[19] While the messiah is the central figure in
lines 1–3,[20] God himself is the acting subject in lines 4–14, which closely
follow Ps 146:7–10 as hypotext. However, the mighty deeds that God
will do belong to the messianic age. The suffix on bə'abodatô ("when you
serve him") in line 3 more likely refers to the messiah than God; compare
"obey his anointed" (line 1) and all nations serving (√pəlaḥ) the Son of
Man in Dan 7:14.

---

18. Based on biblical usage, the term məšîḥô ("his anointed") in the singular would refer to the royal messiah. Cf. the usage in the royal/messianic psalms: "your anointed one"
(Pss 2:2; 89:52 [89:51]) and "my anointed one" (132:17). In Isa 45:1, Cyrus is "his anointed,"
the royal redeemer. "Yhwh's anointed" designates the king in Lam 4:20 and 1–2 Samuel
(1 Sam 24:7, 11 [24:6, 10]; 26:9, 11, 16, 23; 2 Sam 1:14, 16; 19:22 [19:21]). In Lam 4:20
and 1–2 Samuel, the thematic context is (not) hurting "Yhwh's anointed," echoed in Ps
89:39 [89:38]. In contrast, in the contemporary Isa 45:1 ("thus says Yhwh to his anointed
[məšîḥô], to Cyrus") and the later Ps 132:17 ("a lamp for my anointed one [məšîḥî]") "my/
his anointed" is a designation of honor.

19. The "holy ones" of 4Q521 may be identified with the angels of Dan 7:10, who
are witnesses to the end-time judgment, implemented according to heavenly commandments. "Commandments of the holy ones" should be compared with "words of the holy
ones" (4:14 [4:17]).

20. Line 3 ends with a paragraph marker, a *vacat*.

In Dan 7:9–14, the focus is the reign given to the Son of Man, while in 7:15–27, it is the restoration of the people of God and the reign given to it by divine intervention. This twofold structure recurs in 4Q521, where lines 1–3 have the messiah in focus, while lines 4–14 describe how God will restore and redeem the elect community. The Son of Man is not mentioned in Dan 7:15–27, neither is the messiah in 4Q521, lines 4–14. In 4Q521, the enthronement of a messiah in heaven will lead to a renewal of God's people on earth.

As many interpreters note, this text (or the tradition it represents) receives sequels in the Gospels, Matt 11:2–6 ‖ Luke 7:18–23 and 4:18–19. However, few have seen that the closest textual echo of "[for hea]ven and earth will obey his anointed . . . when you serve him" is the last words of Jesus in Matt 28:18: "All authority in heaven and on earth has been given to me," preceded by "they worshiped him" (28:17).

The Enochic Son of Man

The texts of the literary collection 1 Enoch were influential in Second Temple Judaism, New Testament writings, and subsequent church tradition. Following a presentation of the poem of the end time judgment that opens 1 Enoch, this section focuses on the Son of Man in the Enochic Book of Parables (chapters 37–71).

Genesis 5:18–24 provides the annalistic records of the life of Enoch, great-grandfather of Noah. According to 5:24, "Enoch walked with God; then he was no more, for God took him [*lāqaḥ 'ōtô*]"—thus, a human figure was moved up to the heavenly realms.[21] This enigmatic statement inspired apocalyptically oriented Judean scribes to write about Enoch's heavenly sojourn and his journeys in the upper world. Enoch, the "righteous scribe" (1 En 15:1) situated in the heavens, communicates to scribes below about his journeys as well as the secrets of the end time.

Either based on Gen 6:1–5 or preserving a parallel tradition, the Book of Watchers (1 En 1–36) describes the revolt of the angels and their descendants the Watchers, the judgment on the Watchers, and Enoch as intermediary between the Watchers and the heavenly judge. The Book of Watchers grew to a literary unit close to its present shape during the third and early second

---

21. *Lāqaḥ* is used four times about God taking a person unto himself: Gen 5:24; 2 Kgs 2:3 (Elijah); Ps 49:16 [49:15]; 73:24 (Elgvin and Kumpmann 2013, 534).

centuries. Nickelsburg suggests that a composite Enochic testament developed in the pre-Maccabean period, consisting of 1 En 1–5; 6–11 (likely); 12–33; 81:1–82:4; 91; plus parts of 92–105. Chapters 1–5 were written in the early second century as the introduction to chapters 6–36 (or 12–36), to prepare the "chosen and righteous ones" (1:1) for the coming judgment and tribulation (Nickelsburg 2001, 25–26, 131–34).

The full text of 1 Enoch is known only from Ethiopian manuscripts from the fifteenth century onward, and the book would necessarily undergo textual and literary changes during its odyssey from Aramaic (partly preserved in eleven fragmentary Qumran manuscripts that cover less than one-fifth of the text) through Greek to Ethiopic (and the Ethiopic textual tradition is also dynamic). Apart from the fragmentary Aramaic evidence, this ancient Jewish collection has survived through Christian transmission, and we do not know to what degree Christian scribes edited and changed the text. A comparison of the Qumran fragments of 1 Enoch and Jubilees with the Ethiopic recensions reveals substantial literary changes.

First Enoch and Jubilees were translated from Greek to Geez around the sixth century as part of the larger project of translating the Bible into Geez (Nickelsburg 2001, 15; Nickelsburg and VanderKam 2012, 30–34). Fragments of a papyrus discovered in a Christian grave in Gizeh, Egypt, in 1887 preserved a Greek translation of 1 Enoch 1–32:6. Then, passages of 1 Enoch in Greek were incorporated into the work of George Syncellus in the early ninth century. A comparison of parallel passages indicates that the Gizeh manuscript generally is close to the Geez version, while Syncellus draws on a different recension. The Book of Parables (1 En 37–71) is preserved only in Ethiopic. More than 120 Ethiopic manuscripts of 1 Enoch are now known (personal communication from Loren Stuckenbruck), dating from the fifteenth to the mid-twentieth century; they can be divided into two textual families (with subdivisions), Eth 1 and Eth 2.

The poetic preamble in 1:3–9 describes the Great Holy One coming with his angelic entourage to judge the world. God himself is the actor; there is no mention of any messiah:

> ³The Great Holy One will come forth from his dwelling,
> ⁴the eternal God will tread from there upon Mount Sinai.
> He will be revealed with his great army,
> will appear in the strength of his might from the heaven of
> heavens.
> All the Watchers will fear and quake,

[5]and those who are hiding in all the ends of the earth will sing.
All the ends of the earth will be shaken,
and trembling and great fear will seize the Watchers unto the
ends of the earth.
[6]The high mountains will be shaken and fall and break apart,
the high hills will be made low and melt like wax before the fire.
[7]The earth will be wholly rent asunder,
and everything on the earth will perish,
[8]and there will be judgment on all.
With the righteous he will make peace.
Over the chosen there will be protection,
and upon them will be mercy.
They will all be God's,
and he will grant them his good pleasure.
Light will shine upon them,
and he will make peace with them.
[9]Behold, he comes with the myriads of his holy ones
to execute judgment on all,
and to destroy all the wicked and to convict all flesh
for all the wicked deeds they have done,
and the proud and hard words that wicked sinners spoke against
him. (1 En 1:3–9, translation Nickelsburg 2001, 142)[22]

First En 1–5 in general, and this poem in particular, evinces a prophetic self-understanding with the author (Nickelsburg 2001, 132–33). The judgment will lead to a universal re-creation, with all nations becoming righteous and honoring God (10:16–11:2; 5:7–9; cf. Elgvin 2003, 95–96).

While there is no messiah in the Book of Watchers, this will change in the latest section of 1 Enoch, the Book of Parables (also denoted Similitudes) in 1 En 37–71.

The Book of Parables can be subdivided: introduction (1 En 37), first parable (1 En 38–44), second parable (1 En 45–57), third parable (1 En 58–69),

22. Nickelsburg's translation of 1 Enoch is eclectic, comparing the Ethiopic text with the more fragmentary Greek and Aramaic. 1 Enoch 1:1–6 is represented by two small pieces of 4QEn[a] (around twenty words are preserved). The oracle relates transtextually to biblical theophanies (e.g., Deut 33:2; Ps 68:8–9, 18 [68:7–8, 17]), words of judgment (e.g., Isa 24:19–21; 34:1–4; Jer 25:30–31), oracles of future salvation (e.g., Isa 4:2–6; 24:14–16), and the Aaronic blessing (Num 6:24–26). An interpretative sequel to this text appears in the Son of Man theophany in Matt 24:30–31.

and ending (1 En 70–71). The Parables add to the stories of Enoch's sojourn in the heavenly realms. In 1 En 45–69, Enoch sees a heavenly viceroy, a "Son of Man" walking alongside God ("the Lord of Spirits," "the Head of Days") and being set by God on the heavenly throne.

There are affinities between the image of the Son of Man in the Parables and synoptic sayings on the end-time coming of the Son of Man. The evangelists are either dependent on the Parables or a common tradition of a heavenly mediator. I side with scholars who trace this synoptic tradition back to Jesus himself. In his survey of the Book of Parables, Wisdom 1–6, 4 Ezra 11–13, and 2 Baruch, Nickelsburg (1992) identifies a shared tradition about a transcendent judge and redeemer that developed ideas from Dan 7 and royal traditions in Ps 2 and Isa 11—a tradition used by the Synoptics.

The date of composition of the Parables is contested. They are absent from the Aramaic and Greek manuscripts and are not quoted in patristic literature.[23] A scholarly consensus has slowly drifted toward a date of the Parables between 40 BCE and 1 BCE, while a minority clings to a date between 1 CE and 70 CE.[24] At a certain stage, the Parables were included in a collection of Enochic books that later was translated from Greek into Geez. The many parallels between the Parables and the Book of Watchers stimulated this literary growing together.

A qualification is needed in our discussion of Parables as an early Jewish text: while the core of Parables may be dated around the turn of the era, interpreters need to remember that details in the text known to us could be colored by much later Christian scribes in the Greek and Ethiopic traditions. Thus, God-like features attributed to the Son of Man in 1 En 45–69 could have been inserted or sharpened by scribes who let their Christology give color to the Son of Man envisioned by Enoch.

23. There are affinities between the Parables and the later mystical *hekhalot* literature. Suter (2007, 426–28, 440) argues that the Parables were transmitted in mystical Jewish circles and therefore had a path of transmission separate from the other Enochic books, which soon found their way into Christian codices.

24. For a comprehensive discussion of the scholarly literature, see Suter 2007. Nickelsburg and VanderKam (2012, 58–63) date the Parables to the latter part of Herod's reign, as do Hannah 2007, Eshel 2007, and Arcari 2007. Eshel and Arcari convincingly argue that 1 En 56:5–57:3 symbolically depicts the Parthian invasion of Judea in 40 and the physical maiming of Hyrcanus II by his nephew Matthias Antigonus, to make the former unfit for the high-priestly office. For Suter (2007, 439–43), the Parables underwent a literary growth parallel to the synoptic Son of Man tradition during the first century CE, with Matthew being literarily dependent on the Parables.

Different biblical images converge in the Parables' image of the Son of Man. The title and heavenly character echo Dan 7:13–14. Being set on the heavenly throne develops the Danielic text and Ps 110. "My chosen one" and "light for the nations" (1 En 45:3–4; 48:6; 49:2; 51:3; 61:5, 8) point to the servant of Yhwh (Isa 42:1, 6). Righteousness dwells with the Son of Man, similar to the messianic shoot and suffering servant in Isaiah (1 En 46:3; 49:2; Isa 11:1–5; 53:11). He is "the anointed one" like the royal messiah (1 En 48:10; Ps 2:2).

In 1 En 45, 61, 62, and 69, the Son of Man is set on the throne of glory, receives praise and laudation, and presides at the end-time judgment—it is the Son of Man who sits on the throne, not the Head of Days. Sinners and iniquity will be destroyed, while the righteous will be resurrected to a blessed life on a renewed earth.

Toward the end of the literary growth of the Parables, an appendix (1 En 70–71) was added. Here, Enoch receives the surprising message that the enthroned Son of Man is no other than himself:

> [14]You are the Son of Man who was born for righteousness,
> and righteousness dwells on you,
> and the righteousness of the Head of Days will not forsake you.
>
> . . .
>
> [16]And all will walk on your path since righteousness will never
>   forsake you,
> with you will be their dwellings and with you, their lot,
> and from you they will not be separated forever and ever.
> [17]And thus, there will be length of days with that Son of Man,
> and there will be peace for the righteous, and the path of truth
>   for the righteous,
> in the name of the Lord of Spirits forever and ever. (1 En 71:14, 16–
>   17, translation from Nickelsburg and VanderKam 2012, 321)

In 1 En 45–71, the Son of Man is portrayed as mediator between God and humankind, a heavenly source of redemption and righteousness. While subordinate to the Lord of Spirits, he has godlike or divine features. He is preexistent and hidden in God's abode (48:3–6; 62:7); his glory will last forever (48:2); all who dwell on the earth will fall down and worship before him (48:5; 61:11–12; 62:6–9).

The Parables understand Dan 7:9–14 as an unfinished hypotext that is in need of a continuation. The judgment scene in 7:9–11 is elaborated throughout the Parables. According to 7:14, "all shall serve him"—recurring in the worship of the Son of Man (1 En 48:5; 62:6–9).[25] Another point of reference could be the use of *'ĕlōhîm* for the messiah in Ps 45:7 [45:6]: "Your throne, *'ĕlōhîm*, endures forever and ever, your royal scepter is a scepter of equity" (see pp. 163–65).

The People of God as the End-Time Messianic Community

The texts of Ben Sira, Tobit, and 11QPs[a]Zion surveyed above envision a glorious future for Jerusalem without any mention of the son of David. Then there are texts that continue biblical traditions of Yhwh as the sole actor in the end-time drama (e.g., 1 En 1–11). In some texts, the people of God appear as the eschatological messianic community (cf. Isa 55:1–5, where the Davidic promises are bequeathed to the nation in its return to Zion). In Dan 7:15–27, the sequence of the vision of the Son of Man, the people of the holy ones (those allied with the angels) are refined through trials and given eternal reign.

Monti defines the concept "collective messianism" as following: messianic expectations express the certainty of the coming of a new fortunate world, established through one or more mediators of salvation endowed with special gifts of God. In collective messianic expectations, redemption occurs through the action of the people of God (Monti 2004, 28; Sayyad Bach 2020, 238–39).[26]

A Daniel-related text from the second century is a prime example of this line of interpretation. This Aramaic text is commonly called "the Son of God text" and has become famous due to parallels with Gabriel's words during the annunciation (Luke 1:32–35). 4Q246 (4QApocryphon of Daniel ar) preserves a full column and a half of the preceding one from a larger scroll. The text, with my suggested reconstructions, runs as follows:[27]

25. The verb *pəlaḥ* ("to serve") can have connotations of liturgical service or worship (as *'ābad* has in 4Q246 I 8 and perhaps in 4Q521 2 II 3).

26. In her discussion of collective messianism, Sayyad Bach (2020, 239) notes that the Bible twice uses "his/your anointed" in the singular when referring to the people of God (Ps 28:8: "Yhwh is the strength of his people; he is the saving refuge of his anointed"; Hab 3:13: "You went out for the salvation of your people, to save your anointed"). However, these two hymnic passages do not have an eschatological horizon.

27. My translation is indebted to Justnes, Cook, and Fitzmyer. In I 2–3, *'atā* should (with Cook 1995) be read as the word "come," not "you." In I 4, I read (with Justnes) the

^{I.1}[fear] came [u]pon him. He fell before the throne of

²[the king   I said, "Live,] O king, forever! Wrath comes, and your years

³[are counted   revealed in] your vision, everything that shall come forever.

⁴[be b]attles, and oppression will come over the earth.

⁵[carnage in the land], and great slaughter in the provinces,

⁶[brought about by] the king of Assyria, [and E]gypt[28]

⁷[will be hit hard   this king] will be great on the earth,

⁸[him all will] worship and all will serve,

⁹[son of the g]reat [God] he shall call himself, by his name he shall designate himself.

^{II.1}He shall call himself son of God, and they shall call him son of the Most High.

Like the meteors ²that you saw, so shall their rule be changi[ng]:

they shall rule over ³the earth and trample everything down:

people shall trample upon people, province trample upon [pro]vince,

⁴   until the people of God will rise and make everything rest from the sword.

⁵Its kingdom shall be an everlasting kingdom and all its paths in righteousness.

It shall jud[ge] ⁶the land in truth and make everything whole.

The sword shall cease from the earth, ⁷and all the provinces shall pay it homage.

The great God is its strength, ⁸he himself shall wage war for it.

---

first word as *[q]rabîn* ("battles"). In I 8, *ʿābad* is interpreted as "worship." In II 2, I restore (with Justnes) *šany[ʾā]* ("changing") rather than *šanî[n]* ("year[s]").

28. Most scholars read "the king of Assyria and Egypt" or "the kings of Assyria and Egypt." Only Fitzmyer (1994) correctly recognizes that "and Egypt" introduces a new sentence. My interpretation of lines 6–7 would fit the intrusions by Antiochus, "the king of Assyria," into Egypt in 170–169 and 168.

> He shall give peoples in its hand and [9]cast them all down
>> before it.
> Its dominion shall be an everlasting dominion, and all the
>> deeps of

The scholarly discussion on the text is vast. Various and contrasting reconstructions have been proposed for the lacunas in column I. My main line of interpretation follows Justnes (2009, 29–178).

This text is a hypertextual sequel to Dan 7:7–9, 11–12, 15–27, authored sometime between 164 (the commonly assumed final date for Dan 7) and 100, preferably soon after 164. In the text, a prophetlike person is called to the court to interpret the king's vision, similar to Joseph before pharaoh. The imaginary king could be the Ptolemaic ruler (cf. my interpretation of I 6–7).

The parallels with Dan 7 indicate that the main figure in I 5–II 1 is neither a messiah nor a heavenly being, but rather an ungodly king. The boasting king is modeled on or written as a recast of Antiochus Epiphanes, but also has features of an antichrist.[29] In the second century, the Isaianic term "king of Assyria" is reinterpreted as the contemporary king in Damascus and concretely as Antiochus Epiphanes (see pp. 193–94, 224). 4Q246 II 2–3 refers to the political struggles among the Seleucids and between the Seleucids and Ptolemies in the early second century. The rise and fall of these earthly kingdoms are likened to meteors that had appeared in the king's vision: the "career" of a meteor rapidly changes; it shines brightly in the heavens but will soon collapse (Justnes 2009, 128–32; Sayyad Bach 2020, 229).

The parallels with Luke 1:32–35 do not make the ruler of 4Q246 I 4–II 1 a messiah. They rather demonstrate the closeness between Luke's messianic terminology and royal ideology in the ancient Near East. The Gospels were written at a time when the imperial cult was intensified, not the least in the eastern parts of the Roman Empire (cf., e.g., Josephus, *Jewish War* 4.168; Brent 1999, 66–72; Hørning Jensen 2020, 26–32, 38). The words of the annunciation certainly relate to Davidic texts in the Bible. But this text, as many others in the Gospels, vibrates with tension vis-à-vis Roman imperial

---

29. For a survey of scholarship, see Justnes 2009, 32–73. The figure called "Son of God" is identified as an ungodly king such as Alexander Balas (150–145) by Milik; as a royal messiah by Cross, Fitzmyer, Kuhn, Puech, and Collins; as an antichrist figure by Flusser; as an angelic liberator by García Martínez; and as Antiochus Epiphanes by Cook, Steudel, Puech, and Justnes. In his early publications, Puech favors a messianic reading, while he later (1999) identifies the Son of God with Antiochus Epiphanes.

ideology. Thus, 4Q246 remains important for the interpretation of Luke 1:32–35 and New Testament proclamation of Jesus as messiah.[30]

4Q246 II 4–9 presents a crux. The earthly actor who has God as his strength is consistently referred to with a singular suffix—its/his, which can be read either as a divinely blessed king or the end-time people of God. My translation follows the latter option. Line 4 opens with a paragraph marker (a *vacat*), which indicates the new era, the restoration of the people of God.[31] The text of col. II is complete; no king or messiah is introduced before lines 5–9 elaborate on the end-time kingdom given to God's people. As in Dan 7:15–27, the people of God, which has been through turmoil and suffering, emerges as the victor of the end time. According to 4Q246 II 5–6, the elect nation either "rules the land in righteousness" or "judges the land in truth."[32] In this text, the restored people of the end time is portrayed as God's messianic community.[33]

The Hasmonean Kingdom and Messianic Expectations

The Maccabean project started as a guerrilla revolt for Torah, temple, and Israelite purity. It developed into a state-building project with an organized

---

30. The same Jewish tradition on the evil king with antichrist features appears in the *Oracle of Hystaspes* (early first century CE; see pp. 301–2): the oracle foresees an evil king arising from Syria, taking dominion of the empire, invading the holy land and attempting to destroy the temple. This king will be a prophet of lies who will take on a divine name and demand to be worshiped as the Son of God. Flusser (1980, 36–37) notes this parallel.

31. Puech, Steudel, Justnes, and Sayyad Bach understand line 4 as a heading for the following, but it is not correct that the line is framed by a *vacat* on each end (contra Justnes 2009, 84, 134; Sayyad Bach 2020, 230)—the first word of line 5 is too long for the empty space available at the end of line 4.

32. *Dîn baqašôt* means either "rule in righteousness" or "judge in truth." For the latter option, cf. other Jewish texts describing the elect community in the role of judging the nations or the ungodly (Matt 19:28 ‖ Luke 22:30; Rev 20:4) and texts from the second century: 1 En 27:2–3: "Here all the cursed will be gathered . . . at the last times, in the days of righteous judgment in the presence of the righteous of all times"; 1 En 91:12 (= 4Q212 IV 15–16): "An eighth week of righteousness, in which a sword will be given to all the righteous, to execute judgment on all the wicked"; 4Q418 (4QInstr^d) 69 II 7–8: "The seekers of truth will wake up to the judgments [of . . .], all the foolish of heart will be destroyed, and the sons of iniquity will not be found anymore"; 1QH^a XIV 29–30: "And then the sword of God will come quickly at the time of judgment. All the children of truth will rouse themselves to extermin[ate] wickedness, and all the children of guilt will be no more."

33. In reading II 4–9 collectively on the people of God, I follow García Martínez, Steudel, Justnes, and Sayyad Bach (see bibliography).

army, territorial ambitions, and a military expansionist policy vis-à-vis the surrounding nations (see Elgvin 2016b, 2021b).

The expansion of the tiny Seleucid province of Judea began under Jonathan (160–142) and Simon (142–135). The eulogy for Simon in 1 Macc 14:5–7 praises Simon for "taking Joppa and making it his harbor, an entranceway to the islands of the sea" and "extending the borders of his nation and gaining full control in the land." In Jerusalem, he "conquered the Citadel and cast out the unclean things from it"—finally evicting the Seleucid garrison from the Acra, the fortress built by Antiochus Epiphanes in the upper part of the City of David ridge.[34]

John Hyrcanus (135–105) took over from his father Simon. Thus, a sequence of Maccabean brothers as rulers was transformed into a Hasmonean dynasty. Soon after the death of Antiochus VII in 129, Hyrcanus conquered lands east of the Jordan. Then he turned his eyes to the north. Textual and archaeological evidence suggest that most of lower and eastern Galilee and of the Golan was Judaized already by Hyrcanus,[35] with the conquest of Beth-shan (Scythopolis) in 108 as his final great achievement in the north (*Antiquities* 13.280). In 112, he burnt Shechem and the sanctuary at Mount Gerizim, occupied all of Samaria in 108, and conquered Idumea with its capital Maresha in 107.[36] During his short reign, Aristobulus (105–104) expanded the territory in the north, while Jannaeus (104–76) conquered the Golan and northern Gilead as well as Moabite territory east of the Dead Sea. The two latter called themselves king—in itself a pointer to the preexilic Davidic kingdom.

The Hasmonean expansion of territory led to forced conversion of the Idumeans in the south in 107[37] and probably of all gentiles who remained in the conquered territories.

---

34. The Givati excavations south of the Temple Mount have unearthed sections of the Acra (Ben-Ami and Tchekhanovets 2015; Ben-Ami 2015). See figure 8, p. 214.

35. Leibner 2012, 468–69. More than three hundred coins of Hyrcanus suggest that Gamla was settled by Judeans during his reign, with Jannaeus overthrowing the local ruler of Gamla around 80 (Josephus, *Jewish War* 1.103–6; *Antiquities* 13.394). Coins minted by Aristobulus are primarily found in Galilee and Golan, corroborating reports by Josephus that during his short reign Aristobulus acted mainly in the north (*Antiquities* 13.318–19; Syon 2015, 151–70).

36. The destruction layers in Shechem and Mount Gerizim are dated to 112/111, in the city of Samaria to 108/107, and in Maresha to 107/106.

37. Josephus, *Antiquities* 13.257–58, 395–97. Josephus's report of forced conversion of Iturean settlements in the north by Aristobulus in 105–104 (*Antiquities* 13.318–19) has not been confirmed by archaeologists.

With the military conquests of Hyrcanus, Aristobulus, and Jannaeus, an Israelite state was established that matched the biblical accounts of the united kingdom and—according to historians and archaeologists—by far superseded the size of the territory ruled by David and Solomon, or the Northern and Southern Kingdoms of the ninth century together. Jerusalem was rebuilt and the temple compound restored. Under the Hasmoneans, the population of Jerusalem grew from less than 1,500 to 6,000 inhabitants (Geva 2007, 2015). Such remarkable achievements after more than four hundred years of subjugation under world empires would lead to messianic fervor in some circles and to critical reflection in others.

Hasmonean and Anti-Hasmonean Use of Scriptures

A number of Yahad texts are critical toward the Hasmoneans critique against the "Wicked Priest" (an acronym either for Jonathan, Simon, or a sequence of Hasmonean rulers). They address the misuse of wealth; a wicked, divisive, and violent leadership; and disobedience to halakhic rules of purity, but any criticism of the Hasmonean expansion of the state is hard to find.

The Temple Scroll may not be a composition of the Yahad, but it aligns closely with Yahad ideology. The treatise of kingship in 11QT^a (11Q19) 56–59 prescribes that the king shall be subject to a council of chiefs, priests, and Levites (57:12–15). This alternative version of the Deuteronomic law of the king may be read as a critique of Alexander Jannaeus, tacitly tolerating his claim to kingship but setting severe limitations on the king's prerogatives. 11QT^a may be the only Qumran text that criticizes the expansionist policy of the new Judean commonwealth: 58:3–11 limits the commitment of troops for warfare against external enemies to a specified percentage of the total force, giving priority to the defense of the cities in the homeland. Unlike other rules in this treatise, this nonexpansionist policy lacks scriptural support; it may be a critique triggered by Jannaeus's military practice.

Hasmonean rulers and their supporters enlisted the Torah, the Prophets, and Davidic Psalms as legitimation for their new state, a Judea with messianic pretensions. Scriptures combined with a belief in divine election were used to legitimate a leadership that used an iron fist both against external and internal threats. Even the apocalyptic book of Daniel was brought to bear: 1 Macc 2:59–64 enlists Daniel and his three friends as types and ideals for the Hasmonean cause.

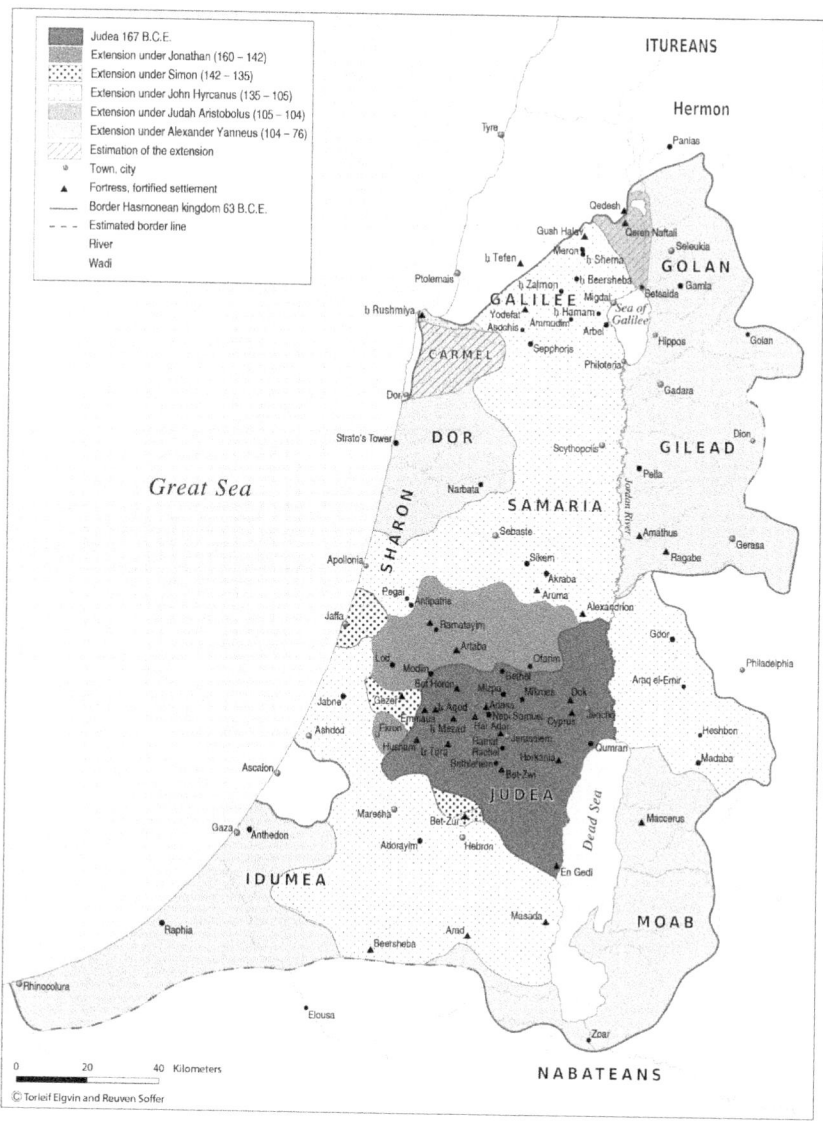

Figure 7. The growth of Judea under the Hasmoneans.

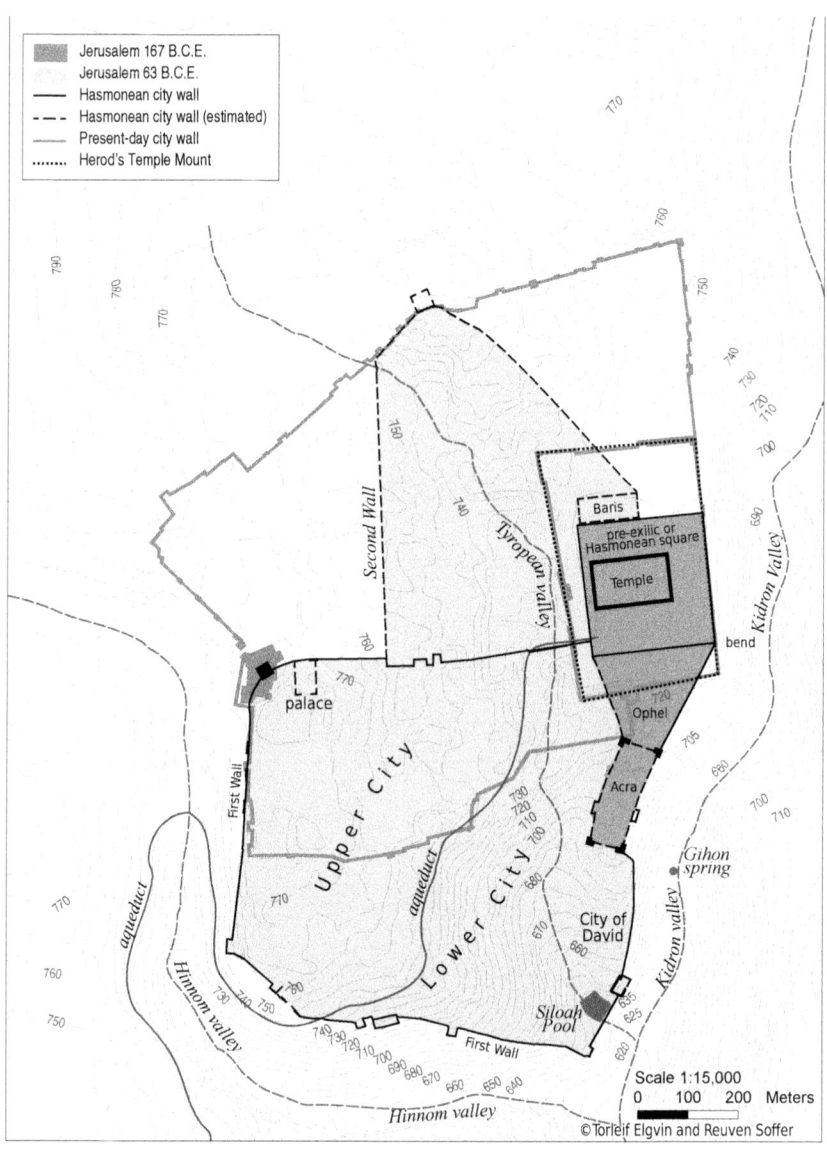

Figure 8. The growth of Jerusalem under the Hasmoneans.

With its first recension from the 120s, 1 Maccabees is a consistent apology for the Hasmoneans as elect deliverers of the Judean nation. They are the "men to whom was given salvation to Israel by their hand," as David was in his time (1 Macc 5:62, echoing 2 Sam 2:17; Goldstein 1987, 80). First Macc 13:41 ("the yoke of the gentiles was lifted from Israel") sees the liberation from the Seleucid Empire—the latter-day Assyria—by the hand of Simon, as fulfillment of Isa 10:27 and 14:25 (Goldstein 1987, 77). Through their actions, the Maccabees restored the righteousness and independence of Israel.

The Hasmoneans saw themselves as an integral part of biblical history, walking in the footsteps of David and Solomon. This is evidenced in two poetic eulogies honoring Judah the Maccabee and Simon after their deaths (1 Macc 3:3–9; 14:4–15), which contain a number of echoes or allusions to biblical texts on the son of David and the future Davidic kingdom (Goldstein 1976, 244, 490–91; Horbury 2003, 49). These anointed priestly rulers were hailed as small messiahs, bringing to some kind of fulfillment Davidic prophecies from the Bible as well as general prophecies on God turning the fate of his people (keywords recur from Gen 49:9; 1 Sam 17:5, 38; 1 Kgs 5:3–5 [4:23–25]; 8:13; Isa 11:4; Mic 4:4; 5:3–5 [5:4–6]; Zech 9:10; Pss 2:10; 45:18 [45:17]; 72:4, 17–19; 110:5–6). First on Judah the Maccabee:

> ³He extended the fame of his people.
> He put on the breastplate like a giant,
> girded on his war harness and waged battles,
> protecting the camp by his sword.
> ⁴He was like a lion in his deeds,
> like a lion's cub roaring for prey.
> ⁵He searched out and pursued those who broke the law,
> he burned those who troubled his people.
> ⁶Lawbreakers shrank back for fear of him,
> all the evildoers were confounded,
> and deliverance prospered by his hand.
> ⁷He brought bitterness to many kings
> and rejoicing to Jacob by his deeds,
> his memory is blessed forever.
> ⁸He went through the cities of Judah,
> he destroyed the ungodly out of the land,
> turning away wrath from Israel.
> ⁹His name resounded to the ends of the earth,
> he gathered in those who were lost. (1 Macc 3:3–9, my translation)

Then on Simon:

> [4]The land was at peace throughout the days of Simon.
> He sought the good of his nation
> his rule was pleasing to them,
> as was his fame throughout his life.
> [5]With great honor he took Joppa and made it his harbor,
> an entranceway to the islands of the sea.
> [6]He extended the borders of his nation,
> and gained full control in the land.
> [7]He gathered a host of captives,
> he conquered Gazara, Beth-zur, and the Citadel,
> and cast out the unclean things from it,
> and no one could resist him.
> [8]They farmed their land in peace,
> the land gave its produce,
> the trees of the plain their fruit.
> [9]Old men sat at ease in the streets,
> they all talked together of good things,
> the young men put on splendid military attire.
> [10]He supplied the towns with food,
> and furnished them with means of defense,
> his fame resounded to the ends of the earth.
> [11]He established peace in the land,
> and Israel knew great joy.
> [12]Each man sat under his own vine and fig tree,
> and there was none to make them afraid.
> [13]No enemy was left in the land to fight them,
> and the kings were crushed in those days.
> [14]He gave help to all the needy among his people,
> he strove to observe the law,
> and cleared away every lawless and wicked man.
> [15]He gave new splendor to the temple,
> replenishing it with sacred vessels. (1 Macc 14:4–15,
>   my translation)

Judah "was like a lion in his deeds, like a lion's cub roaring for prey"—an echo of the blessing of Judah in Gen 49:9. Judah the Maccabee is thus the

"Lion of Judah" of his time.[38] The transition from a ruler of the "tribe of Judah" in 49:8–12 to the "warrior Judah the Maccabee" is easily done; his acts align with the fighter envisioned in 49:8–9. The proclamations that "his memory is blessed forever" and "his name resounded to the ends of the earth" bring to mind the royal/messianic Ps 72:8, 17. "He gathered in those who were lost" would recall prophecies of the ingathering of the dispersed ones (Ezek 34:12–13; 36:24; Mic 4:6). The description of Judah's armor recalls that of Goliath, Saul, and David (1 Sam 17:5, 38).

When Simon made Joppa "an entranceway to the islands of the sea and extended the borders of his nation," he fulfilled prophecies of the future Davidic rule reaching "from the sea to the sea" and "from the River to the sea," (Ps 72:8; Zech 9:10; Ps 89:26 [89:25]. "They farmed their land in peace," "each man sat under his own vine and fig tree," and "he established peace in the land" allude to Mic 4:4 and 5:3–4 [5:4–5]. "No enemy was left in the land to fight them, and the kings were crushed in those days" echoes Ps 2:9 and 110:2, 5. "His fame resounded to the end of the earth" recalls Ps 72:8.[39] And "he gave help to all the needy among his people" points to the messianic promise in Isa 11:4. When Simon "gave new splendor to the temple, replenishing it with sacred vessels," this brings to mind David's instructions to Solomon on the temple equipment in 1 Chr 28:11–18 and the listing of the temple vessels in Ezra 1:7–10. When Simon is praised for "crushing the kings in those days," this could echo Ps 110:5–6: "He [God] will strike kings on the day of his wrath . . . he will strike leaders throughout the land." When Judah "brought bitterness to many kings," the eulogy would allude to royal psalms such as Ps 2:1–4, 10–12 and 110:1–2, 5–6.

These two laudatory poems probably existed before their present literary context: in their poetic form they stand out from the surrounding prosaic storyline, and they are more expressed in their allusions to biblical passages

---

38. For the men of the Yahad, Jannaeus was the perverted "Lion of Wrath," as he is called in the Nahum pesher (4Q169 I 5–8).

39. Ps 72 is a psalm "by/for Solomon." As a messianic figure, Solomon—the son of David par excellence—might have been controversial in the Hellenistic period when the high priest was both the religious and civil leader in Judah. However, Sir 47:11–22 and the apocryphal psalm in 11QapocrPs (11Q11) attest to Solomon's popularity. According to 11Q11 I 3–6, Solomon was given both wisdom and gifts of healing and exorcism (cf. Josephus, *Antiquities* 8.44–45). The use of Ps 72 and Ps 110 suggests that Hasmonean reign was connected to Davidic texts already before Aristobulus and Jannaeus took the title "king" beginning in 105.

than the rest of 1 Maccabees. The poem on Judah the Maccabee may have been written during the rule of Jonathan (160–142) or Simon (142–135), serving as legitimation for the continued rule of his brothers, or both were written together soon after Simon's death.

Another indication that the Hasmoneans incorporated Davidic prerogatives is found in the repeated referral to "Judah and his brothers" in 1 Maccabees. This phrase consciously recalls the same form of reference in Genesis, which sets the patriarch Judah (David's ancestor) apart as the leader of Israel (37:26; 38:1; 44:14; 49:8; 1 Chr 5:2; 1 Macc 3:25, 42; 4:36, 59; 5:10, 61, 63, 65; 7:6, 10, 27; cf. "Judah the Maccabee and his brothers" in 1 Macc 8:20 and 2 Macc 2:19).

Ruler and High Priest Forever

By their deeds, the Hasmoneans established themselves not only as rulers but also as legitimate high priests. Phinehas's zeal for the purity of Israel is set as a paradigmatic ideal in 1 Macc 2:24–28. By repeating the deeds of "Phinehas our father," Mattathias and his sons earn God's favor: "And he became zealous in the law as Phinehas had done" (2:26, 54). The covenant of Phinehas, which gave legitimacy to the high priesthood of the house of Zadok, was superseded by the new covenant with the house of the Hasmoneans (Collins 2003, 12–13; Horbury 2003, 48–50).

From 152, the Hasmonean rulers occupied the double office of high priest and civil leader.[40] During the Ptolemaic and Seleucid periods, the high priest had been both civil and religious leader of the Judean province.[41] Ruling priests who downplayed the hope of a Davidic messiah were, therefore, no *novum* with the Hasmoneans. The memory of the Oniads ruling the province of Judea made it easier for governing Hasmonean priests to implement harsh measures against dissidents.

40. The first two generations did not take the title "king." This could have been seen as a provocation by both the Seleucids and Judean opponents. Cf. Mic 4:6–7, which foresees a restored rule from Zion and ingathering of the dispersed, but with Yhwh alone as king of his people—while the editorially added 4:8 would specify that Yhwh's future rule would be implemented through an earthly king (see pp. 102–3).

41. VanderKam (2004, 122–57) argues that the high priests from 320 (Onias I) to 192 (Simon II) functioned as political leaders of the Judeans. According to Lange (2012, 100–105), the expanded proto-Masoretic recension of Jeremiah may reflect third-century criticism of the Oniads as ruling high priests.

Psalm 110 with its priestly king would be a natural reference text for the supporters of the Hasmoneans. In 140, the Judean assembly gave full powers to Simon:

> The Judeans and the priests were pleased that Simon would be their *leader* and high *priest* forever, until a trustworthy *prophet* would arise, and that he would be commander over them . . . over the country and over the armed forces and over the fortresses, and that the responsibility would be upon him concerning the holy places, and that he would be obeyed by all and that all documents in the country would be written in his name. . . . And no one of the people or the priests will be able to set aside any of these resolutions or to dispute anything said by him or to convoke a gathering in the country without his permission. . . . But whoever acts against or sets aside any of these resolutions shall be culpable. . . . And Simon accepted and was pleased to be high priest and commander and ethnarch of the Judeans and priests and to protect them all. (1 Macc 14:41–47, my translation)

The words "leader and high priest forever" consciously echo the royal/messianic Ps 110:4: "You are a priest forever according to the order of Melchizedek." Psalm 110 is here used as legitimation for the Hasmonean rulers and priests. Another apology for this double office can be traced in the reworking of Aramaic Levi into the (hypothetical) second-century source of the Testament of Levi, where Levi the patriarch—the ancestor of the priests—is portrayed with both military and sacerdotal power (Kugler 1996, 224–25).

Simon's edict acknowledges the three offices of ruler, priest, and prophet: two of them were already in function, while the office of prophet was postponed to the future. The collection of scriptures in the sectarian 4Q175 (4QTestimonia) would represent a silent protest:[42] the present anointed leadership is illegitimate; the Yahad still waits for the right prophet together with the anointed ones of Aaron and Israel: "Until the prophet and the anointed ones of Aaron and Israel will arise" (1QS 9:11; see chap. 7 on the futuristic hopes of the Yahad).

There were opponents to Hasmonean priestly rulers also outside the Yahad. First Maccabees repeatedly refers to opponents of the Hasmoneans as "impious and lawless men" who allied themselves with external enemies

---

42. I use the term "sectarian" with the meaning "related to the Yahad/written within the Yahad," without any sociological connotations.

(7:23–24; 9:23–26, 73; 10:14, 61). The nonsectarian 4QpsDan^c (4Q245), written around 100, contains two separate lists of kings and high priests, presupposing a separation of these offices. The lists conclude before the rule of Alexander Jannaeus, who was the second to identify himself both as king and high priest (after the short rule of his brother Aristobulus).[43]

A talmudic text with parallel in Josephus refers to a Pharisaic critique against Jannaeus (Talmud) or Hyrcanus (Josephus), asking him to be satisfied with the office of ruler and leave that of high priest (Babylonian Talmud, tractate *Qiddushin* 66a; Josephus, *Antiquities* 13.288–92). Both texts refer to a rumor that his mother had been a wartime captive, thereby rendering the son unfit for priestly office. According to the Talmud, this disagreement led to the king's violent persecution of the sages.

Two Josephean texts suggest that Hyrcanus countered opposition by claiming also the third office, that of the prophet. Josephus and his pro-Hasmonean source saw Hyrcanus "accounted by God worthy of three of the greatest privileges: the rule of the nation, the office of high priest, and the gift of prophecy" (*Antiquities* 13.299–300). Elsewhere Josephus reports a prophetic revelation given to Hyrcanus in the temple during his priestly service (*Antiquities* 13.282–83), a tradition positively affirmed in the Tosefta (tractate *Sotah* 13.5). These three texts should be seen as Hasmonean counterpropaganda, responding to criticism from movements such as the Yahad and other oppositional voices still waiting for the eschatological prophet to arise with the anointed priest and anointed ruler.

Updating the Scriptures from Hasmonean Facts on the Ground

The territorial expansion of the Judean state under Hyrcanus, Aristobulus, and Jannaeus would by many Judeans be interpreted as a sign of the messianic or proto-messianic age. The inclusion of the Idumeans and other gentiles into the Jewish commonwealth would bring to mind texts such as Amos 9:12, Isa 2:1–4, and Zeph 3:9, which foresee the inclusion of Edom and other neighboring peoples in the Israelite faith and commonwealth. Hyrcanus's razing to the ground of the Samaritan city of Shechem and the temple on

---

43. Wise (2005, 339) sees these lists, which deliberately separate priest from prince, as a silent critique of the Hasmoneans. The lists significantly made no mention of Alexander Jannaeus and seemingly set the eschaton in his reign. Two or three of the Hasmoneans are mentioned as priests, not rulers—a feature suggesting an origin outside the Yahad.

Mount Gerizim in 112 (*Antiquities* 13.254–56; *Jewish War* 1.62–63) would easily be connected to texts that featured the son of David's victory over the enemies of God's people (Pss 2; 110; Mic 5:1–5 [5:2–6]). His conquest of Idumea in 107 would recall the Balaam oracle (Num 24:17–19), as would Jannaeus's conquest of Transjordanian Edom in the 80s.

This expansion set its stamp on the Scriptures. Geographical, topographical, and demographic descriptions in the Bible reflect Hasmonean-era scribes who backdated realities of the Hasmonean state to earlier biblical times. The scribal editors may have considered the Judean nation of their own times as in principle being part of the return of the sixth and fifth centuries, performing an updating of the description of the stories to fit present-time reality (the Passover verses in Exod 12:26–27 reflect the same idea, as later generations became partakers in the exodus).[44]

Such scribes polished the book of Joshua and updated his conquests in the land to concur with the new Judean reality (de Troyer 2018). Scribes also added substantial sections to the books of Nehemiah, Ezra, and Chronicles, so that the description of the expansion of Judah, its borders, fortresses, cities, and inhabitants in preexilic times would fit the reality of Hyrcanus's rapidly growing state: "This means that Chronicles (at least 2 Chr 10–36) was written (or significantly expanded) in the late second century BCE. . . . The solution that I would advocate is to date parts of the books dealt with in this volume to the late Persian or early Hellenistic periods and other parts to Hasmonean times. In the former, I can think, for example, of the Nehemiah Memoir and the description of an ideal Monarchy in 1 Chr 10–2 Chr 9" (Finkelstein 2018, 157, 162).

Topographical lists in Joshua, Chronicles, and Nehemiah as well as genealogies in Ezra were written or revised to reflect the rapidly growing Judea under the Hasmonean rulers Simon (142–135) and Hyrcanus (135–105). Finkelstein notes that the large numbers of returnees in Ezra 2:1–67 and Neh 7:6–68 does not match the limited settlement identified by archaeologists in sixth- and fifth-century Yehud. Neither does the description of the builders of Jerusalem and their districts in Neh 3 match reality in Jerusalem and Judea before 140 (Finkelstein 2018, 3–70). For Finkelstein, this means that the books of Ezra and Nehemiah were developing into the early Hasmonean period. This suggests a relatively short period of time from the finalizing of these books to their earliest extant copy (one scroll, 4QEzra [4Q117], from the mid-first century).[45] If Ezra and Nehemiah were indeed finalized or pol-

---

44. For the following, cf. Carr's detailed discussion (2011, 158–79).

45. The international team I have been leading discovered two fake Nehemiah frag-

ished in the early Hasmonean period, the responsible editors may have been close to the Hasmonean top echelon. This could explain the limited circulation of these books within the Yahad (the Qumran community)—only one extant scroll—and possibly in Judea at large.

Lee-Sak (2017) argues that the lists of Levitical towns in Josh 21 and 1 Chr 6:39–66 [6:54–81] fit only the mid- or late-Hasmonean period, the time before Hyrcanus conquered Idumea, Samaria, and the central highlands in the years 112–107. A number of the sites mentioned in these biblical lists fit the territory of Hyrcanus, while some were captured by Jannaeus in the 90s and 80s. Lee-Sak therefore suggests the lists were composed as propagandist maps for the Hasmonean territorial expansion under Hyrcanus and Jannaeus. The historical books report that King David's conquered and ruled Edom and Moab:

> He [David] put garrisons in Edom; throughout all Edom he put garrisons, and all the Edomites became David's servants. And Yhwh gave victory to David wherever he went. (2 Sam 8:14 ‖ 1 Chr 18:13 NRSV adapted)

> He defeated Moab, and the Moabites became subject to David and brought tribute. (1 Chr 18:2 ≈ 1 Sam 8:2–3)

These reports can hardly stand up to historical scrutiny. David may have campaigned in the east, but a permanent rule there cannot be argued from extra-biblical sources. These verses better describe the ninth-century rule of the Omrides or the times of Hyrcanus and Jannaeus and may reflect scribal polishing around 100, when Moab and Edom had been incorporated in Greater Judea.

Other biblical texts proclaiming that Edom or Moab will be defeated might represent post-129 or post-107 editing. First, the early first-century translation of Ps 60:7b–8 has Hasmonean shading:

MPs 60:9b–10 [60:7b–8]	GPs 59:9–10
Judah is my scepter,	*Ioudas* is my king,
Moab is my washbasin;	Moab a cauldron of my hope;
on Edom I hurl my shoe;	on Idumea I will put my sandal;
over Philistia I shout in triumph.	to me allophyles were subjugated.

ments, one in Norway and one in Washington. See Davis et al. 2017, 221–26; Davis 2017, 246n53, 248, 260–61, 263; Tov, Davis, and Duke 2016, 17–18, 22, 25–27, 33, 210–21; and press release from Museum of the Bible, October 22, 2018.

The Greek rendering of *yǝhûdâ* as *Ioudas* (instead of the expected *Iouda* or *Ioudaia*) and "king" for "scepter" may be a hidden reference to Judah the Maccabee, the first leader of the princely Hasmonean family. Further, Moab is connected to "hope" rather than being the humiliated washbasin of Israel and its God. The foreigners of Idumea have not only been beaten in war (as in M) but have been subjugated—showing that Moab and Idumea were annexed to Judea at the time of this translation.

Second, a composite Balaam oracle from Num 24 seems to reflect Hasmonean triumph and subjugation of Idumea and the demise of the Seleucid empire:

> [17]What I see is not yet,
> what I behold is not near:
> A star shall come out of Jacob,
> a scepter shall rise out of Israel,
> he shall crush the borderlands of Moab,
> and the territory of all the Shethites.
> [18]Edom will become a possession,
> Seir a possession of his enemies,
> while Israel performs valiantly.
> [19]One out of Jacob shall rule,
> and destroy the survivors of the city. . . .
> [23]Again he uttered his oracle, saying:
> Alas, who shall live when God does this?
> [24]Ships shall come from Kittim
> and afflict Asshur and Eber,
> also he shall perish forever. (Num 24:17–24, my translation)

These verses fit Israelite dominion over their neighbors only with the ninth-century Omri dynasty's expansion into Edom (Finkelstein 2013, 97–112) or in Hasmonean times, and Balaam indeed sees far into the future when a princely ruled Israel shall subdue the neighboring nations to the east. The Nabateans ("his enemies") had pushed the Edomites westward from the fourth/third century, and Israel indeed "performed valiantly" when Hyrcanus conquered the northern part of Perea after 129 and subjugated Idumea in 107. The War Scroll quotes a shorter and likely earlier version of v. 18 without mention of Edom or Seir (1QM XI 6–7).

The last oracle of Balaam (Num 24:23–24) foresees that "ships from Kittim" will afflict Asshur. In the Bible, "Kittim" is used of Greek coastlands in the Mediterranean (Gen 10:4; Isa 23:1, 12; Jer 2:10; Ezek 27:6). Josephus identifies Kittim with Cyprus (*Antiquities* 1.128). In Qumran scrolls, the Kittim are identified with the Romans and their armies. The "ships of Kittim" appear in a Danielic oracle of salvation (11:25–35 at 11:30). This force is commonly identified with the Roman fleet that caused Antiochus Epiphanes to retreat from Cyprus and Egypt during his second Egyptian campaign in 168. I therefore suggest that the last Balaam oracle (Num 24:23–24) with "ships of Kittim" was added in the late second century, the only century where this phrase is otherwise documented.

Second- and first-century texts such as Greek Isaiah and Qumran pesharim can use "Asshur" for Seleucid Syria—with Antiochus IV taking the role of the violent king of Asshur (GIsa 7:17, 18, 20; 8:7–8; 10:12–13, 24; 4QpIsaᵃ [4Q161] frgs. 2–4, 6–10; 4QpIsaᶜ [4Q163] frgs. 2–3; frgs. 4–7 II 2–6, 21 [interpretation of Isa 8:7; 10:12–13, 24–27]). And Seleucid Syria remained the main military enemy of the Hasmoneans throughout the second century. Verses 23–24 hardly fit preexilic times, as the oracle expects ships from the west (= the Romans) to confront Asshur (= Seleucid Syria), which will suffer and thereafter come to an end as a kingdom. These verses were likely added to the Balaam cycle when the empire gradually fell apart after the death of Antiochus VII in 129. (In 63 it finally fell to Pompey.)

Within the Balaam cycle, the king of Israel appears in the oracles of chapter 24 (24:3–9, 15–19, 20, 21, 23–24). Verses 18 and 24 (possibly also v. 19) evince a messianic rereading and extension of the oracles with the Hasmonean conquest of Idumea in 107 and the falling apart of the hostile Seleucid empire. The Hasmonean princely rulers represent a fulfillment of Balaam's prophecy—and the Star of Jacob indeed appears on the coins of Jannaeus (see figure 6, p. 183).

The *Tendenz* of 1 Maccabees with its laudatory poems on Judah and Simon, the use of Ps 110 to provide legitimation for Simon as ruler and high priest forever, and the rereading of Balaam's royal oracles—all this together evinces a down-to-earth realized messianism, not a futuristic or utopic messianic hope. However, for the Hasmoneans and their supporters such a realized eschatology did not exclude a more comprehensive future fulfillment of the prophecies: Simon (and implicitly his descendants) would be high priest and civil leader for all time only "until a faithful prophet would arise." The Hasmoneans and their reign were probably seen as a nucleus of an awaited messianic kingdom.

Blessing King Jannaeus and Gathering the Dispersed

The Prayer for King Jonathan (Jannaeus's Hebrew name), preserved in a Qumran document (4Q448 [4QApocryphal Psalm and Prayer]),[46] testifies to messianic connotations connected to the Hasmonean kingdom. This blessing was preserved alongside a hymn to Zion—and Jannaeus indeed ruled from Zion (my translation):[47]

> [II.2]Awake, Holy One, [2]for King Jonathan
> [3]and all the congregation of your people [4]Israel,
> [5]who is dispersed to the four [6]winds of heaven!
> [7]Let peace be on all of them [8]and on your kingdom!
> [9]May your name be blessed!
> [III.1]In your love I am firmly founded [and will sing][48]
> [2]all through the day until evening. From he[aven look down,]
> [3]come close and be in [their midst. Your people,]
> [4]remember them with blessing and m[ercy. Have compassion]
> [5]for your name that is called [over them and over]
> [6]the kingdom, to bless [them. Visit them]
> [7]on the day of war and b[ring victory]
> [8]to Jonathan the kin[g and your people Israel.
> [9]May [your name] be ble[s]sed!

46. The appearance of a pro-Hasmonean blessing at Qumran is noteworthy, as the Yahad generally was at odds with the Hasmonean leadership. In the 90s, a bloody conflict developed between Jannaeus and the Pharisees. Could a persecuted Pharisee have found refuge at Qumran, bringing with him a scroll from Jerusalem? Yahad texts polemize against the Pharisees ("the seekers of smooth things"). Thus, the Yahad may have sided with Jannaeus in this conflict, resulting in a temporary détente between them.

47. The beginning of this scroll is preserved in its full height—the thong used for binding the scroll is still attached to the fragment. The upper half of the fragment preserves the beginning of a Zion hymn in large letters in a rough scribal hand (column I). The Prayer for King Jonathan appears in the lower half, inscribed by another rough scribal hand. Column II is completely preserved, while we lack the end of the lines of column III. The reconstruction is indebted to Qimron (2014, 186). In III 4–5, I restore *[ḥamal] ʿal šimkā* ("show compassion for your name"), for which cf. Ezek 36:21.

48. Column III 1 remains a crux. *Bəʾahăbatkā* ("in your love") is clear. On the earliest photo (Palestine Archaeological Museum #40.619) one can thereafter read *aleph, taw, waw/yod*, and *samek*, followed by a vertical downstroke (*waw, resh*, or *dalet*?) before the lacuna. Qimron (2014, 186) suggests reading *bəʾahăbatkā ʾityassēr* ("by your love I will be disciplined"). However, God's love and "disciplining" is not a likely pair. Tentatively, I suggest *bəʾahāvatkā ʾityassēd [wəʾāšîr]* ("in your love I am firmly founded [and will sing]").

The praise of God's kingdom in column II is echoed in the blessing on the Judean kingdom in column III. This text sees Jannaeus's wars, territorial expansion, and ingathering of the exiles as fulfillment of biblical promises such as Ezek 34:12–13; Mic 5:3–5 [5:4–6]; Zech 2:10–14 [2:6–10]. The reference to the assembly of Israel spread with the four winds of heaven connects Jannaeus with the ingathering of the exiles; for example, Zech 2:10 [2:6]: "Up, up! Flee from the land of the north, says Yhwh; for I have spread you abroad like the four winds of heaven, says Yhwh" (NRSV adapted). Zechariah 2:10–11 [2:6–7] refers to Zion, and column I of 4Q448 is indeed a Zion psalm.

The ongoing ingathering of Judeans from the diaspora to the Hasmonean kingdom is described in hymnic form in one of the Psalms of Solomon. Inspired by texts from Deutero-Isaiah, Pss Sol 11 illustrates the return of the dispersed and the resettling of the people, seen from a Jerusalem perspective. This is likely no prophecy about an unspecified future but a description of the influx of Judean immigrants to the steadily growing Judea in the early first century:

> ¹Sound in Zion the trumpet of the sanctuary;
> announce in Jerusalem the voice of one bringing good news,
> for God has been merciful to Israel in watching over them.
> ²Stand on a high place, Jerusalem, and look at your children,
> from the east and west assembled together by the Lord.
> ³From the north they come in the joy of their God;
> from far distant islands God has assembled them.
> ⁴He flattened high mountains into level ground for them;
> the hills fled at their coming.
> ⁵The forests shaded them as they passed by;
> God made every fragrant tree to grow for them.
> ⁶So that Israel might proceed under the supervision of the glory
> of their God.
> ⁷Jerusalem, put on (the) clothes of your glory,
> prepare the robe of your holiness,
> for God has spoken well of Israel forevermore. (Pss Sol 11:1–7,
> translation from Wright 1985, 661–62)

The migration is seen as fulfillment of Isaianic oracles (40:3–4, 9–11; 49:11–12; 52:7–9; 60:4), so a messiah is not mentioned. Full redemption may not be there, but one senses the outpouring of end-time blessings. Different from other psalms in the collection, this hymn does not signal any criticism of the

Hasmonean rulers of the land and their military enterprise, and we may be close to the pro-Hasmonean ideology of 1 Maccabees.

Psalms of Solomon 11 can be brought in dialogue with the large number of Jewish settlements in Galilee and Golan from this time period, which suggests also that returnees from the diaspora settled in the north. This psalm possibly predates Jannaeus's harsh treatment of opposition circles in the 90s (cf. Josephus, *Antiquities* 13.372–76, 379–83); it is lauding God's presence in the land and his gathering new people to settle it.

Apart from a couple of references in Josephus and the Talmud (see p. 220), voices critical to the Hasmoneans and their proto-messianic pretensions have primarily been preserved for posterity in the Dead Sea Scrolls. The scrolls also provide windows into eschatological thinking in second- and first-century Judea.

The Messiahs of the Scrolls

Two apocalyptic or eschatological texts from Qumran (4Q246 and 4Q521), a Zion hymn (11QPsᵃZion), and the Prayer for King Jonathan (4Q448)—all presectarian or extrasectarian texts—were discussed in chapter 6 for thematic and diachronic reasons. We now discuss messianism in the relevant Yahad texts. Further, both thematically and chronologically, the Psalms of Solomon from the mid-first century BCE are an interesting countermatch for the Yahad texts.

One should not expect a homogeneous messianism or eschatology throughout the texts from Qumran. Texts covered in this chapter may be dated from the mid-second century to the late first century. Most are written within the Yahad (the so-called Qumran community).

Qumran and Its Community in Context

The Yahad and its learned center at Qumran must be placed in context. It is contested when the Yahad came into being. Most early scholars dated the founding figure, the Teacher of Righteousness, and his opponent, the Wicked Priest, around the mid-second century. The most common candidates suggested to "fill the shoes of the Wicked Priest" were the early Hasmonean rulers Jonathan (160–142) and his brother Simon (142–135). Some recent scholars argue for a later dating and suggest identifying the Wicked Priest with Hyrcanus II, high priest after the death of his father Jannaeus in 76 (Wise, Abegg, and Cook 1996, 26–34; Collins 2010b, 88–121; Ableman 2021).[1]

---

1. Abelman (2021) argues that there are only three possible candidates to identify with the Wicked Priest: the Hasmonean brothers Aristobulus II and Hyrcanus II, competing

Such a late dating is problematic. The Teacher and the Wicked Priest were contemporary and antagonists, meeting each other at least once, when the former was harassed by the latter on his day of fasting (1QpHab IX 8–12; XI 4–8). With the sectarian movement coming into being in the mid-second century or shortly thereafter, it hardly gives meaning to move a founding figure of the community to the 60s, even if the clash with the Wicked Priest could have occurred late in his career.

As I see it, a mid-second-century origin of the Yahad is suggested by the early date of some central sectarian scrolls. According to paleographic analysis, three luxury scrolls from Cave 1 were penned around 100: the Community Rule (1QS), the Thanksgiving Hymns (Hodayot, 1QH[a]), and the Great Isaiah Scroll (1QIsa[a]).[2] Mineral analysis of small pieces of 1QS and 1QIsa[a] demonstrate that the high-quality parchment of these two sectarian-written scrolls were processed in the same workshop with the same advanced technology (Rabin 2016, 66–67)—and strangely they ended up as "bedfellows" for 1900 years in the same jar in Cave 1. 1QIsa[a], 1QS, and 1QH[a] were luxury scrolls likely produced for archival storage or to be "librarian copies/master copies," and there is a complex literary history behind 1QS and 1QH[a]. Therefore, the prehistory of the Serekh and Hodayot traditions must go back well into the second century. And both have siblings or cousins in Serekh and Hodayot copies in Cave 4.

Some sectarian texts were written in cryptic script, and one of them is likely even earlier. In Midrash Sefer Moshe (4Q249), the opening title is written in a square script—a script that hardly can be later than the mid-second century.[3]

Who then could be the Wicked Priest? This sobriquet clearly refers to a Hasmonean ruling high priest. I would point to Simon the Hasmonean, who

---

for the leadership of the nation in 67–40 (the former was high priest 67–63, the latter 63–40), or Aristobulus's son Matthias Antigonus (high priest 40–37). Among these, he finds only Hyrcanus II fulfilling the criteria that can be drawn from the pesharim on Habakkuk and Psalms.

2. The same scribal signs are used in 1QS and 1QIsa[a], demonstrating that the Isaiah scroll was written by two sectarian scribes. Cross (1961, 167, 198n116) dates 1QIsa[a] to around 100 and 1QS to 100–75. A Cave 4 copy of the Hodayot, 4QH[b] (4Q428), is also given an early paleographic date (100–75).

3. deadseascrolls.org.il/explore-the-archive/image/B-371494. The editor of the text, Stephen Pfann, dates the script no later than 150 (DJD 25:4–5, plate II). Michael Langlois (personal communication) notes that with such a small number of letters, a precise dating within the timespan 250–150 is difficult. If written by a conservative scribe who preserved older forms or by an untrained one, the script could be slightly later than 150.

profiled himself as a tough leader. The decree proclaimed at his inauguration forbids any gathering or assembly in the country without his permission:

> The Judeans and the priests were pleased that Simon would be their *leader* and high *priest* forever, until a trustworthy *prophet* would arise, and that he would be commander over them . . . and that the responsibility would be upon him concerning the holy places, and that he would be obeyed by all and that all documents in the country would be written in his name. . . . And no one of the people or the priests will be able to set aside any of these resolutions or to dispute anything said by him or to convoke a gathering in the country without his permission. (1 Macc 14:41–45, my translation)

This means that Simon tried to suppress or control opposition groups, and oppositional priests are specifically mentioned. The Yahad was indeed a priestly-led group in opposition to the Hasmonean leadership. This decree is mirrored in Yahad texts that reveal an outspoken opposition to such a leadership with a double office. If there was only one Wicked Priest, in my view Simon may be the best candidate (thus Milik 1959, 61–64; Eshel 2008, 63–89). However, the widely different times allotted to the Teacher of Righteousness and the Wicked Priest by scholars would not lead to large differences in the interpretation of messianic texts penned within the Yahad. One should not try to explain differences in emphasis among these texts by their date(s) or asserted context(s) within Second Temple history in Judea.

When did the Yahad establish its center at Qumran? Most recent scholars follow Magness (2002, 64–65): based on an analysis of pottery and coins, she suggests that the Yahad founded their center at Qumran in the 90s or 80s of the first century. In contrast, Taylor argues that the community took over a Hasmonean fort in the 30s (2013, 250–61; cf. the debate between these two: Magness 2014; Taylor 2014). A fort established around 100 would concur with the rapid expansion of the Hasmonean state between 112 and 90. Before Jannaeus conquered the southern part of the Moabite region in the 80s, a fort at Qumran would sit at the border.

Based on a comparison of the original ground plan of Khirbet Qumran with contemporary mansions elsewhere in the Levant, Humbert (2017) argues that the center was established as a mansion around the time of Salome Alexandra (76–67) and taken over by Essenes during the early years of Herod.

I side with Taylor and Humbert: the Yahad likely took over a previous center early in Herod's reign.[4] While the Yahad had been in tough opposition to the Hasmonean rulers, Josephus preserves texts that suggest that Herod entertained a positive attitude to the Essenes (Taylor 2013, 93–94). The Yahad was likely an organized elite group within a larger Essene movement. This community had one of its centers at Qumran, perhaps a center with particular scribal and library assignments.

The Yahad left us with a large and partly pluriform collection of texts. Based on a survey of 825 identifiable manuscripts, Crawford (2021) gives the following estimate: 25 percent of the scrolls represent classical (biblical-to-be) literature, 25 percent are sectarian, 17 percent sectarian related, and 18 percent are general Jewish texts reflecting the Judean society at large. (The remaining 15 percent are too small or fragmentary for any classification.) The Qumran texts discussed in chapter 6 belong to the latter category (presectarian or extrasectarian); they do not represent the more narrow and well-organized community of the Yahad.

A Prophet and Two Anointed Ones

The vision in Zech 4 of two sons of oil was foundational for the dual messianism we encounter in three important texts of the Yahad: the final version of the Community Rule, the Rule of the Congregation, and 4QTestimonia.

4QTestimonia (4Q175) is a thematic collection of scriptures. The composition is short; filling out one column only, its thirty lines are almost completely preserved. After an introduction on obeying God and his commandments (lines 1–4: Exod 20:21 [20:24]; Deut 5:25–26 [5:28–29]), the quoted texts outline the offices of prophet like Moses (lines 5–8: Deut 18:18–19),[5] Davidic ruler (lines 9–13: Num 24:15–17), and priest (lines 14–20: Deut 33:8–11). Lines 21–30 quote Joshua's curse on the man who rebuilds "this city" (= Jericho in Josh 6:26). Only this passage is followed by a commen-

---

4. For this dating of the sectarian settlement, cf. the appearance of the "scroll jars," typical for Qumran and almost nonexistent elsewhere. These cylindrical jars with bowl-shaped lids appear only in post-31 archaeological contexts at Khirbet Qumran as well as in the nearby caves (Magness 2004, 151–68). The jars were designed primarily for storing food stuff to comply with the purity concerns of the sect, and secondarily they were used as archive jars for scrolls (Elgvin in Elgvin, Davis, and Langlois 2016, 427–35).

5. Acts 3:20–26 also reads Deut 18:15–19 about the prophet of the end times; cf. John 1:21.

tary, which applies Josh 6:26 as a curse on two generations of Hasmonean builders of "this city."

Can "this city" still be Jericho? In the late Second Temple period the city of Jericho was not concentrated in one locality, but spread out in the form of a garden city, between the many orchards and plantations. The grandiose building projects of the Hasmoneans and Herod were not within the city but were south of it, on both sides of Wadi Kelt (Netzer 2001, 13–14). Therefore, I think the scroll identified "this city" with Jerusalem, not the garden city of Jericho (Elgvin 2016b, 332).[6]

4QTestimonia may be construed as a critical response to the twofold office of Hasmonean rulers, reflected in Simon's edict from 142 that proclaimed Simon and his descendants as high priests and rulers of the Judeans "until a trustworthy prophet would arise" (1 Macc 14:41), and Hyrcanus likely claimed all three offices. The collection of scriptures in 4Q175 represents a silent protest: the officially anointed leadership is illegitimate; the Yahad, enlightened by God's holy spirit, still waits for the right prophet together with the anointed ones of Aaron and Israel.

Lines 9–13 quote the Balaam oracle from Num 24:15–17, an oracle that would be read as a messianic prophecy on the last days. This would indicate that the scriptures of 4QTestimonia are read on the end time—and the sectarians indeed saw themselves as living on the threshold of the last days.

The same threefold hope is expressed in the Community Rule, as it appears in its final recension from Cave 1:

> At that time, the men [6]of the Yahad shall set apart a holy house for Aaron, to form a most holy community and a house of communion for Israel, for those who walk in perfection. [7]The sons of Aaron alone shall have authority in matters of justice and property, and every rule concerning

---

6. 4QTestimonia (4Q175) and 4QApocryphon of Joshua (4Q378–4Q379, quoted as authority in 4Q175) describe two evil brothers who rebuild *the city* and fall under Joshua's curse over Jericho (4Q175 1 21–30; 4Q379 22 II 7–15; cf. Josh 6:26). Their father is described as an evil man of Belial, and the sons as having brutally shed blood in Jerusalem. Many scholars connect these texts with Hyrcanus's sons Aristobulus I, Antigonus, and/ or Jannaeus, and "the city" with Hasmonean Jericho, but Milik's suggestion (1959, 61–64) that the brothers are Jonathan and Simon who fortified and rebuilt Jerusalem remains a valid option. In these two texts, neither of these figures are called "the Wicked Priest." Even if Jericho was intended, a restoration of the holy city by a ruler in Jerusalem would easily be interpreted as a sign of the messianic age. These two texts are sectarian countertexts to Hasmonean claims of being anointed rebuilders of the Israelite state.

the men of the Yahad shall be determined according to their word. [8]As for the property of the men of holiness who walk in perfection, it shall not be merged with that of the men of injustice, who [9]neither purified their life by separating from iniquity nor walk in perfection. They shall depart from none of the teachings of the law to walk [10]in all the stubbornness of their hearts, but shall be ruled by the original precepts by which the men of the Yahad were first instructed, [11]until there shall come the prophet and the anointed ones of Aaron and Israel. (1QS IX 5–11, my translation)

The clause "until there shall come the prophet and the anointed ones of Aaron and Israel" is not preserved in any of the Cave 4 Serekh copies and appears as a later attachment to a long section of regulations for the men walking in perfection (1QS VIII 20–IX 10) and then for the Instructor (IX 12–25). A shorter and earlier version of the passage above appears in 4QS[d] (4Q258) 2 II 6–9. This means that the scribe who prepared the master copy of 1QS saw the need to qualify these statutes with a proclamation of the end-time hope of the Yahad. Before the making of the luxury scroll of the Community Rule, this eschatological clause was not part of the Serekh tradition.

The Rule of the Congregation (1QSa [1Q28a]) is the first of two appendices to the Community Rule.[7] The designations "Charter for Israel in the Last Days" (Wise, Abegg, and Cook 1996, 143) or "The Messianic Rule" (Vermes 1997, 157) are more fitting. The well-preserved text was formatted in two columns, introduced by "This is the rule for all the congregation of Israel in the last days." A fragmentary papyrus copy in cryptic script, 4Q249a, was found in Cave 4.[8] The composition is a blueprint for the military organization in the end-time war, which may be compared with the War Scroll.

7. Physical testing of small pieces of 1QS and its second appendix 1QSb (the Rule of Benedictions) indicates that they were part of the same scroll, as the parchment in these two sections has close to identical mineral characteristics (Rabin 2016, 66–67). The same would be the case for 1QSa, which was sewn between the two other texts. These three texts were written by the same scribe (Cross 1961, 198n116). The Cave 4 copies of Serekh did not include 1QSa and 1QSb, which again demonstrates the special character of 1QS as a master scroll.

8. 4Q249a preserves some textual differences compared to 1QSa (Ben-Dov, Stökl ben Ezra, and Gayer 2017; cf. the new edition of 1QSa in Bloch, Ben-Dov, and Stökl Ben Esra 2019). 4Q249a testifies to an earlier and shorter text of column I, indicating that the textual tradition of 1QSa (as that of 1QS) had been under development for some time (Bloch, Ben-Dov, and Stökl Ben Esra 2019, 27).

The last section describes the sacred meal when the royal messiah appears, a meal presided by the anointed high priest. Thus, the text introduces two anointed ones in the end time:

> [11]This is the order of the [ass]embly of the men of renown, [summoned] for the gathering, for the council of the community: when [God] fathers[9] [12]the messiah among them: [the Priest,] head of the entire congregation of Israel, shall enter first, trailed by all [13][his] brot[hers, the sons of] Aaron, the priests [summoned] for the gathering of the men of renown. They are to sit [14]be[fore him] by rank. Then the [mess]iah of Israel may en[ter,] and the heads [15]of [their] th[ousands] are to sit before him by rank, according to [their] st[anding] in their camps and their marches. Last, all [16]the heads of [the con]gregation's cl[ans,] with [their] sage[s and wise men] shall sit before them by [17]rank.
>
> W[hen] they gathe[r at the tabl]e of the community, [to set out bread and new w]ine and arrange the table [18]of the community, [and to pour the] new wine for drink[ing, nobody [should stretch out] his hand to the first portion [19]of the bread or [the new wine] before the Priest. For [he] shall [bl]ess the first portion of the bread [20]and the new win[e and stretch out] his hand for the bread first. And afterw[ard,] the messiah of Israel [shall st]retch out his hands [21]to the bread. [Finally,] the entire congregation of the community [shall bl]ess, each o[ne] according to his rank. This regulation shall govern [22]every me[al,] provided at least ten men are ga]thered together. (1QSa II 11–22, largely following Bloch, Ben-Dov, and Stökl Ben Esra 2019)

The term "the entire congregation of Israel" combines the term 'ēdâ, commonly used for the Yahad, with the restored nation of the end time. The Yahad is thus conceived as the nucleus of the future nation.

The term "messiah of Israel" is fully preserved in line 20 and partly in line 14. His priestly counterpart, the one who presides at the table and is given liturgical priority, is not designated "messiah/anointed." However, appearing in an appendix to the Community Rule, "the Priest" in this text must be

9. "When God fathers the messiah" (lit., "when God causes the messiah to be born") refers to Ps 2:7: in the act of coronation God "conceives" the new king and adopts him as son. I do not follow scholars who emend the confirmed reading *yôlîd* ("to cause to be born") to *yôlîk* ("to lead") (Milik, Barthélemy, Ben-Dov [Bloch, Ben-Dov, and Stökl Ben Esra 2019, 38–39]). These two imperfect forms are graphically similar. Cf. Cross 1995, 76n3 (arguing for a double causative: "cause to be born").

identified with "the anointed one of Aaron" (1QS IX 11). Further, "the Priest" can be used as a term designating the high priest. The meal is presided by the high priest of the end times, also coming out of the Yahad. In the table liturgy, the Priest is ranked above the messiah of Israel. Further, there is a relation between the now and the eschaton: the common meal of the Yahad is set forth as a liturgical anticipation of the messianic banquet (lines 21–22; Cross 1995, 77).

The breaking-in of the last days is the time "when [God] fathers the messiah among them." The ancient coronation text in Ps 2 is applied to the messiah and his public appearance or intronization, not to a supernatural birth of the king of Israel.[10] The two columns of the Rule of the Congregation combine the mustering of the Yahad for the end-time war with the coming of the royal messiah. As copresider at the eschatological banquet he appears in a peaceful role, but a military role for the messiah would be presupposed (cf. column I).

This text gives color to and provides the regulation for the appearance of the two anointed ones listed in 1QS IX. Since 1QSa had a literary prehistory (and lines 11–18 are paralleled in 4Q249a), I suggest that the joining of this appendix to the Community Rule caused the scribe to add "until there come the prophet and the anointed ones of Aaron and Israel" to the prescriptions in 1QS IX, prescriptions known from the wider Serekh tradition. Thus, 1QSa II is no sequel to 1QS IX 11 as hypotext; rather, 1QSa causes the introduction of this clause into 1QS.

During this literary process, the terms "the Priest" and "messiah of Israel" (1QSa) were rephrased into "the anointed ones of Aaron [mentioned first] and Israel" (1QS). Further, the tradition we encountered in 4QTestimonia and Simon's edict (1 Macc 14:41)—three end-time figures—was known to the scribe of 1QS and caused him to include also the eschatological prophet in the short clause of the last days. The Community Rule was penned as a master scroll on costly parchment around 100, close in time to the reign of Hyrcanus, a ruler claiming that God had blessed him with the offices of ruler, priest, and prophet. The theological confrontation with the Hasmoneans caused Yahad circles to supplement the collective messianism of the Serekh texts with the expectation of three end-time agents still to come and to consciously attach the Messianic Rule (1QSa) as an appendix to this scroll.

10. I disagree with Wise, who states that if the text indeed reads *yôlîd*, "then this Qumran text is describing a messianic figure who is in a special way a 'son of God'" (Wise, Abegg, and Cook 1996, 144).

This literary development suggests that, during the first two generations of the Yahad, some texts advocated a collective messianism with the community as the central end-time actor, while other texts (such as 1QSa) reflect a dual messianism, foreseeing two individual figures of redemption. The focus on the Shoot of David as the main eschatological agent, evinced in exegetical texts of the first century BCE, may be a later development.

The Shoot of David

Some sectarian texts foresee a royal messiah, a Davidide, without mentioning (at least in the preserved parts) any priestly messiah.

4QCommentary on Genesis A (4Q252) is a partly preserved biblical paraphrase. It contains six columns, written on one sheet with a length of 60 cm. Apart from column I, the lower part of the scroll is not preserved; only 25–30 percent of the text is extant.[11] Stories from Genesis are retold, the biblical text is quoted and interspersed with commentary, at times with supporting references from other biblical books. Columns I–II paraphrase the story of Noah and the flood (Gen 6–9). The text then jumps to Abraham in columns II–III (Gen 11, 15, 17, 18, 22). Column III continues with Isaac's blessing of Jacob (Gen 28:3–4). Column IV preserves a passage on Amalek (Gen 36:12), and the remainder of the scroll paraphrases Jacob's tribal blessings (the preserved text refers to Reuben, Judah, Asher, and Naphtali; see DJD 22:186–90). 4Q252 is a unified composition with patriarchal blessings and their fulfillment as overarching theme (Tzoref 2012). The covenants with Noah, Abraham, Isaac, and Jacob form a prelude to the coming Davidic messiah and his "men of the Yahad."

Column V is a paraphrase of Jacob's blessing of Judah (Gen 49:8–12), from which only the exegesis of 49:10 is preserved:

> [1]*The scepter [shall not] depart from the tribe of Judah.* Whenever Israel rules, [2]*there shall [not] fail to be a descendant of David upon the throne* [Jer 33:17], for *the staff* is the covenant of kingship, [3][and the cla]ns of Israel are the divisions, until the messiah of *righteousness comes, the Shoot of David*

11. The scroll is early Herodian, i.e., written ca. 40–10. The Schøyen Collection holds tiny remnants of what could be another copy of 4QCommGen A from the same time period, preserving a few words parallel to 4Q252 I 8–10 (paraphrasing Gen 8:3–4; see Elgvin, Davis, and Langlois 2016, 291–94).

[Jer 23:5]. ⁴For to him and his seed is granted the covenant of kingship over his people for everlasting generations, since ⁵he observed the [. . . statutes and precepts of] the law with the men of the Yahad. For ⁶[. . . *the obedience of the people]s* is the assembly of the men of ⁷[the Yahad who submit to him(?)]. (4Q252 V 1–7, my translation)

These lines refer both to the present ("whenever Israel rules") and to the messianic future ("kingship over his people for everlasting generations"). If this commentary was written in the first half of the first century, it would follow that the present rulers, the Hasmoneans, unlawfully occupied the throne. The same would go for their successor, Herod, appointed by the Roman senate as "king of the Judeans."

The Davidic messianism is underlined by bringing in Jer 33:17 and 23:5 as supporting references. The words of 23:5 are dynamically rendered: Jeremiah's *ləḏāwīḏ ṣemaḥ ṣadîq* ("for David a righteous shoot") is rephrased as *məšîaḥ haṣṣedeq ṣemaḥ dāwīḏ* ("the messiah of righteousness, the Shoot of David"). The designation "Shoot of David" echoes scriptures such as Isa 11:1; Jer 23:5–6; Zech 3:8; 6:12; and Jer 33:14–16 (not present in G).

The preserved lines do not refer to any military task or a messiah at war. However, the end of the preceding column likely contained an interpretation of Gen 49:8–9.[12] These verses describe Judah with his hand on the neck of his enemies and as a young lion hunting for prey and suggest a military interpretation.

The fragment breaks off before the last two verses of the blessing on Judah (Gen 49:11–12). But toward the end of the preserved passage, we learn that the dynastic promise to David was given because of his Torah observance: "Since he observed the [. . . statutes and precepts of] the law with the men of the Yahad"—which means that David and the community shared the same interpretation of the law (at least according to this scribe). 4Q252 is a composition of the Yahad. Similar to the Rule of the Congregation, the Yahad is perceived as the nucleus of the future nation under the Davidic messiah. Thus, there is a relation between the troublesome days the men of the Yahad may experience in the present and the promised messianic eschaton.

---

12. The last sixteen lines of column IV would have contained most of the interpretation of the blessing of Reuben, the biblical text of the blessings of Simeon and Levi with interpretation, and the text of Gen 49:8–9 with interpretation. The biblical text itself would fill five of these sixteen lines.

The sectarian pesharim are exegetical commentaries where the biblical text is interpreted on the present and related to the history of the land and the Yahad. The term "pesher" ("the interpretation of…") refers to a hidden meaning of the biblical text that can be unraveled by a spirit-filled exegete of the community. Most pesharim providing commentary to the running biblical text are commonly dated to the first half of the first century.

4Q161 (4QpIsa^a) preserves pesher interpretation on Isa 10:20–11:5. In column II, the commentator reads Isa 10:22–34 as a prophecy on the end-time war of the gentiles (the Kittim = the Romans) against Jerusalem. During the time of war, the Prince of the Congregation (*neśî' hā'ēdâ*) will return to Zion from the wilderness of the nations (II 14–15). Column III 11–16 quotes Isa 11:1–5, then follows the interpretation of these verses:

> [17][Its interpretation: this is the Shoot of] David, who shall arise at the end o[f days, … [18]…] his enemies; and God will support him with [a spirit of] strength [… [19]… and will give him] a throne of glory, a crown [of holiness,] and elegant garments. [20][… He will put a scepte]r in his hand, and he shall rule over all the n[atio]ns, even Magog [21][and his army …] his sword shall judge [all] the nations. As for the saying, *he will not [22][judge by what his eyes see] or pass sentence by what his ears hear,* this means that [23][he will be advised by the Zadokite priests,] and as they instruct him, so will he judge, and as they order, [24]so will he pass sentence.] One of the priests of renown shall go out with him, in whose hand shall be the garments of [   ]. (4Q161 III 17–24, my translation)

As in 4Q252, the royal messiah is designated "the Shoot of David." The military role of the messiah was not outlined in the Rule of the Congregation, while 4Q161 is more elaborate on the role of the messiah in the eschatological war. The hypotext Isa 11:1–5 portrays a peaceful messiah, ruling and judging his people in the land in righteousness. However, the sectarian scribes read 11:1–5 together with the preceding verses that describe a war campaign as a joint prophecy on the last days, which would necessarily imply a military role for the messiah, who will judge and rule the nations with his sword. "He shall strike the land with the rod of his mouth, and with the breath of his lips, he shall kill the wicked" (11:4) is transformed into "he shall rule over all the n[atio]ns, even Magog [21][and his army …] his sword shall judge [all] the nations."

For the commentator, "he will not judge by what his eyes see or pass sentence by what his ears hear" (11:3) prescribes that the king should relate to what *others* would see and hear. For this priestly dominated community, the messianic king would need to listen to and submit to the advice of a group of priests, and "priests of renown" would likely come out of the Yahad.[13]

4Q174 (4QFlorilegium) is a thematic pesher that deals with more than one biblical book. The scroll contains a collection of various biblical verses followed by commentary, an interpretation with the end time in focus (Ps 89:23 [89:22]; 2 Sam 7:10–14; Amos 9:11; Pss 1:1; 2:1–2; Isa 8:11; Ezek 44:10; Dan 12:10; 11:32). Most of the first column of the scroll is preserved.

Lines 1–9 deal with the end-time temple and the sons of light's victory over the men of Belial; lines 10–13 deal with the royal messiah, lines 14–17 with the ways of the righteous and their community led by the priests:

> [1.10]*The Lord decl[ares] to you that he will build you a house* [2 Sam 7:11c]; *and I will raise up your offspring after you* [2 Sam 7:12b]; *and I will establish the throne of his kingdom* [11][fore]ver. I will be a father to him, and he will be my son* [2 Sam 7:13b–14a]—this is the Shoot of David, who shall arise with [12]the Interpreter of the Torah, who will [arise] in Zi[on in the la]st days, as it is written, *And I shall raise up the booth of David that is fallen* [Amos 9:11]—this is the fallen booth of [13]David that will arise to deliver Israel. . . .
>
> [18][*Why*] *do the nations [con]spire, and the peoples plo[t] in vain? The kings of the earth s]et themselves, [and the ru]lers take counsel together against Yhwh and his* [19][*anointed one*] (Ps 2:1–2). Its in]terpretation: [that the na]tions [shall set themselves] and con[spire vainly against] the chosen ones of Israel in the last days—[II.1]this is the time of trials that is to co[me upon the house of J]udah. (4Q174 I 10–II 1, my translation)

The Shoot of David will "arise to deliver [*ləhôšîaʿ*] Israel." In biblical terminology, Yhwh is the one who delivers his people (e.g., Deut 20:4: "Yhwh your God . . . will deliver you [*ləhôšîaʿ ʾetkem*]"). But he can also send his agents to deliver Israel. The same phrase (*ləhôšîaʿ ʾet-yiśrāʾēl*) is used about deliverers raised by God in Judg 10:1 and 13:5, and close to identical terms appear in Judg 3:9, 15, 31.

In 4Q161, the royal Shoot of David was prescribed to listen to a council of priests. In this text, the Davidide is accompanied by the "Interpreter of the Torah." Thus, there are two leaders of the end-time nation. The Interpreter

---

13. The same idea appears in the treatise of kingship in the Temple Scroll (11QT[a] [11Q19] 56–59), which prescribes that the king shall be subject to a council of chiefs, priests, and Levites (57:12–15).

of the Torah is likely the high priest, who will continue the teaching ministry of the priestly Teacher of Righteousness. Neither of these two figures are called "anointed," and the "anointed one" of Ps 2:2 is identified with the elect nation. The terminology is clearly different from "the anointed ones of Aaron and Israel" in 1QS IX 11.

4Q174 I 18–19 relates to Ps 2:1–2 as hypotext, a text addressing the conspiracy "against Yhwh and his anointed one." However, the anointed king is not thematized in the interpretation in I 19–II 1. The "anointed one" is the elect nation; the hypotext is read on the end-time war of the nations against "the chosen ones of Israel," "the house of Judah." Thus, the text advocates both collective and individual messianism—the latter with two end-time figures.

The same terminology as in 4Q174 appears in the Damascus Document, but here with another hypotext, the Balaam oracle, Num 24:17: "The *star* is the Interpreter of the Torah, who shall come to Damascus as it is written, *A star shall come out of Jacob, a scepter shall rise out of Israel.* The *scepter* is the Prince of all the Congregation. When he comes he shall *crush all the Shethites*" (CD-A VII 18–21). The natural reading of Num 24:17 would be to see both "scepter" and "star" as royal symbols. But here this word pair is used as argument for a dual messianism. "Scepter" is necessarily a royal symbol, while the term "star" is less clear in itself. Thus, star is a foretelling of the end-time Interpreter of the Torah who will stand alongside the Prince of the Congregation, the scepter in the Balaam prophecy.

Similar to the Serekh tradition, the War Scroll textual tradition was fluid (see below on its collective messianism). And the royal messiah does appear in 4Q285 (4QSefer ha-Milhamah). There is no textual overlap between 4Q285 and the War Scroll (1QM); these texts seem to preserve parallel but not identical traditions on the end-time war to come:

²[. . . Prin]ce of the Congregation and all Isr[ael . . . ³. . . just as it wa]s written [in the book of Ezekiel the prophet, *And I will strike your bow from your left hand*] ⁴[*and bring down your arrows from your right. You shall fall*] *upon the mountains of I[srael, you and all your troops and the peoples that are with you* [Ezek 39:3–4] . . . ⁵. . . the king of the] Kittim and [. . . ⁶. . . the Pr]ince of the Congregation [shall pursue them] all the way to the [Great] Sea [. . . ⁷. . .] And they [shall flee] from Israel at that time [. . . ⁸. . . And] he shall stand against them and they shall be stirred against them [. . . ⁹. . .] and they shall return to the dry land at th[at] time [. . .

[10]. . .] then they shall bring him before the Prince of [the Congregation . . .]. (4Q285 4 2–10, my translation)

In this text we encounter a messiah at war, similar to Ps 2 and Ps 110. As in 4Q161, he is "Prince of the Congregation" (nesî' hā'ēdâ), but he also musters the forces of "all Israel." Hā'ēdâ ("the Congregation") is another term for the Yahad. The royal messiah, coming out of the Yahad and leading all Israel, will muster his armed forces against the Kittim (= the Romans) in battle. The fragment ends with the commander (or king) of the enemy forces being brought before the messiah to receive his judgment.

A Sacrificing and Suffering Priest

4Q541 (4QApocryphon of Levi[b]?) is preserved only in separate minor fragments (Elgvin 2020a, 89–98). This is a pre-Yahad composition written in Aramaic; the copy was penned toward the end of the second century (DJD 31:213–16, 227). Various fragments describe a figure with a unique teaching role who passes through trials:

> [1]] wounds upon w[ounds] . . . [2]. . . you will be found innocent(?) in your] case, and you will not be guil[ty . . . [3]. . .] the tracks of your wounds wh[ich] (4Q541 6)

> The hid[den mysteries] he shall reveal [. . .] [2][for the one] who does not understand he shall write [. . .] [3]the Great Sea shall be calmed because of him [. . .] [4]Then the books of wis[dom] shall be opened [. . .] [5]his command; and like [. . . his] wis[dom . . .] [6][his t]eaching [ ] (4Q541 7)

> [3]you shall receive a blow [. . .] [4]I will bless you. The burnt offering [. . .] [6]because [he is] wise [. . .] [8]he persecuted him and sought [to devour him . . .] (4Q541 2 II 3–8)

The text foresees an eschatological high priest (DJD 31:213–16). Its editor, Puech, points to parallels in the later Testament of Levi:

> You shall kindle the light of knowledge in Jacob, and you shall be as the sun for all the posterity of Israel. (Testament of Levi 4:3, my translation)

And then the Lord will raise up a new priest
to whom all the words of the Lord will be revealed.
He shall implement the judgment of truth over the earth for
   many days.
And his star shall rise in heaven like a king,
kindling the light of knowledge as day is illuminated by the sun.
And he shall be extolled by the whole inhabited world.
This one will shine forth like the sun in the earth,
he shall take away all darkness from under heaven,
and there shall be peace in all the earth. (Testament of Levi
   18:2–4, my translation)

4Q541 9, the longest preserved passage in 4Q540–41, may continue the line from MJer 30:20–24 (see pp. 150–52). But instead of God's wrath being poured out on the nations and a restoration and renewed covenant for Israel only, this text sees an end-time priest as a tool for universal renewal:

¹[all] the children of his generation[. . . ². . .] his [w]isdom. He shall make atonement for all the children of his generation, and he shall be sent to all the children of ³his peo[ple]. His words are like the words of heaven, and his teaching like the will of God. His everlasting sun¹⁴ will shine, ⁴its fire will give warmth unto the ends of the earth. It will shine on darkness, darkness will vanish ⁵from the earth and mist [fr]om the dry land.

They will speak against him many words and many ⁶[lie]s, invent fables about him, and speak all kinds of shameful things about him. His generation will be evil and perverted ⁷[so that] it will be [rejected.] Lies and violence will be his office, in his days the people will go astray and be confounded. (4Q541 9 I 1–7, my translation)

The second paragraph must refer to a period before the breakthrough of universal renewal. There is internal strife in the people; the priest is controversial and a victim of slandering and perhaps persecution. Are the 170s seen as a blueprint for the end times? Could Onias III, who was killed by enemies,

---

14. The suffix on "his everlasting sun" is more likely to refer to the priest than to God. Seeing the priestly figure as originator of the everlasting sun would, however, be unique for this text. Accordance emends *šemeš ʿalmʾâ* to *šemeš ʿalmʾā*, which would yield "the sun everlasting"; cf. the phonetic similarity between *aleph* and *ayin*.

be some kind of type for this figure, or perhaps his son Onias IV, who found refuge in Egypt and built the temple in Heliopolis?

Isaiah 53 plays in the background (cf. Brooke 2005, 140–51): "be sent to all the children of his peo[ple]" recalls the "we-group" of Isa 53; "in his days the people will go astray" echoes "all we like sheep have gone astray" (53:6); "they will speak against him many words and many [lie]s, invent fables about him, and speak all kinds of shameful things about him" recalls "he was despised and rejected by men . . . he was despised, and we did not recognize him" (53:3); and "you will grow and see and rejoice in eternal light" (4Q541 24 II 6) may echo "through his soul's anguish he shall see light" (Isa 53:11, reading "light" with 1QIsa[a,b], G).

This Levitical priest shall make atonement for all of "his generation"—perhaps a reference to the eschatological day of atonement (Brooke 2005, 151). In contrast to Isa 53, MJer 30, and Zech 13, the text does not signal the sacrifice of his life. The priest will teach powerfully: "His words are like the words of heaven, and his teaching like the will of God." His ministry will have cosmic consequences, the godlike teaching and sacrificial ministry of the priest will open a cosmic renewal.

The words "his everlasting sun will shine, its fire will give warmth unto the ends of the earth. It will shine on darkness, darkness will vanish [5]from the earth and mist [fr]om the dry land" can be compared with a similar description of light's end-time victory over darkness in the contemporary Book of Mysteries, where there is no personal messianic agent (see below, pp. 256–57).

The image of Noah may have colored the description of this end-time priest. Noah is the first biblical sage to bring forth an animal sacrifice, and the third-century Aramaic Levi portrays him as progenitor of Levi and the priestly line. There are parallels between the priestly image of 4Q541, the portrayal of the elect in 4QBirth of Noah ar (4Q534–36),[15] and descriptions of Noah in 1 En 106 and the Genesis Apocryphon.[16] While

---

15. The elect in 4Q534–36 is not named; the figure is often identified with Noah. Peeters (2008, 101) doubts that the main actor in 4Q541 is eschatological and finds more likely a teaching figure merging priestly features of Noah and Levi. Cook, however, doubts the identification with Noah and (with many scholars) regards the figure as a future messiah. The testamentary form does suggest a future figure.

16. Wise, Abegg, and Cook 1996, 539–40; Peeters 2008, 100–106; Jones 2018. In 1Qap-Gen V–XV the righteous Noah is contrasted with the wicked ones of humankind: his eyes shine like the sun (V 12; cf. 1 En 106:5), he is given wisdom and separates from the ways of deceit that lead to everlasting darkness (VI 1–6), and he atones for all the earth (X 13–17).

4Q541 was copied well before 1QapGen and 4Q534–36, they may draw on a common tradition.

There is no Davidide in the eschatological hope of 4Q541; the priest is God's only agent, as may be expected in a patriarchal testament coming out of priestly circles. The author may have found the motive of opposition, trials, suffering, and atonement in Isa 50 and 53; the central role of the priestly leader in Ezek 40–48; his role in redemption in MJer 30:18–24 and perhaps Zech 13; and wisdom, teaching, and sacrifice in Noah traditions. But in contrast to the Jeremiah and Zechariah oracles, he has a universal perspective. In the context of universal renewal (lines 3–5), the statement "he shall make atonement for all the children of his generation" probably encompasses the nations.

A sequel to the image of the eschatological priest in 4Q541 appears in the sectarian Self-Glorification Hymn—the former text written in Aramaic, the latter in Hebrew. This text is preserved in two recensions and four manuscripts: two copies of the Thanksgiving Hymns and two texts from the Milhamah (War Scroll) tradition (1QH^a XXV–XXVI; 4QH^a [4Q427] 7 I; 4Q491 11; 4Q471b). The text below is from 4Q491, which has its own recension; the righthand column adds variants from 4Q471b and 4Q427:

5[To me is given] a mighty throne
in the angelic council [for]ever.
No king of yore can sit on it,
neither can their nobles.
[Wh]o can be compared [to 6me?]
None can compare to my glory,
none has been exalted save myself,
and none can accompany me.
7[   ] I am reckoned with the angels,
My dwelling is in the holy council.
[My] desi[re] is not of the flesh,
[for] everything precious to me
is in the glory of 8the holy [hab]itation.
Who has been despised like me,   [Who] has been shunned [by men]
                                                           like me?

yet who is like me in my glory?

[9][   ] Who has born[e all] afflictions
like me,

Who compares to me [in endur]ing
evil?

Never have I been instructed,

yet no teaching compares [10][to mine.]

Who could cut off m[y words?]

And who could measure the flow of
my speech?

Who can associate with me and compare with my judgment?

[11][. . . Fo]r I am reckoned with the angels,	I am the beloved of the King
my glory is with the sons of the king.	and companion of the holy ones,
Neither [with gol]d nor with refined gold [I will be adorned (4Q491 11 5–11)	Neither with gold I will crown myself,
	nor with refined gold [I will be adorned.]

Who is the imagined speaker of this hymn? An early proposal identifies him as the archangel Michael. But angels do not suffer trials, nor is a teaching role on earth prominent in their job description. Most scholars now say that the imagined singer is the high priest of the last days: "The figure does not seem to be of angelic origin, but rather a human being who has been elevated to share the lot of the angels" (Eshel 1999, 626–35 at 628). His unique teaching suggests a priestly figure, as teaching was part of the job description of the priests. As was the case in 4Q541, this teacher experiences trials and suffering.

The singer can be compared to the Teacher of Righteousness. The exalted teacher of the hymn should be identified with the one who would "teach righteousness at the end of days" (CD-A VI 11) (as the Teacher had done in his days) and the end-time "Interpreter of the Law" of 4QFlorilegium (cf. Collins 2010c, 122–23, 149–64). The Teacher Hymns in the Hodayot evince that the Teacher had experienced suffering and trials and was harassed by the Wicked Priest on his day of fasting (1QpHab XI 4–8).

Collins understands the elevation of the singer as transformation to some kind of divine status:

> The way the boasts of exaltation function in the self-glorification hymn can be understood by analogy with such figures as the Son of Man in the Similitudes of Enoch or the exalted Christ in the New Testament.
>
> The figure in 4Q491 is also reckoned among the gods, *'ēlîm*. In no case does this "divinization" impinge on the supremacy of the Most High, the God of Israel. But it clearly involves the exaltation of some human figures to a status that is envisaged as divine and heavenly rather than human and mortal. (Collins 2010c, 163, 164)

I disagree. The singer's elevation to the heavens does not eliminate his humanity. In his officiating ministry he performs before the heavenly king and is enthroned on high, but his teaching ministry is still vis-à-vis other humans. As an analogy we can compare how the sect, drawing on temple traditions, envisioned the officiating priest performing at the same time on earth and in the heavens. The Rule of Blessings conceives the priest as spiritually residing in heaven while continuing his earthly ministry (Eshel 1999, 631–33):

> III 25May he set you as a glorious ornament in the midst of 26the holy ones. [May he re]new the covenant of [everlasting] priesthood for you. . . .
>
> IVMay you 25be like an angel of the presence in the holy residence for the glory of the God of host[s. . . . May you] attend the service in the royal 26temple, ordering destiny with the angels of the presence, in communion [with the holy ones for] everlasting ages and for all perpetual periods, for [all] 27his judgments [are true.] May he make you holy among his people, and an [eternal] light [to illuminate] the world with knowledge and to enlighten the face of the congregation 28[in your teaching. May he] crown you to the holy of holies, for [you are made] holy for him and shall glorify his name and his holiness. (1QSb III 25–26; IV 24–28)

The priest blessed in 1QSb III may be the regular priest; in his officiating ministry he can be perceived as being in line with the heavenly sanctuary. The priest blessed in 1QSb IV should likely be understood as the eschatological high priest (Eshel 1999, 631–33). At the same time, the inclusion of the Rule of Blessings as an appendix to the Community Rule suggests some kind of liturgical communion between the ideal end-time priest and the priests officiating in the prayers of the Yahad.

Eshel concludes (1999, 635):

> The [Self-Glorification] Hymn was spoken in the name of this Eschato-
> logical High Priest. This type of literature might be combined with hymns
> of praise to God who brings about this elevation, i.e., the hymn which
> follows the Self-Glorification Hymn [in the Hodayot]. . . .
>
> For the followers of the Teacher of Righteousness it was probably very
> difficult to accept the scenario that such a significant figure as the Teacher
> of Righteousness would disappear from the historical stage. It is possible,
> therefore, that some followers of the Teacher of Righteousness identified
> him with an eschatological figure, to be revealed at the End of Days. The
> resemblance between the Teacher of Righteousness and the Eschatologi-
> cal High Priest could have led some scribes to incorporate the Hymn of
> Self-Glorification, which was composed in the name of the Eschatological
> High Priest, into the Hodayot Scroll.

That the Self-Glorification Hymn was included in the Hodayot suggests that
the singers of the Yahad and their liturgical cantor (perhaps the Instructor,
hammaśkîl) perceived themselves as partaking in the imagined end-time
communion with the heavens, similar to their singing the Teacher Hymns
and identifying with the subject of these prayers.

We have seen that Isa 50 and 53 gave color to the portraits of the end-time
priest in 4Q541 as well as in the Self-Glorification Hymn. Was this the primary
understanding of the songs of the suffering servant both in the presectarian
priestly circles behind the Levi testament 4Q541 and within the Yahad?

To answer this question, we turn to the midsection of the Thanksgiving
Hymns. In columns IX–XVIII of the Hodayot we encounter a singer with a
strong sense of a God-given vocation who conveys to those around him the insight, blessing, and revelation he has received himself. Suffering and persecution
have been part of his odyssey. These hymns are commonly designated Teacher
Hymns—perceived as either being written by the Teacher of Righteousness or
written with his life story and career in mind (cf. the biblical psalms that drew
unto themselves the heading *lǝdāwīd*). Throughout the Teacher Hymns are numerous echoes of biblical psalms of lament as well as the songs of the suffering
servant, in the mouth of a singer calling himself "your servant" (XV 16; XVII
11; Elgvin 2005, 32–33, cf. Isa 50:4, 53:2, 3, 5, 8, 11) (all translations my own):

> [I will proclaim in the assembly of the] simple ones the judgments of my
> afflictions. (1QHᵃ IX 33)

I became a trap for offenders, but healing for all who turn away from offense. (1QHᵃ X 8–9)

I was rejected by them, they did not esteem me. (1QHᵃ XII 8)

When I lean on you, I remain resolute and rise above those who scorn me. (1QHᵃ XII 22)

Through me you have enlightened the face of the many. (1QHᵃ XII 27)

You have . . . made my tongue like that of your disciples. (1QHᵃ XV 10)

The Lord Yhwh has given me the tongue of disciples to straighten my steps . . . to walk before you in the land of the living. (1QHᵃ XV 14)

You made me a fountain in dry ground . . . the tree of life at the secret fountain . . . shall make a shoot grow. (1QHᵃ XVI 4–6)

My residence is with the sick, my heart knows afflictions. (1QHᵃ XVI 26–27)

My spirit hides with the dead, for my life has gone down to the pit. (1QHᵃ XVI 29)

The voice of my disciple-tongue . . . shall sustain the weary with a word. (1QHᵃ XVI 36)

The evidence of the Teacher Hymns indicates that the two Isaiah songs of the suffering servant were not read as one-dimensional prophecies of the end-time priest. These songs were likely read in Qumran as foretelling the suffering of different righteous individuals, not necessarily one specific end-time image. With these songs coloring the Teacher Hymns, it was natural for an inspired poet of the Yahad to draw from these songs in his portrayal of the end-time priest, in part perceived as a Teacher of Righteousness *redivivus*.

I noted on pp. 139–40 that the scribe who penned the second half of the large Isaiah scroll may have consciously added a *yod* to the text of his *Vorlage* in Isa 52:14, to make it clear that the suffering servant is anointed, like Cyrus (45:1), and the prophet proclaiming his own vocation in 61:1: "So I anointed [*māšaḥtî*] his appearance above any man, and his form above any sons of man" (1QIsa[a] 52:14). With such a reading, the anointed servant of the Isaiah text would prefigure the priestly Teacher of Righteousness and the end-time high priest, both anointed servants of God.

The Messianic Community of the Last Days

The War Scroll (1QM) is a detailed description of the coming end-time war where the sons of light confront the sons of darkness, the army of Belial, which is denoted Edom, Moab, Ammon, Philistia, and the Kittim of Asshur (= the Romans).

A messiah is not mentioned in this well-preserved scroll, which may be compared with the Community Rule and the Hodayot Scroll from Cave 1 as an archival or "librarian copy" of high quality. The Balaam oracle on the star of Jacob and scepter of Israel is quoted in XI 6–7. The interpretation of the oracle, however, does not focus on a royal messiah, but rather reads the oracle as a prophecy of the end-time war with the destruction of Moab, the sons of Seth, and other enemies. David appears earlier in this column but only as an example and ideal of warriors who trust in God's intervention. The high priest is given a liturgical role in columns XII–XVIII. He appears as leader of the corps of army chaplains following the battle, cursing the enemy and blessing and inspiring the troops.

The War Scroll thus advocates a collective messianism (Monti 2004, 28; Sayyad Bach 2020, 238–39). The restored nation—identified with the sons of light—appears as the messianic actor. Redemption will be brought forth through the action of the people of God, assisted by the angels with whom they are in communion.

In the Serekh scrolls the collective messianism is more reflected and pronounced. The Community Rule sees the Yahad as a spiritual temple and God's agent in the eschatological history:

> [4]When such men as these come to be in Israel, [5]then shall the council of the Yahad truly be established, an everlasting plantation, a house of holiness for Israel and assembly of supreme [6]holiness for Aaron. They shall be truthful witnesses to the judgment and the chosen ones of (God's) goodwill, who shall atone for the land and pay to [7]the wicked their reward. They will be *the tested wall, the precious cornerstone* [Isa 28:16] whose [8]foundations shall neither rock nor sway in their place, the dwelling of supreme holiness [9]with Aaron. All of them will know the covenant of justice

and shall offer up sweet fragrance. They shall be a house of perfection and truth in Israel, [10]establishing a covenant according to everlasting precepts. They shall be an acceptable sacrifice, atoning for the land and determining the judgment of wickedness, and there shall be no more iniquity. When these men have been confirmed for two years in perfection of way in the foundation of the Yahad, [11]they shall be set apart as holy within the council of the men of the Yahad. And the Interpreter [12]shall not conceal from them, out of fear of the spirit of desertion, any of those things hidden from Israel that have been discovered by him. (1QS VIII 4–11 // 4Q258 2 I 1–6, 4Q259 II 11–III 3, my translation)

The Yahad is "the everlasting plantation," a term for the elect community with an active role as the end times unroll. When 1QS was penned, the men of the Yahad were likely excluded from the temple, which was in Hasmonean hands, or they had excluded themselves from sacrifices in Jerusalem. Coming out of a priestly tradition and viewing the present physical temple as defiled, the idea of the community as a spiritual temple would naturally develop.

The priestly led Yahad with its council is *not compared* with the temple; it *is the temple* and embodies the "assembly of supreme holiness for Aaron": an abode for the divine presence, with the sons of Aaron as guardians and liturgical servants. As such, the spiritual temple is called to "offer up sweet fragrance" and "be an acceptable sacrifice, atoning for the land." The Yahad's atoning for the land would again open for the purification and restoration of the people of Israel in the land, with the Yahad as the nucleus of the renewed nation.

The same collective messianism may be reflected in a festival prayer that likely was part of the Pentecostal liturgy of the Yahad with its covenant renewal (Vermes 1997, 368; Falk 1998, 178–80).[17] The Festival Prayers of the Yahad drew on liturgical traditions from Judea at large but were adapted and edited to fit the self-understanding of the community.[18]

---

17. Weinfeld (1978) demonstrates that the Sinai covenant was celebrated at the Feast of Weeks already in biblical times, as is evinced in the blowing in the horn on the festival day (Ps 81:4 [81:3]) and the Sinai-like theophany connected to Zion in 50:1–6. In the first century BCE, Jubilees 6 and 14–15 prescribe a festival of covenant renewal during the Feast of Weeks (cf. 6:11–17; 15:3–9). For the understanding of Jubilees as a literary tradition developing throughout the first century, either within the Yahad or circles close to it, cf. Monger 2014, 2017, 2018a, 2018b.

18. Falk 1998, 155–87. The Festival Prayers are preserved in 1Q34 and 4Q507–9. A

The passage below follows a reflection on man's trespassing the laws of God:[19]

> [5]But in the time of your goodwill you chose for yourself a people. For you remembered your covenant, [6]you u[nited] them and set them apart from all the peoples as holy to yourself. And you renewed for them your covenant through a glorious vision and the words of [7]your holy [spirit], by the works of your hands and the writing of your right hand, that they might know the glorious instructions and the deeds that lead to eternity. [. . . [8]You raised up] for them a faithful shepherd, M[oses your servant, a ma]n of humility and gr[eat mer]cy. (1Q34 3 II 5–8, my translation)

The liturgy recalls Israel's first shepherd, Moses—the sectarians saw themselves as walking in his footsteps. In the text, there is a seamless transition from the Sinai revelation and covenant to the Yahad's celebration and self-understanding. The "renewal of your covenant" refers to both the covenant at Sinai and the yearly covenant renewal of the Yahad, which *is* the community of the new covenant. As Israel from the Sinai event was set apart from the nations, thus the community is in the present set apart from ungodly Judah at large.

For the sectarians, this is confirmed and experienced in their spirit-filled liturgy and exegesis. The liturgy expresses a strong confidence of being the elect community of the end times, the people of the renewed covenant (Jer 31) that enjoys God's goodwill. They are "the sons of your goodwill" or "men of [his] goodwill" (1QH[a] XIX 12; 4Q418 81 10).[20] The singers have experienced the presence of God's holy spirit and are a holy community before him. Only to them have been revealed the "glorious instructions" and the "deeds that lead to eternity" (*yisûrê kābôd, ma'ăśê 'ôlām*). As in 1QS VIII, they appear as a messianic community, as God's elect actor as the end times unroll.

---

sectarian edge can be perceived in concepts such as "the time of God's goodwill," the renewal of the covenant, a consciousness of being unrighteous from the mother's womb (4Q507 1 2), and God "knowing the hidden and the revealed things" in a festival context (4Q508 2 4). In the Bible, this word pair appears only in Deut 29:28 [29:29] (only God knows the future). For the Yahad, God has revealed hidden things only to them (1QS V 11–12; CD-A III 14; 1QH[a] XIX 20; XXVI 15).

19. Reading line 7 with Parry and Tov 2005, 5.268. Reconstruction of line 8 with Qimron 2013, 392; cf. Num 12:3: "the man Moses was very humble."

20. These are Hebrew equivalents of Luke's *anthrōpois eudokias* ("men of goodwill"; Luke 2:14).

Melchizedek: A Heavenly Redeemer

In Dan 7 and 4Q521, the savior is related to the heavenly realms. In a similar vein, three priestly writings foresee a heavenly figure as the acting redeemer, while the elect community on earth appears as a more passive recipient of salvation.

Here God's angelic viceroy is Melchizedek—a figure known from Gen 14 and Ps 110. 11QMelchizedek (11Q13) was written or copied around 75–50. A sectarian scribe lays out his expectation of the last days through a pesher commentary on select biblical passages, opening with the year of Jubilee (Lev 25:13, paired with Deut 15:2 on "a remission of God"):

> [4][The interpretation of these verses] refers to the final days and the captives . . . [5] . . . they are the inheritan[ce of Melchize]dek [6]who will make them return. Liberty shall be proclaimed to them, to free them from [the debt of] all their iniquities. . . . [7] . . . And the D[ay of Atone]ment mar[ks] the e[nd of] the tenth [ju]bilee—[8]then atonement will be made for all the sons of [light,] the men [of] the lot of Mel[chi]zedek . . . for [9]this is the time decreed for the *year of favor* of Melchizedek [Isa 61:2] and [his] arm[ies, the nati]on [of] the holy ones of God . . . as it is written [10]about him in the songs of David: *'ĕlōhîm shall [sta]nd in the ass[em-bly of the godlike ones and judge in the midst of the divine ones* [Ps 82:1]. About him it is said, *'el shall judge the nations* [Ps 7:9 (7:8)] . . . [13]And he, Melchizedek, will carry out the vengeance of Go[d]'s judgments. [On that day he will f]r[ee them from the hand of] Belial and all the s[pirits of his lot.] [14]All the angels [of justice] shall come to his help; and he [will muster] all the angels. . . . [15]This is the day of peace on which [Isa]iah the prophet said: *How beautiful* [16]*on the mountains are the feet of the messenger who announces peace, the messenger of good who announces salvation and says to Zion, your 'ĕlōhîm is king* [Isa 52:7]. . . . [23] . . . It is about him it is written, *your 'ĕlōhîm is king* [Isa 52:7]. . . . [24] . . . And *your 'ĕlōhîm is* [25][. . . , Melchizedek, who will fr]ee [them from the han]d of Belial. (11Q13 II 4–25, my translation)

Following biblical texts (e.g., Ps 8:6 [8:5]) that use *'ĕlōhîm* for angelic beings, the pesher interprets *'ĕlōhîm* of 82:1 and *El*, the divine judge of 7:9 [7:8], as God's second-in-command, Melchizedek. The proclamation "your *'ĕlōhîm* is king" (Isa 52:7) is read about Melchizedek, not the Lord, and "the year of *'ĕlōhîm's* favor" (61:2) is rendered as "the year of favor of Melchizedek."

Melchizedek appears as the semidivine redeemer, chief of the heavenly armies, who leads the battle against the evil powers.[21]

Melchizedek is instrumental when, during the end-time Yom Kippur, "atonement will be made for all the sons of [light]"—a climax of his performing bloodless Yom Kippur sacrifices accompanying the earthly sacrifices in the temple. Melchizedek executes the end-time judgment on the evil forces and redeems the elect "sons of light," those who are of the "lot of Melchizedek."

11Q13 likely quoted from Gen 14 and Ps 110, although such references are not preserved. Psalm 110:1–4 was probably read as an address by God to Melchizedek, closing with "on my decree you are priest forever, Melchizedek" (Aschim 1999, 136–37).

Two earlier nonsectarian texts cast light on the portrayal of Melchizedek in 11Q13. 4QVisions of Amram (4Q543–4Q549), written in Aramaic in the second century, is a priestly testament put in the mouth of Amram (father of Moses and Aaron and precursor of the Levites). The conflict between the prince of light and the prince of darkness, the two angelic powers ruling over humans, is revealed to Amram through a vision. The prince of darkness is named Melchiresha ("My king is evil"). The name of his counterpart is not preserved; he was no doubt called Melchizedek ("My king is righteousness"). This angelic ruler of the sons of light belongs to the divine realm; he brings healing and saves men from the power of death:

> [1.12]"We rule over all the sons of Adam." . . . [13][One] of them had a dr[ead]ful appearance and his [cl]o[th]ing was colored and obscured by darkness. . . . [14][The other,] and behold, [he was bright] in his appearance and his face was smiling.
>
> [2.2][Then I asked him,] "This [Watcher,] who is he?" And he said to me, "This (dark) one is called [. . .] [3]and Melchiresha." . . . [5] . . . "And he rules over all darkness." . . . [6] . . . "But I rule over all that is bright. . . . I have been made ruler [over all the sons of lig]ht." (4Q544 1 12–14; 2 2–6, my translation)

> [3][God will redeem] them by their healer, [[4]deliver] them from death and an[nihilation. . . . [9] . . . [For the sons of light] [10]will be brilliant, and all

---

21. The nonpriestly War Scroll displays a different image and terminology for the angelic forces. In 1QM IX 15–16, Michael appears as the first of the four archangels, with Gabriel, Sariel, and Raphael; and 1QM XVII 6–7 portrays Michael as the highest angel—God will send redemption by his hand.

the sons of darkness will be dark. . . . [13] . . . [The sons of light] will go to light, to [everlasting] happiness [and rejoicing]. (4Q548 1 3–4, 9–13, my translation)

Songs of the Sabbath Sacrifice is a liturgy found in nine copies at Qumran and one at Masada. Here the conductor of the Levitical temple choir below also directs the praises of the angels above. One of the angels is referred to as "[. . .]zedek, priest in the assemb[ly of God"—to be restored as "[Melchi]zedek" (4Q401 11 3). Melchizedek appears as an angel with a priestly ministry in the heavenly sanctuary, probably as a counterpart to the service of priests in the earthly temple.

Seen together, Songs of the Sabbath Sacrifice, Visions of Amram, and 11QMelchizedek testify to the concept of an angelic Melchizedek, priest and prince in God's assembly, and the two latter texts outline his end-time ministry of deliverance and judgment. An analogous picture of Melchizedek emerges in 2 Enoch, a Jewish apocalypse from the first century CE (2 En 23).

The idea of a heavenly Melchizedek probably crystallized in priestly exegesis of Gen 14:18–20 and Ps 110:4 before the formation of the Yahad. The names of Abraham's antagonists were read symbolically: the king of Gomorra, Birsha (*birša‘*), is read as "son of wickedness," while the king of Sodom, Bera (*bera‘*), was read as "son of evil" (Gen 14:2). Such a reading facilitated the understanding of Melchizedek as heavenly warrior fighting against evil powers. Genesis 14 was then read as an earthly visit by the priestly angel Melchizedek, who helped Abraham in his fight against the evil powers, an interpretation probably shared by Hebrews.

The letter to the Hebrews, itself a priestly/Levitical treatise, should be read as a sequel to these priestly texts.[22] Hebrews 5:6, 10; 6:20 introduce Melchizedek as antetype of Jesus as end-time high priest before the theme is unfolded in Heb 7: Melchizedek is "without father or mother . . . without beginning of days and end of life, like the Son of God he remains priest forever"; in contrast to earthly priests who are mortal, he is "declared to be living" (7:3, 8)—features that prefigure Jesus. Jesus appears as a priest like Melchizedek, not because of his ancestry (he was not of the tribe of Levi), but "on the power of an indestructible life" (7:15–16). And Jesus is proclaimed "priest forever, according to the order of Melchizedek" (5:10; 6:20).

22. For this reading of Hebrews, cf. Aschim 1999; Mason 2008, 8–39, 138–203; Elgvin, "Melchizedek" (forthcoming).

Hebrews 2:10–18 portrays Jesus in conflict with the devil and sent to redeem the enslaved. The author likely draws on the tradition of Melchizedek as heavenly warrior and redeemer of the elect. As is the case in 11QMelch, Hebrews reinterpret the atoning rituals of Yom Kippur in terms of eschatological redemption, making the temple ritual temporal or disposable. Thus, the author of Hebrews connected the Melchizedek tradition and the Jesus event: the angelic Melchizedek prefigures the priestly ministry of Jesus who brought himself forth as a sacrifice, concurrently on earth and in the heavenly sanctuary (9:24).

Universal Renewal

In the Bible and Qumran many texts promise redemption only to the elect nation. However, some texts foresee universal renewal and redemption also for the nations.

In 1 En 6–11, a section that likely was part of an Enochic testament by the early second century (Nickelsburg 2001, 25–26; Elgvin 2003, 96–97), we find God's command to the archangel Michael to destroy wickedness:[23]

> [10:16]Destroy all perversity from the face of the land,
> and let every wicked deed be gone,
> and let the plant of righteousness be planted forever with joy.
> [17]And then, all the righteous will escape,
> and they will live until they beget thousands,
> and all the days of their youth and their old age will be completed
>   in peace.
> [18]Then all the earth will be tilled in righteousness,
> all of it will be planted with trees and filled with blessing,
> [19]all the trees of joy will be planted on it.
> They will plant vines on it,
> and every vine that will be planted on it will yield a thousand
>   jugs of wine,
> of every seed that is sown on it, each measure will yield a thou-
>   sand measures,
> and each measure of olives will yield ten baths of oil.

23. For commentary on this passage, see Nickelsburg 2001, 225–28; Elgvin 2003, 92–95.

²⁰Cleanse the earth from all impurity and from all wrong,
from all lawlessness and all sin,
and remove godlessness and all impurities that have come upon
    the earth!
²¹And all the sons of men will become righteous,
all the peoples will worship and bless me and prostrate
    themselves.
²²All the earth will be cleansed from defilement and uncleanness,
and I shall not again send upon them any wrath or scourge for
    the generations of eternity.
¹¹:¹Then I shall open the storehouses of blessing that are in heaven
and make them descend upon the earth,
upon the works and the labor of the sons of men.
²Truth and peace shall be united together
for all the days of eternity and all generations of men. (1 En
    10:16–2:2, translation from Nickelsburg 2001, 216)

In this end-time scenario, wickedness and the ungodly will be eliminated. Then, the "plant of righteousness" crystallizes on earth. The plant is the community of the elect, perceived as the nucleus of the restored humankind that will live in peace and experience a paradisiac earth. All nations will recognize the God of Israel, bless him, and prostrate before him (cf. Isa 45:23).

This Enochic text can be compared with two texts that date to approximately the same time: the composite wisdom text 1Q/4QMysteries (1Q27/4Q299–301) and 4QTime of Righteousness (4Q215a) (Elgvin 2003, 94–98; 2004, 69–77).

⁵This shall be the sign that it shall come to pass:
When the begotten of unrighteousness are shut up,
wickedness shall be banished by righteousness
as darkness is banished by ⁶light,
so shall wickedness perish forever
and righteousness be revealed like the sun governs ⁷the world.
All who cleave to the mysteries of wickedness²⁴ shall be no more.
But knowledge shall fill the world and folly exist no longer.
    (1QMyst 1 I 5–7, my translation)

---

24. Reading *razê pešaʿ* ("mysteries of wickedness") with Qimron 2013, 130; cf. Palestine Archaeological Museum #40.527.

In this passage, the images of light and darkness are prominent, as in 4Q541. As in the Levi text, the universal renewal is compared to the dominion of the sun. All the wicked will be shut up and wiped out, and justice and light penetrate the world—but there is no personal messianic agent in this breakthrough. Humankind will live in righteousness and all will know Yhwh. The foretelling that "knowledge shall fill the world" echoes Isa 11:9: "The earth will be full of the knowledge of Yhwh" ("knowledge," i.e., knowing Yhwh and relating to him).

The hope for universal renewal appears also in 4QTime of Righteousness (4Q215a), a fragmentary scroll copied by a sectarian scribe around the turn of the era. The work itself is likely older:[25]

> 2]for the heart of men ponder wickedness.
> They will be purified in the furnace of [miser]y
> 3with distress and oppression and the ordeal of the pit.
> Through this they will be refined to become the elect of
>   righteousness,
> and he will wipe out all their wickedness 4because of his loving
>   kindness.
> For the period of wickedness has been completed, all injustice
>   will [pass aw]ay.
> For] 5the time of righteousness has come,
> and the land has been filled with knowledge and praise of God in
>   [his] bea[uty.[26]
> For] 6the age of peace has come, and the laws of truth and the
>   testimony of justice,
> to instruct [men] 7in the ways of God,
> and [they will reflect] on his mighty deeds forever and ever.
> Every tong[u]e 8shall bless him, every man prostrate before him.
> [And] they [will be of] on[e hea]rt.
> For he [prepared] 9their actions before they were created,
> for the deeds of righteousness he assigned boundaries
> [and borderlines] 10throughout their generations.
> For the dominion of goodness has come,

---

25. For the translation, cf. Elgvin 2003, 89–90; and Qimron 2014, 37. For a wider interpretation, cf. Elgvin 2003, 92–95; and Justnes 2009, 281–386.

26. Qimron's reading *bapi k[ôl]* is not materially possible. I read *bayōp[yô]*; cf. Isa 33:17.

> the throne [of holiness][27] he has exalted [11]on high.
> Knowledge, prudence, and insight are tested by [his] holy
> desi[gn]. (4Q215a 1 II 2–11)

4Q215a is a poetic work on the end times. There is a periodization of history, and the creator has preordained the deeds of all people throughout their generations. The text opens with the purification of the elect group. Then, all wickedness and injustice will be eliminated, and the ultimate time of righteousness and age of peace will break through. God will sit on his throne and humankind will be transformed. Each and every person will bless the Lord and prostrate before him, as foresaid in Isa 45:23. Jeremiah 32:39 and Ezek 11:19 foresee that God will transform the Israelites and give them one heart.[28] In 4Q215a, however, the one heart will be given to all humankind. The universal outlook is different from that of the Yahad and more similar to 1 En 10 and 1Q/4QMysteries.

The three texts surveyed here are all considered presectarian or extra-sectarian. Their inclusion of all nations in renewed humankind differs from the narrower expectations of the Yahad. Eschatological war is not outlined, nor is there any messiah with a particular role as the end times unroll.

A Davidic Messiah in the Psalms of Solomon

A contemporary group of psalms that never made it into the collection at Qumran, the Psalms of Solomon, were known in antiquity[29] but became known in the West only in the early seventeenth century. The text is pre-served in Greek and Syriac. Joosten (2015) challenges the traditional view of a Hebrew original, arguing for a Judean author writing in Greek heavily influenced by the Septuagint.

Most of the psalms were written in the years following the Roman takeover of Judea in 63. As liturgical texts, the psalms were formative com-munity texts with transformative power upon the individual (Atkinson

---

27. One can reconstruct terms such as "throne of [holiness]" or "throne of [judg-ment]," less likely "throne of the [messiah]."

28. In both verses G reads "another heart" (*lēb ʾaḥēr* for M's *lēb ʾeḥād*; cf. the graphical similarity between *resh* and *dalet*), while Syriac reads "a new heart" (followed by Hebrew manuscripts in Ezek 11:19).

29. Codex Alexandrinus concludes its table of contents with the Psalms of Solomon without including the work itself.

2015; Werline 2015). Deposed priests and dissident scribes were part of these circles that were critical to the lascivious lifestyle of the Hasmonean rulers. Psalms of Solomon 1, 2, 7, 8 deplore the sins and impure deeds of the city's inhabitants, priests, and leaders. Some verses lament the impurity and destiny of the temple. Prayer and fasting are seen as means of atonement (3:8), which led previous scholars to link the community to Pharisaic circles.

The final recension of the Psalms of Solomon is consciously formatted, opening with a Jerusalem psalm (Pss Sol 2) and ending with two messianic texts. The presence of Pss Sol 11 in the collection, a hymn that hails the return of the dispersed to the Hasmonean kingdom, evinces some pluriformity among the authorial circles—even if this psalm could be a leftover from a preceding generation (see pp. 226–27).

The two last psalms describe and praise the Davidic messiah (17:4, 21–46; 18:1–9). Mainly written in the period 63–37, the psalms underline the expectation of a Davidic messiah, not a return to power by the Hasmonean family. Embry (2006; 2015, 63) suggests that an author with a prophetic self-understanding utilized the image of Solomon as a prophetic figure to convey his vision of a Davidic restoration of Israel. After a proclamation of the covenant with David, Pss Sol 17 continues with God's judgment on the Hasmoneans by the hand of Pompey:

> 4Lord, you chose David to be king over Israel,
> and swore to him about his descendants forever,
> that his kingdom should not fail before you.
> 5Those to whom you did not make a promise they took away
>   by force,
> those who had not honored your glorious name.
> 6With pomp they had set up a haughty monarchy,
> they despoiled the throne of David with arrogant shouting.
> 7But you, O God, overthrew them, and uprooted their descen-
>   dants from the earth,
> for against them rose a man from the nations. . . .
> 9According to their deeds, God showed no mercy to them,
> he hunted down their descendants and did not let even one of
>   them go. (Pss Sol 17:4–9, my translation)

The psalm continues with a lament of the decay under the last Hasmonean rulers, and concludes with a long messianic hymn:

²¹O Lord, raise up for them their king,
the son of David, to rule over your servant Israel
in the time known to you, O God.
²²Gird him with strength to destroy unrighteous rulers,
to purge Jerusalem from gentiles who trample her to destruction,
²³—with wisdom and righteousness, to drive out sinners from the
    inheritance,
to smash the arrogance of sinners like a potter's jar,
²⁴to shatter all their substance with an iron rod,
to destroy lawless nations with the word of his mouth.
²⁵At his warning, nations will flee from his presence,
he will condemn sinners by the thoughts of their hearts.
²⁶He will gather a holy people whom he will lead in
    righteousness.
He will judge the tribes of the people
that has been made holy by the Lord their God.
²⁷He will not tolerate unrighteousness to pause among them
or any wicked man to live with them.
For he shall know them, that they are all children of their God.
²⁸He will distribute them throughout the land according to their
    tribes,
no alien or foreigner will live near them.
²⁹He will judge peoples and nations in the wisdom of his
    righteousness,
³⁰gentile nations will serve under his yoke.
He will glorify the Lord all through the land
and purify Jerusalem to be holy as it was in the beginning.
³¹Nations will come from the ends of the earth to see his glory,
to bring as gifts her children who had been driven out,
to see the glory of the Lord who has glorified her.
³²He will be a righteous king over them, taught by God.
There will be no wickedness among them in his days,
all shall be holy, and their king the Lord messiah.
³³He will not rely on horse and rider and bow,
nor will he collect gold and silver for war,
nor will he build up hope among men for a day of war.
³⁴The Lord himself is his king, he has a strong hope in his God.
He shall be compassionate to all the nations
who stand reverently before him.

³⁵He will strike the earth with the word of his mouth,

he will bless the Lord's people with wisdom and happiness.

³⁶He will be free from sin, to rule a great people.

He will expose officials and drive out sinners by the strength of
his word.

³⁷He will not weaken in his days, relying upon his God,

for God made him powerful in the holy spirit,

wise in the counsel of understanding with strength and
righteousness.

³⁸The blessing of the Lord will be his strength,

he will not weaken, ³⁹his hope will be in the Lord.

Who will succeed against him,

⁴⁰mighty in actions and strong in the fear of God?

He will be a faithful and righteous shepherd of the Lord's flock,

he will not let any of them stumble in their pasture.

⁴¹He will lead them all in holiness,

there will be no arrogance among them, nobody will be
oppressed.

⁴²This is the beauty of the king of Israel,

known by God to be raised over the house of Israel, to discipline
it.

⁴³His words will be purer than the finest gold,

he will judge the peoples in the assemblies, the tribes that are
sanctified.

His words will be as the words of the holy ones among sanctified
peoples.

⁴⁴Blessed are those born in those days to see the good fortune of
Israel

that God will bring to the assembly of the tribes.

⁴⁵May God dispatch his mercy to Israel,

may he deliver us from the pollution of profane enemies!

⁴⁶The Lord himself is our king forevermore! (Pss Sol 17:21–46,
my translation)

The hymn abounds with echoes of Davidic texts (Pss 2; 72; 110; 2 Sam 5:2; Jer 23:5–6; Isa 9:5 [9:6]; 11:1–5; Zech 9:9–10) and oracles of the future of Zion (Isa 2:1–5; 60:3–6). The messiah is a central actor in God's redemption of Zion. He appears as a mediator of God's presence and blessings, as the king is portrayed in Ps 72. Psalms of Solomon 17:23–24, 31, 36 recasts the role of the Davidic king as described in Ps 72:1–14; while Pss Sol 17:29–31 and 17:35 describe the messiah's powerful role vis-à-vis other nations as in Ps 2:8–12 and Ps 110.

This messianic hymn expresses a weariness of Hasmonean rulers who were levying taxes on the people in order to finance their lascivious lifestyle and wars. The ideal is a future son of David who will inaugurate a time of peace, prosperity, and blessing.

The messiah will have his trust in God, not in his military strength, as did the Hasmonean rulers. "He will not rely on horse and rider and bow" (Pss Sol 17:33) is an echo of Hos 1:7: "I will save them by Yhwh their God; I will not save them by bow, or by sword, or by war, or by horses, or by horsemen"; and of 14:4 [14:3]: "Assyria shall not save us, no more will we ride on steeds" (NJPS).

When the messiah will "destroy lawless nations with the word of his mouth" (Pss Sol 17:24), he takes on God's own role, as seen in scriptures describing the might of God's voice that causes fear and destruction (Isa 30:30; Jer 25:30; Amos 1:2). But a similar role is ascribed to the Davidide in Isa 11:4 ("he shall strike the land with the rod of his mouth, and with the breath of his lips, he shall kill the wicked").

As shepherd of God's flock (Pss Sol 17:40) he will mirror the divine shepherd (Ezek 34:11–16; Isa 40:11) and fulfill the prophecies of the son of David shepherding his people (2 Sam 5:2; Ezek 34:23–24; Mic 2:12; 5:1–8 [5:2–9]).

In the end-time texts of the Yahad, the community plays the role as nucleus of the renewed nation, a purified nation where the ungodly have been eliminated. In contrast, this messianic hymn displays a national hope—the nation at large will be redeemed. The hymn can be compared with the Zion psalms in Sir 36, Tob 13, and 11QPsªZion. But different from these texts, the Davidic messiah is an essential God-sent actor in the end times. He "gathers a holy people" (Pss Sol 17:26), "he will purify Jerusalem to be holy as in the beginning" (17:30), "he will bless the Lord's people with wisdom and happiness" (17:35), "he will be a faithful and righteous shepherd of the Lord's flock, he will not let any of them stumble in their pasture" (17:40), "he will lead them all in holiness" (17:41).

Jerusalem will be purified; while the temple, its liturgy, or sacrifices are not mentioned, this hymn is no priestly text. Other psalms in the collection deplore the looting of the temple and its impurity, lamenting that the sacrifices had been profaned, so that no sweet candor rose before God (Pss Sol 2:3–4; 7:2; 8:11–12). But in Pss Sol 17 and 18, the glory of the Davidic messiah outshines the temple and its ministry.

Jewish Messianism
after the Turn of the Era

F ew studies of Hebrew Bible messianism include Jewish texts from the first millennium CE, and the subject is rarely included in theological curricula. Christian studies may include the New Testament with the Old, but that is not my task in this book. As New Testament writings are in their own way, other Jewish writings also represent a continuation and interpretation of texts and traditions from the Hebrew Bible and Second Temple literature.

I present a selection of relevant texts from the late first century to the seventh century CE, using the first Islamic century as a natural dividing line to end my discussion. This chapter is primarily a survey of texts and lines of development, and I hope that readers will find here an attractive foretaste of a fascinating and pluriform textual world.

The Great Revolt and Its Aftermath

Josephus describes messianic fervor during the Great Revolt:

> What more than all else incited them to the war was an ambiguous oracle found in their sacred scriptures: at that time one from their country would become ruler of the world. This they understood to mean someone of their own race, and many of their wise men went astray in their interpretation of it. (Josephus, *Jewish War* 6.312–13, my translation)

The oracle Josephus refers to is most likely the Balaam prophecy of Num 24:17–19, according to which the messiah shall subdue enemy nations. He also mentions a prophetic oracle about miraculous salvation given during the last days of the siege and onslaught on Jerusalem:

The people owed their destruction to a false prophet who had, on that very day, declared to the people of the city that God ordered them to go up to the temple courts to receive there the signs of their deliverance. Many prophets had been induced in these days by the rebel leaders to deceive the people by exhorting them to wait for help from God and thereby to reduce the flow of deserters, as well as buoy up with hope those who were beyond fear or precaution. . . .

This is how the unhappy people were beguiled at this stage by charlatans and false messengers of God. (Josephus, *Jewish War* 6.285–86, 288, my translation)

This specific prophetic voice in 70 CE is one of many first-century Jewish prophets who promised miraculous signs from God (Gray 1993, 120–44). A coordinated alliance between zealot leaders and charismatic prophets, as Josephus implies, sounds unlikely. But desperate situations like that of Jerusalem under siege would easily encourage such enthusiastic voices.

The people of Jerusalem had been in a similar situation when Herod besieged the city in 37. At this time too, there were prophecies that Jerusalem could not be conquered:

Considerable agitation seized the Jewish masses in the city. . . . Congregating around the temple, the feebler folk sought divine guidance while their spiritual leaders predicted wise "prophecies" to fit the occasion. (Josephus, *Jewish War* 1.347, my translation)

According to these prophecies, God would guard and save his temple, leading the people to believe that God would give them victory in their zealous fight against Herod (*Antiquities* 14.470). Commenting on the Oracle of Hystaspes from the subsequent century (see pp. 301–2), Flusser (1988, 392) notes that "already in the year 37 B.C. an apocalyptic hope existed that the temple would not fall under any circumstances."

Earlier in his narrative from Jerusalem under siege, Josephus records the story of Menahem, another messiahlike figure in the days of the revolt (*Jewish War* 2.433–48). Menahem, son of the Zealot leader Judah the Galilean, captured Masada, which enabled him to arm the brigands that followed him. He "returned like a king to Jerusalem, became the leader of the revolution, and took charge of the siege of the palace" (4.434). After successfully repelling a Roman onslaught, Menahem's gang killed the high priest Ananias and his brother, seemingly leaving Menahem as head of the rebels without any rivals. He then entered the temple "with a brilliant display of splendor to worship, decked with kingly robes and an entourage of armed zealots" (4.443–44); such an appearance suggests some kind of messianic aspirations and evinces messianic fervor among his followers. Menahem's conflict with the priestly leadership shows their dislike of such a messianic profile (Schäfer 2012, 225–26).

However, Menahem's success was not long-lived. In the temple he was attacked by the zealot group of Eleazar and was pelted with stones by the people. Menahem was subsequently tracked down, tortured, and killed by Eleazar's men. A relative of Menahem (also named Eleazar) escaped to Masada and took command there.

The fall of the temple would lead to anguish, despair, and lament, to reflections on the defeat and bloodshed, and to prayers for rebuilding Jerusalem and the temple.

Two pseudepigraphic writings reflect on the fall of the temple in the disguise of the fall of the First Temple, with Baruch and Ezra as recipients of revelation. Fourth Ezra is a composite Jewish apocalypse written during the first decades after the fall of the temple. At the time of its writing, Zion lies in ruins (10:20, 49). As is the case with other Jewish pseudepigrapha, 4 Ezra has been preserved through Christian transmission, which means that there may be Christian interpolations in the text. Fourth Ezra was likely written in Hebrew, translated into Greek, and from the Greek the book found its way into the Latin, Armenian, Syriac, and Arabic traditions; it appears as an appendix to the Vulgate.

In the book, Ezra the scribe mourns the corruption of humankind and the loss of the temple. During his dialogue with God, Ezra is led to new confidence in God's covenant with Israel. In parallel visions, he receives revelation on the end times. According to the third vision, there will be signs in heaven and earth and trials for all humankind. The messiah will be revealed, and a millennium of four hundred years will follow:

> [28]For my (son the) messiah shall be revealed with those who are with him, and those who remain shall rejoice four hundred years.[1] [29]And after these years my (son the) messiah shall die, and all who draw human breath. (4 Ezra 7:28–29, my translation)

---

1. "My son the messiah" (Syriac, Arabic[1]), "my servant the messiah" (Arabic[2])—the Arabic translations were made from Syriac. Other witnesses read "the messiah," "my messiah," "God's messiah," "my son Jesus" (Latin). Schäfer (2012, 78–79) suggests that the Hebrew original used either "my son the messiah" or "my servant the messiah" (referring to the Isaianic Servant Songs). For the "millennium" of four hundred years, compare Rev 20.

Figure 9. *Judea capta* ("Judea conquered") coin, minted by Vespasian, 70–78. A victorious Roman soldier counters the defeated "Lady Judah."

The designation "my son the messiah" may reflect the pen of a later Christian scribe, but such words are not incomprehensible in a Jewish hand (cf. 2 Sam 7:14; Ps 2:7). The words "my messiah shall be revealed" indicate that the messiah was preexistent, a feature made explicit in other passages (4 Ezra 12:32; 13:26, 32; Stone 1987, 214; Laato 1998, 360–65).

With the death of the messiah, God remains as the sole end-time actor. Following the end of the millennium, the world will be transformed, a new paradisiac era will begin, humankind will be resurrected, and the final judgment take place.

Fourth Ezra 11–12 (Ezra's fifth vision) follows a more detailed eschatological scenario. In the symbolic vision, a demonic and cruel eagle (= Rome) will be annihilated by a lion (= the Davidic messiah). This means that the messiah will appear to judge and destroy the ungodly nations and to redeem the remnant of Israel. His messianic reign will last until the day of judgment (12:26–35).

The sixth vision appears in 4 Ezra 13, which (for the first time in the book) thematizes the end-time attack of the nations on Zion and the messiah: a human figure rises from the sea and soars with the clouds of heaven (cf. Dan 7:13). When he is attacked by a multitude of humans, he stands against them on Mount Zion; fire will stream out of his mouth and annihilate his enemies. Afterward he gathers a great multitude around himself as his own flock. Ezra then receives the interpretation from God: the man from the sea is the preexistent messiah ("my son") who will appear after the violence and wars of the end time. He will annihilate the attacking gentile peoples and gather around himself the remnant of the northern tribes from the east and the Judeans left in the land.[2]

While Israel has failed in observing the Torah, the Torah itself will remain in glory (4 Ezra 9:11, 36–37). A restored Zion appears in only one of Ezra's visions (10:27, 44–55), but temple and sacrificial service is not mentioned.

Second Baruch (or Syriac Baruch) is contemporary with 4 Ezra. As is the case with 4 Ezra, the reign of Domitian (81–96) may provide the historic background. There exists only one complete Syriac manuscript, from the late sixth or early seventh century. Second Baruch was known and read in some circles of the West Syriac (Jacobite) church. Parts of the text of 4 Ezra and 2 Baruch are included in five Syriac lectionaries from the thirteenth and fifteenth centuries, which means that these two books were considered on a par with Old Testament books.[3]

Among its eighty-seven chapters (some are very short), the messiah and the messianic times are thematized in parallel visions or revelations in 2 Bar 25–30, 35–40, 70–74. History runs its preordained path. There will be a long sequence of tribulations on earth, the preexistent messiah will be revealed and introduce a paradisiac era on earth, and the world will be renewed. At the end of times, God will send the messiah, who will redeem Israel from subjugation. Any rebuilding of the temple and restoration of the sacrificial ministry is not mentioned in the messianic times. In the present time one is called to live by the Torah.

According to 2 Bar 25–30, the messiah will be revealed after the great tribulations, but he is mentioned in passing in only two verses. When he appears, nature will be transformed, and paradisiac conditions will follow. When the period of the messiah has reached its fullness, the righteous will rise at the end of times.

Second Bar 35–40 takes up the scheme of four consecutive kingdoms from Dan 7. The last one is Rome, which surpasses its predecessors in cru-

---

2. With a diachronic reading of the book, the messiah dies with humankind in ch. 7 but appears again on the scene in chs. 11–12 and 13. Such a reading may have inspired the two-stage messianism where Messiah of Ephraim is a precursor for Messiah son of David (see pp. 305–11).

3. The lectionaries prescribe for reading the following texts: 2 Bar 44:9–15; 72:1–73:2; 4 Ezra 6:18–28; 7:26–42; 12:31–38. Four thirteenth-century lectionaries are from the Syriac monastery in Wadi al-Natrun in Egypt. A manuscript dated 1423 is from the Qartmin Monastery in Tur Abdin in southeast Asia Minor. I am indebted to Liv Ingeborg Lied for this information; cf. Lied 2021.

elty. When the time of fulfillment approaches, "my messiah will be revealed," the enemy forces will be annihilated, and their leader led in chains to Mount Zion, where the messiah will pronounce the judgment and kill him. In this section, the messiah is a militant warrior. After the annihilation of the enemies, the messiah will guard the elect nation, and the messianic times will last until the final periods of history have been fulfilled.

In the scenario of 2 Bar 70–74, nations will rise against nations, and many will be devoured. Those living in the land will be spared from the tribulations. The messiah will appear as judge and rule the world from his throne. The nations that have not inflicted evil on Israel will be saved and submit to the seed of Jacob. During the reign of the messiah there will be paradisiac conditions on earth until the world passes into its ultimate, incorruptible state.

Some pseudepigrapha with Jewish-Christian interpolations from the first half of the second century provide relevant material (Elgvin 2007, 286–99). The *Testaments of the Twelve Patriarchs* has a Jewish *Grundschrift* with roots in the second century BCE and was polished by Jewish-Christian editors around the mid-second century CE (Jervell 1969). For these Jewish-Christian scribes, the hostile kingdom will be brought to an end; all Israel will be saved in the end time, be ingathered to the land, and enjoy millennial blessings with Christ as their earthly king.

Fourth Baruch has a Jewish *Grundschrift* written around 120 and was interpolated soon after the Bar Kokhba war by a Christian hand (Herzer 1994, 177–98). For this book, Israel shall stay separate from the gentiles, be obedient to God, and return to the land where the temple cult will be renewed.

The Tannaitic Amidah

The Amidah (or Eighteen Prayers) have roots before 70, while its final forms were shaped after the fall of the temple. Kimelman (1997) dates the vision of national redemption in blessings 10–15 to the tannaitic period (70–200; the tannaim are the rabbis of the Mishna). The full text is first known from 860, in the Siddur (common prayer book) of Amram Gaon, the rabbinic leader in Abasside Babylon. However, the motifs, structure, and sequence of the Amidah are discussed in the Mishnah and both Talmuds. A version commonly identified as an early Palestinian recension was found in the Cairo Genizah. In the Siddur, blessings 10–12 and 14–15 run as follows (my translation):

[10]Blow the great *shofar* and redeem us. Raise a banner and gather our exiles, gather us from the four corners of the earth. Blessed be you, O Lord, who gathers the exiles of your people Israel!

[11]Restore our judges as in former times and our counselors as in the beginning. Remove from us trouble and anguish. Reign over us, you alone, O Lord, in kindness and mercy! Blessed are you, O Lord, who loves justice and righteousness!

[12]May the informants have no hope and all the sectarians [*minîm*] instantly perish, and all your enemies speedily be cut off. And may the wicked kingdom be uprooted and broken and vanquished in our days.[4] Blessed are you, O Lord, who breaks enemies and vanquishes the wicked![5] . . .

> [14]And to Jerusalem, your city, return in mercy, and dwell in it as you have spoken!
> Rebuild it forever, soon in our days, and speedily establish in it the throne of David.
> Blessed are you, O Lord, who rebuilds Jerusalem!
> [15]Speedily cause the sprout of your servant, David, to flourish!
> Let his horn be exalted by your salvation, for we wait daily for your salvation.
> Blessed are you, O Lord, who causes the horn of salvation to flourish!

In the Siddur there are separate blessings for Jerusalem and the Shoot of David (14 and 15). In contrast, in the Palestinian (Genizah) version, the blessings of Jerusalem and the Shoot of David appear together:

4. In tannaitic times, "the wicked kingdom" would commonly be identified with Rome.
5. With the insertion of a twelfth member, the Eighteen Prayers ended up with nineteen subunits. According to the Babylonian Talmud, tractate *Berakhot* 28b, *birkat ha-minim* ("the curse of the sectarians") was included in the existing Amidah by the sages of Yabne in the late first century (I regard the first half of the second century as more likely). A genizah version runs: "May the apostates have no hope, and may the wicked kingdom be uprooted in our days, and the *nōṣrîm* (Nazarenes/Christians) and the sectarians instantly perish. Let them be erased from the Book of Life and not be recorded alongside the righteous. Blessed are you, O Lord, who vanquishes the wicked!" Scholars disagree on whether the *nōṣrîm* of the Palestinian version refers to Jewish Christians only or to Christians in general. According to Justin Martyr (writing around 160), the Jews curse Christ in their prayer. By the fourth century, Epiphanius and Jerome specify that Christians are cursed three times a day (Skarsaune 2007, 482–85; cf. Flusser 2007, 84–85).

> Have compassion, O Lord, our God, in your abundant mercy, on Israel your people, on Jerusalem your city, on Zion, the abode of your glory, and upon the royal seed of David, your justly anointed. Blessed are you, O Lord, God of David, rebuilder of Jerusalem![6]

The rebuilding and restoration of Zion is at the center of the prayer for redemption. That God shall "dwell in it" points to a rebuilt temple, as does "the abode of your glory" in the Palestinian version. Whether blessings 14–15 were formulated before or after Bar Kokhba remains an open question for Kimelman; I see a pre–Bar Kokhba date as the most likely.

In blessings 10–15, the Davidide is subordinated to the divine intervention (thus Kimelman 1997, 319). Blessing 11 highlights God's exclusive rule. He alone is the redeemer and rebuilder of Jerusalem. The appearance of the Shoot of David in blessing 15 is more a manifestation of divine power than an expression of acute messianism. "The key player, indeed virtually the only player, is God."

Such a downplaying of human agency in the coming redemption fits the tannaitic period. The same point is stressed in the third-century midrash *Mekilta of Rabbi Ishmael* to Exod 12:10, where God is the only actor: "*And I will smite*—not through an angel nor through a messenger."[7]

Targum to Isaiah 53: A Victorious Son of David

The interpretation of Isa 53 in Targum Jonathan is without parallel in other texts. The targumist who wrote the interpretative Aramaic version of Isa 53 presupposes that the suffering servant is a portrait of the messiah, something he might have learned from earlier tradition (cf. 1QIsaᵃ to Isa 52:14; see pp. 139–40). As the song opens with the elevation of the servant (52:13–15), he

---

6. This Palestinian practice is confirmed by the Tosefta (tractate *Berakhot* 3.25): "In the Eighteen blessings . . . one inserts (the blessing) *for David* in (the blessing) *builder of Jerusalem*."

7. Lauterbach 1933, 1.97. This statement would soon be included in the Passover liturgy: "*And the Lord brought us out of Egypt*—not by an angel, nor by a seraph, nor by a messenger, but the Holy One, blessed be He, by himself." The *Mekilta of Rabbi Ishmael* and early Haggadah tradition testify to the second/third-century separation from the Jewish Christians, who saw Moses and the exodus as types for Christ and the Christian Passover and also could advocate an angelic Christology (Yuval 2006, 68–91).

understands this messiah as the Davidic messiah, and he knows that the son of David is a victorious one.[8] This leads him to rewrite the text, so that the suffering is first experienced by the people and then laid on the enemy nations. In all of this, the servant of the Lord emerges victorious, and his exaltation is a feature throughout the text (Chilton 1983, 91–96; Ådna 2004; Himmelfarb 2017, 91–96):

> [52:13]Behold, my servant the messiah will prosper; he shall be exalted and be great and mighty. [14]Just as the house of Israel hoped for him for many days—and their appearance was wretched among the nations, and their countenance beyond that of the sons of men—[15]so shall he scatter many nations, kings shall be silent because of him. They will put their hand over their mouth—what was not told them, they have seen, what they have not heard, they have perceived.
>
> [53:1]Who has believed this message of ours? And to whom has the mighty arm of the Lord been so revealed? [2]The righteous shall grow up before him as budding shoots, as a tree sends forth its roots by channels of water, so shall the holy generations increase in the land that waited for him. His appearance is not a common one, fearing him is different from fearing ordinary men, his countenance shall be holy, for all who see him will recognize him.
>
> [3]Then the glory of all the kingdoms will become a disgrace and be cut off, they will be weak and sick even as a man of sorrows and one destined for sickness. As when the Shekhinah was taken away from us, they will be despised and not esteemed.
>
> [4]Then he will entreat for our sicknesses, and our iniquities will be forgiven for his sake, even though we were accounted smitten, stricken by the Lord, and afflicted. [5]He shall rebuild the sanctuary that was defiled by our sins and handed over because of our iniquities. By his teaching the peace will be great for us, by our devotion to his words, our transgressions will be forgiven.
>
> [6]We were all scattered like sheep, we had wandered off, each on his own way, but it was pleasing to the Lord to forgive all our transgressions for his sake. [7]He entreats and is answered, before he opens his mouth he is accepted.

---

8. A passage in the later Midrash Tanhuma (Toledoth, 14) may be inspired by this targum: the great mountain before Zerubbabel is the Davidic messiah (Zech 4:7), and Isa 52:13 refers to his elevation. This parasha contains no further reference to Isa 53.

He will hand over the mighty ones of the nations like lamb to the slaughter, and as a ewe that is silent before her shearers, so no one will open the mouth before him to speak a word.

[8]From suffering and punishment he will bring near our exiles. Who can proclaim the miracles that will be done for us in his days? For he will remove the rule of the nations from the land of Israel. Sins that my people have sinned, he will put on the nations. [9]He will hand over the wicked to Gehenna, and those who have become rich through robbery to death and destruction, for the evildoers will not stand and will not any more speak deception.

[10]But for the Lord it was pleasing to refine and purify the remnant of his people, so that he could cleanse them from sin. They will look upon the kingdom of their messiah. They shall multiply sons and daughters and have their days prolonged, and those who do the Torah of the Lord will succeed by his favor.

[11]He will deliver them from the servitude under the nations. They will see that their enemies are punished, they will be satiated with the spoil of their kings. By his wisdom he will justify the righteous and subject many to the Torah, and he will entreat for their transgressions. [12]Then I will divide unto him the spoil of many peoples and the riches of strong cities, he shall divide the booty, because he handed his life over to death and subjected the rebellious to the Torah. He will entreat for many transgressions, and the rebellious will be forgiven for his sake. (adapted from Stenning 1949, 178–80)

To some degree, the job description of this Davidic messiah is traditional and corresponds to that of the Amidah. The messiah shall gather the dispersed and free them from servitude, fight against enemy nations and overcome them, and build the temple.

In some details, the hypotext puts its stamp on the sequel. Being hit by sickness and sorrow, going like sheep to the slaughter, being silent without opening one's mouth—these traits are applied to the leaders of enemy nations. But Israel as well is painted as carrying sicknesses, being beaten and afflicted with blows from the Lord, as they deserved because of their sin and iniquities.

A rare feature is the teaching office of a Davidic messiah ("he will subject many to the Torah"; Isa 53:5, 11, 12) and the call to follow *his* words instead of phrasing the call as heeding the words of the Lord (53:5). Instead of the traditional "fearing the Lord," the nation shall "fear him, but different from fearing ordinary men" (53:2).

Then, in 53:4–7, 11–12, there is an emphasis on purification and forgiveness of sins, forgiveness for the sake of the messiah, he who intercedes for his people and even for rebellious Israelites (Ådna 2004, 214–22). Finally, "he handed his life over to death" (53:12) is faithfully rendered—meaning either risking one's life or giving it—a rare statement in Davidic messianism. Such an expression of the messiah's readiness to die could be indebted to a portrayal of Moses as intercessor, ready to vicariously take upon himself the punishment for the nation's sin (Exod 32:30–34; Num 11:14–15; Deut 9:18–29), as is evinced by *Mekilta of Rabbi Ishmael* to Exod 12:1.[9]

The targumist's portrayal of the messiah reflects a conscious theological conception developed by a daring interpreter. Features that in Qumran texts were connected to different end-time figures are here combined into an all-encompassing job description for the messiah as mediator of salvation: he will defeat the enemies, gather the dispersed, build the temple, restore the nation and teach them the Torah, intercede for the sins of the nation so that they will be forgiven for his sake, and be ready to die for the people (Ådna 2004, 222–24). But through all this, the Lord remains the ultimate savior who through his messiah reveals his mighty arm. It is God himself who forgives Israel's transgressions "for his sake," for the sake of the messiah (Isa 53:2, 6).

What is the time of origin for this targumic text? Targum Jonathan contains diverse material of different age and origin, from the first to the fifth century. The main redaction was done in Mesopotamia in the third to fifth centuries, while some passages were edited up to the ninth century. According to Chilton (1983, 92–99), the messianism and eschatology of the full Isaiah Targum point to tannaitic times: writing soon after the fall of the temple, the translator has a vivid hope for restoration; and he does not discern clearly between the messianic age and the world to come. Chilton compares the messianism with that of the Amidah and arrives at a probable dating between 70 and 130, with some later amendments in Amoraic times.[10] He even suggests

---

9. "The patriarchs and the prophets offered their lives on behalf of Israel. As to Moses, what did he say: But now, if you will only forgive their sin! But if not, blot me out of the book that you have written (Exod 32:32)—I cannot carry all this people by myself, for it is too much for me. If you would deal thus with me, kill me rather, I beg you, and let me see no more of my wretchedness! (Num 11:14–15)" (Lauterbach 1933, 1.10). *Mekilta of Rabbi Ishmael* is an early halakhic midrash to select chapters of Exodus, with a core going back to the school of Rabbi Ishmael (teaching 120–40 CE). Undergoing a series of redactions throughout the third century, Mekilta's final form should be dated to the late third century (Strack and Stemberger 1992, 277–79).

10. Himmelfarb (2017, 92–93, 189–90) finds Chilton's precise dating of the Isaiah tar-

that "such a portrait of the messiah may have driven Bar Kokhba, and inspired rabbis to take his lead, he was even willing, as the Targumic messiah, to risk his life, subjecting the rebellious to the law (cf. Tg. Is. 53.12)" (1983, 95).

The targum was written too early to contain any conscious anti-Christian exegesis of Isa 53 (Ådna 2004, 190–94). The connection of the messiah with Torah recurs in another prophetic targum (Targum to Jer 23:5; 33:1), as does the vindication of the righteous and the punishment of the wicked in Gehenna (Targum to 1 Sam 2:8–10; Chilton 1983, 94, 96, 100–101).

For Chilton, this text may be dated anywhere between 70 and 130, while Ådna (2004, 194–97) concludes that the text likely was composed shortly before the Bar Kokhba Revolt: Isa 53:5 and 53:8 presuppose that the land is occupied by gentiles, but these two verses and the text in general are carried by a glowing messianic expectation that this disastrous state soon will come to an end. Such a hope for imminent redemption is largely different from the mode of rabbinic rethinking in the generations following the catastrophe of the messianic Bar Kokhba war.

The targumist hardly knows the tradition of a second messiah from the tribe of Ephraim (a fighting or suffering one, and then dying before the son of David enters the scene; see pp. 303–10). Had he known, his job in reinterpreting Isa 53 might have been easier. Thus, he writes before the idea of a messiah son of Ephraim crystallized, an idea that perhaps developed in the second part of the second century CE. Further, he was not aware of the mid-third-century messianic reading of Isa 53 as "the sick" or "the leper" among Palestinian rabbis (Himmelfarb 2017, 96; see pp. 294–96). Ådna's dating of the text to the years before the Bar Kokhba Revolt seems well founded.

Bar Kokhba: A Militant Messiah

The Prehistory of the Revolt

Jerusalem proper was in ruins after the Great Revolt, barren of any civil population and guarded by Roman soldiers (Geva 1997; 2007, 58–59).[11] The Romans allowed, however, the construction of a high-class neighborhood

---

gum too optimistic; she argues that the Isaiah targum, as other parts of Targum Jonathan, took shape over centuries.

11. There was a large Roman army camp close to today's Binyenei Haumma, and a smaller one close to the Temple Mount, unearthed in the recent Givati excavations.

3 km north of Jerusalem: salvage excavations in Shuafat in 2003 revealed a high-standard Jewish neighborhood, even with a Roman bathhouse. Five mold-made inkwells were unearthed here (Sklar-Parnes, Rapuano, and Bar-Nathan 2004). If this was the closest to Jerusalem the Romans allowed the priestly elite, the scribal milieu associated with the temple may have continued to exist. According to rabbinic sources, the main scribal centers were Lod and Yavne; the latter was the seat of the Sanhedrin up to the Bar Kokhba Revolt. To a large extent, the rural communities in Judea recovered within a generation.

Rabbi Akiva, possibly a later supporter of Bar Kokhba, had hoped for a rapid rebuilding of Jerusalem. The Mishnah quotes him with words soon included in the Passover Haggadah. If the ascription of these words to Akiva holds true, this prayer should be dated before the revolt and can be compared with blessings 14 and 15 of the Amidah. They exemplify the hope shared by wide circles in the nation in the period between the two revolts:

> O Lord our God and God of our fathers, bring us in peace to the feasts and festivals coming to meet us, while we rejoice in the building-up of your city and rejoice in worshiping you. May we there eat of the sacrifices and the Passover lambs whose blood has reached with acceptance the wall of your altar. Let us praise you for our redemption and for redeeming our soul. Blessed are you, O Lord, who redeems Israel! (Mishnah, tractate Pesahim 10.6, my translation)

The Diaspora Revolt, 115–117 CE

The sources for the revolt in the diaspora are diverse and fragmentary. They include Roman historian Cassius Dio (third century), church father Eusebius (early fourth century), and Egyptian papyri (Schürer, Vermes, and Millar 1973, 529–34; Mendels 1992, 385–86). The revolt may have been prompted by a general Jewish frustration over the particular tax imposed on Jews all over the empire after 70 and Roman refusal to permit the rebuilding of the temple, while other nations within the empire were allowed to build their sanctuaries (Goodman 1992; 2003, 25–28). Emperor Nerva (ruled 96–98) displayed a more lenient attitude toward the Jews than his predecessors, while Trajan (98–117) did not assent to Jewish hopes.

In 115, while the emperor and large Roman forces were fighting the Parthians in the east, the Jews of Cyrene and Egypt rose against their Greek countrymen. According to Cassius Dio, the rebels killed large numbers of gentiles and destroyed pagan temples. While attacking the Greeks and destroying their temples, the Jews of Cyrene crowned their leader "king of the Jews." When Roman forces intervened to stop the riots, the conflict evolved into real battles. In Egypt, the Jews defeated the Roman prefect in a battle and caused the Greeks involved to flee to Alexandria, where many local Jews subsequently were massacred. A papyrus refers to a Jewish victory over Roman forces late in 116 and the calling in of another Roman legion. Other papyri refer to confiscation of Jewish property after the revolt and to an Oxyrhynchus celebration of the anniversary of the victory over the Jews as late as 200.

Trajan sent the experienced General Marcius Turbo to Cyrene. He put down the revolt and killed thousands of rebels. In the meantime, the revolt had spread to Cyprus. Temples were destroyed, large numbers of Greeks killed, and the capital Salamis ravaged. Afterward, Jews were forbidden access to the island.

With Trajan fighting the Parthians at their capital Ctesipon, the Jews of Mesopotamia seized the moment and revolted. Commissioned by Trajan, the moorish commander Lucius Quietus beat down the rebels and killed thousands of them.

The sources are meager when it comes to Judea's role during the revolt, but some sources indicate there were upheavals also in Judea. Hadrian's biographer Spartianus notes there were daring rebels in Palestine; this may find support in a Jewish source that calls the revolt "the war of Quietus."[12] Further, precautions taken after the war indicate that the Roman authorities saw the need for tightly controlling the people in Judea. The choice of Quietus as new governor of Judea is telling.

Battles were still going on when Hadrian became emperor in 117. Following the revolt, Jewish communities that had been involved were devastated to the degree that the Romans had to resettle the localities with other groups. Alexandrian Jews were made subject to large-scale massacres—the beginning of the end of Jewish presence in Egypt (Collins 2010c, 222–24).

Some localities in Galilee were likely involved in the uproar. Subsequently, the Romans extended the road system in the region in a way that

12. Listing wars in the land of Israel, *Seder Olam* 2.66 counts fifty-two years from the war of Vespasian to "the war of Quietus," and sixteen years from this war to that of Ben Koziba, which again lasted three-and-a-half years. The term "the war of Quietus" suggests there were tough battles also in Judea. *Megillat Ta'anit* 29 notes "the day of Trajan," 12 Adar, as a day of mourning, giving a legendary story of Trajan persecuting Jews in Laodicea as the reason.

enabled them to cut communication between Jews in Galilee and Judea—new roads from the coast all through the land could seal Galilee off from the south (Mor 2003, 127). While settlements in Galilee built underground hideouts in the years preceding the Bar Kokhba Revolt, the next revolt never extended to Galilee (Shahar 2003).

Bar Kokhba's War for the Redemption of Israel

The Bar Kokhba Revolt (132–36) is the most distinctive messianic movement within the Jewish people in the first millennium. Its catastrophic repercussions would be formative for the subsequent development of central features of rabbinic thinking. It is therefore pertinent to give a broad presentation of the revolt.

The sources to the prehistory and development of the war are diverse: a few Latin texts, writings by church fathers, and legendary hints in rabbinic writings. From 1952 onward, documents, coins, and artifacts were found in Judean Desert caves where the rebels took refuge. Subsequently, the knowledge of subterranean hideouts and places of concealment of rebel coins has steadily increased.[13] Together, these sources enable a rather comprehensive understanding of the revolt.

Frustration over direct military rule in parts of Judea may have grown over time. After the Great Revolt, independent farmers were reduced to the status of sharecroppers (Eshel and Zissu 2019, 8–12). While most settlements had slowly recovered after the Great Revolt, Roman precautions after the diaspora revolt were felt in Judea. Toward the end of his reign, Trajan made Judea a regular consular province and stationed a second legion there. Another legion was ensconced in Arabia, the province to the east. These moves show that the Romans were concerned that the Judeans were prone to initiate new rebellions (Goodman 2003, 27–29). With the seventy-year anniversary of the fall of the temple approaching, Jeremiah's prophecy of "seventy years" passing from the fall of the temple to the restoration (Jer 29:10) likely stimulated eschatological hopes—and seventy years had indeed passed from the fall of the First Temple to its reconstruction.

13. For the following, see in particular the contributions in Schäfer 2003 and Eshel and Zissu 2019. The latter was published in Hebrew in 2015, primarily being researched until the death of Hanan Eshel in April 2010.

In contrast to the revolt of 66–70, the Bar Kokhba Revolt was concentrated in central Judea. Galilee and the coast were not involved (not a single Bar Kokhba coin has been found in Galilee). According to Roman historian Cassius Dio (third century), the revolt was provoked by Hadrian's decision to make Jerusalem a Roman *colonia*, with a sanctuary for Jupiter on the Temple Mount. Hadrian founded Aelia Capitolina during his visit to Judea in 130 and marked its borders through a symbolic act. Different from other Roman colonies, the founding of Aelia Capitolina was no honorary act toward a local population. Hadrian's intention was to settle non-Jews there and initiate non-Jewish religious rites. "Within Hadrian's great policy of urban reconstruction, with the foundation of many cities, Aelia Capitolina is unique in its use of the new colony not to flatter but to suppress the natives" (Goodman 2003, 29). This provocative act was an ultimate blow to Jewish hopes for rebuilding the temple and pushed nationalistic Judeans from slowly preparing for a fight against the Romans to active planning of military action in the close future. Aelia Capitolina coins found together with Bar Kokhba coins in a rebel cave confirm that such coins were minted in Jerusalem before the outbreak of the war (Eshel and Zissu 2019, 139–40).

The putative banning of circumcision is also proposed as a cause of the revolt. According to the Hadrian section of the *Augustan History* (fourth century?), "the Jews went to war because they were forbidden to mutilate their genitals," and some rabbinic sayings might be interpreted in the same direction. Scholars argue about the scope and time of a decree proscribing circumcision—if it was proclaimed before the revolt or afterward as a means of punishment, and whether it was decreed by Hadrian or his successor Antoninus Pius (138–61). Today, few scholars would date such a Roman decree before the revolt (Eshel and Zissu [2019, 15] belong to the minority). The law of Antoninus Pius states: "Jews are permitted to circumcise only their sons. If anyone should commit it on one who is not of the same religion, he shall suffer the punishment of a castrator."[14]

Oppenheimer (2003) surveys the relevant rabbinic material and concludes that the few sayings that clearly relate to tough anti-Jewish legislation were pronounced by rabbis active in Galilee *after* the revolt. From a Roman perspective it would be difficult to enact a general prohibition against Jewish

14. The point of reference for Antoninus's law was not an existing ban on circumcision. Rather, earlier legislation proscribing castration of slaves was used as point of reference for a legal approval of Jewish circumcision (the first ever in Roman law), while restricting it to the Jewish nation (Abusch 2003, 84–91).

circumcision and subsequently implement it only in Judea. Abusch (2003) concurs that no Latin source ascribes a ban on circumcision to Hadrian. The late *Augustan History* is colored by anti-Jewish sentiments and speaks about "mutilating their genitals"—hardly a legal terminology. The emperor did implement tough anti-Jewish measures in Judea after the war, but legislation on circumcision was initiated by Antoninus Pius and was directed against circumcising non-Jews.

The revolt was hardly a spontaneous act. Many Judean settlements had been preparing for war, building networks of subterranean hideouts for refuge and guerilla warfare. In central Judea, archaeologists have identified four hundred underground hideouts in more than 160 localities. Many hideouts show an architectural uniformity of the tunnel-system structures that point to strategic planning by underground authorities in the years preceding the revolt. The hideouts were ingeniously constructed, and it would have been extremely difficult for enemy soldiers to penetrate these systems. Building large hideouts would necessarily take time and must have begun before Hadrian's decision to build Aelia Capitolina. Further, such an endeavor evinces a socioeconomic recovery in the region, as local Judean communities were able to direct large resources of manpower into building these subterranean structures. The hideouts are located from Shiloh and the Modiin/Lod district in the north and almost to Beer-sheba in the south, with the tightest cluster west of the Bethlehem/Hebron ridge (Eshel and Zissu 2019, 48–61). A large number of hideouts were constructed in Galilee (forty sites, seventy complexes), but these were not in active use during the revolt (Shahar 2017). However, Galileans did join Bar Kosba's forces in the south.

The revolt started early summer 132, and the outbreak of the revolt may be the starting point for the rebels' calculation of years: "Year X of the redemption of Israel" is the common dating of financial documents found in the refuge caves and of coins minted by the rebels.

After sustaining heavy losses in the beginning of the war, in 134 Hadrian called in the experienced commander Julius Severus, headhunted from the Roman forces in Britain, to lead the campaign. Other top commanders were also called in. Ten or eleven legions were involved, indicating that the forces in Judea numbered more than 50,000. Severus changed tactics, divided his forces into smaller units that tracked down enemy groups, and besieged the fortified sites (thus Cassius Dio). After a lengthy siege, Bar Kokhba's headquarters Betar fell to the Romans in late summer 135, early in Year 4.

Cassius Dio writes that due to the heavy losses, in Hadrian's report to the senate, he omitted the usual clause: "I and the legions are in good health."

Another Latin source from the 160s notes that large number of soldiers were killed by the Judeans during Hadrian's reign. The recruitment of thousands of soldiers in the west and Asia Minor in 133–35 was possibly needed to fill the ranks after the many casualties in Judea.[15] Severus received the highest military ornament after the campaign, and honors were also awarded the governors of Syria and Arabia, which means that forces from the neighboring provinces were called in to support Severus's forces (Eshel and Zissu 2019, 144–51).

In the latter part of the revolt, fighters and civilians fled from their fortifications and homes to refuge caves, primarily in the Judean Desert. So far, thirty-seven refuge caves have been identified, and a further twenty may belong to this category. Of these thirty-seven caves, twenty-one are located to the east along the Dead Sea Fault Escarpment, nine are found in the upper part of the riverbeds flowing eastward, and seven are located in the Judean Hills west of the watershed. The Roman forces invested huge efforts in hunting down the rebels. A transport path was constructed from Nahal Arugot to the more remote Nahal Hever, and siege camps were constructed on both sides of Nahal Hever above two refuge caves (Cave of Letters and Cave of Horror). Most of these rebels were likely hunted down by the Romans in the winter of 136 (Eshel and Zissu 2019, 62–83).

Documents from the insurgents have been unearthed by Bedouin and archaeologists in Judean Desert wadis: Wadi Murabbaʻat, Nahal Hever, and Nahal Seiyal. These texts clarified the actual name of the leader of the revolt: Bar Kosba or Kosiba (the Greek transliteration is *Xōsiba*), with Kosba more likely referring to his place of origin rather than being his father's name. The documents found in the caves include forty undated letters from actors in the revolt. Fifteen letters were sent from Bar Kosba's headquarters to the commanders of En Gedi and two to Herodium. One letter is written *to* Bar Kosba, while six others refer to the ongoing war, to battles and losses.[16] Bar Kosba appears as a tough commander who regularly threatened those who disobeyed his orders, for example, putting them in fetters. In some letters, Bar Kosba explicitly designates himself *nāśî' yiśrā'ēl* ("Prince of Israel")—while nothing in the texts would suggest that he belonged to the (royal) tribe of Judah.

---

15. Thus Eck 1999; Eck and Cotton 2001; Eshel and Zissu 2019, 160–61. Mor (2003) disagrees, deeming the evidence insufficient.

16. Cf. formulations such as "the nations . . . brothers were destroyed" (Hever/Seiyal 30), "they have no chance . . . were lost . . . from those that fell by the sword" (Murabbaʻat 45), "he should come to me in En Gedi . . . the poor people and bury the dead" (Murabbaʻat 46), "even though the gentiles are closing in on us . . . so that I could not come to you" (Murabbaʻat 42).

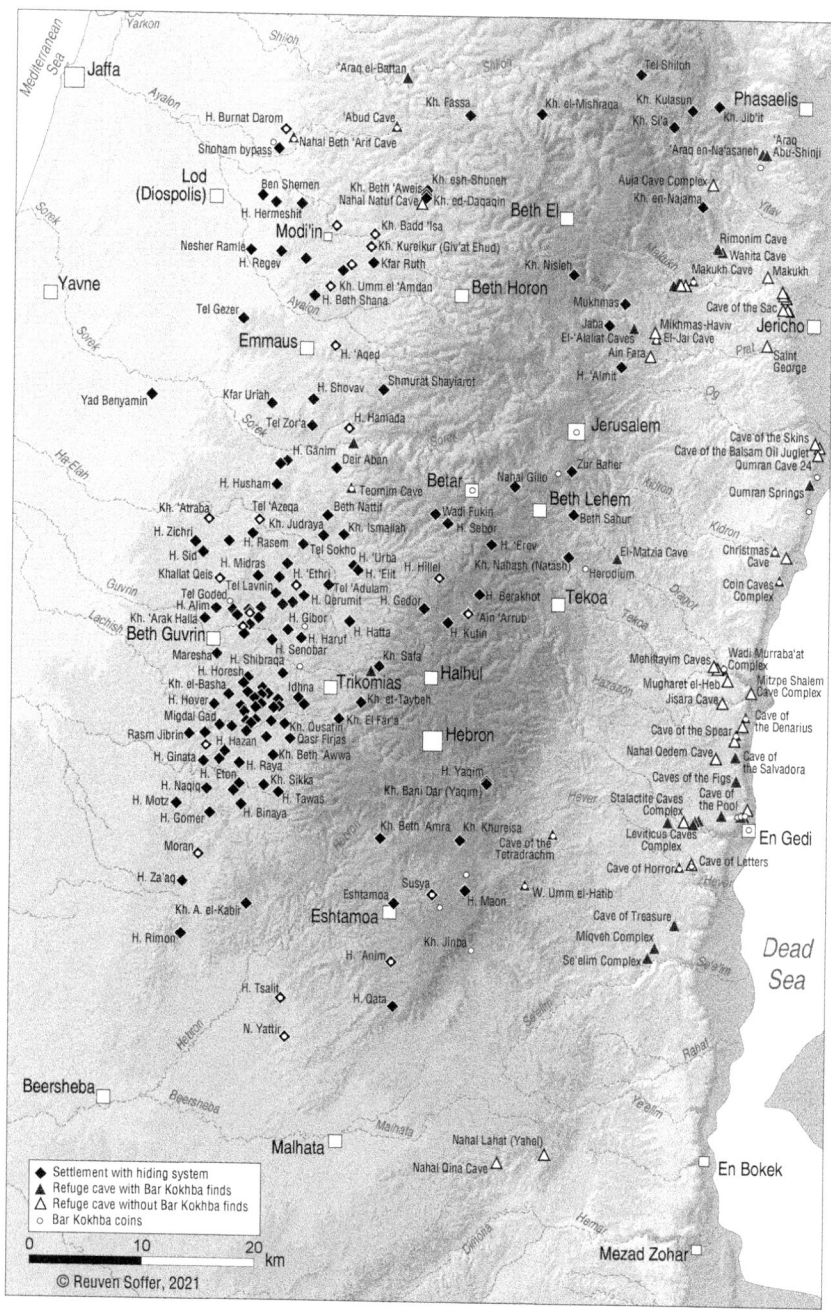

Figure 10. The Bar Kokhba Revolt.

The letters are written in Hebrew, Aramaic, and Greek. Some prescribe that provisions should not be transported on the Sabbath, another gives orders for bringing the "four species" needed for proper Sukkot celebration from En Gedi to the headquarters. Thus, observing Jewish commandments was important for the commander and his forces (Eshel and Zissu 2019, 84–93, 102–13).

In two letters, "House of Israel" is used of the liberated part of the land under Bar Kosba's control (cf. the document dated to "Year 4 after the destruction of the House of Israel," p. 289 below). A governmental system was organized, with local commanders and financial officers.

Among the large number of documents related to property, finances, and family matters, fourteen are from the years of the revolt and dated according to the timetable of the rebels. They regularly open with the following formula: "On the X (date) of Y (month), Year Z of the redemption of Israel by Shimon bar Kosba nasi Yisrael." Alternatively they could open with "Year X of the freedom of Jerusalem," demonstrating that the war was a battle for a new temple and a liberated nation led by the prince of Israel.

The place names referred in the letters and documents include Tekoa, Herodium ("Herodis"), Hakharamat and Ir Nakhash (both near Herodium), Beth-mashko and Mezad Hasidin (two unidentified sites near Herodium), Kfar Baruch and Kiryat Arbaya (somewhere between Betar and En Gedi), and En Gedi.[17]

Two documents (XHever/Seiyal 8, 8a) were written in the village Kfar Baruch east of the Dead Sea (north of Maccerus), which belonged to Judean Perea. Both are dated to Adar of "Year 3 of the freedom of Israel in the days of Shimon bar Kosba, prince of Israel, in Kfar Baruch." These documents suggest that the revolt extended to Perea, with this region still being controlled by Bar Kosba in early 135 (Cotton 2003, 149–52; Eshel and Zissu 2019, 104, 113).

A letter from Bar Kosba with instructions for Sukkot (in 134?) was penned in Greek by Simonos the scribe, "because of our inability to write in Hebrew (script)"—writing in Hebrew was clearly the ideal. Simonos was among Nabateans from the east who took part in the revolt; they spoke Aramaic but did not know the Hebrew script.[18] Non-Jewish participation in the re-

---

17. Other documents were written in Mahoza, an ethnically mixed village close to the southeastern shore of the Dead Sea. This was the home of Babatha, whose archive was found in the Cave of Letters (she moved to En Gedi in August 132 CE).

18. Simonos was a common Nabatean name. Cotton (2003, 143–52) argues that Si-

volt was noted by Cassius Dio: "Many from other nations were joining the Judeans for eagerness of gain, and the whole earth, one might almost say, was being stirred up over the matter." Cotton (2003, 150–52) suggests that the Nabateans in the Roman province of Arabia initiated their own revolt when news reached them of Bar Kosba's early victories.

Galileans had indeed joined Bar Kosba's forces. In a letter to the Herodium commander, Shimon warns him: "If anyone of the Galileans who are with you be har[m]ed(?), I will put fetters on your feet as I did to ben Aphlul" (Murabba'at 43).[19]

A large number of coins minted under Bar Kosba is important evidence (Eshel and Zissu 2019, 122–41). All the coins were recycled Roman coins overstruck by new motifs. These coins could be used only inside rebel-controlled territory; thus they reveal the territory conquered by Bar Kokhba. At the largest, his "House of Israel" encompassed most of Judea proper, from the northern Negev to southern Samaria, from the Shephelah to the Dead Sea, and parts of Perea as well. Jerusalem, however, remained in Roman hands—of 15,000 coins found by archaeologists in Jerusalem, only four are Bar Kokhba coins (Eshel and Zissu 2019, 140–41). In the sites close to Modiin and Lod, many coins from the first two years were found, but only one from Year 3 (summer 134–summer 135), and this was the year the Bar Kokhba administration produced the largest number of coins. These finds suggests that the rebels had lost control in the northern Judean hills by the summer of 134.

The coins use paleo-Hebrew script for the inscriptions, as was the case with early Hasmonean coinage. Coins proclaim: "Year 1 for the redemption of Israel," "Year 2 for the freedom of Israel," and "Year 3 for the freedom of Jerusalem." Most of the coins are inscribed "Shimon" or "Shimon nasi Yisrael," but some bear the name "Elazar hakohen." A priest being involved in the leadership of the revolt shows the clear aim to liberate Jerusalem and initiate sacrifices on the Temple Mount (cf. Rabbi Akiva's prayer; see p. 275).

---

monos was not the only Nabatean involved; the same was likely the case for Agrippa, who delivered this letter, as well as Aelianus, the scribe of the second Greek letter. The cultural inheritance of the Nabateans had affinities with that of the Jews, as both spoke Aramaic. Nabateans likely revolted because they too felt threatened by Hadrian's cosmo-Hellenistic policies and were provoked by Hadrian's relocation of the province capital from Petra to Bozrah.

19. The last letter is missing from a verb likely in the *niphal*. Restoring *yippās[ēq]* would yield "be harmed/destroyed" (√pasaq = "to cut, break"). Alternative translations are "unless you destroy the Galileans" or "unless you mobilize the Galileans."

Many coins picture a stylized temple façade with the showbread table. Other motifs are a wreath, a date palm tree, a cluster of grapes, a harp, a lyre, two trumpets, an amphora, the four species for Sukkot, and a jug with a willow branch (a motif connected with the temple's water-drawing ceremony during Sukkot). In some cases, a star or plus sign is placed above the temple façade, interpreted by some scholars as an emblem of "the son of the star," Bar Kokhba.

Eusebius and Jewish sources agree that the war ended with Bar Kokhba and his men making a final stand at the fortress of Betar south of Jerusalem. Surrounded on three sides by the Nahal Refaim riverbed and rising 150 m above it, Betar provided a natural base for fortification. Bar Kokhba forces had in haste surrounded the top of the hill with a wall with towers, buttresses, gates, and a moat at the weakest point of defense.

The fortified site covered approximately 130 dunams, including the acropolis of 30 dunams. With a population estimation of twenty-five persons per dunam, there would be around 3,250 residents in times of peace. In a time of war, with refugees seeking shelter between the walls, the total number would be much higher (personal communication by Boaz Zissu).

From the side of the Roman forces, archaeologists have uncovered a siege wall 4 km long, five army camps, small fortresses, and an assault ramp crossing the moat. Roman slingstones (5 cm in diameter) and a ballista stone projectile were found at the site (Eshel and Zissu 2019, 118–21).

Eusebius's report of the war runs as follows:

> [1]The rebellion of the Jews progressed in character and extent, and Rufus, the governor of Judea, when military aid had been sent him by the emperor, moved out against them, treating their madness without mercy. He destroyed in heaps thousands of men, women and children, and, under the law of war, enslaved their land. [2]The Jews were at that time led by a certain Barchochebas, which means "star," a bandit and murderous man that relied on his name, treating others as slaves, claiming to be a luminary from heaven that magically should enlighten those who were in misery. [3]The war reached its height in the eighteenth year of Hadrian in Betar, which was a strong citadel not far from Jerusalem. The siege lasted a long time before the rebels were driven to final destruction by famine and thirst, and the instigator of their madness paid the penalty he deserved. Hadrian then commanded that by a legal decree the whole nation should be absolutely prevented from entering even the district around Jerusalem, not even from a distance should they see their ancestral home. (*Ecclesiastical History* 4.6.1–3, my translation)

Figure 11. Bar Kokhba silver tetradrachm from the third year of the revolt. Temple façade with showbread table and the six-pointed star (of Jacob), with the inscription "Shimon." Reverse: The four species for Sukkot celebration, with the inscription "For the freedom of Jerusalem."

The conquest of Betar was cruel and bloody. Jewish sources narrate that when Betar fell "men, women, and children were slain until their blood ran into the Great Sea," while another story tells of students and sages being wrapped in the scrolls and burned to death (Babylonian Talmud, tractate *Gittin* 57a). Rabbi Akiva was executed for defying the subsequent Hadrianic ban on public study of Torah (Babylonian Talmud, tractate *Berakhot* 61b):

> 50 of their most important outposts and 985 of their most famous villages were razed to the ground. 580,000 men were slain in the various raids and battles, and the number of those that perished by famine, disease, and fire was past finding out. . . . Nearly the whole of Judea was made desolate. (Cassius Dio, *Roman History* 69.14.1–2, my translation)

> Jerusalem was completely destroyed, and the Jewish nation massacred in large groups at a time, with the result that they were even expelled from the borders of Judea. . . . That being the time when Barcochebas, the leader of the Jews, was crushed and Jerusalem demolished to the ground. (Jerome, *Commentary on Daniel* 9, my translation)

The number of 580,000 slain Judeans is exaggerated but gives an indication of the massive destruction of the "house of Israel" by the hand of the Romans. As Galilee had not been part of the revolt, this region was left undisturbed. Galilee and Golan could continue to offer the Jewish nation a homeland.

285

Bar Kokhba's Messianic Pretensions

Schäfer questions the historical reality of the great Rabbi Akiva supporting the revolt and proclaiming Bar Kosba as the king messiah. The primary text appears in two sources: the early fifth-century Jerusalem Talmud and the contemporary *Lamentations Rabbah*.[20] The Jerusalem Talmud reads:

> (a) Rabbi Shimon bar Yohai taught, "My teacher Akiva used to expound, *a star shall go out from Jacob*: Kozba goes out from Jacob.
> (b) When Rabbi Akiva saw Bar Kozba, he exclaimed, "This one is the king messiah!"
> (c) Rabbi Yohanan ben Torta answered him, "Akiva, grass will grow on your cheeks (i.e., on your grave), and still the son of David will not have come." (Jerusalem Talmud, tractate *Ta'anit* 4.5, my translation)

The parallel text in *Lamentations Rabbah* runs:

> (a') Rabbi Yohanan said: *Rabbi* used to expound, *a star shall go out from Jacob*: read not *kokab* (star) but *kozab* (liar).
> (b') When Rabbi Akiva saw Bar Kozba, he exclaimed, "This one is the king messiah!"
> (c') Rabbi Yohanan ben Torta answered him, "Akiva, grass will grow on your cheeks, and he will still not have come." (*Lamentations Rabbah* 2.4, my translation)

In (a), (b), and (b'), (*Bar*) *Kozba* ("Son of the Lie") is a later rabbinic pun on the name *Bar Kosba* and its messianic rephrasing *Bar Kokhba* ("Son of the Star"). Shimon bar Yohai, a younger contemporary and disciple of Akiva, survived the revolt, so the chain Akiva → Shimon bar Yohai is a plausible one. However, the midrash attributes the *Bar Kozba* pun not to Akiva but to *Rabbi*, that is, Judah haNasi, the final compiler of the Mishna in early third-century Galilee—transmitted through Rabbi Yohanan, a disciple of Judah haNasi teaching in the mid-third century. Rabbi Yohanan ben Torta is a rare authority, appearing in only two other early sources (Jerusalem Talmud, tractate *Yoma* 1.1; Tosefta, tractate *Menahot* 13.22);

---

20. Strack and Stemberger (1992, 309–11) date the basic shape of *Lamentations Rabbah* to the first half of the fifth century but note that the textual form was dynamically transmitted for many centuries thereafter.

his appearance in this text is likely a later invention to neutralize the messianic proclamation.

Through a literary-critical analysis, Schäfer suggests that the original statement is preserved in (a) and (c), but that the proclamation "Kosba goes out from Jacob" from the beginning was attributed to an anonymous author and only later connected with Akiva.[21]

Schäfer notes that Bar Kosba regarded himself as sovereign owner of the country and the yields of the land. A land lease (Murabba'at 24b) contains the formulation "I, Eleazar, have leased from you, Hillel, some of the fields in Ir Nahash, in the leased land you have leased from Shimon nasi Yisrael." Bar Kosba's preoccupation with Sukkot may be explained by the connotations of military victory and breaking-in of the last days connected with this festival, as evinced by Hasmonean history and texts such as Zech 14:16–20 and John 7:37–38. In Schäfer's view, it is mistaken to understand Bar Kosba as belonging to the nascent rabbinic movement; legal traditions from before 70 are a more likely background, and Bar Kokhba likely viewed himself as a successor of the Hasmoneans (Schäfer 2003, 8–15).

There should be no doubt that Bar Kosba *was* proclaimed the king messiah—either by Akiva or another rabbi. The composite text on the Star of Jacob was indeed transmitted in rabbinic circles, so Akiva remains the best candidate for such a proclamation. The change of *Bar Kosba* to *Bar Kozba* as well as the reproof put in the mouth of ben Torta represent the later rabbinic evaluation of the messianic fervor of the revolt.

Two early Christian sources evince that Bar Kosba claimed to be the messiah and persecuted Jewish Christians in the land, who likely felt, "this is not our messiah, this is not our war." According to Justin Martyr, Bar Kosiba persecuted Christians unless they denounced Christ (*First Apology* 31.6). Justin, a native of Samaria, writes in the shadow of the Bar Kokhba war and makes

---

21. Schäfer (2003, 2–7) notes that members (a) and (c) are formulated in Hebrew, while (b) is in Aramaic, a feature that suggests a process of literary compilation. He suggests (a) and (c) as the kernel, with (a) originally positively claiming Bar Kosba as messiah and attributed to an unknown author, followed by the repudiation in (c). After the failure of the revolt, Judah haNasi reinterpreted the positive statement in (a) negatively, as presented in (a'). Subsequently, "Rabbi" was understood as "my teacher" instead of being a sobriquet for Judah haNasi, and the names of two rabbis contemporary with Bar Kosba were inserted. Thus, "Rabbi Yohanan said: *Rabbi* expounded" was changed to "Rabbi Shimon bar Yohai taught, My teacher Akiva expounded." The Aramaic middle part (b) is a final explicative addition. I struggle to see the plausibility of such a misreading of "Rabbi" (= Judah haNasi) in the generations following Rabbi Yohanan.

a point that the Star of Jacob must be from the tribe of Judah and the root of Jesse,[22] which confirms that Shimon bar Kosba was proclaimed to be the Star of Jacob and that he was not of Davidic descent (Skarsaune 2007, 383–89).

The *Apocalypse of Peter* was possibly written during the revolt by a Jewish Christian living in the land (Bauckham 1998, 254–58; Skarsaune 2007, 381–89). The book is set as instruction given by Jesus to his disciples between the resurrection and ascension. In *Apocalypse of Peter* 1–2, the base text is Matt 24:30–34. The sign of the coming of the Son of Man will be clear to all, it will be the sign of the cross in the skies. The meaning of the parable of the fig tree is that immediately before the parousia, the tree of Israel will bear fruit by producing many martyrs at the hand of a false messiah: "But this deceiver is not the messiah. And when they reject him, he will kill with the sword and there will be many martyrs. Then shall the boughs of the fig tree sprout, and there shall be many martyrs by his hand: they shall be killed and become martyrs" (*Apocalypse of Peter* 2).

As Bauckham and Skarsaune read the text, persecution and martyrdom have already begun, and more is expected. The false messiah is not yet exposed as a false one, he is still active and is a real threat to Jesus believers in Israel who may be tempted to join his forces. The apocalypse was likely written in Greek, and the false messiah was called a "liar." This suggests the author knew Hebrew and that Jewish opponents of the revolt had already turned the name Bar Kosba into Bar Kozba, "Son of the Lie."

The mid-second-century 5 Ezra testifies to the same traumatic experience for Jewish Christians. The book was probably written closely after the revolt by a Jewish-Christian as an interpretative prescript to 4 Ezra. The people of Israel "has hands that are stained with blood," and there will be martyrs (1:26; 2:45). The "people soon to come" will suffer hardship and are admonished to persevere (2:24–32; Stanton 1992, 256–77; Elgvin 2007, 300–301).

The Posthistory of the Revolt

The devastation after the Bar Kokhba Revolt by far superseded that of the Great Revolt. The inhabitants of central Judea were killed or exiled. Thou-

---

22. "The scepter shall not be taken away from Judah, nor the ruler from his thigh, until he comes for whom it is reserved. . . . A star shall rise out of Jacob, and a flower shall spring from the root of Jesse, in his arm nations shall trust [Gen 49:10; Num 24:17; Isa 11:1; 51:5]" (*First Apology* 32.1, 12).

sands were sold at slave markets in Hebron and Egypt. Jerusalem was permanently converted into the pagan city of Aelia Capitolina and Jews forbidden to enter it. A temple for Jupiter was built on the Temple Mount, and a temple for Venus on the place pilgrims connected with Jesus's death and resurrection (the place of the later Church of the Holy Sepulchre). The name of the province was changed from Provincia Judea to Provincia Syria Palestina. Henceforth, the centers of Jewish cultural and religious life would be in Galilee and Babylon, not in Judea. The Sanhedrin was relocated from Yavne to Usha in Galilee.

A papyrus document outlining the financial settlement after a divorce, likely looted from a cave east of Hebron in the early 2000s, was written in "Year 4 after the destruction of the house of Israel," that is, 140.[23] The phrase "the destruction of the house of Israel" shows how deeply the defeat and its aftermath was experienced and recalls the naming of the Bar Kosba–ruled entity as "House of Israel" in two letters from the revolt. The place of concealment shows that survivors were finding refuge in a desert cave four years after the revolt to evade the restrictions imposed on Jewish life by the Romans.

Many rabbinic sources reflect the deep trauma of the defeat:

On the ninth of Av, it was decreed upon our ancestors that they would not be allowed to enter the Land of Israel, the First and Second Temples were destroyed, Betar was captured, and the city of Jerusalem was plowed over.[24] (Mishnah, tractate *Ta'anit* 4.6, my translation)

The emperor Hadrian slew 80,000 myriads of men at Betar. 80,000 trumpeters besieged Betar. . . . For three and a half years emperor Hadrian surrounded Betar. . . . Bar Kozba was convinced that Rabbi Eleazar wanted to surrender the city (Betar). . . . He flew into a rage, kicked him with his foot, and killed him. . . . The sins (of the people) caused Betar to be captured. Bar Kozba was slain and his head taken to Hadrian. . . . They slew the inhabitants until the horses waded in blood up to the nostrils. . . . The brains of three hundred children (were dashed) upon one stone. (*Lamentations Rabbah* 2.4, my translation)

23. Eshel, Eshel, and Yardeni 2011. The document was confiscated by the antitheft unit of Israel Antiquities Authority in 2009. It may derive from the Cave of the Tetradrachm 10 km southeast of Hebron.
24. The emperor would determine the borders of the city by the symbolic act of plowing with two oxen around the intended area, as was done by Hadrian in 130.

A philosophical reflection on how God could allow the Romans to slaughter the Judeans, appears in a midrash that has been read anew after the Holocaust:

> Commenting on the verse, *the sound of your brother's blood cries to me from the ground* [Gen 4:10], Rabbi Shimon bar Yohai said: I find what I have to say very difficult, but nevertheless, I have to say it. The matter can be compared to two gladiators fighting to death in the arena. Finally, one gladiator gets the better of the fight, and he is about to run his sword through his victim. Before doing so, however, he looks up to the emperor who is sitting in the royal seat watching the bloody contest. Everyone knows that if the emperor shows "thumbs down," the victor has royal assent to kill his victim. But if the emperor shows "thumbs up," the victim is spared. As the gladiators look up to the emperor, the Roman ruler who has the fate of the unfortunate loser literally in his hands, shows the sign of condemnation. Then, before he is slain, the victim calls out to the emperor, "If you had wished, you could have spared me: Now my blood will cry out, accusing you of my murder." (*Genesis Rabbah* 4.10, my paraphrase)

There is deep anguish in this midrash. It reflects the close memory of the Roman "gladiator" that wiped out his opponent, the nation of Israel in central Judea. Its ascription to Shimon bar Yohai, a leading rabbi who survived the revolt, might be historically precise. The defeat in the two revolts is not, as in other midrashim, seen as the result of the nation's sin and internal division. Here, Cain and Abel symbolize Rome vis-à-vis Israel. Shimon bar Yohai knows that God could have saved his people if he had willed, if he had shown "thumbs up." In his cry of anguish, Shimon accuses God of silence and passivity in the face of Jewish suffering. As may be done in midrash, the biblical verse is turned upside down: in Genesis, the blood of the fallen cries out to heaven and accuses the earthly murderer. Here, the blood of the fallen nation cries out to heaven and accuses God. The God of Israel allowed the slaughter of his people, and the blood of the stricken nation will from now on cry out and accuse God himself of murder (Pearl 1997, 64–65).

In Jewish thinking, the fall of the temple was the beginning of the time of the diaspora. However, in a sociopolitical reading, the second revolt had more far-reaching consequences for the Judean nation. The double defeat in these two revolts and their outcome were combined in Jewish memory.

The catastrophic outcome of the second revolt was a major impetus for the development of rabbinic theology, for the writing down of the Mishnah and the rabbinic writings that followed. With the crushing of the Bar Kokhba Revolt, Jewish expectations for rebuilding the temple and the coming of the messiah were postponed indefinitely into the future. It became urgent to put into writing all that could be recalled about temple procedures so that a blueprint for a possible third temple would be in place. In the interim, prayers would take on the role of the temple sacrifices, and a nation sanctified by obeying the Torah came into focus. In the Mishnah, messianic expectations play hardly any role, and the importance of the Torah is emphasized. As Neusner (1984, 20) phrases it: "The Mishnah presents us with a kind of Judaism that has an eschatology without the Messiah, a teleology beyond time. ... The point of insistence is sanctification and not salvation."

A classic rabbinic response to the fall of the temple is found in one of the many legendary stories that in hindsight were connected with Yohanan ben Zakkai, the great Pharisaic leader of the 60s and 70s:

> Once as Rabban Yohanan ben Zakkai was coming forth from Jerusalem, Rabbi Joshua followed after him and saw the temple in ruins.
>
> "Woe unto us!" Rabbi Joshua cried, "that this, the place where the iniquities of Israel were atoned for, is laid waste!"
>
> "My son," Rabban Yohanan said to him, "be not grieved; we have another atonement as effective as this. And what is it? It is acts of loving-kindness, as it is written, *For I desire mercy and not sacrifice* [Hos 6:6].
> (*Avot of Rabbi Nathan* 4, adapted from Goldin 1955, 34)

This response, written down in the third/fourth century, is laid in the mouth of Yohanan ben Zakkai at the sight of the temple soon after its destruction. Such reflection shows that some generations have passed since the fall of the temple and that the hope for a rapid rebuilding of the temple is hardly there anymore. In Israel's cry to heaven for atonement, Israel now has prayer and alms in their hands as substitute for bloody sacrifices on the altar—a basic pillar in rabbinic theology.

Jewish faith in tannaitic times is more than the ahistoric eschatology of the Mishnah. The hope for David and rebuilding of the temple still resounded in the daily prayer: "Have compassion, O Lord, our God, in your abundant mercy, on Israel your people, on Jerusalem your city, on Zion, the abode of your glory, and upon the royal seed of David, your justly anointed. Blessed are you, O Lord, God of David, rebuilder of Jerusalem!"

Justin Martyr's *Dialogue with Trypho*, written around 160, testifies to a living Jewish hope for the coming of a Davidic messiah and to intense discussion between Jews and Christians in Roman Palestine on messianism and the right exegesis of the Bible they had in common.

Talmudic Messianisms

Rabbinic writings are no unified corpus when it comes to teaching on the end times, the messianic age, or the characteristics of the messiah. As in 4 Ezra, 2 Baruch, Mark 13 ‖ Matt 24, there will be signs of the end times, "birth pangs of the messiah": signs in the skies, earthquakes, war and tumults among nations, ethical decay, disobedience to the Torah. According to some sayings, there are prerequisites for the coming of the messiah: "The son of David will not come until. . . ."

Some rabbinic sayings discern between the messianic age and the world to come; in others these ages seem more conflated. There are different opinions on how long the messianic age will last; some hold four hundred years (e.g., 4 Ezra). Based on Mal 3:23–24 [4:5–6], mishnaic sayings expect a specific role for Elijah in the end times: "Let it be left until Elijah comes," "let no one touch them until Elijah comes," "Elijah will come to declare (priestly families) unclean or clean" (Mishnah, tractate *Baba Metzi'a* 1.8; 2.8; 3.4; Mishnah, tractate *Eduyyot* 8.7). According to some sayings, the messiah is preexistent or present in heaven before he is revealed on earth.

In Babylonian Talmud, tractate *Sanhedrin* 97–99 we find a messianic smorgasbord, with a wide range of messianic sayings gathered together. Here is a representative selection (translation follows Soncino edition with slight adaptations):

> Rabbi Judah said: In the generation of the messiah's coming, the council chamber shall be given to fornication, Galilee shall be laid waste, and the borderlands made desolate. The people of the frontiers shall wander from city to city without any showing pity to them. The wisdom of the scribes will become insipid, God-fearing men will be despised, and truth will be nowhere found, as it is written, *Truth is lacking, and whoever turns from evil is despoiled* [Isa 59:15].
>
> Rabbi Nehemiah said: In the generation of the messiah's coming, impudence will increase, esteem perverted, the vine will yield its fruit, yet wine will be costly, and the empire will be converted to heresy without

any to rebuke them.[25] This supports Rabbi Isaac who said: The son of David will not come until the whole world is converted to the faith of the heretics.

Rabbi Zera would say: Three come unawares: messiah, a found article, and a scorpion. (Babylonian Talmud, tractate *Sanhedrin* 97a)

Tanna debe Eliyahu teaches: The world is to exist six thousand years. In the first two thousand there was desolation; two thousand years the Torah flourished; and the next two thousand years is the messianic era, but through our many iniquities all these years have been lost. (Babylonian Talmud, tractate *Sanhedrin* 97a–b)

Rabbi Hanan ben Tahlifa sent word to Rabbi Joseph: 4,231 years after the creation, the world will be orphaned. The following years—some will be the war of the sea monsters, some will be the war of Gog and Magog, the remaining will be the messianic era. The Holy One will renew the world only after 7,000 years.

Elijah said to Rab Judah: The world shall exist not less than 85 Jubilees, and in the last Jubilee the son of David will come. (Babylonian Talmud, tractate *Sanhedrin* 97b)

Rabbi Hama ben Hanina said: The son of David will not come until the pettiest kingdom ceases to have power over Israel. (Babylonian Talmud, tractate *Sanhedrin* 98a)

Rabbi Ze'iri said in the name of Rabbi Hanina: The son of David will not come until there are no conceited men in Israel, as it is written, *I will take away from your midst those who rejoice in your pride* [Zeph 3:11].

Rabbi Yohanan said: The son of David will come only in a generation that is either altogether righteous or altogether wicked.

Rabbi Joshua ben Levi opposed two verses, as it is written, *See, one like a Son of Man came with the clouds of heaven* [Dan 7:13], while elsewhere it is written, *See, your king comes to you, humble and riding upon an ass* [Zech 9:9]. This means, if they are meritorious, he will come with

25. Nehemiah is a second-century rabbi, but "the empire shall fall into heresy" is likely a post-Constantine saying. This saying and the preceding one of Rabbi Judah are included in a postmishnaic section added to Mishnah, tractate *Sotah* 9.15, based on the Bavli, but without reference to Rabbi Nehemiah or Rabbi Judah.

the clouds of heaven; if not, humble and riding on an ass. (Babylonian Talmud, tractate *Sanhedrin* 98a)

Rabbah Joseph said: Let the messiah come, and may I be worthy of sitting in the shadow of the saddle of his ass. Rabbah said: Let the messiah come but let me not see him. Abaye responded: Why do you say so, because of the birth pangs of the messiah? (Babylonian Talmud, tractate *Sanhedrin* 98b)

Rabbi Hillel maintained that there will be no messiah for Israel, since they already enjoyed him during the reign of Hezekiah.[26]

Rab Judah said in Rab's name: The Holy One will raise up for us another David, as it is written, *they shall serve the Lord their God and David their king, whom I will raise up for them* [Jer 30:9]. . . . Rabbi Papa said to Abaye: it is written, *my servant David shall be their prince forever* [Ezek 37:25]—so there will be an emperor and a viceroy (i.e., two David's, one being king and the other prince [*nāśî'*]).

Abimi son of Rabbi Abbahu learned: the days of Israel's messiah shall be seven thousand years, as it is written, *as the bridegroom rejoices over the bride, so shall your God rejoice over you* [Isa 62:5]. Rab Judah said in Samuel's name: the days of the messiah shall endure as long as from creation until now, as it is written, *as the days of heaven upon earth* [Deut 11:21]. (Babylonian Talmud, tractate *Sanhedrin* 99a)

Rabbi Hiyya ben Abba said in Rabbi Yohanan's name: all the prophets prophesied only in respect of the messianic era, while as for the world to come, *no eye has seen, O God, but you, who act for those who trust in you* [Isa 64:3 (64:4)]. He disagreed with Samuel who said: This world differs from the days of the messiah only in respect of servitude to foreign powers. (Babylonian Talmud, tractate *Sanhedrin* 99b)

In this list of messianic sayings in the Talmud, sages ask about the name of the messiah. One of the names mentioned is "the sick" (later changed to "the leper"), names inspired by the suffering servant:

Rab said: The world was created for David's sake. Samuel said: For Moses's sake. Rabbi Yohanan said: For the sake of the messiah.

---

26. The same interpretation is found in *Exodus Rabbah* 18.5. The tradition is known in the second century; cf. Justin Martyr, *Dialogue with Trypho* 43.

What is the name of the messiah?—The school of Rabbi Shila said: His name is Shiloh, for it is written, *until Shiloh comes* [Gen 49:10].

Others say: His name is Yinnon, a name that endures forever, as long as the sun lasts it will get offspring [*yinnôn* (Ps 72:17 *qere*)].

Others say: His name is Menahem son of Hezekiah, for it is written, *for a comforter [mənaḥēm] that would relieve my soul, is far from me* [Lam 1:16].

Those from the house of Rabbi say: The sick is his name, as it is written:[27] *Surely, he has borne our sicknesses and carried our diseases; yet we accounted him stricken, struck down by God, and afflicted* [Isa 53:4]. (Babylonian Talmud, tractate *Sanhedrin* 98b)

The last saying may be the only talmudic text about a messiah who vicariously suffers for his people. It remains open whether this suffering would include giving his life for the nation (as per Isa 53:12). The chain of transmission carried authority, as the original text was ascribed to successors of Judah haNasi. Himmelfarb (2017, 66–69) locates this saying and the legendary story below to mid-third-century Palestine.

Slightly earlier in the list, the third-century Rabbi Joshua ben Levi contrasted Dan 7:13 with Zech 9:7. The same rabbi is a main actor in a legendary story on the leprous messiah:[28]

Rabbi Joshua ben Levi met Elijah standing by the entrance of Rabbi Shimon bar Yohai's tomb (in the Galilee). He asked him, "Do I have a portion in the world to come?" He replied, "If this master desires it." . . . He then asked Elijah, "When will the messiah come?" "Go and ask himself," was his reply. "Where is he sitting?"—"At the city gates."[29]—"And how can I recognize him?"—"He is sitting among the poor lepers. The others re-

27. "Those from the house of Rabbi (i.e., Judah haNasi) say: The *sick* is his name." This is the more original text, preserved in a medieval pamphlet (name and prooftext fit together)—a text that later was changed to "his name is the leper from the house of Rabbi," which would cover in fog the vicarious suffering of this messiah, a feature confirmed by the Scripture reference (Schäfer 2012, 253; Himmelfarb 2017, 68–69).

28. In an exchange between two early tannaitic rabbis, Eliezer ben Hyrkanos maintains that the time of redemption depends on Israel's Torah obedience, while Rabbi Joshua holds that the time has been determined once and for all by God (Jerusalem Talmud, tractate *Ta'anit* 1.1.16; Babylonian Talmud, tractate *Sanhedrin* 97b).

29. Some witnesses read "at the gates of Rome" (i.e., Constantinople) (Himmelfarb 2017, 67, 181n31, 75).

move all their bandages at once, before they rebandage themselves. But this one, he only removes one bandage at the time and puts on a new before he continues with the next, thinking, 'Should they want me to come, I must be ready to come at once.'" Joshua found the messiah and greeted him, "Peace to you, master and teacher." "Peace to you, son of Levi," he replied. "When will you come, master?" he asked. "Today," was his answer.

When Joshua returned to Elijah, the latter enquired, "What did he say to you?"—"Peace to you, son of Levi." Thereupon Elijah concluded, "Thereby he assured both you and your father of a portion in the world to come." "But he lied to me," Joshua exclaimed, "he stated that he would come today, but he hasn't." Then Elijah explained, "He referred to the scripture that says, *today, if you listen to his voice* [Ps 95:7]. (Babylonian Talmud, tractate *Sanhedrin* 98a)

The narrative does not pretend to render any encounter that really happened. But legendary stories may hide deep truths: Israel has a messiah that already exists somewhere. He is a leper, a wounded one; and the hypertextual relation with Isa 53 would indicate that he bears his wounds for others. This messiah must be prepared to come immediately when Israel calls on him or is ready to receive him. However, the time of his coming depends on Israel's obedience to God's voice and commandments. In this legend we encounter a messiah hit by sickness, but his suffering is not vicarious, his wounds are not caused by Israel's sins. In another saying (Babylonian Talmud, tractate *Sanhedrin* 93b), God loads upon the Shoot of Jesse "good deeds and suffering as millstones," that is, the burden and suffering connected with good deeds, not a vicarious suffering (Schäfer 2012, 254).

Is the suffering and leprous messiah in these two texts identical with the anointed son of David, or is another anointed figure in focus? Is he the only end-time messiah, or is there more than one? A clear answer is not provided in these two texts. But they show that some rabbis interpreted Isa 50 and 53 as referring to an anointed end-time figure, a reading evinced as early as 100 BCE when the Great Isaiah Scroll read the figure described in Isa 52:14 as anointed. A similar interpretation may belong to the background of Targum Jonathan's understanding of Isa 53 as a text of a militant victorious messiah.

Rabbis do ask whether biblical texts expect more than one anointed servant of God in the end times. They provide different and contrasting answers. Most of the sayings in the long messianic list in Babylonian Talmud, tractate *Sanhedrin* 97–99 refer to the Davidic messiah; two sayings expect the anointed redeemer in the image of the suffering servant.

The diverse opinions on the messiah, the preceding birth pangs, and the characteristics of the messianic age in Babylonian Talmud, tractate *Sanhedrin* 97–99, are placed alongside each other. All are seemingly valid interpretations of biblical prophecies and hopes. No rabbi is reproached for his interpretation, neither is any conclusion or ultimate interpretation brought at the end. The future remains open and in God's hands. In the Bavli (i.e., Babylonian Talmud), there is no high-strung expectation of redemption in the close future.

However, a prominent rabbi is indeed reproached for a saying on the messianic king. The Bavli ascribes to Rabbi Akiva an interpretation of Dan 7 where a heavenly throne is given the messiah at the right hand of God:

> (a) It is written, *his throne was fiery flames* [Dan 7:9], and the same verse says, *until thrones were set in place, and One that was Ancient of Days took his seat*. There is no contradiction here, one throne is for God, and one for David—these are the words of Rabbi Akiva.
>
> (b) Rabbi Jose the Galilean reproached him: Akiva, how long will you profane the divine presence? The meaning is: (God has) one throne for justice and one for mercy. . . .
>
> (c) . . .
>
> (d) Then, Rabbi Eleazar ben Azariah said: Akiva, keep to halakhah, you are no master of aggadah (narratives)! The one is the throne where God takes his seat, the other a footstool to support his feet. (Babylonian Talmud, tractate *Hagigah* 14a, slightly stylized)

In (a), Akiva affirms that the Danielic "thrones" in plural means there will be one throne for God and another for the Son of Man—the latter he identifies with the Davidic messiah. The Bavli connects his saying with reproaches from two other second-century rabbis. Akiva is warned that he is close to blasphemy when he provides the son of David with a heavenly throne alongside God himself. His two respondents agree that a human messiah cannot sit on a heavenly throne but provide alternative interpretations of "thrones" in plural. In (b), Rabbi Jose provides God with two thrones: God sits on one when he allocates mercy to humans, on the other when he executes his judgment. In the long section (c), which is not quoted here, Akiva ultimately submits to the view of Jose the Galilean. Strangely, this is followed by (d), where Eleazar is not happy with either of his two colleagues. Allowing separate thrones for attributes of the divine may be dangerous, as such an interpretation may be exploited by the heretics. God can have only one throne, so Eleazar makes away with Akiva's literal interpretation of Dan 7:9–14.

Akiva advocates a literal reading of 7:9–14—the ultimate power given to the Son of Man indicates that the second throne was given him as God's viceroy. In the next interpretative step, Akiva identifies the Son of Man with the Davidic messiah, a view that is not self-evident from the biblical text. Akiva's saying is not the only one that identifies the Son of Man with the messiah. Rabbi Berekiah (fourth-century Palestine) identifies the Son of Man with "the king messiah" without mention of the heavenly thrones, an interpretation he ascribes to Rabbi Samuel (third-century Babylon), and some texts call the messiah "Son of a cloud."[30]

I follow Schäfer's brilliant analysis (2012, 37, 68–84) of this and related passages. In Babylonian Talmud, tractate *Sanhedrin* 38b, the third-century Rabbi Yohanan discusses verses that may problematize the oneness of God. The Bavli editor concurs with Yohanan, but states that the Galilean rabbi does not solve the crux of the thrones of Dan 7:9 and concludes that the text evinces one throne for God and another for David. This statement is not followed by any correction, which appears only in the wider discussion in Babylonian Talmud, tractate *Hagigah* 14a. We find neither of these passages in Palestinian sources before the Bavli; they rather reflect Babylonian interaction with Christianity. Akiva and his contemporaries are called forth as witnesses to the polemic dialogue between church and synagogue in fifth/sixth-century Mesopotamia.

Schäfer comments (2012, 80–81): "The Son-of-Man expectation of Second Temple Judaism is eminently messianic—from Daniel through to the Similitudes of the Ethiopic Book of Enoch and the Son of Man vision of the Fourth Book of Ezra to its climax in the New Testament." The Bavli editors are aware of this Jewish chain of tradition, still endorsed by Jewish countrymen. But the Bavli is also aware that Dan 7 is exploited by the church. With the editors giving Akiva a role in the play, a great Jewish proponent of this interpretation is brought forth and subsequently refuted. Akiva is already known for sticking his head forth with courageous words and then being reproached (cf. his proclamation of Bar Kosba being the Son of the Star, the king messiah).

---

30. Segal 1977, 47–49n22. For Segal, "the messianic controversy over Dan. 7:13 is probably from R. Akiva's time; the mercy-justice revision is probably from his students" (1977, 49). "Two powers" (in heaven) seems to be one of the basic issues over which Judaism and Christianity separated" (1977, 262).

The Birth of the Messianic Child and Its Mother

In the Yerushalmi (the Jerusalem Talmud, edited in Tiberias in the early fourth century), there is a strange story about the birth of the messiah (Schäfer 2012, 215–35). The story runs as follows:

(a) A Jew was plowing when his cow laid down. An Arab passing by told the farmer to unharness his ox, as the temple had been destroyed. When the cow laid down again, he repeated, "Son of a Jew, harness your ox again, for the king messiah is born." Asked about the name of the messiah, the Arab answers "Menahem son of Hezekiah," and adds that he is born in the royal city of Bethlehem.

(b) The farmer sold his ox and became a wandering peddler of diapers for babies. Finally arriving in Bethlehem, all the mothers made purchases except Menahem's mother. When the others asked her to buy, she answered, "I would rather like to strangle the enemies of Israel, for on the day he was born, the temple was destroyed." The peddler replied, "If it was destroyed at his coming, we trust it will be rebuilt close on his coming too." Pushing her to buy diapers, she answered she has no money. The peddler gave her the clothes, saying he could get the payment later.

(c) When he returned to the town, he asked the mother how her baby was doing, and she replied, "The winds and the whirlwinds came and snatched him out of my hands."

(d) Rabbi Bun commented: We do not need the testimony of the wise Arab, for it is written, *Lebanon will fall for the mighty one* [Isa 10:34], immediately followed by *A rod shall come out from the stump of Jesse* [Isa 11:1].[31] (Jerusalem Talmud, tractate *Berakhot* 2.4.12–14 ‖ *Lamentations Rabbah* 1.16 §51)

The original narrative is contained in the first three units. Unit (d) is a later rabbinic exegetic reflection: Jewish sages should know from Isa 10–11 that the fall of the temple and the coming of the Davidic messiah are interrelated, so one does not need an Arab with supernatural knowledge for such a revelation.

Partly following Hasan-Rokem (2000), Schäfer (2012, 223–35) reads this narrative as a parodistic inversion of the birth story of Jesus in Matthew and Luke. The story is filled by echoes of the Jesus narrative. The rabbinic story will undermine the Christian message that the true messiah was the

---

31. In rabbinic symbolism, "Lebanon" is a chiffre for the temple.

child Jesus born in Bethlehem, the city of David. This child cannot be such a messiah as the Christians say, since after his birth he was soon snatched away by the whirlwinds and disappeared.

The words of the mother, "I would rather like to strangle the enemies of Israel," reflects an earlier "I would rather like to strangle him because of the enemies of Israel": the mother hates her baby and wants to kill him. In the mouth of the Christians, Jesus was killed by his fellow Jews. The Yerushalmi narrator has it differently: the mother, as representative of the Jewish people, admits she wanted to kill the baby, but she didn't. She hates her baby because he is destined to become a danger to his own people—his followers would relate the fall of the temple to his coming and hold that the sanctuary had been rebuilt in a new, spiritual temple.

The story never hints that the baby is a false messiah who deserved to be killed. Therefore, the baby messiah was carried off by the winds to heaven, as Elijah was. And he will remain in heaven until the time is ready for him to come to redeem the Jewish nation.

Himmelfarb (2017, 46–47) notes that Schäfer's reading requires a willingness on the part of the rabbis to recognize at least some aspects of Christian messianic claims for Jesus, a presupposition she is not prepared to accept. Recognizing the parody of the gospel story, she asserts that the primary target for the narrative's sarcasm is a popular Jewish nativity story for a messiah named Menahem, where the mother is portrayed in a heroic role. Her evidence for the circulation of such a narrative is much later than the turn of the fifth century—thus I prefer Schäfer's reading of the story.

Since the mid-1990s, scholars such as Yuval, Schäfer, and Boyarin have demonstrated the close interaction between Christian and Jewish sages and texts in the early centuries. Jewish ideas develop in polemic reception of Christian theology—and it goes the other way too. The Yerushalmi story is a prime example of this dialectic process.

This rabbinic story has a close parallel in Rev 12:1–6: a woman is about to give birth, is clothed with the sun, has the moon under her feet and a crown of twelve stars on her head. When she is about to deliver, a dragon is ready to devour the baby. The woman gives birth to a baby that one day will rule all the nations by an iron rod. Immediately after his birth he is snatched away and lifted up to God's throne. Subsequently the woman flees into the desert, to a place prepared by God, to wait there for the appointed time to come.

In Revelation, the mother is Israel—virgin Zion who will give birth. The baby messiah needs to be protected from his enemies, that is, Rome. The world empires would know that the messiah is their great enemy by whom they may be overcome. In contrast, in the Yerushalmi, the baby messiah needs to be protected from his own mother (Schäfer 2012, 228–29).

Is the Yerushalmi story based only on the Christian texts it parodies (Luke 1–2; Matt 1–2; Rev 12)? Or can the author at the same time draw on earlier Jewish tradition of the birth of the messiah, a question not discussed by Schäfer? Werman (2009) argues convincingly that the motif of the woman giving birth to the messiah in Rev 12 goes back to an earlier Jewish apocalyptic text. In a Christian text like Revelation, it is strange that the messianic baby is taken to heaven after his birth, if this was not already an element in John's source. For Werman, the Jewish *Vorlage* must be the *Oracle of Hystaspes*, which Flusser (1988, 390–453) demonstrates to be a central source for Revelation (Rev 11:1–2, 3–12; 13:11–17; 14:1–5).

A Jewish apocalyptic book, the *Oracle of Hystaspes* predicts the downfall of the Roman Empire and the invasion of Jerusalem by a foreign invader, who never will conquer the innermost part of the temple (cf. Rev 11:1–2). This would indicate that the oracle was written before the fall of the temple, likely early in the first century. Flusser (1988, 394–401, 448) argues it was written in Greek in Asia Minor or Parthia. Elaborating on an early Iranian source, the author drew upon and transformed earlier Jewish material.

By the mid-second century, Justin Martyr refers affirmatively to the oracle as a genuine prophetic book (*First Apology* 44). The contents of the oracle are primarily known from its broad retelling by the Christian Latin writer Lactantius in his *Divine Institutions*, condensed some years later in his *Epitome* (in the latter, he polishes his extract of the oracle where Revelation deviates from it). The main elements of the oracle go as follows:

> A symbolic dream given to the Persian King Hystaspes is interpreted by a young boy in the form of a long prophecy. A wicked ruler will arrive from the north, he will kill the three kings who were in power and conquer Asia. He will then abolish the (Roman) empire and transfer its rule of the world to Asia. After years of chaos and natural disasters, the nation of God will pray to the Lord for help, and God sends a prophet to preach and bring the people to repentance. Then, an evil king will arise from Syria and take dominion of the empire. He will invade the holy land and attempt to destroy the temple. This king is a prophet of lies, he takes on a divine name and demands to be worshiped as the Son of God.[32] God's prophet

32. The "Son of God" text (4Q246) reflects the same tradition, drawing upon Dan 7 and Antiochus Epiphanes as the archetypal evil king (see pp. 208–10).

will be slain by the evil king, his body left unburied, but then on the third day he is resurrected and called back to heaven [cf. Rev 11:3–12]. After years of terror, the righteous will flee and separate themselves from the wicked. The evil king will besiege the mountain of the righteous, whose only hope is to implore the aid of heaven. Then God will send a great king who descends from heaven with his angelic forces to rescue and free the righteous. This heavenly king will initiate the last judgment and destroy all the wicked with fire and sword. (Lactantius, *Divine Institutions* 305–10, my paraphrase)

Werman (2009, 285–93) argues that the oracle also included the birth story of the messiah, a human being born of a human mother. Being under threat, he escapes to heaven immediately after his birth. The messiah will then reside in heaven until he is sent down to earth at the end of days accompanied by his angelic entourage. As a Christian, Lactantius would consciously omit from his *Vorlage* the birth and early ascension of the boy messiah, which would have contradicted the Jesus story in the Gospels.

The presence of the messiah in heaven is not uncommon in the first century; this idea is presupposed by the late first-century apocalypses 4 Ezra and 2 Baruch. Werman (2009, 290) points to parallels to the Yerushalmi story in Rev 12. In both, the baby is in danger on earth and taken up to dwell with God, and there is a struggle between destruction and salvation. In Revelation, Rome threatens the life of the baby, while in Yerushalmi, the boy must be saved from his mother, who perceives him as agent of her nation's destruction. In Werman's reconstruction of *Hystaspes*, the antichrist (Rev 13) opposed the helpless baby messiah (12:1–6) and the vulnerable prophet (11:3–12); this evil ruler will ultimately be killed by the powerful messiah returning from heaven at the end of days. Similar motifs appear in the *Apocalypse of Elijah*, a second-century Christian work based on a Jewish *Vorlage*, and the much later *Sefer Zerubbabel*.[33]

A story of the birth of the messiah with his mother as a key player is thus a Jewish motif, present in Jewish tradition when Matthew, Luke, and John of

---

33. In *Apocalypse of Elijah* 4, three faithful witnesses preach against the antichrist and are slain by him, a virgin and two prophets. The bodies of the latter two lie exposed for three-and-a-half days before they are resurrected, preach against the evil ruler, and are taken up to heaven.

Patmos penned their books by the late first century. In the coming centuries this motif would be recirculated by Jewish and Christian authors, at times in polemic reception of the stories of their colleagues or competitors in the other camp (cf. Himmelfarb 2017, 35–59).

Messiah Son of Joseph: Fighting, Dying, Suffering

Sometime during the first five centuries of the common era, the idea of two consecutive end-time messiahs comes to the surface—a messiah son of Joseph/Ephraim will precede the coming of the son of David. It remains an open question *when* the understanding of such a messiah developed. Billerbeck (1924, 292–93) finds sayings of the messiah son of Ephraim from the mid-second century onward.

A talmudic passage shows that in the sixth century the idea of a messiah son of Joseph as precursor of the Davidic messiah is well known:

(a) *And the land shall mourn, every family apart; the family of the house of David apart, and their wives apart* [Zech 12:12]. . . . Rabbi Dosa and the rabbis differ on the cause for the mourning. One explained, "The cause is the slaying of the messiah son of Joseph," while the other explained, "the cause is the slaying of the evil inclination." The explanation that the cause is the slaying of the messiah son of Joseph runs easily, it agrees well with the verse, *and they shall look upon me whom they have pierced, and they shall mourn for him as one mourns for one's only son* [Zech 12:10].

(b) [Here follows a lengthy discussion on the evil inclination and God's end-time annihilation of it, with the wicked and the righteous as onlookers. Even the righteous will weep, understanding the force of the evil inclination also in their lives.]

(c) Our rabbis taught, The Holy One will say to the messiah son of David, "Ask me for anything, and I will give it to you," as it is said, *I will tell of the decree of the Lord. He said to me, you are my son, today I have begotten you. Ask me and I will make the nations your heritage* [Ps 2:7–8]. But when he sees that the messiah son of Joseph is slain, he will say to God, "Lord of the Universe, I ask from you only the gift of life." "As to life," God would answer him, "Your father David has already prophesied this about you," it is said, *He asked you for life, you gave it to him—length of days forever and ever* [Ps 21:5 (21:4)]. (Babylonian Talmud, tractate *Sukkah* 52a, my translation)

The passage discusses the interpretation of Zech 12:12, interpreted on the end time. Part (a) provides two possible reasons for the mourning described here, either the slaying of the messiah son of Joseph or God's final annihilation of the evil inclination. In part (b) follow rather strained explanations for the second option, while part (c) appears as a free-floating text on the two messiahs, which editors found convenient to insert here.

Part (a) connects the mourning of separate groups (Zech 12:12) with the earlier verse on the pierced one (12:10). The pierced one is the messiah son of Joseph. According to the biblical verse, the piercing is not caused by enemy swords, since Israelites will mourn for a figure whom they had pierced. If the Bavli shared this reading of 12:10, the suffering servant and the "we-group" of Isa 53 may play in the background, without this text being mentioned in the discussion. Such a reading would explain the nation's deep mourning. Alternatively, the verse may be reread in midrashic style—with Israel mourning for a messiah that had been pierced by enemies (see below on the targum to Zech 12:10).

In part (c) we learn about the ultimate fate of the messiah son of Joseph from the perspective of his successor, the Davidic messiah—in dialogue with God through verses of royal-messianic psalms. The son of David will enter the scene when his predecessor is slain, likely by enemy armies. Psalm 2 is read eschatologically with the son of David in focus. Since God's promise to him in 2:7–9 includes the words "ask me," the son of David, afraid to be killed, asks God to be spared for the fate of his predecessor and be granted lasting life. The answer is given by the Davidic/messianic Ps 21, which shows that God has already granted his request.

The messiah son of Joseph may have been perceived as the commander of Israel's armies in the end-time battle against the enemies and being slain during the battle. The Davidic messiah will not suffer the same fate—as messianic psalms granted him life "forever and ever" and decreed that domination of the nations will be given him as inheritance.

Himmelfarb (2017, 111–13, 195) notes that the Yerushalmi parallel (Jerusalem Talmud, tractate *Sukkah* 5.2) refers to mourning for an unnamed messiah; his death is not explicitly mentioned. Here, Zech 12:12 is quoted, but not 12:10.

For Himmelfarb, this Bavli text is in conscious dialogue with contemporaries who follow another messiah son of a Joseph, a messiah slain on a cross. If God had granted life to this Davidic messiah, he would not have been slain. Thus, Zech 12:10–12 refers to a messiah, but that messiah cannot be Jesus.

Himmelfarb rightly locates part (c) as a text in critical dialogue with church Christology. As for part (a), it is not clear whether the Bavli conceived of a messiah taunted and pierced by his own people or by his enemies. If the former was the case, this talmudic text would evince two contrasting images of the messiah of Ephraim existing side by side in the sixth century.

The Warrior Messiah of Ephraim

Laato (1998, 392) notes that the blessing of Joseph in Gen 49:22–26 would offer scriptural support for such a militant messiah: a strong fighter from the tribe of Joseph will stand at the head of his brothers (see pp. 69–71). Moses's blessing of Joseph would underline the same:

> [13]Blessed by Yahweh be his land,
> with the choice gifts of heaven above. . . .
> [16]with the choice gifts of the earth and its fullness,
> and the favor of him who dwells on Sinai.
> Let these come on the head of Joseph,
> on the brow of the prince among his brothers.
> [17]A firstborn bull—majesty is his!
> His horns are the horns of a wild ox;
> with them he gores the nations,
> driving them to the ends of the earth;
> such are the myriads of Ephraim,
> and the thousands of Manasseh. (Deut 33:13, 16–17
>   NRSV adapted)

Thus, the blessings of Joseph by Jacob and especially by Moses would provide the necessary textual base for developing the idea of a militant and victorious messiah of Ephraim (Billerbeck 1924, 292–94; Flusser 1988, 424).

In addition to Babylonian Talmud, tractate *Sukkah* 52a, there are a few rabbinic references to the militant messiah of Ephraim (Billerbeck 1924, 292–99; Schäfer 2012, 236, 317–18nn3, 5):

- Jacob's oxen and asses (Gen 32:5 [32:6])—the ox is the anointed for war coming from Joseph (Deut 33:17), while the ass is the king messiah who rides upon an ass (Zech 9:9). Edom will be defeated by the anointed for war, a descendant of Joseph (*Genesis Rabbah* 75.6; 99).
- The messiah son of Joseph will defeat Gog and Magog at the end of time (Targum Pseudo-Jonathan to Exod 40:11).

- The warrior messiah is of the tribe of Joseph; his partner is the messiah of the tribe of Judah (Midrash Tanhuma, *Wayyigash* 3).
- "Esau (i.e., Rome) will fall by the hand of Rachel's descendants, as it is written, *the young ones of the flock will drag them [Edom] away. The young ones* are Rachel's sons who are the younger among the tribes" (*Pesiqta Rabbati* 29a).
- There will be two future redeemers, the messiah son of David and the messiah son of Ephraim (Targum Canticles 4:5; 7:4).
- Zechariah 12:10 depicts the messiah son of Ephraim who will be killed by Gog in the final battle at the gates of Jerusalem; the nation will then look to God and ask him why the nations pierced the messiah son of Ephraim, and mourn for him (Targumic additions to the Prophets, Sperber 1962, 495).
- The messiah son of Ephraim, precursor of the messiah son of David, will die at the gates of Jerusalem (Midrash to Ps 60:3: "God, you have rejected us and broken our defenses; you have been angry, now restore us!").

Most of these references to the militant messiah are difficult to date, but none can be securely dated before the fifth century.[34] *Genesis Rabbah* and Targum Pseudo-Jonathan, which may be dated not later than the fifth century, describe a victorious messiah son of Ephraim without mention of his death, while two sources refer to his death in the end-time war against the nations.

Klausner (1955, 483–501) discerns two contrasting images of the messiah in the Bible: a militant warrior and a peaceful and humble interpreter of the Torah in the land. After the fall of the temple and the catastrophic Bar Kokhba Revolt, this tension would be solved by introducing two distinct messiahs, a warring one from the tribe of Ephraim would precede the son of David. But since there can be only one messiah at a time, the messiah son of Joseph would have to die before his successor could take up the scepter and complete the job.

Heinemann (1975) sees the messiah of Ephraim as one of many messianic images prevalent in the Second Temple period; its particular characteristic

---

34. Strack and Stemberger date the final redaction of *Genesis Rabbah* to the first half of the fifth century (1992, 303–4); Midrash to Psalms 1–118 is composite and may have grown from the third to the thirteenth century, the bulk may be Palestinian from the fourth/sixth century (1992, 350–51); Tanhuma is a homiletic compilation, perhaps growing into the ninth century (1992, 332–33); and the same goes for *Pesiqta Rabbati*. Targum Pseudo-Jonathan mainly contains material from the first to fifth centuries, while Targum to Canticles is early medieval.

is a messiah who will die in battle. However, only some sources speak of his fatal end, while others seem to be unaware of it. Thus, for the early sources he is a militant messiah only; later this image was transformed into a dying messiah. The tradition of the militant and victorious anointed of Ephraim is certainly pre-Hadrianic, while the transformation into a dying one occurred after Bar Kokhba. Only a dramatic event could cause such a transformation; its likely cause is the defeat and death of Bar Kokhba—as suggested earlier by Billerbeck (1924, 294) and Jacob Levy. In the aftermath of the revolt, rabbinic disciples of Akiva would by all means try to find a way to uphold Bar Kokhba as a messiah in spite of his failure. Thus, they created the legend about a militant messiah doomed to fall in battle, who would nevertheless be some kind of a redeemer since he would be the forerunner of the son of David.

Flusser (1988, 424) concurs that the earlier sources do not narrate the death of the messiah son of Ephraim. The first reference to this idea may be the church father Hippolytus. According to his *Refutation of the Heresies* (ca. 330), the Jews expect a militant Davidic messiah who will fight the nations, restore Jerusalem to his nation, and after a short period of peace be slain in the next war. The earliest Jewish reference is Babylonian Talmud, tractate *Sukkah* 52a, which at best could go back to the late third century, the time of the amoraic Rabbi Dosa.

Flusser finds the earliest evidence of two messianic figures as early as Maccabean times: according to 1 En 90:37–38, a white bull (a Davidic messiah) will come forth from the flock; over time, all the flock will be transformed to white bulls, and the first among them will be a wild ox with strong horns. In Deut 33:17, the main rabbinic text of reference for the messiah of Ephraim, Joseph is the wild ox that will gore the nations with his horns.

Here Flusser overplays the evidence. The text of 1 En 90 is silent about any subsequent deeds of the wild ox, and no parallel is drawn between the white bull and the horned ox. In chapters 4–7 I have outlined the pluriform messianic hopes from the exile onward, including the expectation of two anointed ones side-by-side in some Qumran texts. But a Davidic messiah preceded by a militant messiah of Joseph cannot be found in texts before the third century.

Heinemann rightly underlines the "different faces" of the messiah son of Ephraim. If Bar Kokhba indeed belonged to the house of Joseph, Levy's and Heinemann's explanations would be particularly meaningful—but the tribal background of Bar Kosba is not mentioned in any text. And Heinemann ignores that some texts portray this messiah as pierced by his own nation who later is brought to remorse.

If Billerbeck, Levy, and Heinemann hit the mark, the posthistory of Bar Kosba would be twofold. First, his name and its messianic rephrasing would be converted to Bar Kozba, Son of the Lie—a perversion of a true messiah. Second, in a contrasting interpretation, Bar Kosba would appear as type for a fighting messiah of the end times. Giving his life in the battle against the enemies, he would pave the way for the victorious son of David. In this perspective, Bar Kosba would not be a perverted messiah, and his death was not in vain. Thus, two highly contrasting interpretations of Bar Kosba were held by different rabbis in the second and third centuries.

I suggested above (p. 274) that the targum to Isa 53, likely from the early second century, was written before the idea of a messiah son of Ephraim was known—as the job description provided by the targumist combines the tasks of the militant messiah son of Ephraim and the son of David in the later tradition. This would fit a post–Bar Kokhba appearance of the two-messiah conception, which possibly from the outset included the death or slaying of the messiah of Ephraim.

Billerbeck notes (1924, 297) that nowhere in rabbinic literature is the death of the messiah of Ephraim understood as expiation for sin; Isa 53 is never brought in as interpretative text.

The suffering image of Messiah Ephraim would be narrated in detail in *Pesiqta Rabbati*, while the full narrative of the militant messiah of Ephraim is first documented in two writings from the seventh/eighth century: *Secrets of Rabbi Shimon bar Yohai* and *Sefer Zerubbabel*. They narrate the same story, which is told in more detail in the latter. *Sefer Zerubbabel* narrates a visionary revelation given to the biblical Zerubbabel, with the main elements running as follows (Reeves 2005, 51–66):

> First appears a suffering and broken one who introduces himself as God's Davidic messiah, son of Hezekiah, imprisoned until the end. At Zerubbabel's question, "When will the light of Israel (i.e., the messiah) come," the other is transformed into a strong man and addresses him as Michael, the chief of God's army, and as Metatron (God's viceroy), and informs him:
>
> This messiah, named Menahem ben 'Amiel, was born in King David's time, and then by the winds carried off and hidden until the end time. Then his mother Hephṣibah enters the scene, led by a star, and kills two evil kings. A king of Rome will rise and destroy the Second Temple.
>
> After 570 years, redemption will come through Nehemiah ben Hushiel, the messiah of Ephraim. He will gather Israel, and for four years they

offer sacrifices to the Lord. In the fifth year, the king of Persia will attack Israel and its messiah. Israel will suffer, but the evil Persian king will fall.

Then appears a sculpture of an indecent woman. Through intercourse with Satan she gives birth to a son, Armilus, who will rule over all the world (a foil of emperor Heraclius), make war against the holy ones and kill the messiah son of Joseph. Israel will mourn for him in the time of trials.

Suddenly the Davidic messiah, Menahem ben 'Amiel, will appear, meeting the elders of Israel in the valley of Arbel as a despicable man in rags and being mocked by them. He will then don garments of vengeance and go to the gates of Jerusalem. There, his mother gives him the rod of war and the messiah of Ephraim appears alive again. Israel will then acknowledge Menahem ben 'Amiel as messiah, and Elijah the prophet will appear.

After a mighty earthquake God will descend on the Mount of Olives and make battle against the enemies, a battle where the Davidic messiah will slay the evil King Armilos. The surviving enemies will gather and be overcome by the forces of the messiah of Ephraim and Elijah, "with you, Zerubbabel, as their head."

In the presence of Elijah, the dead will be resurrected; Menahem ben 'Amiel, Nehemiah ben Hushiel and all Israel will gather in Jerusalem where the heavenly temple will come down from above and God descend on the Mount of Olives that will crack open before him.

The references to the wars between Persia and the Byzantines place the composition of the book to the tumultuous years of the early seventh century, with hefty wars waged between Persia and Byzantium from 614 to 629 (Reeves 2005, 47). In the subsequent centuries there would be a notable impact of the two-messiah tradition and *Sefer Zerubbabel* in Jewish tradition (Himmelfarb 2017, 121–43)

The dialogue with Christianity can be perceived in a dying messiah who is eventually resurrected, but this messiah son of Joseph is subordinate to the son of David. It is the latter who is the suffering messiah, and it is he who brings his predecessor back to life—a deed that confirms his messianic status. Thus, in contrast to Christian tradition, a suffering messiah can play a major role without dying. As it was noted in Babylonian Talmud, tractate *Sukkah* 52a: if God, as promised in Ps 21, had granted life to the "son of David," a true Davidic messiah should never see death (Himmelfarb 2017, 85). The suffering of the messiah is not vicarious for others.

Further, a particular critique of Byzantine tradition is transparent. The sculpture of the indecent woman is a foil of the Virgin; in the critique of *Sefer Zerubbabel*, Christianity is indeed a continuation of pagan idolatry (Himmelfarb 2017, 57).

Hephṣibah, the militant mother of the messiah, is a *novum* in Jewish tradition. Sivertsev (2014, 88–90, 101–4) argues that she is a Jewish antitype to the Virgin. The Virgin Mary indeed played an important role in Byzantine warfare, with icons of the Virgin following the troops. Further, the Virgin was the patron and protector of Constantinople—as Hephṣibah appears a fighter for Israel and defender of Jerusalem. Himmelfarb (2017, 38–39, 58–59) notes that, different from the Virgin, Hephṣibah operates independently of her son. She protects Jerusalem after the slaying of the messiah son of Joseph. But when her own son finally appears, she turns over the staff and disappears—perhaps an indication of a certain ambivalence toward the idea of the mother of the messiah.

A contemporary to *Sefer Zerubbabel*, the liturgical poem "That Very Day" from the 630s sees Muhammad as a God-sent precursor of the messiah, a "Cyrus" of the last days who will conquer the land for Israel:[35]

> The king from the west and the king from the east will confront
> each other. . . .
> A king from Arabia will march out, his armies will conquer
> the land. . . .
> Israel will be redeemed from all their sins
> and not anymore be excluded from the place of prayer. . . .
> Ismael and Edom (i.e., the Byzantines) will battle in the Valley
> of Achor. . . .
> Israel will head east from the holy city. . . .
> Their messiah will be revealed,
> they will be comforted and praise their king,
> while the evil ones cannot be standing on the day of judgment.
> (Lewis 1974)

35. A related idea appears in the *Secrets of Rabbi Shimon bar-Yohai*, a text with seventh-century sources: "The Holy One will bring about the kingdom of Ishmael only for the purpose of delivering you from the wicked one (i.e., Byzantium). He shall raise up over them a prophet, he will conquer the land for them, and they shall come and restore it with grandeur" (Shoemaker 2012, 28). The understanding of Muhammad in this poem and the *Secrets of Rabbi Shimon bar-Yohai* concurs with early and partly contemporary sources that seem to indicate that Muhammad did not die peacefully in Medina in 632, but rather while he was leading the Arab forces toward Palestine in 634–35 (Shoemaker 2012, 18–72).

In subsequent tradition this piyyut is followed by another section with clear echoes of *Sefer Zerubbabel* (Himmelfarb 2017, 52–55): the first end-time figure to appear is Hephṣibah, the mother of the messiah. She is the staff of Israel's salvation, fighting and killing enemy kings in Galilee and preparing the way for her son, Menahem ben ʿAmiel.

In *Sefer Zerubbabel*, this was the name of the Davidic messiah; here Menahem ben ʿAmiel is the messiah of Ephraim. Himmelfarb suggests that the piyyut tries to simplify the image of Hephṣibah in *Sefer Zerubbabel*, where she appears more closely connected with the messiah son of Joseph than with her own son. The continued narrative echoes *Sefer Zerubbabel*: the messiah of Ephraim will lead Israel to Jerusalem, where he will be killed by enemy forces, and then the Davidic messiah will appear and be recognized as the messiah when he resurrects his predecessor.

The Suffering Messiah of Pesiqta Rabbati

Only a few rabbinic texts describe a suffering messiah. Two talmudic texts depict the messiah as sick or leprous with reference to Isa 53. In the first, his name is "the sick one" who "has borne our sicknesses and carried our diseases." The second is the legendary story about the messiah sitting at the gates (of Rome/Constantinople) and waiting to be called to his people, a messiah sitting among the poor and the lepers and treating his wounds. Then, Babylonian Talmud, tractate *Sukkah* 52a contains a composite text on the messiah son of Joseph, where the first part identifies him as the pierced one of Zech 12:10 who is mourned by the nation. In the second part, the son of David appears as the successor of the messiah son of Joseph who has been slain, most likely by hostile nations in the end-time war. In *Sefer Zerubbabel* the son of David is portrayed as a suffering messiah until he finally puts on the garments of glory.

Pesiqta Rabbati is a late rabbinic collection of homilies. Chapters 34, 36, and 37 bear the stamp of the early seventh century and are thus contemporary to *Sefer Zerubbabel*. These three homilies depict the suffering messiah in a unique way:[36] Messiah Ephraim is the only messiah, "there is no other with him." For Himmelfarb (2017, 87), the author is aware of the two-messiah tradition but rejects it. Features that earlier tradition connects to different mes-

---

36. The following is mainly paraphrased from Schäfer 2012, 236–71; cf. also Himmelfarb 2017, 86–91.

sianic figures are here subsumed into the one and only messiah—the Davidic one who is named "Messiah Ephraim." His name is evinced in Scripture: when repentant Israel returns to God, he will declare: "I have become a father to Israel, and Ephraim is my firstborn" (Jer 31:9). The suffering messiah is thus the son of David—as he is in the contemporary *Sefer Zerubbabel*.

Messiah Ephraim is the humble messiah riding on a donkey (Zech 9:9), humbled by years in prison while being scorned by the sinners of Israel. In *Pesiqta Rabbati* 34, the author criticizes the rabbinic ideal of Torah obedience if it is not accompanied by "love of God's kingdom," the expectation of imminent redemption. Thus, he castigates a main line of thinking in rabbinism after Bar Kokhba. He idealizes the "mourners for Zion," those who long for a restoration soon-to-come and are haunted by other Jews—Isa 53 colors both the description of Messiah Ephraim and that of the righteous ones. God will send angels of destruction to punish the mockers, and he will vindicate the mourners.

According to *Pesiqta Rabbati* 36, the messiah was present with God before the time of creation, and he remains hidden beneath the Lord's throne of glory until God's appointed time. The words at the creation, "God saw that the light was good," refer to the light of the messiah that was there from the beginning.

Before the act of creation there is a dialogue between these two, alluding to Jer 31:18 (Ephraim pleading with God: "You chastised me, and I was chastised"). God asks the messiah if he is prepared to carry Israel's future sins, a heavy yoke that will weigh him down and exhaust him: "Will my suffering last many years?"—"for a week of seven years which I have decreed." The spirit of the messiah will choke under the burden of their sins; his tongue will stick to his palate (cf. Ps 22:16 [22:15]).

If Messiah Ephraim is not prepared to take upon himself the sins of humankind, God will revoke his decision to create humankind that is destined to sin. Rabbinism maintained that human repentance could bring expiation for sins. For this preacher, however, atonement is possible only through the messiah, and all future life revolves around him. The voluntary suffering that the messiah takes upon himself provides salvation for Israel.

The image of Messiah Ephraim is colored by verses from the Psalms and prophets; Isa 53 clearly is some kind of base text, most visible in *Pesiqta Rabbati* 34. One element in Isa 53 is lacking, however, the servant giving his life (53:8–12). Messiah Ephraim does not die; through his suffering he secures life for himself and for Israel.

Messiah Ephraim agrees to take the suffering upon himself so that no one in Israel should perish. His acceptance of expiatory suffering for Israel *is* redemption; it is not a means that will bring redemption.

Appearing on the earth, the messiah will suffer for seven years. He cries and weeps and laments to God that his suffering is unbearable, echoing the steadily recurring laments in Ps 22 (as they do in the Gospels' depiction of the crucifixion). God answers him that he himself suffers with his people and his messiah.

Subsequently, at the time determined by God, the messiah will reveal himself, standing on the roof of the temple and proclaiming to Israel: "Your redemption has come, my light rises upon you, *Arise, shine, for your light has come, and the glory of the Lord has risen upon you* [Isa 60:1]."[37] Then, Israel will see his light, and ultimately the nations will acknowledge the messiah and become Israel's servants. The messiah will be lifted up to the heavens, be seated on the throne of glory and clothed in God's own glory.

In his concluding analysis, Schäfer (2012, 264–71) reviews the many parallels with the New Testament Gospels. In polemic reception, these three homilies represent a daring alternative to the Christology of the church; they perform a *Heimholung* of the messiah.

Himmelfarb (2017, 88–89) finds a "higher Christology" in *Pesiqta Rabbati*'s Messiah Ephraim than in any other Jewish text on a suffering messiah. In contrast to the legendary story on the sick messiah at the city gates (Babylonian Talmud, tractate *Sanhedrin* 98a) and the Davidic messiah in *Sefer Zerubbabel*, the suffering of Messiah Ephraim will not begin until the dawn of the eschaton and will last only a week of years. With echoes of Ps 22, his trials are painted in more detail than in any other Jewish text on a suffering messiah. And his being given the throne of glory is a concrete echo of Christian tradition.

Pesiqta Rabbati 36 provides a clue for the dating of the homilies: "In the year in which the king messiah reveals himself ... the king of Persia will make war against the king of Arabia, and this king of Arabia will go to Edom to take council from the Edomites. Thereupon the king of Persia will again lay the whole world waste." This is a description of the wars between the Parthians and the Byzantine Empire in 614–29. Emperor Heraclius defeated the Parthians in 628 and retook Jerusalem in 629. The "king of Arabia" is clearly a reference to Muhammad and the first two caliphs. The Muslim incursions into Edom (modern Jordan) occur in the years 629–35, and the Muslim wars

---

37. "It is not the *light* that brings about redemption but solely the expiatory suffering of the Messiah, or, to put it differently, it is not God who brings about redemption—he only determines its exact moment—but the Messiah. Such a statement is unheard of within the taxonomy of rabbinic Judaism" (Schäfer 2012, 257).

against the Parthians are waged in 636–39, with the capital Ctesiphon being firmly in Muslim hands from 639. These historical references suggest a date soon after 636 for the homilies of *Pesiqta Rabbati*—close in time to *Sefer Zerubbabel* and the liturgical text that viewed Muhammad as a precursor to the messiah.

The messiah image of *Pesiqta Rabbati* remains a unique voice within Jewish tradition. It is the militant messiah of Ephraim and even more the son of David that remain in the center of Jewish messianic hopes, as evinced by Maimonides's thirteen articles of faith and his outline of the messiah's job description in *Mishneh Torah*.[38] However, three of the greatest exegetes of the synagogue—Ibn Ezra, Rashi, and Radak—would interpret the pierced one of Zech 12:10–12 as the messiah son of Joseph.

And Isa 53 was not forgotten by the synagogue. In the *Zohar*, the preexistent messiah is the one who was wounded for the transgressions of the people and crushed for their iniquities. A messiah image similar to that of *Pesiqta Rabbati*, with echoes of Isa 53, is included in a prayer in the Sephardi Yom Kippur liturgy (Santala 1992, 206–8; Himmelfarb 2017, 89, 188n33):

Messiah, our righteousness, has turned away from us. We are shaken, and find no one who can justify us. We are burdened under the yoke of our iniquity and sins, but he was wounded for our trespasses, the suffering of our sins he carried on his shoulders, there is forgiveness for our sins, by his wounds we were healed. It is time for a new creation forever: bring him back from afar, back from Seir, so that we may hear him in Lebanon, hear him anew through Yinnon.[39] He is our God and Father, he is our king and savior, he will redeem and save us for a second time and proclaim in the presence of all: I will save you in the end as in the beginning and be your God.

The theme of vicarious expiation in this prayer and *Pesiqta Rabbati* 34–37 can be compared with another "polemic echo" of Christian tradition: the

---

38. "He will be a righteous king of the stock of David, he will study the Torah and inspire Israel to follow it, conduct the wars of the Lord, gather the dispersed, and build the temple. And through him the nations will be brought to acknowledge and serve God" (*Mishneh Torah* 14.11–12; Birnbaum 1944, 329–31). The thirteen articles of faith were later included in the daily prayer. The twelfth article runs: "I declare faith with complete trust in the coming of the messiah—though he may tarry, I will nevertheless daily wait for him to come."

39. Lebanon is a chiffre for the temple. Yinnon is one of the names of the messiah (Babylonian Talmud, tractate *Sanhedrin* 98a, p. 295).

interpretation of the binding of Isaac in Midrash Tanhuma, a midrash that "fills out" what is perceived missing in the biblical text. In this text, roughly from the same time period as *Pesiqta Rabbati* 34–37, Isaac is portrayed as a vital teenager who willingly submits to being bound and sacrificed:

> As Abraham was about to slaughter him, Isaac cried out, "Father, bind my hands and feet, for my will to live is strong, so that I will not tremble at the sight of the knife and the sacrifice become blemished and defective. . . . The Holy One opened the sky and the cloud and said: "*By myself have I sworn.*" "You have sworn," Abraham replied, "and now I swear that I shall not descend from this altar until I have said what I wish to say." . . . "So far, I have not challenged you, but now I do: when Isaac's descendants submit to sin or oppression, recall the binding of Isaac, reckon it as if his ashes had been piled upon the altar, and pardon them and release them from their anguish!" The Holy One answered, ". . . In the future Isaac's descendants will sin against me, and I will judge them on Rosh Hashanah. If they want me to recall for their advantage the binding of Isaac, let them blow upon this shofar." Abraham asked: "What shofar?" The Holy One said, "Turn around!" Then, *Abraham looked up and saw a ram, caught in a thicket by its horns* (i.e., a shofar to be made from its horns). (Midrash Tanhuma, *Wayyera* 23; cf. Gen 22:13, 16)

As we have seen in this survey of messianic texts, there is a high degree of pluriformity among scribes and rabbis of the first seven centuries of the common era. The catastrophic fallout of the Great Revolt and the Bar Kokhba Revolt had a lasting impact on the framing of rabbinic theology in general and eschatological and messianic ideas in particular. It can further be noted that every text from the Hebrew Bible that is interpreted in a messianic sense in New Testament writings recurs with a messianic edge somewhere in the rabbinic corpus, resulting in a large number of texts that may be characterized as polemic echoes of Christian texts or themes.

Bibliography

Abelman, Oren. 2021. "The Wicked Priest and the Romans: Reading Pesher Habakkuk as a Unified Text." Paper presented at University of Pretoria's international conference "The Origin of the Sectarian Movement in the Dead Sea Scrolls," May 12.

Abusch, Raʿanan. 2003. "Negotiating Difference: Genital Mutilation in Roman Slave Law and the History of the Bar Kokhba Revolt." Pages 71–91 in *The Bar Kokhba War Reconsidered: New Perspectives on the Second Jewish Revolt against Rome*. Edited by Peter Schäfer. Tübingen: Mohr Siebeck.

Ådna, Jostein. 2004. "The Servant of Isaiah 53 as Triumphant and Interceding Messiah: The Reception of Isaiah 52:13–53:12 in the Targum of Isaiah with Special Attention to the Concept of the Messiah." Pages 189–224 in *The Suffering Servant: Isaiah 53 in Jewish and Christian Sources*. Edited by Bernd Janowski and Peter Stuhlmacher. Translated by Daniel P. Bailey. Grand Rapids: Eerdmans.

Aḥituv, Shmuel, and Esther Eshel (eds.). 2015. *To Yhwh of Teman and His Ashera: The Inscriptions and Drawings from Kuntillet ʿAjrud (Ḥorvat Tēman) in Sinai*. [In Hebrew.] Jerusalem: Israel Exploration Society and Yad Ben-Zvi.

Albertz, Rainer. 2004. *Israel in Exile: The History and Literature of the Sixth Century B.C.E.* Translated by D. Green. Studies in Biblical Literature 3. Leiden: Brill.

Alt, Albrecht. 1950. "Jesaja 8,23–9,6: Befreiungsnacht und Königstag." Pages 29–49 in *Festschrift Alfred Bertholet zum 80. Geburtstag gewidmet*. Edited by Walter Baumgartner. Tübingen: Mohr.

Anava, Sarit et al. 2020. "Illuminating Genetic Mysteries of the Dead Sea Scrolls." *Cell* 181:1–14. DOI: https://www.cell.com/cell/fulltext/S0092-8674(20)30552-3.

Arav, Rami. 2020. "The Forgotten Kingdom of Geshur." Lecture at virtual conference "'The Land That I Will Show You': Recent Archeological and Historical Studies of Ancient Israel," New York University and Israel Antiquities Authority, October 25.

Arcari, Luca. 2007. "A Symbolic Transfiguration of a Historical Event: The Parthian Invasion in Josephus and the Parables of Enoch." Pages 478–86 in *Enoch and the Messiah Son of Man: Revisiting the Book of Parables*. Edited by Gabriele Boccaccini. Grand Rapids: Eerdmans.

Arie, Eran. 2008. "Reconsidering the Iron Age II Strata at Tel Dan: Archaeological and Historical Implications." *Tel Aviv* 5/1:6–64. DOI: https://doi.org/10.1179/tav.2008.2008.1.6.

Aschim, Anders. 1999. "Melchizedek and Jesus: 11QMelchizedek and the Epistle to the Hebrews." Pages 129–47 in *The Jewish Roots of Christological Monotheism: Papers from the St. Andrews Conference on the Historical Origins of the Worship of Jesus*. Edited by Carey C. Newman, James R. Davila, and Gladys S. Lewis. Journal for the Study of Judaism Supplement 63. Leiden: Brill.

Aster, Shawn Zelig. 2018. "Reflections of Empire in Isaiah 11:1–10." Paper presented at SBL Annual Meeting, Denver, November 18.

Atkinson, Kenneth. 2015. "Perception of the Temple Priests in the Psalms of Solomon." Pages 79–96 in *Psalms of Solomon: Language, History, Theology*. Edited by Eberhard Bons and Patrick Pouchelle. Atlanta: SBL Press.

Aubin, Henry Trocmé. 2002. *The Rescue of Jerusalem: The Alliance between Hebrews and Africans in 701 B.C.* New York: Soho Press/Toronto: Doubleday (2003: Anchor Canada).

Balogh, Csaba. 2014. "Historicising Interpolation in the Isaiah-Memoir." *Vetus Testamentum* 64:519–38.

Barth, Hermann. 1977. *Die Jesaja-Worte in der Josiazeit: Israel und Assur als Thema einer produktiven Neuinterpretation der Jesajaüberlieferung*. Wissenschaftliche Monographien zum Alten und Neuen Testament 48. Neukirchen: Neukirchener Verlag.

Bauckham, Richard. 1998. *The Fate of the Dead: Studies on the Jewish and Christian Apocalypses*. Novum Testamentum Supplement 93. Leiden: Brill.

Becker, Uwe. 2000. "Die Reichsteilung nach I Reg 12." *Zeitschrift für die alttestamentliche Wissenschaft* 112:210–29.

Beentjes, Pancratius C. 2003. *The Book of Ben Sira in Hebrew: A Text Edition of All Extant Hebrew Manuscripts and a Synopsis of All Parallel Hebrew Ben Sira Texts*. Vetus Testamentum Supplement 68. Leiden: Brill.

Bellis, Alice Ogden. 2021. "Did an Academic Outsider Determine What Saved Jerusalem from Conquest by the Assyrian Emperor Sennacherib in

701 BCE?" *Ancient Near East Today* 9. DOI: asor.org/wp-content/up loads/2021/07/Bellis-July-2021-ANEToday.pdf.

Bellis, Alice Ogden (ed.). 2019. "Jerusalem's Survival, Sennacherib's Departure, and the Kushite Role in 701 BCE: An Examination of Henry Aubin's *Rescue of Jerusalem*." *Journal of Hebrew Scriptures* 19, article 7. DOI: 10.5508 /jhs29552.

Ben-Ami, Doron. 2016. "The Excavations at the Givati Parking Lot." Private lecture, Jerusalem, February 10.

Ben-Ami, Doron, and Yona Tchekhanovets. 2015. "'Those in the City of David in Jerusalem, Who Had Built Themselves a Citadel' (1 Macc 14:36): The Seleucid Fortification System at the Givati Parking Lot, City of David." [In Hebrew.] *New Archaeological Discoveries in Jerusalem and Its Surroundings* 9:313–22.

Ben-Dov, Jonathan, Daniel Stökl ben Ezra, and Asaf Gayer. 2017. "Reconstruction of a Single Copy of the Qumran Cave 4 Cryptic-script Serekh Haedah." *Revue de Qumran* 29:21–77.

Ben-Yosef, Erez, Brady Liss, Omri A. Yagel, Ofir Tirosh, Mohammad Najjar, and Thomas E. Levy. 2019. "Ancient Technology and Punctuated Change: Detecting the Emergence of the Edomite Kingdom in the Southern Levant." DOI: 10.1371/journal.pone.0221967.

Ben-Yosef, Erez, Ron Shaar, Lisa Tauxe, and Ron Hagai. 2012. "A New Chronological Framework for Iron Age Copper Production at Timna (Israel)." *Bulletin of the American Schools of Oriental Research* 367:31–71.

Ben-Zvi, Ehud. 2000. *Micah*. Forms of Old Testament Literature 21B. Grand Rapids: Eerdmans.

Berges, Ulrich. 2008. *Jesaja 40–48: Übersetzt und ausgelegt*. Herders Theologischer Kommentar zum Alten Testament. Freiburg: Herder.

Billerbeck, Paul. 1924. *Kommentar zum Neuen Testament aus Talmud und Midrasch*, vol. 2. By Hermann Strack und Paul Billerbeck. Munich: Beck.

Biran, Avraham. 1994a. "Tel Dan 1992." [In Hebrew.] *Hadashot Archeologiyot*, 3–6.

———. 1994b. "More Fragments from 'David' Stela Found at Dan." In "BARlines." *Biblical Archaeology Review* 1994/5:20, 22, 66.

Biran, Avraham, and Joseph Naveh. 1995. "The Tel Dan Inscription: A New Fragment." *Israel Exploration Journal* 45:1–18.

Birnbaum, Philip. 1944. *Mishneh Torah: Maimonides' Code of Law and Ethics*. Abridged and translated from the Hebrew by Philip Birnbaum. New York: Hebrew Publishing Company. Reprinted 1974.

Blenkinsopp, Joseph. 2016. "The Sacrificial Life and Death of the Servant (Isaiah 52:13–53:12)." *Vetus Testamentum* 66:1–14.

Bloch, Yigal, Jonathan Ben-Dov, and Daniel Stökl ben Esra. 2019. "The Rule of the Congregation from Cave 1 of Qumran: A New Edition." *Revue des Études Juives* 178:1–46.

Blum, Erhard. 2009. "Der leidende Gottesknecht von Jes 53: Eine kompositionelle Deutung." Pages 138–59 in *Gottes Wahrnehmungen: Helmut Utzschneider zum 60. Geburtstag*. Edited by Stefan Gehrig and Stefan Seiler. Stuttgart: Kohlhammer.

———. 2010. "Solomon and the United Monarchy: Some Textual Evidence." Pages 59–78 in *One God—One Cult—One Nation: Archaeological and Biblical Perspectives*. Edited by Reinhard G. Kratz and Hermann Spieckermann. Berlin: de Gruyter.

———. 2020. "The Israelite Tribal System: Literary Fiction or Social Reality?" Pages 201–22 in *Saul, Benjamin, and the Emergence of Monarchy in Israel: Biblical and Archaeological Perspectives*. Edited by Joachim J. Krause, Omer Sergi, and Kristin Weingart. Ancient Israel and Its Literature 40. Atlanta: SBL Press.

Bogaert, Pierre-Maurice. 1986. "Les deux rédactions conservées (LXX et TM) d'Ezéchiel 7." Pages 21–47 in *Ezekiel and His Book: Textual and Literary Criticism and Their Interrelation*. Edited by Johan Lust. Bibliotheca Ephemeridum Theologicarum Lovaniensium 74. Leuven: Peeters.

———. 2005. "La datation par souscription dans les rédactions courte (LXX) et longue du livre de Jérémie." Pages 137–59 in *L'apport de la Septante aux études sur l'Antiquité: Actes du colloque de Strasbourg, 8–9 novembre 2002*. Edited by Jan Joosten and Philippe Le Moigne. Lectio Divina 203. Paris: Cerf.

Bohak, Gideon. 1996. *Joseph and Aseneth and the Jewish Temple in Heliopolis*. Early Judaism and Its Literature 10. Atlanta: Scholars Press.

Brent, Allen. 1999. *The Imperial Cult and the Development of Church Order: Concepts and Images of Authority in Paganism and Early Christianity before the Age of Cyprian*. Vigiliae Christianae Supplement 45. Leiden: Brill.

Brooke, George J. 2005. *The Dead Sea Scrolls and the New Testament*. Minneapolis: Fortress.

Broshi, Magen. 1974. "The Expansion of Jerusalem in the Reigns of Hezekiah and Manasseh." *Israel Exploration Journal* 24:21–26.

Bunimovitz, Shlomo, and Zvi Lederman. 2017. "Swinging on the 'Sorek Seesaw': Tel Beth-shemesh and the Sorek Valley in the Iron Age." Pages 27–43 in

The Shephelah during the Iron Age: Recent Archaeological Studies. Edited by Oded Lipschits and Aren M. Maeir. Winona Lake, IN: Eisenbrauns.

Burnett, Joel S. 2007. "A Plea for David and Zion: The Elohistic Psalter as Psalm Collection for the Temple's Restoration." Pages 95–113 in *Diachronic and Synchronic: Reading the Psalms in Real Time; Proceedings of the Baylor Symposium on the Book of Psalms.* Edited by Marion Grau. London: Bloomsbury.

Carlson, Rolf August. 1974. "The Anti-Assyrian Character of the Oracle in Is. ix 1–6." *Vetus Testamentum* 24:130–35.

Carr, David M. 2011. *The Formation of the Hebrew Bible: A New Reconstruction.* Oxford: Oxford University Press.

———. 2020. *The Formation of Genesis 1–11: Biblical and Other Precursors.* Oxford: Oxford University Press.

Childs, Brevard S. 2001. *Isaiah.* Old Testament Library. Louisville: Westminster John Knox.

Chilton, Bruce D. 1983. *The Glory of Israel. The Theology and Provenience of the Isaiah Targum.* Sheffield: JSOT Press.

Clements, Ronald Ernest. 1983. "The Isaiah Narrative of 2 Kings 20:12–19 and the Date of the Deuteronomic History." Pages 209–20 in *Essays on the Bible and the Ancient World: Isac Leo Seeligmann Volume,* part 3. Edited by Alexander Rofé and Yair Zakovitch. Jerusalem: E. Rubinstein's Publishing House.

Cline, Eric H. 2020. "1177 BC Revisited: The Late Bronze Age Collapse and Its Immediate Aftermath." Lecture at virtual conference "'The Land That I Will Show You': Recent Archeological and Historical Studies of Ancient Israel," New York University and Israel Antiquities Authority, October 27.

Cole, Steven, and Peter Machinist. 1998. *Letters from Priests to the Kings Esarhaddon and Assurbanipal.* State Archives of Assyria 13. Helsinki: Helsinki University Press.

Collins, John J. 1993. *Daniel: A Commentary on the Book of Daniel.* Hermeneia. Philadelphia: Fortress.

———. 2003. "The Zeal of Phinehas, the Bible, and the Legitimation of Violence." *Journal of Biblical Literature* 122:3–22.

———. 2010a. "The Sign of Immanuel." Pages 225–44 in *Prophecy and Prophets in Ancient Israel.* Edited by John Day. New York: T&T Clark.

———. 2010b. *Beyond the Qumran Community: The Sectarian Movement of the Dead Sea Scrolls.* Grand Rapids: Eerdmans.

———. 2010c. *The Scepter and the Star: Messianism in Light of the Dead Sea Scrolls.* Grand Rapids: Eerdmans.

Cook, Edward M. 1995. "4Q246." *Bulletin for Biblical Research* 5:43–66.

Cook, Gila. Undated. "How I Discovered the 'House of David' Inscription." DOI: http://ngsba.org/excavations/tel-dan/.

Cotton, Hannah. 2003. "The Bar Kokhba Revolt and the Documents from the Judean Desert: Nabatean Participation in the Revolt (P. Yadin 52)." Pages 133–52 in *The Bar Kokhba War Reconsidered: New Perspectives on the Second Jewish Revolt against Rome*. Edited by Peter Schäfer. Tübingen: Mohr Siebeck.

Craigie, Peter C. 2004. *Psalms 1–50*. Supplemented by Marvin E. Tate. Word Biblical Commentary 19. Waco: Word.

Crawford, Sidney White. 2021. "Scribes and Scrolls at Qumran: A New Synthesis." Virtual lecture at Faculty of Theology, University of Lugano, March 17.

Cross, Frank Moore. 1961. "The Development of the Jewish Scripts." Pages 133–202 in *The Bible and the Ancient Near East*. Edited by G. Ernest Wright. New York: Doubleday.

———. 1973. *Canaanite Myth and Hebrew Epic: Essays in the History of the Religion of Israel*. Cambridge: Harvard University Press.

———. 1995. *The Ancient Library of Qumran*. 3rd ed. Minneapolis: Fortress.

Crowell, Bradley L. 2007. "Nabonidus, as-Sila', and the Beginning of the End of Edom." *BASOR* 348:75–88.

———. 2021. *Edom at the Edge of Empire. A Social and Political History*. Atlanta: SBL.

Dahood, Mitchell. 1965. *Psalms I*. Anchor Bible 16. New York: Doubleday.

Davis, Kipp. 2017. "Caves of Dispute: Patterns of Correspondence and Suspicion in the Post-2002 'Dead Sea Scrolls' Fragments." *Dead Sea Discoveries* 24:229–70.

Davis, Kipp, et al. 2017. "Nine Suspicious 'Dead Sea Scrolls Fragments' from the 21st Century." *Dead Sea Discoveries* 24:189–228.

Doran, Robert. 2012. *2 Maccabees: A Critical Commentary*. Hermeneia. Minneapolis: Fortress.

Duhm, Bernhard. 1914. *Das Buch Jesaia übersetzt und erklärt*. 3rd ed. Göttingen: Vandenhoeck & Ruprecht.

Durham, John I. 1987. *Exodus*. Word Biblical Commentary 3. Waco: Word.

Eck, Werner. 1999. "The Bar Kokhba Revolt: The Roman Point of View." *Journal of Roman Studies* 89:76–89.

Eck, Werner, and Hannah Cotton. 2001. "The Impact of the Bar Kokhba Revolt on Rome: Another Military Diploma from AD 160 from Syria Palaestina." [In Hebrew.] *Mikmanim* 23:7–22.

Edenburg, Cynthia. 2014. "II Sam 21,1–14 and II Sam 23,1–7 as Post-Chr Additions to the Samuel Scroll." Pages 167–82 in *Rereading the Relecture? The Question of (Post)chronistic Influence in the Latest Redaction of the Books of Samuel*. Edited by Uwe Becker and Hannes Bezzel. Tübingen: Mohr Siebeck.

Ehrlich, Arnold B. 1905. *Die Psalmen: Neu uebersetzt und erklaert*. Berlin: Poppelauer.

———. 1914. *Randglossen zur hebräischen Bibel: Textkritisches, Sprachliches und Sachliches*, vol. 7. Hildesheim: Olms.

Elgvin, Torleif. 2003. "The Eschatological Hope of 4QTime of Righteousness." Pages 89–102 in *Wisdom and Apocalypticism in the Dead Sea Scrolls and in the Biblical Tradition*. Edited by Florentino García Martínez. Bibliotheca Ephemeridum Theologicarum Lovaniensium 168. Leuven: Peeters.

———. 2004. "Priestly Sages? The Milieus of Origin of 4QMysteries and 4QInstruction." Pages 67–87 in *Sapiential Perspectives: Wisdom Literature in Light of the Dead Sea Scrolls*. Edited by John J. Collins, Gregory E. Sterling, and Ruth A. Clements. Studies on the Texts of the Desert of Judah 51. Leiden: Brill.

———. 2005. "The Individual Interpretation of the Servant Songs." *Mishkan* 43:25–33.

———. 2007. "Jewish Christian Editing of the Old Testament Epigrapha." Pages 278–304 in *Jewish Believers in Jesus: The Early Centuries*. Edited by Oskar Skarsaune and Reidar Hvalvik. Peabody, MA: Hendrickson.

———. 2016a. "Texts on Messianic Reign from the Hasmonean Period: 4Q521 as Interpretation of Daniel 7." Pages 169–78 in *The Seleucid and Hasmonean Periods and the Apocalyptic Worldview*. Edited by Lester Grabbe and Gabriele Boccaccini. London: Bloomsbury/T&T Clark.

———. 2016b. "Violence, Apologetics, and Resistance: Hasmonaean Ideology and Yahad Texts in Dialogue." Pages 319–40 in *The War Scroll, Violence, War, and Peace in the Dead Sea Scrolls and Related Literature*. Edited by Kipp Davis et al. Studies on the Texts of the Desert of Judah 115. Leiden: Brill.

———. 2018. *The Literary Growth of the Song of Songs in the Hasmonean and Early-Herodian Periods*. Contributions to Biblical Exegesis and Theology 89. Leuven: Peeters.

———. 2020a. "Trials and Universal Renewal—the Priestly Figure of the Levi Testament 4Q541." Pages 78–100 in *Vision, Narrative, and Wisdom in the Aramaic Texts from Qumran*. Edited by Mette Bundvad and Kasper Siegismund. Studies on the Texts of the Desert of Judah 131. Leiden: Brill.

———. 2020b. "1QSamuel—A Pre-canonical Shorter Recension of 2Samuel." *Zeitschrift für die alttestamentliche Wissenschaft* 132:281–300.

———. 2020c. "Chasing the Hasmonean and Herodian Editors of the Song of Songs." Pages 71–98 in *The Song of Songs in Its Context: Words for Love, Love for Words*. Edited by Pierre van Hecke. Bibliotheca Ephemeridum Theologicarum Lovaniensium 310. Leuven: Peeters.

———. 2021a. "More on 1QSamuel and the Theory of Literary Growth: Response to Benjamin Ziemer." *Zeitschrift für die alttestamentliche Wissenschaft* 133:1–8.

———. 2021b. "Post-exilic History and Archaeology and the Formation of Biblical Literature." Pages 243–79 in *Epigraphy, Iconography, and the Bible*. Edited by Meir Lubetski and Edith Lubetski. Sheffield: Sheffield Phoenix Press.

———. Forthcoming. "Melchizedek." In *The Dead Sea Scrolls*. Edited by Craig A. Evans and Cecilia Wassén. Ancient Literature for New Testament Studies, vol. 3. Grand Rapids: Zondervan Academic.

Elgvin, Torleif, Kipp Davis, and Michael Langlois (eds.). 2016. *Gleanings from the Caves: Dead Sea Scrolls and Artefacts from the Schøyen Collection*. London: Bloomsbury/T&T Clark.

Elgvin, Torleif, and Christina Kumpmann. 2013. "*Lāqaḥ*." Pages 532–37 in *Theologisches Wörterbuch zu den Qumrantexten*, vol. 2. Edited by Heinz-Josef Fabry and Ulrich Dahmen. Stuttgart: Kohlhammer.

Embry, Brad. 2006. "Solomon's Name as a Prophetic Hallmark in Jewish and Christian Texts." *Henoch* 28:47–62.

———. 2015. "Some Thoughts on and Implications from Genre Categorization in the Psalms of Solomon." Pages 59–78 in *Psalms of Solomon: Language, History, Theology*. Edited by Eberhard Bons and Patrick Pouchelle. Atlanta: SBL Press.

Emerton, John A. 1969. "Some Linguistic and Historical Problems in Isa viii 23." *Journal of Semitic Studies* 14:158–60.

Eshel, Esther. 1999. "The Identification of the 'Speaker' of the Self-Glorification Hymn." Pages 619–35 in *The Provo International Conference on the Dead Sea Scrolls: Technological Innovations, New Texts, and Reformulated Issues*. Edited by Donald W. Parry and Eugene Ulrich. Studies on the Texts of the Desert of Judah 30. Leiden: Brill.

Eshel, Esther, Hanan Eshel, and Ada Yardeni. 2011. "A Document from 'Year 4 of the Destruction of the House of Israel.'" *Dead Sea Discoveries* 18:1–28.

Eshel, Hanan. 2007. "An Allusion in the Parables of Enoch to the Acts of Matthias Antigonus in 40 B.C.E.?" Pages 487–91 in *Enoch and the Messiah*

Son of Man: Revisiting the Book of Parables. Edited by Gabriele Boccacini. Grand Rapids: Eerdmans.

———. 2008. *The Dead Sea Scrolls and the Hasmonean State*. Studies in the Dead Sea Scrolls and Related Literature. Grand Rapids: Eerdmans.

Eshel, Hanan, and Boaz Zissu. 2019. *The Bar Kokhba Revolt: The Archaeological Evidence*. Translated by Michael Even-Esh. Jerusalem: Yad Ben-Zvi.

Falk, Daniel K. 1998. *Daily, Sabbath, and Festival Prayers in the Dead Sea Scrolls*. Studies on the Texts of the Desert of Judah 27. Leiden: Brill.

Fantalkin, Alexander, and Israel Finkelstein. 2017. "The Date of Abandonment and Territorial Affiliation of Khirbet Qeiyafa: An Update." *Tel Aviv* 44:53–60.

Faust, Avraham. 2012. "Social, Cultural, and Demographic Changes in Judah during the Transition from the Iron Age to the Persian Period and the Nature of the Society during the Persian Period." Pages 108–34 in *From Judah to Judaea: Socio-Economic Structures and Processes in the Persian Period*. Edited by Johannes U. Ro. Hebrew Bible Monographs 43. Sheffield: Sheffield Phoenix Press.

———. 2013. "The Shephelah in the Iron Age: A New Look on the Settlement of Judah." *Palestine Exploration Quarterly* 145:203–19.

———. 2014. *Israel's Ethnogenesis: Settlement, Interaction, Expansion, and Resistance*. London: Routledge.

———. 2019. "The World of P: The Material Realm of Priestly Writings." *Vetus Testamentum* 69:173–218.

Faust, Avraham, and Haya Katz. 2015. "A Canaanite Town, a Judahite Center, and a Persian Period Fort: Excavating over Two Thousand Year of History at Tel 'Eton." *Near Eastern Archaeology* 78:88–102.

Feldmeier, Reinard, and Hermann Spieckermann. 2011. *God of the Living: A Biblical Theology*. Translated by Mark E. Biddle. Waco: Baylor University Press.

Finkelstein, Israel. 1993. "Environmental Archaeology and Social History." Pages 56–66 in *Biblical Archaeology Today, 1990: Proceedings of the Second International Congress on Biblical Archaeology*. Edited by Avraham Biran and Joseph Aviram. Jerusalem: Israel Exploration Society.

———. 2002. "The Campaign of Shoshenq I to Palestine: A Guide to the Tenth Century BCE Polity." *Zeitschrift des deutschen Palästina-Vereins* 118:109–35.

———. 2006. "Shechem in the Late Bronze and the Iron I." Vol. 2/pages 349–56 in *Timelines: Studies in Honor of Manfred Bietak*. Edited by Ernst Czerny et al. Leuven: Peeters.

———. 2008. "The Settlement History of Jerusalem in the Eighth and Seventh Centuries BC." *Revue biblique* 115:499–515.

———. 2012. "Persian Period Jerusalem and Yehud Rejoinders." Pages 49–62 in *Focusing Biblical Studies: The Crucial Nature of the Persian and Hellenistic Periods*. London: T&T Clark.

———. 2013. *The Forgotten Kingdom: The Archaeology and History of Northern Israel*. Ancient Near East Monographs 5. Atlanta: SBL Press.

———. 2015. "Migration of Israelites into Judah after 720 BCE: An Answer and an Update." *Zeitschrift für die alttestamentliche Wissenschaft* 127:188–206.

———. 2018. *Hasmonean Realities behind Ezra, Nehemiah, and Chronicles: Archaeological and Historical Perspectives*. Ancient Israel and Its Literature 34. Atlanta: SBL Press.

———. 2019. "First Israel, Core Israel, United (Northern) Israel." *Near Eastern Archaeology* 82:8–15.

———. 2020. "Saul and the Highlands of Benjamin Update: The Role of Jerusalem." Pages 33–56 in *Saul, Benjamin, and the Emergence of Monarchy in Israel: Biblical and Archaeological Perspectives*. Edited by Joachim J. Krause, Omer Sergi, and Kristin Weingart. Ancient Israel and Its Literature 40. Atlanta: SBL Press.

Finkelstein, Israel, and Alexander Fantalkin. 2012. "Khirbet Qeiyafa: An Unsensational Archaeological and Historical Interpretation." *Tel Aviv* 39:38–63.

Finkelstein, Israel, and Neil A. Silberman. 2006a. *David and Solomon: In Search of the Bible's Sacred Kings and the Roots of the Western Tradition*. New York: Free Press.

———. 2006b. "Temple and Dynasty: Hezekiah, the Remaking of Judah and the Rise of the Pan-Israelite Ideology." *Journal for the Study of the Old Testament* 30/3:259–85.

Fitzmyer, Joseph A. 1994. "The Aramaic 'Son of God' Text from Qumran Cave 4." Pages 163–78 in *Methods of Investigation of the Dead Sea Scrolls and the Khirbet Qumran Site: Present Realities and Future Prospects*. Edited by Michael O. Wise et al. New York: New York Academy of Sciences.

Fleming, Daniel E. 2012. *The Legacy of Israel in Judah's Bible: History, Politics, and the Reinscribing of Tradition*. Cambridge: Cambridge University Press.

Flint, Peter. 2014. "The Contribution of Gerald Wilson toward Understanding the Book of Psalms in Light of the Dead Sea Scrolls." Pages 209–30 in *The Shape and Shaping of the Book of Psalms*. Edited by Nancy L. deClaissé-Walford. Atlanta: SBL Press.

Flusser, David. 1980. "The Hubris of the Antichrist in a Fragment from Qumran." *Immanuel* 10:31–37.

———. 1988. *Judaism and the Origins of Christianity*. Jerusalem: Magnes.

———. 2007. *Judaism of the Second Temple Period*, vol. 1: *Qumran and Apocalypticism*. Grand Rapids: Eerdmans.

Fox, Michael E. 1985. *The Song of Songs and the Ancient Egyptian Love Songs*. Madison: University of Wisconsin Press.

Fried, Lisbeth. 2002. "Cyrus the Messiah? The Historical Background to Isaiah 45:1." *Harvard Theological Review* 95:373–93.

Gadot, Yuval. 2019. "The Iron I Settlement Wave in the Samaria Highlands and Its Connection with the Urban Centers." *Near Eastern Archaeology* 82:32–41.

Gadot, Yuval, and Yiftah Shalev. 2019. "Persian and Hellenistic Jerusalem: Evidence from the Givati Excavations." Paper presented at ASOR Annual Meeting, San Diego, November 21.

García Martínez, Florentino, and Eibert Tigchelaar. 1997. *The Dead Sea Scrolls Study Edition*, vol. 1. Leiden: Brill.

———. 1998. *The Dead Sea Scrolls Study Edition*, vol. 2. Leiden: Brill.

Garfinkel, Yosef. 2017. "The Iron Age City of Khirbet Qeiyafa." Pages 115–31 in *The Shephelah during the Iron Age: Recent Archaeological Studies*. Edited by Oded Lipschits and Aren M. Maeir. Winona Lake, IN: Eisenbrauns.

———. 2020. "The 10th Century BCE: A 'United Monarchy' or a Kingdom of Judah?" Lecture at virtual conference "'The Land That I Will Show You': Recent Archeological and Historical Studies of Ancient Israel," New York University and Israel Antiquities Authority, October 27.

Garfinkel, Yosef, and Madeleine Mumcuoglu. 2016. *Solomon's Temple and Palace: New Archaeological Discoveries*. Jerusalem: Bible Lands Museum and Biblical Archaeological Society.

Genette, Gérard. 1997. *Palimpsests: Literature in the Second Degree*. Translated by Channa Newman and Claude Doubinsky. Lincoln: University of Nebraska Press.

Gerstenberger, Erhard. 1988. *Psalms*, part 1: *With an Introduction to Cultic Poetry*. Forms of Old Testament Literature 14. Grand Rapids: Eerdmans.

Gese, Hartmut. 1977. "Der Messias." Pages 128–51 in *Zur biblischen Theologie: Alttestamentliche Vorträge*. Munich: Kaiser.

———. 1983. "The Messiah." Pages 141–66 in *Essays in Biblical Theology*. Minneapolis: Fortress.

Geva, Hillel. 1997. "Searching for Roman Jerusalem." *Biblical Archaeology Review* 23.6:35–45, 72–73.

———. 2007. "Estimating Jerusalem's Population in Antiquity: A Minimalist View." [In Hebrew.] *Eretz-Israel* 28:50–65.

———. 2015. "Hasmonean Jerusalem in the Light of Archaeology—Notes on Urban Topography." [In Hebrew with English abstract.] *Eretz-Israel* 31:57–75, 184*.

Givon, Shmuel. 2008. "Tel Ḥarasim." Pages 1766–67 in *New Encyclopedia of Archaeological Excavations in the Holy Land*. Edited by Ephraim Stern. Jerusalem: Israel Exploration Society.

Glessner, Uwe. 1992. "Das Textwachstum von Ps 89." *Biblische Notizen* 65:55–73.

Goldin, Judah. 1955. *The Fathers according to Rabbi Nathan*. New Haven: Yale University Press.

Goldstein, Jonathan. 1976. *I Maccabees: A New Translation with Introduction and Commentary*. Anchor Bible 41. New York: Doubleday.

———. 1987. "How the Authors of 1 and 2 Maccabees Treated the 'Messianic' Promises." Pages 97–109 in *Judaisms and Their Messiahs at the Turn of the Christian Era*. Edited by Jacob Neusner et al. Cambridge: Cambridge University Press.

Goodman, Martin. 1992. "Diaspora Reactions to the Destruction of the Temple." Pages 27–38 in *Jews and Christians*. Edited by James D. G. Dunn. Tübingen: Mohr Siebeck.

———. 2003. "Trajan and the Origins of the Bar Kokhba War." Pages 23–29 in *The Bar Kokhba War Reconsidered: New Perspectives on the Second Jewish Revolt against Rome*. Edited by Peter Schäfer. Tübingen: Mohr Siebeck.

Gosse, Bernard. 2010. *David and Abraham: Persian Period Traditions*. Supplement to Transeuphratène 16. Pendé, France: Gabalda.

———. 2015. *L'espérance messianique davidique et la structuration du Psautier*. Supplement to Transeuphratène 21. Pendé, France: Gabalda.

Granerød, Gard. 2010a. "A Forgotten Reference to Divine Procreation? Psalm 2:6 in Light of Egyptian Royal Ideology." *Vetus Testamentum* 60:323–36.

———. 2010b. *Abraham and Melchizedek: Scribal Activity of Second Temple Times in Genesis 14 and Psalm 110*. Beihefte zur Zeitschrift für die alttestamentliche Wissenschaft 406. Berlin: de Gruyter.

———. 2016. *Dimensions of Yahwism in the Persian Period: Studies in the Religion and Society of the Judaean Community at Elephantine*. Beihefte zur Zeitschrift für die alttestamentliche Wissenschaft 488. Berlin: de Gruyter.

Gray, Rebecca. 1993. *Prophetic Figures in Late Second Temple Jewish Palestine: The Evidence from Josephus*. Oxford: Oxford University Press.

Greenfield, Jonas C., Michael E. Stone, and Esther Eshel. 2004. *The Aramaic Levi Document: Edition, Translation, Commentary*. Leiden: Brill.

Gzella, Holger. 2015. *A Cultural History of Aramaic from the Beginnings to the Advent of Islam*. Handbuch der Orientalisk 111. Leiden: Brill.

Hackett, Jo Ann. 1992. "Deir ʿAlla, Tell." Vol. 2/pages 126–30 in *Anchor Bible Dictionary*. Edited by David Noel Freedman et al. Garden City: Doubleday.

Halpern, Baruch. 2001. *David's Secret Demons: Messiah, Murderer, Traitor, King*. Grand Rapids: Eerdmans.

Hannah, Darrel D. 2007. "The Book of Noah, the Death of Herod the Great, and the Date of the Parables of Enoch." Pages 469–77 in *Enoch and the Messiah Son of Man: Revisiting the Book of Parables*. Edited by Gabriele Boccacini. Grand Rapids: Eerdmans.

Harrelson, Walter. 1962. "Nonroyal Motifs in the Royal Eschatology." Pages 147–65 in *Israel's Prophetic Heritage*. Edited by Bernhard W. Anderson and Walter Harrelson. New York: Harper.

Hasan-Rokem, Galit. 2000. *Web of Life: Folklore and Midrash in Rabbinic Literature*. Translated by Batya Stein. Stanford: Stanford University Press.

Hays, Christopher B. 2019a. *The Origins of Isaiah 24–27: Josiah's Festival Scroll for the Fall of Assyria*. Cambridge: Cambridge University Press.

———. 2019b. "Make Peace with Me: The Josianic Origins of Isaiah 24–27." *Interpretation* 73:143–57.

Heinemann, Joseph. 1975. "The Messiah of Joseph and the Premature Exodus of the Tribe of Ephraim." *Harvard Theological Review* 8:1–15.

Hendel, Ronald. 2007. "Plural Texts and Literary Criticism: For Instance, 1 Samuel 17." *Textus* 23:97–114.

Hendel, Ronald, and Jan Joosten. 2018. *How Old Is the Hebrew Bible? A Linguistic, Textual, and Historical Study*. Anchor Yale Bible Reference Library. New Haven: Yale University Press.

Hermisson, Hans-Jürgen. 1984. "Voreiliger Abschied von den Gottesknechtliedern." *Theologische Rundschau* 49:209–22.

Herzer, Jens. 1994. *Die Paralipomena Jeremiae: Studien zu Tradition und Redaktioneiner Haggada des frühen Judentums*. Texte und Studien zum antiken Judentum 43. Tübingen: Mohr.

Herzog, Ze'ev. 2010. "Perspectives on Southern Israel's Cult Centralization: Arad and Beer-sheba." Pages 169–99 in *One God—One Cult—One Nation: Archaeological and Biblical Perspectives*. Edited by Reinhard G. Kratz and Hermann Spieckermann. Berlin: de Gruyter.

Hillers, Delbert R. 1984. *Micah: A Commentary on the Book of Micah*. Hermeneia. Philadelphia: Fortress.

Himmelfarb, Martha. 2017. *Jewish Messiahs in a Christian Empire: A History of the Book of Zerubbabel*. Boston: Harvard University Press.

Høgenhaven, Jesper. 1987. "On the Structure and Meaning of Isaiah viii 23b." *Vetus Testamentum* 37:218–21.

Horbury, William. 2003. *Messianism among Jews and Christians: Biblical and Historical Studies*. London: T&T Clark.

Hørning Jensen, Morten. 2020. "The Gospel of Reconciliation in the Gospel of Mark." Pages 23–44 in *Reconciliation: Christian Perspectives—Interdisciplinary Approaches*. Edited by Tobias Faix, Johannes Reimer, and Cobus J. van Wyngaard. Vienna/Zurich: LIT.

Hossfeld, Frank-Lothar, and Erich Zenger. 1993. *Die Psalmen 1–50*. Herders Theologischer Kommentar zum Alten Testament. Würzburg: Echter.

———. 2005. *Psalms 2: A Commentary on Psalms 51–100*. Hermeneia. Minneapolis: Fortress.

———. 2008. *Die Psalmen 101–150*. Herders Theologischer Kommentar zum Alten Testament. Freiburg: Herder.

———. 2011. *Psalms 3: A Commentary on Psalms 101–150*. Hermeneia. Minneapolis: Fortress.

Humbert, Jean-Baptiste. 2017. "L'architecture de Qumrân avant les esséniens." Lecture at University of Lausanne, April 26.

Jerusalem Bible. 1966. London: Darton, Longman & Todd.

Jervell, Jacob. 1969. "Ein Interpolator Interpretiert: Zu der christlichen Bearbeitung der Testamente der Zwölf Patriarchen." Pages 30–61 in *Studien zu den Testamenten der Zwölf Patriarchen*. Edited by Walter Eltester. Beihefte zur Zeitschrift für die neutestamentliche Wissenschaft 36. Berlin: Töpelmann.

Joannès, Francis, and André Lemaire. 1996. "Contrats babyloniens d'époque achéménide du Bît-Abî-Râm avec une épigraphe araméenne." *Revue d'assyriologie et d'archéologie orientale* 90:41–60.

Johnson, Benjamin J. M. 2015. *Reading David and Goliath in Greek and Hebrew*. Forschungen zum Alten Testament 2.82. Tübingen: Mohr Siebeck.

Jones, Barry Alan. 2020. "The Book of the Twelve in the Septuagint." Pages 286–304 in *The Book of the Twelve: Composition, Reception, and Interpretation*. Edited by Lena-Sofia Tiemeyer and Jakob Wöhrle. Vetus Testamentum Supplement 184. Leiden: Brill.

Jones, Robert. 2018. "A Priest like Noah: 4Q541 in Its Qumran Aramaic Context." Paper presented at SBL Annual Meeting, Denver, November 18.

Joosten, Jan. 2015. "Reflections on the Original Language of the Psalms of Solomon." Pages 31–47 in *Psalms of Solomon: Language, History, Theology*. Edited by Eberhard Bons and Patrick Pouchelle. Atlanta: SBL Press.

Joyce, Paul M. 1998. "King and Messiah in Ezekiel." Pages 323–37 in *King and Messiah in Israel and the Ancient Near East*. Edited by John Day. Journal for the Study of the Old Testament Supplement 270. Sheffield: Sheffield Academic Press.

Justnes, Årstein. 2009. *The Time of Salvation: An Analysis of 4QApocryphon of Daniel ar (4Q246), 4QMessianic Apocalypse (4Q521 2), and 4QTime of Righteousness (4Q215a)*. Frankfurt: Peter Lang.

Kartveit, Magnar. 2009. *The Origin of the Samaritans*. Vetus Testamentum Supplement 128. Leiden: Brill.

Keel, Othmar, and Christoph Uehlinger. 1998. *Gods, Goddesses, and Images of God in Ancient Israel*. Translated by Thomas H. Trapp. Edinburgh: T&T Clark.

Kimelman, Reuven. 1997. "The Messiah of the Amidah: A Study in Comparative Messianism." *Journal of Biblical Literature* 116:313–20.

King, Philip J. 1959. *A Study of Psalm 45 (44)*. Rome: Pontifical University Press.

Kisilevitz, Shua. 2015. "The Iron IIA Judahite Temple at Moẓa." *Tel Aviv* 42:147–64.

Kisilevitz, Shua, and Oded Lipschits. 2020. "Another Temple in Judah: The Tale of Tel Moẓa." *Biblical Archaeology Review* 46/1:40–49.

Klausner, Joseph. 1955. *The Messianic Idea in Israel: From Its Beginning to the Completion of the Mishnah*. New York: Macmillan.

Kleiman, Assaf. 2018. "Comments on the Archaeology and History of Tell el-Farʿah North (Biblical Tirza) in the Iron IIA." *Semitica* 60:85–104.

Koch, Ido. 2017. "Settlements and Interactions in the Shephelah during the Late Second through Early First Millennia BCE." Pages 181–207 in *The Shephelah during the Iron Age: Recent Archaeological Studies*. Edited by Oded Lipschits and Aren M. Maeir. Winona Lake, IN: Eisenbrauns.

———. 2020. "On Philistines and Early Israelite Kings: Memories and Perceptions." Pages 7–32 in *Saul, Benjamin, and the Emergence of Monarchy in Israel: Biblical and Archaeological Perspectives*. Edited by Joachim J. Krause, Omer Sergi, and Kristin Weingart. Ancient Israel and Its Literature 40. Atlanta: SBL Press.

Koehler, Ludwig, Walter Baumgartner, and Johann Stamm. 1995–2000. *The Hebrew and Aramaic Lexicon of the Old Testament*. 3rd ed. Leiden: Brill.

Koh, Shmuel S.-J. 2018. "Manasseh's Birth, One of the Catalysts for the Proclamation of Isa 11:1–5." Paper presented at SBL Annual Meeting, Denver, November 19.

Kooij, Arie van der. 1983. "On the Place of Origin of the Old Greek of Psalms." *Vetus Testamentum* 33:67–74.

Kratz, Reinhard. 1991. *Kyros im Deuterojesaja-Buch: Redaktionsgeschichtliche*

Untersuchungen zu Entstehung und Theologie von Jes 40–55. Forschungen zum Alten Testament 1. Tübingen: Mohr Siebeck.

———. 2010. "The Idea of Cultic Centralization and Its Supposed Ancient Near Eastern Analogies." Pages 121–44 in *One God—One Cult—One Nation: Archaeological and Biblical Perspectives.* Edited by Reinhard G. Kratz and Hermann Spieckermann. Berlin: de Gruyter.

Krause, Joachim J. 2020. "A Historical Hypothesis on the Reign of Rehoboam." Pages 111–31 in *Saul, Benjamin, and the Emergence of Monarchy in Israel: Biblical and Archaeological Perspectives.* Edited by Joachim J. Krause, Omer Sergi, and Kristin Weingart. Ancient Israel and Its Literature 40. Atlanta: SBL Press.

Kugler, Robert A. 1996. *From Patriarch to Priest: The Levi-Priestly Tradition from Aramaic Levi to Testament of Levi.* Atlanta: Scholars Press.

Kuhrt, Amélie. 2007. *The Persian Empire: A Corpus of Sources from the Achaemenid Period.* London: Routledge.

Laato, Antti. 1992. *Josiah and David Redivivus: The Historical Josiah and the Messianic Expectations of Exilic and Postexilic Times.* Coniectanea Biblica: Old Testament 33. Stockholm: Almqvist & Wiksell.

———. 1998. *A Star Is Rising: The Historical Development of the Old Testament Royal Ideology and the Rise of the Jewish Messianic Expectations.* Atlanta: Scholars Press.

———. 2016. "'When He Comes to Shiloh' (Gen 49, 8–12)—An Approach to the Books of Samuel." Pages 511–19 in *The Books of Samuel: Stories—History—Reception History.* Edited by Walter Dietrich. Bibliotheca Ephemeridum Theologicarum Lovaniensium 284. Leuvens: Peeters.

Lange, Armin. 2009. "Satanic Verses: The Adversary in the Qumran Manuscripts and Elsewhere." *Revue de Qumran* 24:35–48.

———. 2010a. "The Textual Plurality of Jewish Scriptures in the Second Temple Period in Light of the Dead Sea Scrolls." Pages 43–96 in *Qumran and the Bible: Studying the Jewish and Christian Scriptures in Light of the Dead Sea Scrolls.* Edited by Nora Dávid and Armin Lange. Contributions to Biblical Exegesis and Theology 57. Leuven: Peeters.

———. 2010b. "2 Maccabees 2:13–15: Library or Canon?" Pages 155–67 in *The Books of the Maccabees: History, Theology, Ideology.* Edited by Géza G. Xeravits and József Zsengellér. Journal for the Study of Judaism Supplement 118. Leiden: Brill.

———. 2012. "The Covenant with the Levites (Jer 33:21) in the Light of the Dead Sea Scrolls." Pages 95–116 in *"Go Out and Study the Land" (Judges 18:2): Archaeological, Historical, and Textual Studies in Honor of Hanan Eshel.*

Edited by Aren M. Maeir, Jodi Magness, and Lawrence H. Schiffman. Journal for the Study of Judaism Supplement 148. Leiden: Brill.

Langlois, Michael. 2019a. "The Kings, the City, and the House of David on the Mesha Stele in Light of New Imaging Techniques." *Semitica* 61:23–47.

———. 2019b. "The Book of Jeremiah's Redaction History in Light of Its Oldest Manuscripts." Pages 9–29 in *Jeremiah in History and Tradition*. Edited by Jim West and Niels P. Lemche. London: Routledge.

Lauterbach, Jakob Z. 1933. *Mekilta de-Rabbi Ishmael*. 3 vols. Philadelphia: Jewish Publication Society. Reprinted 1961.

Lee-Sak, Yitzhak. 2017. "The Lists of Levitical Cities (Joshua 21, 1 Chronicles 6) and the Propagandistic Map for the Hasmonean Territorial Expansion." *Journal of Biblical Literature* 136:783–800.

Leibner, Uzi. 2012. "The Origins of Jewish Settlement in Galilee in the Second Temple Period: Historical Sources and Archaeological Data." [In Hebrew.] *Zion* 77:437–70.

Lemaire, André. 1994. "'House of David' Restored in Moabite Inscription." *Biblical Archaeology Review* 20.3:30–37.

Levenson, Jon D. 1976. *Theology of the Program of Restoration of Ezekiel 40–48*. Atlanta: Scholars Press.

Levine, Baruch A. 1981. "The Deir 'Alla Plaster Inscriptions." *Journal of the American Oriental Society* 101:195–205.

Levy, Thomas E. 2020. "David, Solomon, and Edom: Reflections from the Edom Lowlands Archaeology Project." Lecture at virtual conference "'The Land That I Will Show You': Recent Archeological and Historical Studies of Ancient Israel," New York University and Israel Antiquities Authority, October 25.

Levy, Thomas E., Mohammed Najjar, and Erez Ben-Yosef. 2014a. *New Insights into the Iron Age Archaeology of Edom, Southern Jordan*, vol. 1. Los Angeles: Cotzen Institute of Archaeology.

———. 2014b. *New Insights into the Iron Age Archaeology of Edom, Southern Jordan*, vol. 2. Los Angeles: Cotzen Institute of Archaeology.

Lewis, Bernard. 1974. "On That Day: A Jewish Apocalyptic Poem on the Arab Conquest." Pages 197–200 in *Mélanges d'islamologie*. Edited by Pierre Salmon. Leiden: Brill.

Lied, Liv Ingeborg. 2021. *Invisible Manuscripts: Textual Scholarship and the Survival of 2 Baruch*. Tübingen: Mohr Siebeck.

Lipschits, Oded. 2020. "Benjamin in Retrospective: Stages in the Creation of the Territory of the Benjamin Tribe." Pages 161–200 in *Saul, Benjamin, and the Emergence of Monarchy in Israel: Biblical and Archaeological Per-*

spectives. Edited by Joachim J. Krause, Omer Sergi, and Kristin Weingart. Ancient Israel and Its Literature 40. Atlanta: SBL Press.

Lipschits, Oded, Yuval Gadot, Benjamin Arubas, and Manfred Oeming. 2017. *What Are the Stones Whispering? Ramat Rahel: 3000 Years of Forgotten History*. Winona Lake, IN: Eisenbrauns.

Lust, Johan. 1986. "The Use of Textual Witnesses for the Establishment of the Text: The Shorter and Longer Texts of Ezekiel, an Example: Ez 7." Pages 7–20 in *Ezekiel and His Book: Textual and Literary Criticism and Their Interrelation*. Edited by Johan Lust. Bibliotheca Ephemeridum Theologicarum Lovaniensium 74. Leuven: Peeters.

Magness, Jodi. 2002. *The Archaeology of Qumran and the Dead Sea Scrolls*. Grand Rapids: Eerdmans.

———. 2004. *Debating Qumran: Collected Essays on Its Archaeology*. Leuven: Peeters.

———. 2014. "The Essenes and the Qumran Settlement." Online review of Joan E. Taylor's *The Essenes, the Scrolls, and the Dead Sea*. DOI: marginalia.lareviewofbooks.org/the-essenes-and-the-qumran-settlement-by-jodi-magness/.

Malamat, Avraham. 1980. "A Mari Prophecy and Nathan's Dynastic Oracle." Pages 66–82 in *Prophecy: Essays Presented to G. Fohrer on His Sixty-fifth Birthday, 8th September 1980*. Edited by John A. Emerton. Beihefte zur Zeitschrift für die alttestamentliche Wissenschaft 150. Berlin: de Gruyter.

Mason, Eric F. 2008. *"You Are a Priest Forever": Second Temple Jewish Messianism and the Priestly Christology of the Epistle to the Hebrews*. Studies on the Texts of the Desert of Judah 74. Leiden: Brill.

Mason, Rex. 1998. "The Messiah in the Postexilic Old Testament Literature." Pages 338–64 in *King and Messiah in Israel and the Ancient Near East*. Edited by John Day. Journal for the Study of the Old Testament Supplement 270. Sheffield: Sheffield Academic Press.

Mazar, Amihai. 2010. "Archaeology and the Biblical Narrative: The Case of the United Monarchy." Pages 29–58 in *One God—One Cult—One Nation: Archaeological and Biblical Perspectives*. Edited by Reinhard G. Kratz and Hermann Spieckermann. Berlin: de Gruyter.

———. 2016. "Culture, Identity, and Politics Relating to Tel Reḥov in the 10th–9th Centuries BCE (with an Excursus on the Identification of Tel Reḥov)." Pages 89–119 in *In Search of Aram and Israel: Politics, Culture, and Identity*. Edited by Omer Sergi, Manfred Oeming, and Izaak J. de Hulster. Oriental Religions in Antiquity 20. Tübingen: Mohr Siebeck.

———. 2020. "Jerusalem in the 10th Cent. B.C.E.: A Response." *Zeitschrift des deutschen Palästina-Vereins* 136:139–51.

Mazar, Amihai, and Shmuel Aḥituv. 2011. "The Inscriptions from Tel Rehov and Their Contribution to Research on Script and Writing in the Iron Age 2a." [In Hebrew.] *Eretz-Israel* 30:300–316.

Mazar, Benjamin. 1985. "The Temple Mount." Pages 463–68 in *Biblical Archaeology Today: Proceedings of the International Congress on Biblical Archaeology, Jerusalem, April 1984.* Jerusalem: Israel Exploration Society.

Mendel-Geberovich, Anat, Ortal Chalaf, and Joe Uziel. 2020. "The People behind the Stamps: A Newly-Found Group of Bullae and a Seal from the City of David, Jerusalem." *Bulletin of the American Schools of Oriental Research* 384:159–82.

Mendels, Doron. 1992. *The Rise and Fall of Jewish Nationalism.* New York: Doubleday.

Meshel, Ze'ev. 2012. *Kuntillet 'Ajrud (Ḥorvat Teman): An Iron Age II Religious Site on the Judah-Sinai Border.* Jerusalem: Israel Exploration Society.

Mettinger, Trygve N. D. 1983. *A Farewell to the Servant Songs: A Critical Examination of an Exegetical Axiom.* Lund: Gleerups.

Milik, Joseph T. 1959. *Ten Years of Discovery in the Wilderness of Judaea.* London: SCM.

———. 1969. *The Books of Enoch. Aramaic Fragments of Qumrân Cave 4.* Oxford: Clarendon.

Monger, Matthew P. 2014. "4Q216 and the State of Jubilees at Qumran." *Revue de Qumran* 26:595–612.

———. 2017. "The Development of Jubilees 1 in the Late Second Temple Period." *Journal for the Study of the Pseudepigrapha* 27:83–112.

———. 2018a. "4Q216—A New Material Analysis." *Semitica* 60:308–33.

———. 2018b. "4Q216: Rethinking Jubilees in the First Century BCE." PhD diss., Norwegian School of Theology.

Monroe, Lauren, and Daniel E. Fleming. 2019. "Earliest Israel in Highland Company." *Near Eastern Archaeology* 82:16–23.

Monti, Ludwig. 2004. "Attese messianiche a Qumran: una communità alla fine della storia." *Henoch* 26:25–62.

Mor, Menahem. 2003. "The Geographical Scope of the Bar-Kokhba Revolt." Pages 108–31 in *The Bar Kokhba War Reconsidered: New Perspectives on the Second Jewish Revolt against Rome.* Edited by Peter Schäfer. Tübingen: Mohr Siebeck.

Morag, Shlomo. 1996. "Language and Style in Miqsat Maase Ha-Torah: Did Moreh ha-Sedeq Write This Document?" [In Hebrew.] *Tarbiz* 65:209–23.

Moule, C. F. D. 1982. *Essays in New Testament Interpretation.* Cambridge: Cambridge University Press.

Na'aman, Nadav. 1991. "The Kingdom of Judah under Josiah." *Tel Aviv* 18:3–71.

———. 1996. "Sources and Composition in the History of David." Pages 170–86 in *The Origins of the Ancient Israelite States.* Edited by Volkmar Fritz and Philip R. Davies. Sheffield: Sheffield Academic Press.

———. 2007. "When and How Did Jerusalem Become a Great City? The Rise of Jerusalem as Judah's Premier City in the Eighth–Seventh Centuries B.C.E." *Bulletin of the American Schools of Oriental Research* 347:21–56.

———. 2014. "Dismissing the Myth of a Flood of Israelite Refugees in the Late Eighth Century BCE." *Zeitschrift für die alttestamentliche Wissenschaft* 126:1–14.

Netzer, Ehud. 2001. *The Palaces of the Hasmoneans and Herod the Great.* Jerusalem: Yad Ben-Zvi and Israel Exploration Society.

Neusner, Jacob. 1984. *Messiah in Context: Israel's History and Destiny in Formative Judaism.* Philadelphia: Fortress.

New English Translation of the Septuagint and Other Greek Translations Traditionally Included under That Title. 2007. Edited by Albert Pietersma and Benjamin G. Wright. New York: Oxford University Press.

Nickelsburg, George W. E. 1992. "Son of Man." Vol. 6/pages 137–50 in *Anchor Bible Dictionary.* Edited by David Noel Freedman et al. Garden City: Doubleday.

———. 2001. *1 Enoch 1: A Commentary on the Book of 1 Enoch, Chapters 1–36; 81–108.* Hermeneia. Minneapolis: Fortress.

Nickelsburg, George W. E., and James C. VanderKam. 2012. *1 Enoch 2: A Commentary on the Book of 1 Enoch, Chapters 37–82.* Hermeneia. Minneapolis: Fortress.

Nogalski, James. 1993. *Literary Precursors to the Book of the Twelve.* Beihefte zur Zeitschrift für die alttestamentliche Wissenschaft 217. Berlin: de Gruyter.

Noth, Martin. 1926. "Zur Komposition des Buches Daniel." *Theologische Studien und Kritiken* 98/99:143–63.

Notley, R. Stephen, and Mordechai Aviam. 2020. "Searching for Bethsaida: The Case for el-Araj." *Biblical Archaeological Review* 1/2020:2–13.

Oppenheimer, Aharon. 2003. "The Ban of Circumcision as a Cause of the Revolt: A Reconsideration." Pages 55–69 in *The Bar Kokhba War Reconsidered: New Perspectives on the Second Jewish Revolt against Rome.* Edited by Peter Schäfer. Tübingen: Mohr Siebeck.

Ortiz, Steven M., and Samuel R. Wolff. 2012. "Guarding the Border to Jerusalem: The Iron Age City of Gezer." *Near Eastern Archaeology* 75:4–19.

———. 2017. "Tel Gezer Excavations 2006–2015: The Transformation of a Border City." Pages 61–102 in *The Shephelah during the Iron Age: Recent Archaeological Studies*. Edited by Oded Lipschits and Aren M. Maeir. Winona Lake, IN: Eisenbrauns.

Oswald, Wolfgang. 2020. "Possible Historical Settings of the Saul-David Narrative." Pages 93–109 in *Saul, Benjamin, and the Emergence of Monarchy in Israel: Biblical and Archaeological Perspectives*. Edited by Joachim J. Krause, Omer Sergi, and Kristin Weingart. Ancient Israel and Its Literature 40. Atlanta: SBL Press.

Otto, Eckhart. 2012. *Deuteronomium*. Herders Theologischer Kommentar zum Alten Testament. Freiburg: Herder.

———. 2013. "The History of the Legal-Religious Hermeneutics of the Book of Deuteronomy." Pages 211–50 in *Law and Religion in the Eastern Mediterranean: From Antiquity to Early Islam*. Edited by Anselm Hagedorn and Reinhard G. Kratz. Oxford: Oxford University Press.

Pakkala, Juha. 2010. "Why the Cult Reforms in Judah Probably Did Not Happen." Pages 201–35 in *One God—One Cult—One Nation: Archaeological and Biblical Perspectives*. Edited by Reinhard G. Kratz and Hermann Spieckermann. Berlin: de Gruyter.

Panitz-Cohen, Nava, and Robert A. Mullins. 2016. "Aram-Maacah? Arameans and Israelites on the Border: Excavations at Tell Abil el-Qameh (Abel-beth-maacah) in Northern Israel." Pages 139–67 in *In Search of Aram and Israel: Politics, Culture, and Identity*. Edited by Omer Sergi, Manfred Oeming, and Izaak J. de Hulster. Oriental Religions in Antiquity 20. Tübingen: Mohr Siebeck.

Panov, Lida Leonie. 2019. *Hiskijas Geschick und Jesajas Beistand: Heilstheologische Verarbeitungen der Jesaja-überlieferung in den Hiskija-Jesaja-Erzählungen*. Abhandlungen zur Theologie des Alten und Neuen Testaments 110. Zürich: TVZ.

———. 2021. "Scribal Experiences of Salvation—Aspects of Formation Processes in the Hezekiah-Isaiah Narratives." *Zeitschrift für die alttestamentliche Wissenschaft* 133.3:312–28.

Parry, Donald W., and Emanuel Tov (eds.). 2005. *The Dead Sea Scrolls Reader*, vols. 3–6. Leiden: Brill.

Patrich, Yosef. 2020. "The Temple and the Temple Mount: Their Location and Form." [In Hebrew.] Pages 263–326 in *The Book of Jerusalem in Second Temple Times, 332 BCE–70 CE*. Edited by Isaiah Gafni, Ronny Reich, and Joshua Schwartz. Jerusalem: Yitshaq ben Zvi.

Paul, Shalom M. 1979–80. "Adoption Formulae: A Study of Cuneiform and Biblical Legal Clauses." *Maarav* 2:173–85.

———. 2012. *Isaiah 40–66: Translation and Commentary*. Grand Rapids: Eerdmans.

Pearce, Laurie E. 2006. "New Evidence for Judeans in Babylonia." Pages 399–411 in *Judah and the Judeans in the Persian Period*. Edited by Oded Lipschits and Manfred Oeming. Winona Lake, IN: Eisenbrauns.

Pearce, Laurie E., and Cornelia Wunsch. 2014. *Documents of Judean Exiles and West Semites in Babylonia in the Collection of David Sofer*. Cornell University Studies in Assyriology and Sumerology 28. Bethesda: CDL.

Pearl, Chaim. 1997. *Theology in Rabbinic Stories*. Jerusalem: Carta/Peabody, MA: Hendrickson.

Peeters, Dorothy M. 2008. *Noah Traditions in the Dead Sea Scrolls: Conversations and Controversies of Antiquity*. Atlanta: SBL Press.

Piotrkowski, Meron M. 2019. *Priests in Exile: The History of the Temple of the Oniads and Its Community in the Hellenistic Period*. Studia Judaica 106/ Rethinking Diaspora 4. Berlin: de Gruyter.

Pritchard, James B. (ed.). 1969. *Ancient Near Eastern Texts Relating to the Old Testament*. 3rd ed. with Supplement. Princeton: Princeton University Press.

Puech, Émile. 1999. "Some Remarks on 4Q246 and 4Q521 and Qumran Messianism." Pages 545–65 in *The Provo International Conference on the Dead Sea Scrolls: Technological Innovations, New Texts, and Reformulated Issues*. Edited by Donald W. Parry and Eugene Ulrich. Studies on the Texts of the Desert of Judah 30. Leiden: Brill.

Qimron, Elisha. 2013. *The Dead Sea Scrolls: The Hebrew Writings*, vol. 2. [In Hebrew.] Jerusalem: Yad Ben-Zvi.

———. 2014. *The Dead Sea Scrolls: The Hebrew Writings*, vol. 3. [In Hebrew.] Jerusalem: Yad Ben-Zvi.

Rabin, Ira. 2016. "Material Analysis of the Fragments." Pages 61–77 in *Gleanings from the Caves: Dead Sea Scrolls and Artefacts from the Schøyen Collection*. Edited by Torleif Elgvin with Kipp Davis and Michael Langlois. London: Bloomsbury/T&T Clark.

Rad, Gerhard von. 1947. "Das judäische Königsritual." *Theologische Literaturzeitung* 72:211–16.

———. 1965. *Old Testament Theology*, vol. 2: *The Theology of Israel's Prophetic Traditions*. London: SCM.

Rendsburg, Gary A., and William M. Schniedewind. 2010. "The Siloam Inscription: Historical and Linguistic Perspectives." *Israel Exploration Journal* 60:188–203.

Reeves, John C. 2005. *Trajectories in Near Eastern Apocalyptic: A Postrabbinic Jewish Apocalypse Reader*. Atlanta: SBL Press.

Roberts, Jimmy J. M. 1997. "Whose Child Is This? Reflections on the Speaking Voice in Isaiah 9:5." *Harvard Theological Review* 90.2:115–29.

Rofé, Alexander. 2015. "David Overcomes Goliath (1 Samuel 17): Genre, Text, Origin, and Message of the Story." *Henoch* 37:66–100.

Rosenberg, Gil. 2016. "Hypertextuality." Pages 16–28 in *Exploring Intertextuality: Diverse Strategies for New Testament Interpretation of Texts*. Edited by B. J. Oropeza and Steve Moyise. Eugene, OR: Wipf & Stock.

Rowley, H. H. 1965. *The Servant of the Lord and Other Essays on the Old Testament*. 2nd ed. Oxford: Blackwell.

Sæbø, Magne. 1978. "Von Grossreich zum Weltreich: Erwägungen zu Pss. lxxii 8, lxxxix 26; Sach. ix 10b." *Vetus Testamentum* 28:83–91.

Santala, Risto. 1992. *The Messiah in the Old Testament in the Light of Rabbinical Writings*. Jerusalem: Keren Ahva Meshihit.

Sayyad Bach, Melissa. 2020. "4Q246 and Collective Interpretation." Pages 221–41 in *Vision, Narrative, and Wisdom in the Aramaic Texts from Qumran*. Edited by Mette Bundvad and Kasper Siegismund. Studies on the Texts of the Desert of Judah 131. Leiden: Brill.

Schäfer, Peter. 2003. "Bar Kokhba and the Rabbis." Pages 1–22 in *The Bar Kokhba War Reconsidered: New Perspectives on the Second Jewish Revolt against Rome*. Edited by Peter Schäfer. Tübingen: Mohr Siebeck.

———. 2012. *The Jewish Jesus: How Judaism and Christianity Shaped Each Other*. Princeton: Princeton University Press.

Schaper, Joachim. 1995. *Eschatology in the Greek Psalter*. Wissenschaftliche Untersuchungen zum Neuen Testamentum 2.76. Tübingen: Mohr Siebeck.

Schmid, Konrad. 2012. *The Old Testament: A Literary History*. Minneapolis: Fortress.

Schneider, Thomas. 2010. "Contributions to the Chronology of the New Kingdom and the Third Intermediate Period." *Egypt and the Levant* 20:373–403.

Schniedewind, William. 1999. *Society and the Promise to David: The Reception History of 2 Samuel 7:1–17*. Oxford: Oxford University Press.

———. 2003. "Jerusalem, the Late Judean Monarchy, and the Composition of Biblical Texts." Pages 375–93 in *Jerusalem in Bible and Archaeology: The First Temple Period*. Edited by Andrew Vaughn and Ann E. Killebrew. Leiden: Brill.

———. 2004. *How the Bible Became a Book*. Cambridge: Cambridge University Press.

————. 2019. *The Finger of the Scribe: How Scribes Learned to Write the Bible.* Oxford: Oxford University Press.

————. 2022. "Solomon from Archival Sources to Collective Memory." Plenary address at IOSOT, August 8, 2019. Forthcoming in Vetus Testamentum Supplement Congress Volume Aberdeen 2019. Edited by Joachim Schaper.

Schorch, Stefan. 2010. "The Libraries in 2 Macc 2:13–15, and the Torah as a Public Document in 2nd Century Judaism." Pages 169–80 in *The Books of the Maccabees: History, Theology, Ideology.* Edited by Géza G. Xeravits and József Zsengellér. Journal for the Study of Judaism Supplement 118. Leiden: Brill.

Schuller, Eileen. 2006. "Prayers and Psalms from the Pre-Maccabean Period." *Dead Sea Discoveries* 13:306–18.

Schürer, Emil, Geza Vermes, and Fergus Millar. 1973. *The History of the Jewish People in the Age of Jesus Christ (175 B.C.–A.D. 135),* vol. 1. Revised and edited by Geza Vermes and Fergus Millar. Edinburgh: T&T Clark.

Seeligmann, Isac Leo. 2004. *The Septuagint Version of Isaiah and Cognate Studies.* Edited by Robert Hanhart and Hermann Spieckermann. Forschungen zum Alten Testament 40. Tübingen: Mohr Siebeck.

Segal, Alan F. 1977. *Two Powers in Heaven: Early Rabbinic Reports about Christianity and Gnosticism.* Leiden: Brill. Reprinted 2002.

Sellers, Ovid R. 1958. "The 1957 Campaign at Beth-zur." *Biblical Archaeologist* 21:71–76.

Sellin, Ernst. 1898. *Serubbabel: Ein Beitrag zur Geschichte der messianischen Erwartung und der Entstehung des Judentums.* Leipzig: Deichert.

————. 1930. "Tritojesaja, Deuterojesaja und das Gottesknechtsproblem." *Neue kirchliche Zeitschrift* 41:73–93, 145–73.

————. 1937. "Die Lösung des deuterojesajanischen Gottesknechts-rätsels." *Zeitschrift für die alttestamentliche Wissenschaft* 35:177–217.

Sergi, Omer. 2016. "The Gilead between Aram and Israel: Political Borders, Cultural Interaction, and the Question of Jacob and Israelite Identity." Pages 333–54 in *In Search for Aram and Israel: Politics, Culture, and Identity.* Edited by Omer Sergi, Manfred Oeming, and Izaak J. de Hulster. Oriental Religions in Antiquity 20. Tübingen: Mohr Siebeck.

————. 2017. "The Emergence of Judah as a Political Entity between Jerusalem and Benjamin." *Zeitschrift des Deutschen Palästina-Vereins* 133/1:1–23.

————. 2019. "The Formation of Israelite Identity in the Central Canaanite Highlands in the Iron Age I–IIA." *Near Eastern Archaeology* 82/1:42–51.

————. 2020. "Saul, David, and the Formation of the Israelite Monarchy: Revisiting the Historical and Literary Context of 1 Samuel 9–2 Samuel 5." Pages 57–91 in *Saul, Benjamin, and the Emergence of Monarchy in Israel: Biblical and Archaeological Perspectives*. Edited by Joachim J. Krause, Omer Sergi, and Kristin Weingart. Ancient Israel and Its Literature 40. Atlanta: SBL Press.

Sergi, Omer, and Izaac de Hulster. 2016. "Some Historical and Methodological Considerations Regarding the Question of Political, Social, and Cultural Interaction between Aram and Israel in the Early Iron Age." Pages 1–14 in *In Search for Aram and Israel: Politics, Culture, and Identity*. Edited by Omer Sergi, Manfred Oeming, and Izaak J. de Hulster. Oriental Religions in Antiquity 20. Tübingen: Mohr Siebeck.

Sergi, Omer, and Asaf Kleiman. 2018. "The Kingdom of Geshur and the Expansion of Aram-Damascus into the Northern Jordan Valley: Archaeological and Historical Perspectives." *Bulletin of the American Schools of Oriental Research* 379:1–18.

Seters, John van. 1983. *In Search of History: Historiography in the Ancient World and the Origins of Biblical History*. New Haven: Yale University Press.

Shahar, Yuval. 2003. "The Underground Hideouts in Galilee and Their Historical Meaning." Pages 217–40 in *The Bar Kokhba War Reconsidered: New Perspectives on the Second Jewish Revolt against Rome*. Edited by Peter Schäfer. Tübingen: Mohr Siebeck.

Shai, Itzhaq. 2017. "Tel Burna: A Judahite Fortified Town in the Shephelah." Pages 45–60 in *The Shephelah during the Iron Age: Recent Archaeological Studies*. Edited by Oded Lipschits and Aren M. Maeir. Winona Lake, IN: Eisenbrauns.

Shanks, Herschel. 1999. *Celebrating Avraham: Avraham Biran, the Excavator of Dan at 90*. Washington, DC: Biblical Archaeological Society.

Shoemaker, Stephen J. 2012. *The Death of a Prophet: The End of Muhammad's Life and the Beginnings of Islam*. Philadelphia: University of Pennsylvania Press.

Sivertsev, Alexei M. 2014. *Judaism and Imperial Ideology in Late Antiquity*. Cambridge: Cambridge University Press.

Skarsaune, Oskar. 2007. "Jewish Christian Sources Used by Justin Martyr and Some Other Greek and Latin Fathers." Pages 379–416 in *Jewish Believers in Jesus: The Early Centuries*. Edited by Oskar Skarsaune and Reidar Hvalvik. Peabody, MA: Hendrickson.

Skehan, Patrick W., and Alexander A. Di Lella. 1987. *The Wisdom of Ben Sira: A New Translation with Notes*. Anchor Bible 39. New York: Doubleday.

Sklar-Parnes, Deborah A., Yehudah Rapuano, and Rachel Bar-Nathan. 2004.

"Excavations in Northeast Jerusalem—A Jewish Site in between the Revolts." *New Studies on Jerusalem* 10:35*–41*.

Sparks, Kenton L. 2005. *Ancient Texts for the Study of the Hebrew Bible*. Peabody, MA: Hendrickson.

Sperber, Alexander. 1962. *The Bible in Aramaic*, vol. 3: *The Latter Prophets according to Targum Jonathan*. Leiden: Brill.

Stanton, Graham N. 1992. *A Gospel for a New People: Studies in Matthew*. Louisville: Westminster John Knox.

Stenning, J. F. 1949. *The Targum of Isaiah*. Oxford: Clarendon.

Stone, Bryan J. 1995. "The Philistines and Acculturation: Culture Change and Ethnic Continuity in the Iron Age." *Bulletin of the American Schools of Oriental Research* 298:7–32.

Stone, Michael A. 1987. "The Question of the Messiah in 4 Ezra." Pages 209–24 in *Judaisms and Their Messiahs at the Turn of the Christian Era*. Edited by Jacob Neusner, William S. Green, and Ernest S. Frerichs. Cambridge: Cambridge University Press.

Strack, Hermann L., and Günther Stemberger. 1992. *Introduction to the Talmud and Midrash*. Translated by Markus Bockmuehl. Minneapolis: Fortress.

Stuart, Douglas. 1987. *Hosea–Jonah*. Word Biblical Commentary 31. Nashville: Nelson.

Süssenbach, Claudia. 2005. *Der elohistische Psalter*. Tübingen: Mohr Siebeck.

Suter, David W. 2007. "Enoch in Sheol: Updating the Dating of the Book of Parables." Pages 415–43 in *Enoch and the Messiah Son of Man: Revisiting the Book of Parables*. Edited by Gabriele Boccaccini. Grand Rapids: Eerdmans.

Sweeney, Marvin A. 1996. *Isaiah 1–39, with an Introduction to Prophetic Literature*. Forms of Old Testament Literature 16. Grand Rapids: Eerdmans.

———. 2001. *King Josiah of Judah: The Lost Messiah of Israel*. Oxford: Oxford University Press.

Syon, Danny. 2015. *Small Change in Hellenistic-Roman Galilee: The Evidence from Numismatic Site Finds as a Tool for Historical Reconstruction*. Jerusalem: Israel Numismatic Society.

Tanakh: A New Translation of the Holy Scriptures according to the Traditional Hebrew Text. 1985. Philadelphia: Jewish Publication Society.

Tappy, Ron E. 2017. "The Archaeology and History of Tel Zayit: A Record of Liminal Life." Pages 155–79 in *The Shephelah during the Iron Age: Recent Archaeological Studies*. Edited by Oded Lipschits and Aren M. Maeir. Winona Lake, IN: Eisenbrauns.

Taylor, Joan. 2013. *The Essenes, the Scrolls, and the Dead Sea*. Oxford: Oxford University Press.

———. 2014. "Joan Taylor Responds to Jodi Magness." marginalia.lareviewof books.org/mrblog-joan-taylor-responds-jodi-magness/.

Thareani, Yifat. 2016. "Enemy at the Gates? The Archaeological Visibility of the Arameans at Dan." Pages 169–97 in *In Search of Aram and Israel: Politics, Culture, and Identity.* Oriental Religions in Antiquity 20. Edited by Omer Sergi, Manfred Oeming, and Izaak J. de Hulster. Tübingen: Mohr Siebeck.

———. 2019. "Archaeology of an Imagined Community: Tel Dan in the Iron Age IIa." Pages 263–76 in *Research on Israel and Aram: Autonomy, Independence and Related Issues. Proceedings of the First Annual RIAB Center Conference, Leipzig, June 2016.* Edited by Angelika Berlejung and Aren M. Maeir. Tübingen: Mohr Siebeck.

Tigay, Jeffrey H. 1971. "Adoption." Vol. 2/pages 300–301 in *Encyclopaedia Judaica.* Edited by Cecil Roth. Jerusalem: Keter.

Tov, Emanuel. 1999. *The Greek and Hebrew Bible: Collected Essays.* Leiden Brill.

Tov, Emanuel, Kipp Davis, and Robert Duke (eds.). 2016. *Dead Sea Scrolls Fragments in the Museum Collection.* Leiden: Brill.

Troyer, Kristin de. 2018. *The Ultimate and Penultimate Text of Joshua.* Contributions to Biblical Exegesis and Theology 100. Leuven: Peeters.

Tsafrir, Yoram. 1975. "The Location of the Seleucid Acra in Jerusalem." *Revue biblique* 82:501–21.

Tzoref, Shani. 2012. "4Q252: Listenwissenschaft and Covenantal Patriarchal Blessings." Pages 335–57 in *"Go Out and Study the Land" (Judges 18:2): Archaeological, Historical, and Textual Studies in Honor of Hanan Eshel.* Edited by Aren M. Maeir, Jodi Magness, and Lawrence H. Schiffman. Journal for the Study of Judaism Supplement 148. Leiden: Brill.

Uziel, Joe, and Yuval Gadot. 2017. "The Monumentality of Iron Age Jerusalem prior to the Eighth Century BCE." *Tel Aviv* 44:123–40.

VanderKam, James C. 2004. *From Joshua to Caiaphas: High Priests after the Exile.* Minneapolis: Fortress.

Veijola, Timmo. 1982. *Verheissung in der Krise: Studien zur Literatur und Theologie der Exilszeit anhand des 89. Psalms.* Helsinki: Suomalainen Tiedeakatemia.

Vermes, Geza. 1997. *The Complete Dead Sea Scrolls in English.* London: Allen Lane/Penguin.

Wegner, Paul D. 1992. "A Re-examination of Isaiah ix 1–6." *Vetus Testamentum* 42:103–12.

Weidner, Ernst F. 1939. "Jojachin, König von Juda, in babylonischen Keilschrifttexten." Vol. 2/pages 923–35 in *Mélanges Syriens offerts a monsieur Rene Dussaud.* Paris: Geuthner.

Weinfeld, Moshe. 1972. *Deuteronomy and the Deuteronomic School*. Oxford: Oxford University Press.

———. 1978. "Pentecost as a Festival of the Giving of the Law." *Immanuel* 8:7–18.

Weingart, Kristin. 2019. "'All These Are the Twelve Tribes of Israel': The Origins of Israel's Kinship Identity." *Near Eastern Archaeology* 82/1:24–31.

———. 2020. "Jeroboam and Benjamin: Pragmatics and Date of 1 Kings 11:26–40; 12:1–20." Pages 133–59 in *Saul, Benjamin, and the Emergence of Monarchy in Israel: Biblical and Archaeological Perspectives*. Edited by Joachim J. Krause, Omer Sergi, and Kristin Weingart. Ancient Israel and Its Literature 40. Atlanta: SBL Press.

Werline, Rodney A. 2015. "The Formation of the Pious Person in the Psalms of Solomon." Pages 133–54 in *Psalms of Solomon: Language, History, Theology*. Edited by Eberhard Bons and Patrick Pouchelle. Atlanta: SBL Press.

Werman, Cana. 2009. "A Messiah in Heaven." Pages 281–99 in *Text, Thought, and Practice in Qumran and Early Christianity: Proceedings of the Ninth International Symposium of the Orion Center for the Study of the Dead Sea Scrolls and Associated Literature, Jointly Sponsored by the Hebrew University Center for the Study of Christianity, 11–13. January, 2004*. Studies on the Texts of the Desert of Judah 84. Edited by Ruth A. Clements and Daniel R. Schwartz. Leiden: Brill.

Weyde, Karl William. 2021. "Messianic Expectations and Yhwh's Sanctuary in Ezechiel." Pages 62–84 in *Herald of Good Tidings: Essays on the Bible, Prophecy, and the Hope of Israel in Honour of Antti Laato*. Edited by Pekka Lindqvist and Lotta Valve. Sheffield: Sheffield Phoenix Press.

Wildberger, Hans. 1972. *Jesaja*, vol. 1: *Jesaja 1–12*. Biblischer Kommentar, Altes Testament 10.1. Neukirchen-Vlyun: Neukirchener Verlag.

Willgren, David. 2016. *The Formation of the "Book" of Psalms: Reconsidering the Transmission and Canonization of Psalmody in Light of Material Culture and the Poetics of Anthologies*. Forschungen zum Alten Testament 2.88. Tübingen: Mohr Siebeck.

Williamson, Hugh G. M. 1994. *The Book Called Isaiah: Deutero-Isaiah's Role in Composition and Redaction*. Oxford: Clarendon.

———. 1998. "The Messianic Texts in Isaiah 1–39." Pages 238–70 in *King and Messiah in Israel and the Ancient Near East*. Edited by John Day. Journal for the Study of the Old Testament Supplement 270. Sheffield: Sheffield Academic Press.

Wise, Michael O. 2005 "4Q245 (psDan^c ar) and the High Priesthood of Judas Maccabaeus." *Dead Sea Discoveries* 12:313–62.

Wise, Michael O., Martin Abegg Jr., and Edward Cook. 1996. *The Dead Sea Scrolls: A New Translation*. San Francisco: HarperSanFrancisco.

Wright, R. B. 1985. "Psalms of Solomon." Vol. 2/pages 639–70 in *The Old Testament Pseudepigrapha*. Edited by James H. Charlesworth. New York: Doubleday.

Wunsch, Cornelia. 2018. *Judeans by the Waters of Babylon: New Historical Evidence in the Cuneiform Sources from Rural Babylon: Texts from the Schøyen Collection*. Babylonische Archiv 6. Dresden: ISLET.

Yuval, Israel. 2006. *Two Nations in Your Womb: Perceptions of Jews and Christians in Late Antiquity and the Middle Ages*. Berkeley: University of California Press.

Zevit, Ziony. 2005. "Dating Ruth: Legal, Linguistic, and Historical Observations." *Zeitschrift für die alttestamentliche Wissenschaft* 117:574–600.

Zimmerli, Walther. 1969. *Ezechiel*. Biblischer Kommentar, Altes Testament 13. Neukirchen-Vlyun: Neukirchener Verlag.

Index of Authors

Index of Subjects

Index of Scripture and Other Ancient Sources

JOSEPHUS